The Federation of German Industry in Politics

The Federation of German Industry in Politics

BY GERARD BRAUNTHAL

Associate Professor of Government

University of Massachusetts

Cornell University Press

Ithaca, New York

CORNELL UNIVERSITY PRESS

First published 1965

This work has been published with
the assistance of a grant from the
Ford Foundation

Library of Congress Catalog Card Number: 65-14793

PRINTED IN THE UNITED STATES OF AMERICA
BY THOMAS J. GRIFFITHS SONS, INC.

For my parents

Preface

ALTHOUGH much has been written about the position of the Federal Republic of Germany as a pawn in the Cold War, somewhat less has been written about her domestic politics, and still less about the multitude of her interest groups. The role played in the body politic by one such group, the postwar Federation of German Industry (Bundesverband der Deutschen Industrie, or BDI), is the subject of this case study. It has been charged by Marxist and other critics of West Germany that the "economic plutocrats" are once again powerful there, to the extent of dictating both economic and political policy to the government. On the other hand, proponents of the pluralist thesis maintain that competition among the various groups serves to counteract the pressure exerted by the BDI and other business associations. One purpose of this study is to provide at least the basis for a sober assessment of these conflicting points of view. To this end, the BDI will be studied in relation to the country's political, economic, and social framework, which has undergone profound changes since the epoch that ended with World War II.

In the political realm, the numerous parties of the Empire and of the Weimar Republic, and in its turn the single-party system under the Nazis, have been superseded by the emergence of but two major parties whose ideological commitments are much less rigid. To some extent the new system accounts for the stability of the government and for the protracted rule of Chancellor Adenauer. The narrowing of differences between the parties has tended to make politics more and more a contest between the "outs" and the "ins." The consequence has been that many citizens have become more and more indifferent to political affairs.

In the economic realm, the chaos and destruction of the years immediately following the war have given way to the celebrated *Wirtschaftswunder*, born of the union of United States economic assistance with native hard work: an unprecedented prosperity (though it is not shared equally by all social classes) an enormous concentration of industry, and full employment, to the degree that foreign workers have had to be imported to supplement the labor force. The average monthly income of a West German family has risen from 343 DM (about $83) in 1950 to 759 DM (about $183) in 1960. In terms of 1950 prices, this represents a rise in real income of 86.7 per cent.[1] Of course, such data hide income differentials and the perennial struggle between workers and employers over the sharing of the profits.

In the social realm, class distinctions have become less marked, but have not been entirely replaced by egalitarian attitudes. Economic prosperity has led to some social mobility, and has also produced family dislocations. The drive to achieve status is becoming as important in West Germany as it is in the United States. With the virtual disappearance of the old aristocracy, new elites have arisen in managerial, political, and military affairs. The middle class is rapidly growing in numbers, and to a lesser extent in prestige. There can be no doubt that the patterns of West German society—though this is not yet true of education—increasingly mirror those in America. One consequence is a

[1] German Federal Republic, Presse- und Informationsamt, *Bulletin*, No. 96, May 26, 1961, pp. 927–928 (German ed., hereafter referred to as *Bulletin*).

tendency to maintain the status quo in most areas of public and private life.[2]

Though there are few who desire any revolutionary transformation of government and society, the great majority do seek to protect their interests by means of a wide variety of associations. That such organizations are once again free to articulate their demands and to criticize the government may well prove important in democratizing German politics. At the national level there are currently 1,800 economic and sociopolitical associations—an array of bureaus, officers, and secretariats representing an impressive number of individuals, though the exact number is not easily determined since many are members of more than one association.

Among the business associations, industrial groups such as the BDI—and others to be discussed in Chapter II—represent nearly 100,000 employers. Wholesale and retail trade, transport, banking, insurance, the hotel industry, and artisans have also formed their own national associations.

Of the agricultural organizations that "continue to this day to make claims for special treatment based at least in part on rights accorded their estate during the feudal or preconstitutional periods,"[3] the most important is the German Peasants' Union (Deutsche Bauernverband, or DBV), claiming a membership of about one million, or 77 per cent of the 1.3 million proprietors engaged in agriculture and related occupations.[4] The DBV and other agricultural associations, known collectively as the Green Front, give their support primarily to the conservative parties, are well represented in parliament, and exert a strong influence on the government.

[2] For a perceptive study see Ralf Dahrendorf, *Soziale Klassen und Klassenkonflikt in der industriellen Gesellschaft* (Stuttgart, 1957), translated as *Class and Class Conflict in Industrial Society* (Stanford, 1959).

[3] Arnold J. Heidenheimer, *The Governments of Germany* (New York, 1961), p. 79.

[4] Rupert Breitling, *Die Verbände in der Bundesrepublik* (Meisenheim, 1955), p. 33.

Of the 20.9 million persons who were gainfully employed in 1962, about 6.4 million were included in the German Trade Union Federation (Deutscher Gewerkschaftsbund, or DGB), which consists of sixteen nationwide industrial unions. Most of the DGB's members support the Social Democratic Party (SPD); a minority back the Christian Democratic Union (CDU). In addition to the one million civil service and white-collar employees who belong to the DGB, another million make up two rival organizations, the Deutscher Beamtenbund (DBB) and Deutsche Angestelltengewerkschaft (DAG).[5]

The churches must be numbered among the sociopolitical associations. Members of the Roman Catholic Church, who comprise nearly half the population, are called upon at election time to vote "Christian"—that is, for the CDU. The Protestant churches, on the other hand, have traditionally refrained from endorsing any party, partially because all parties have leading Protestants among their members.

Finally, in addition to a multitude of professional and civic organizations, there are the associations of war veterans, of expellees, of those persecuted under the Nazi regime, of Nazis who have lost their civil service posts, and so on. The aim of the latter groups is to provide not only cohesiveness and strength to their members, but also such specific services as the institution of claims against the government.[6] Although a detailed description of all interest groups lies beyond the scope of the present

[5] On employment: Bundesanstalt für Arbeitsvermittlung und Arbeitslosenversicherung, Nuremberg, March 31, 1962 (excl. Berlin), as quoted in letter from the German Consulate in Boston, May 29, 1962. On trade unions, DGB, *Mitgliederstand*, Dec. 31, 1961. The DBB claimed a membership of 656,630 in Sept. 1961 (letter from Dr. A. Hülden, DBB central office, March 17, 1962) and the DAG 465,000 (letter from DAG central office, April 1962).

[6] Wolfgang Hirsch-Weber, "Some Remarks on Interest Groups in the German Federal Republic," *Interest Groups on Four Continents*, ed. Henry W. Ehrmann (Pittsburgh, 1958), pp. 102–103.

volume, their political and economic role will be noted where it is relevant.

The organization of this book largely follows the recommendations made by the Committee on Comparative Politics of the Social Science Research Council, which has called for an approach to the study of interest groups leading to a truly comparative examination of such groups throughout the world, and to the further development and refinement of a general theory of politics. In the words of a statement by the Committee, "We can now look forward to a situation in the near future in which theories of interest groups, parties, and public opinion can be built up on the basis of a rich collection of intensive studies."[7]

It may be added parenthetically that the recent controversy among political scientists concerning the significance of interest groups, and in particular concerning the theories of Arthur F. Bentley and David B. Truman, only renders more urgent the exploration of those interest groups that have not yet been studied.[8] Each new study will add one more test of the soundness of the hypotheses concerning the nature of interest groups set forth by Bentley and Truman.

A second purpose of this volume is thus to offer a modest contribution toward the large goals outlined by the Social Science Research Council. It is hoped that an intensive case study may contribute to an understanding of one phase of the West German political process—the effect of demands made by a specific group upon public policy. The examination of interest groups is no longer a monopoly of American political scientists. In other countries, too, there has been a shift of focus away from the

[7] Committee on Comparative Politics, Social Science Research Council, *A Comparative Study of Interest Groups and the Political Process*, ed. Gabriel A. Almond (mimeographed; Stanford, 1957), p. 2.

[8] Bentley, *The Process of Government* (Bloomington, Ind., 1949); Truman, *The Governmental Process* (New York, 1960).

formal and legalistic in favor of the dynamic aspects of politics. In other words, interest groups are being recognized as a distinct element in the play of political forces.

In West Germany during the last decade, several authors have pioneered in a broad analysis of major interest groups, although thus far there have been few specific case studies.[9] The work of these authors, plus a few well-publicized scandals, has led to a spirited discussion, both in the press and in scholarly journals, of the place of interest groups in a democratic system. More case studies of these groups will not only provide new fuel for the discussion but also add to the limited store of essential data now available concerning the character and function of the groups themselves.

The BDI is referred to in this study as an "interest group" rather than a "pressure group" or "lobby," because the phrase seemed to the author to reflect its activities most accurately. How, then, is "interest group" to be defined? For Bentley the phrase suggests "so many men, acting, or tending toward action —that is, in various stages of action." He goes on to assert that "there is no group without its interest," and still more boldly, that interest "is the equivalent of a group."[10] More cautiously, Truman defines as an interest group "any group that, on the basis of one or more shared attitudes, makes certain claims upon

[9] Breitling, *Die Verbände in der Bundesrepublik*; Joseph H. Kaiser, *Die Repräsentation organisierter Interessen* (Berlin, 1956); Jacobus Wössner, *Die Ordnungspolitische Bedeutung des Verbandswesens* (Tübingen, 1961); Hirsch-Weber in *Interest Groups on Four Continents*, ed. Ehrmann, pp. 96–116; for other titles see the biographical note to Hirsch-Weber, pp. 114–116. On trade unions see Hirsch-Weber, *Gewerkschaften in der Politik* (Köln und Opladen, 1959); Günter Triesch, *Die Macht der Funktionäre* (Düsseldorf, 1956). A host of books and articles have been written on the theme of interest groups and codetermination. See, *e.g.*, Herbert J. Spiro, *The Politics of German Codetermination* (Cambridge, Mass., 1958), and Abraham Shuchman, *Codetermination: Labor's Middle Way in Germany* (Washington, 1957). A team of political scientists at the Berlin Free University is currently at work on two case studies of the influence of interest groups on specific laws. This author is investigating the Transport Finance Act of 1955 from the same point of view; and Breitling is studying the pressures exerted by the business community upon several legislative acts.

[10] *The Process of Government*, p. 211.

other groups in the society for the establishment, maintenance, or enhancement of forms of behavior that are implied by the shared attitudes."[11] Alfred de Grazia succinctly defines an interest group as "a privately organized aggregation which attempts to influence public policy."[12] To refer to an organization as a "pressure group" may be to place undue emphasis on its political activity. Although much of the work of the BDI does consist of direct pressure upon parties, the government, and the legislature, many of the activities of its membership, as well as its efforts to influence public opinion, cannot be so classified. The connotations of the word "lobby" as a group seeking its ends primarily in the antechambers of a legislature are likewise too limited.

This study will begin with a brief survey of the history of German business associations, followed by an examination of the internal organization of the BDI, its politics and ideology, and its impact upon public opinion through mass media of communication. An assessment will then be made of the techniques and channels of access used by the BDI in reaching its primary targets, namely the decision-makers in the political parties, the legislature, and the executive. Finally, an evaluation will be made of the role played by the BDI in shaping key legislative issues. It will then be possible to begin to answer the questions whether German industry does in fact dominate the political arena and whether the activities of interest groups per se are detrimental or beneficial to democracy in the Federal Republic.

Interest groups by their very nature tend to be secretive concerning their operations. A researcher may encounter many obstacles in his effort to penetrate the mysteries surrounding

[11] *The Governmental Process*, p. 33.

[12] "Nature and Prospects of Political Interest Groups," *The Annals of the American Academy of Political and Social Science*, Vol. 319 (Sept. 1958), p. 114. For a sophisticated theoretical analysis see Harry Eckstein, *Pressure Group Politics: The Case of the British Medical Association* (Stanford, 1960), pp. 15–39.

these groups. However, officials of the Institute of German Industry, the BDI, and the latter's constituent associations have generously granted the author access to their published and many unpublished documents—for example, the minutes of committee meetings. Access to most of the minutes of the presidential and executive boards came from another source. Since these minutes at best only summarize the discussions, and occasionally omit or gloss over sensitive and controversial questions, for an outside observer they are no substitute for sitting in at the meetings. Nevertheless they provide enough data to give the researcher a sense of what makes the organization tick and how it operates in political affairs.

To obtain further data, I met with over one hundred individuals, including officials and staff members of the BDI, its affiliated trade associations and regional offices; parliamentary deputies close to industry; civil servants in the federal and state ministries; officials and staff personnel of the three major parties; and leading industrialists and trade unionists. Since most respondents are either strongly sympathetic or distinctly hostile to the BDI, a detached observer is obliged to weigh the information he receives with the greatest care if he is to remain objective. Gaining access to and rapport with the informants was less difficult than might be imagined. I kept the interviews informal, unstructured, and open-ended, having deemed it advisable not to base them on a questionnaire. With few exceptions the respondents were frank and cordial, although some obviously withheld information that would have been useful. The fact that all were assured anonymity has no doubt enhanced the value of the raw data I have been able to collect. I am most grateful for their cooperation.

I am also indebted to the University of Massachusetts for providing faculty research grants; to the Fulbright Commission for appointing me visiting professor at the University of Frankfurt for 1959–1960; to the dedicated staffs of the libraries and archives at the Institute of German Industry in Cologne and the Bundestag in Bonn; and to Professors Ulrich Scheuner (Bonn), Henry W. Ehrmann (Dartmouth), and Arnold J. Heidenheimer (Florida), Dr. Rupert Breitling (Heidelberg), my father Dr. Alfred Braunthal, Herr Günter Triesch, and Herr Wolf Grabendorf, who read the manuscript in part or in its entirety, for their invaluable criticisms and suggestions. Of course all of them are absolved of responsibility for any errors that may still be found.

I thank Mr. Sun Ki Choe and Miss Emily Marchant for able research and clerical assistance, and the editorial staff of Cornell University Press for many stylistic improvements. I thank also my wife Sabina and our two youngsters, Peter and Stephen, for their patience and fortitude during the long gestation period of the manuscript.

Finally I wish to thank the editors of *Politische Vierteljahresschrift* for permission to use previously published material, and Little, Brown and Company, publishers, for use of the material on cartels which is included in James B. Christoph's *Cases in Comparative Politics.*

GERARD BRAUNTHAL

Amherst, Massachusetts
January, 1965

Abbreviations

AsU	Arbeitsgemeinschaft selbständiger Unternehmer
BDA	Bundesvereinigung der Deutschen Arbeitgeber-verbände
BDI	Bundesverband der Deutschen Industrie
BHE	See GB/BHE
CDI	Centralverband Deutscher Industrieller
CDU/CSU	Christlich–Demokratische Union/ Christlich–Soziale Union
CNPF	Conseil National du Patronat Français
DGB	Deutscher Gewerkschaftsbund
DI	Deutsches Industrieinstitut
DIHT	Deutscher Industrie- und Handelstag
DM	Deutsche Mark
DP	Deutsche Partei
ECSC	European Coal and Steel Community
EEC	European Economic Community

EFTA	European Free Trade Association
FBI	Federation of British Industries
FDP	Freie Demokratische Partei
GB/BHE	Gesamtdeutscher Block/Bund der Heimatlosen und Entrechteten
NAM	National Association of Manufacturers
RDI	Reichsverband der Deutschen Industrie
SPD	Sozialdemokratische Partei Deutschlands
UNICE	Union of Industries of the European Community
VDA	Vereinigung der Deutschen Arbeitgeberverbände
VDMA	Verein Deutscher Maschinenbau-Anstalten

Contents

Tables

PART ONE: INTRODUCTION

I

Industrial Associations:

Their History

THE role of the Federation of German Industry in the postwar Federal Republic cannot be properly assessed without an examination of its predecessors. The necessity for economic groups to provide mutual aid and to protect the interests of their members, especially in the sphere of trade, was recognized in Germany as early as the Middle Ages, with the formation of a number of merchant and craft guilds and of the Hanseatic League—which developed first as a company of traders with foreign lands and then blossomed into a mercantile association holding power in several German and foreign cities.

These gradually declined in importance. Not until the nineteenth century was German economic power revived, as the industrial revolution made its permanent impact on the economy and on the society generally. Mechanization was originally introduced in weaving and mining, and spread rapidly to other industries. During the period from 1825 to 1850 while the output of coal tripled, that of pig iron increased fivefold. What are now familiar industrial names made their debut: Krupp started operations at Essen in 1827, and the Borsig machine works started a decade later. While Saxony and the Rhineland mushroomed as early centers of industrialism, the factory system showed evidence of a movement toward concentration.

As a parallel to this industrial growth, and to its attendant social upheavals, a number of associations were formed to strengthen the power of the individual entrepreneur. In 1819 the Commercial and Industrial Union, made up of merchants and manufacturers in the central and southern states, was organized in order to promote a system of free commerce between the rival German states. In 1829 the Industrial Association of the Kingdom of Saxony was founded to deal with trade policy, technological developments, currency, and economic legislation. By 1846 the Association had already expired because of stagnation in its membership and a failure to extend its organization much beyond Saxony.

The next several decades saw only sporadic activity in the realm of purely industrial organization. For a time the spotlight was on the newly formed chambers of commerce opposing the government. The effectiveness of these chambers was limited, however, by internal schisms between the two interests. Accordingly, some industrial elements once again urged the formation of industrial associations whose more restricted interests would, it was hoped, obviate such schisms. They also warned of the necessity for countering the swiftly growing trade unions.

These arguments were convincing to the industrial community as a whole, especially since it was faced at the time by such added difficulties as the competitive struggle for both domestic and foreign markets, business depressions, the increased interference by the state in economic affairs, and their own need for state aid. It is thus no wonder that coincidentally with the founding of the German Reich, and especially between 1876 and 1880, a feverish outburst of organizational activity occurred in the coal, iron, and textile industries, among others. One of the pioneers was the formidable "Long Name Association" of Rhineland and Westphalia, established in 1871 to deal with a critical coal shortage and disruption in the freight traffic. By the turn of the century some five hundred national and regional associations and twelve hundred affiliates were in existence, many of them handling both economic and social problems.[1]

THE CDI

The antecedents of the BDI may be found in the first confederation (*Spitzenverband*) of associations concerned with raw materials and manufacturing. The Central Association of German Industrialists (Centralverband Deutscher Industrieller) was formed in 1876 for the primary purpose of exerting a greater influence upon those in key governmental positions, and more specifically of counteracting the traditional national free trade policy.[2] The CDI used what were then considered unorthodox pressure tactics, including calls on civil servants—who were more attuned to the interests of the landed gentry than those of industry—the selection or support of candidates for the 1878 election to the Reichstag who in return were pledged to work in favor of high tariffs; and massive lobbying in the legislature. As the veteran socialist leader August Bebel put it: "The lobby of the Reichstag at the time resembled a market place. The

[1] There is much literature on this period: *e.g.*, Gerhard Schulz, "Über Entstehung und Formen von Interessengruppen in Deutschland seit Beginn der Industrialisierung," *Politische Vierteljahresschrift*, II, No. 2 (July 1961), 124–154; Thomas Nipperdey, "Interessenverbände und Parteien in Deutschland vor dem Ersten Weltkrieg," *Politische Vierteljahresschrift*, II, No. 3 (Sept. 1961), 262–280; Fritz Hauenstein, "Die Gründerzeit der Wirtschaftsverbände," *Ordo*, IX (1957), 43–64; Wolfram Fischer, "Das Verhältnis von Staat und Wirtschaft in Deutschland am Beginn der Industrialisierung," *Kyklos*, XIV, Fasc. 3 (1961), 337–363; Theodore S. Hamerow, *Restoration Revolution Reaction: Economics and Politics in Germany 1815–1871* (Princeton, 1958); S. Tschierschky, *Die Organisation der industriellen Interessen in Deutschland* (Göttingen, 1905).

[2] Robert A. Brady. *Business as a System of Power* (New York, 1943), p. 30. Brady errs in setting the date at 1879. For a full description of the CDI see H. A. Bueck, *Der Centralverband Deutscher Industrieller, 1876–1901* (3 v., Berlin, 1902, 1905); Wilhelm Kulemann, *Die Berufsvereine* (6 v., Jena, 1908).

representatives of the most diverse industrial trades and agriculture populated the lobby and the [party] group chambers
of the Reichstag by the hundreds. There were achieved the
compromises which subsequently were sanctioned by the full
assembly."[3] These pressure tactics were in part responsible for
a new protective tariff policy launched by Chancellor Bismarck
in 1879. Indeed, the policy reflected the demands of an alliance
between heavy industry and agricultural interests.

As the CDI expanded the scope of its activities, it ran into
determined opposition by the chemical and processing industries. They accused the CDI of being under the control of
powerful magnates in the textile industry, and in the iron and
steel industries of Rhine-Westphalia, who disregarded the legitimate concerns of other industries. Therefore in 1895 the
processing industries set up a rival confederation, the League of
Industrialists (Bund der Industriellen), which received the support of such regional groups as the powerful Association of
Saxonian Industrialists, led by Gustav Stresemann, later foreign
minister during the Weimar era. Although the chemical industry had left the CDI as early as 1883, for several reasons it failed
to affiliate with the new League, and preferred instead to remain
a third force.[4]

Not to be outdone by its rival, the League put pressure on
administrative and legislative organs, often indirectly by influencing public opinion and the press, and sought to increase
employer representation in the several parliaments. In contrast
to the conservatively oriented CDI, the League supported the
liberal parties, but with mixed success. In Saxony its affiliates
made an impressive showing when through its efforts, out of a

[3] *Aus meinem Leben* (Berlin, 1946), III, 88; cited by Günter W. Remmling, "Die Interessenverbände in der Westlichen Welt," *Zeitschrift für
Politik*, IV (new series), No. 2 (1957), 169.

[4] Hans Brettner, *Die Organisation der industriellen Interessen in
Deutschland* (Berlin, 1924), p. 45; Kurt Apelt, *Die Wirtschaftlichen In-
teressenvertretungen in Deutschland* (Leipzig, 1925), 56; Hauenstein, "Die
Gründerzeit der Wirtschaftsverbände," p. 52.

total membership of 82, 31 industrialists and merchants were elected to the Landtag. But in the Reichstag the ratio was only 26 to 397, and of the twenty-six only five were industrialists.[5] As members of various parties, they sought with only limited success to persuade their respective parliaments to adopt policies favorable to their interests. Stresemann therefore concluded that industry could achieve more power if it founded a party of its own, but abandoned the idea in the face of a schism in the ranks of industry, lack of interest on the part of employers in following active political careers, and the absence of strong electoral support. His next move was to bring about a *rapprochement* between industrialists and politicians. Prominent deputies became members of the executive committees of associations, and public hearings, at which representatives of industry appeared, were held in the legislature.

What impact did the two confederations actually have in the realm of public affairs? Their fierce rivalry, which often led to open clashes of personality, weakened their potential effectiveness against the power of the ministerial bureaucracy. Even though nine-tenths of the work of the Reichstag dealt directly or indirectly with economic affairs, industry was far less adequately represented in it than agriculture.[6] Economic interests,

[5] Brettner, *Die Organisation*, p. 37; *Der Weg zum industriellen Spitzenverband* (Darmstadt, 1956), p. 55. One journal characterized the Saxonian Landtag as a local branch of the Association of Saxonian Industrialists (cited by Brettner, *Die Organisation*, p. 37). Another survey reveals that in the first parliament of 1848 only 6 per cent of the delegates were associated with industry; the number in 1887 rose to 17 and in 1912 fell to 12 per cent. Nikolaus v. Preradovich, "Die politischen und gesellschaftlichen Führungsstrukturen in Deutschland seit dem 18. Jahrhundert," *Politisches Seminar der Staatsbürgerlichen Vereinigung 1954 e.V., Siebte Tagung vom 21. bis 25. Nov. 1960 in Bad Godesberg* (Bergisch Gladbach, n.d. [1961]), p. 15 (hereafter referred to as *Politisches Seminar*, year). The author cites a survey made by Joachim Knoll of the liberal wing of the Reichstag between 1871 and 1912. On an average, from 10 to 20 per cent of the members in this wing were factory owners and merchants, with a low of 9 per cent in 1874 and a high of 27 per cent in 1893. *Ibid.*, p. 16.

[6] *Der Weg*, p. 70.

however, and especially those of heavy industry, began to challenge the entrenched position of the agricultural interests—not only breaking their near-monopoly but actually forming a temporary coalition with them in order to obtain tariffs and other economic legislation—and opened their own channels of access to the government. Personal contacts were established with Bismarck and Kaiser Wilhelm II, who was often a house guest of the Krupp family. Thus industry could look upon the period before World War I with a measure of satisfaction.

Up until 1904 the industrial associations dealt with a broad range of questions concerning economic and labor relations. As major strikes erupted in textile and mining industries, however, the advocates of a functional division of tasks finally won out. The industrial associations were to handle solely economic questions, while two new employers' associations were to handle labor relations. By 1913 the latter had amalgamated into the League of German Employers Associations (Vereinigung der Deutschen Arbeitgeberverbände, or VDA), whose chief purposes were to counteract the power of the trade unions and to fight strikes. It remained in existence until 1933, and was reconstituted in 1949.

A similar functional division is to be found in Great Britain, where the British Employers' Confederation deals with labor relations and the Federation of British Industries with economic policies. On the other hand, the top industrial associations in France (Conseil National du Patronat Français) and the United States (National Association of Manufacturers) combine the two functions. One can make no more than a calculated guess as to why this should happen in some countries and not in others. It would appear that the political structure has no bearing on the question, since in Germany, with a federal government, and Great Britain, with a unitary one, the same functional division prevails. Nor has the nature of the collective bargaining process any more bearing, since that process varies greatly from one country to another. One is thus left with historical developments, the kinds of labor unions, and the views of leading individuals, as possible factors determining the number and constitution of major industrial associations.[7]

In Germany, while the network of associations expanded, several attempts were made to bridge the gap between the League of Industrialists and the CDI. These proved abortive until World War I, when the need for unity in prosecuting the war led to the establishment in August 1914 of a War Committee of German Industry, and in October 1916 of the Council of German Industry. The latter was intended to be an advisory body for the transitional period after the establishment of peace.[8] It was made up of the CDI, the League, and the Chemical Association, whose cooperation proved to be merely a working alliance for the duration of the war, and did not lead to amalgamation.

THE RDI

Nevertheless, the seeds of eventual unity had been sown.[9] In February 1919 the rival industrial organizations finally buried the hatchet, and founded the National Association of German Industry (Reichsverband der Deutschen Industrie), with headquarters in Berlin. The RDI was a superassociation of 26 trade groups, subdivided into 400 national associations and cartels, 58 regional and 70 local associations, over 1,000 individual members and firms, and 70 chambers of industry and commerce.[10]

In this complex structure the national and regional associa-

[7] See Ehrmann, *Organized Business in France* (Princeton, 1957), pp. 124 ff., for a description of the postwar CNPF; and S. E. Finer, "The Federation of British Industries," *Political Studies*, IV, No. 1 (Feb. 1956), 61–84.

[8] *Der Weg*, p. 72.

[9] The employers cooperated among themselves and with the trade unions in a much publicized but short-lived joint venture, the Central Works Committee of German Employers and Employees (*Zentralarbeitsgemeinschaft*), formed on November 15, 1918.

[10] *Der Weg*, pp. 125–126.

tions played a significant role. The central power rested, however, with the president and the 36-member presidential board, who met as often as once a month to work out grand strategy and tactics. A prominent industrialist—such as Dr. Carl Duisberg of I. G. Farben, or Dr. Gustav Krupp von Bohlen and Halbach—occupied the presidential chair. Big business was always well represented on the board by such men as Robert Bosch, Carl von Siemens, and Hugo Stinnes. Significantly, the first managing directors, Dr. Walter Simons and Dr. Hermann Bücher, came to the RDI from the Ministry of Foreign Affairs. (Simons later became foreign minister and president of the Reich Court.)

The other organs of the RDI were of less actual importance. Until 1927 the general assembly met once a year; after that, owing to the expense involved, meetings took place only every other year. With an average attendance of between two and three thousand, the meetings tended to be purely formal affairs. The main committee, consisting of two hundred delegates, primarily from the trade associations, met more frequently; but it was not involved in policy-making. Its members merely heard speeches from the top leaders and engaged in discussions. The executive board consisted of some ninety leading industrial managers, but was not much more effective as a policy or control organ than the main committee.[11]

To achieve the broad objective of producing a climate favorable to its economic interests, the RDI strove to cultivate government and legislative personnel who were shapers of national policy, and to manipulate public opinion through the media of communications. It backed not only conservative cabinets and parties, but also anti-democratic forces committed to preventing

[11] The figures cited are from *Der Weg*, pp. 129–133, and do not necessarily coincide with those found in other sources. See also RDI, *Organisatorischer Aufbau des Reichsverbandes der Deutschen Industrie* (Berlin, 1929).

"dangerous" experiments in bolshevism or socialization. Much of industry supported either the conservative German National People's Party (DNVP), led by Alfred Hugenberg, the former director-general of Krupp, or the German People's Party (DVP). Hugenberg headed a sprawling newspaper empire that reflected the prevailing views of heavy industry, and was opposed to the policies of the Weimar Republic.

The RDI and the conservative parties worked out a mutually favorable arrangement, under which the latter received generous financial support from the RDI and VDA, from corporations, and from banks. As in the United States, contributions were often made by one corporation to several parties simultaneously, in order to reap maximum returns from any conservative cabinet. A committee headed by Hugenberg, whose members were nominated by industrialists, distributed the funds to the parties.

In return, the RDI and the other donors expected the parties to favor economic legislation that would benefit the business community. They also expected the parties to give full support to men from industry who were candidates for legislative office. The parties were eager to oblige, especially when these were wealthy candidates who themselves could make a substantial contribution to party coffers.[12] But aside from Hugo Stinnes and Albert Vögler, few industrialists sat in the Reichstag. The wealthy were too engrossed in becoming wealthier, or simply did not care about politics. Most of the deputies friendly to industry thus came from the second level in the business hierarchy. There were many complaints that these deputies were not active enough on behalf of industry and business, even though they formed a sizable bloc in the Reichstag. (In 1928, for instance, out of 490 Reichstag deputies, they numbered 76, or 16 per cent

[12] Richard Lewinsohn (Morus), *Das Geld in der Politik* (Berlin, 1930), pp. 80 ff; James K. Pollock, *Money and Politics Abroad* (New York, 1932), pp. 240, 242.

of the total.)[13] Since they represented several parties, one member from heavy industry called for an interparty liaison in order to preserve a united front on major questions. Where there was any degree of party discipline, such unity could not easily be achieved. But Director Duisberg of I. G. Farben, along with the banks and others, got around this obstacle by supporting several conservative parties and placing a key man in each of them.

Still another kind of liaison that served to strengthen the ties of industry to politics is implicit in the results of the 1928 election, when sixty-eight of the deputies elected held a total of 275 posts on the boards of directors of corporations. It was not unusual for such a post to be awarded with the expectation that the deputy would be able to reap benefits for the corporation in the public sphere.[14]

The increasingly effective intervention in politics by associations and corporations led to concern in socialist ranks and on the part of some newspapers. Even Stresemann, the minister of foreign affairs, who was at first active in industrial circles but who became more independent of them during the Weimar period, went so far as to remark, in 1928, "We should be inter-

[13] Lewinsohn, *Das Geld in der Politik*, p. 93. On page 94 Lewinsohn gives the following breakdown, by parties, of those deputies elected to the 1928 Reichstag who were close to industry and business:

Parties	Deputies close to industry	Deputies close to business
German National People's	9	9
German People's	15	8
Center	3	6
Democratic	8	3
Bavarian People's	1	1
Economic	1	12
Total	37	39

In another study the percentage of deputies associated with industry is given as only 23, or 4.5 per cent. Ingolf Liesebach, *Der Wandel der Politischen Führungsschicht der Deutschen Industrie von 1918 bis 1945* (Hannover, 1957), pp. 43, 114.

[14] Lewinsohn, *Das Geld in der Politik*, p. 98.

ested in preventing the capitalistic interests from gaining an excessive influence upon the form of the Reichstag."[15] As a remedy he called for state financing of parties; but the government was not receptive. The RDI naturally attempted to deprecate the extent of its own power, but the masses on the left were not convinced.

As a matter of fact, in 1920 the national associations of industry, employers, trade, banking, insurance, handicrafts, and agriculture set up the Central Committee of Employers' Associations (Zentralausschuss der Unternehmerverbände), as an organ for coordinated action. Syndicates, trusts, and cartels further served to consolidate the power of business. To a certain extent the three major trade union federations exerted a countervailing pressure on public policy, but whether they were as successful as their opponents is difficult to gauge.

This is not to say that business was altogether monolithic— far from it. Up until 1921 there were splits even within the RDI; and although after that date there was greater cohesion, the leading industrialists of the RDI were never united in support of any one party, while others of their number had no interest in politics per se.[16] A moderate group headed by Gustav Stresemann and Paul Silverberg was pitted against a more powerful conservative group headed by Fritz Thyssen, Hugo Stinnes, and other Ruhr industrialists. The two groups joined forces in opposing socialization and reparations, however, and in such political questions as the support to be given the central government at the time of the Kapp Putsch in 1921 and the Ruhr occupation in the 1920's. In general, their political activity slackened during periods of economic boom and intensified during those of depression or crisis.

PRELUDE TO NAZISM

During the early 1930's the RDI officially sustained the efforts

[15] Speech to a group of newspapermen, *Kölnische Zeitung*, March 22, 1928, as quoted in Pollock, *Money and Politics Abroad*, p. 259.

[16] August Heinrichsbauer, *Schwerindustrie und Politik* (Essen, 1948), p. 14.

by the various governments to save the Republic, while urging Chancellor Brüning to govern by decree, and warning Chancellor von Schleicher against radical welfare experiments. But in the summer of 1931 some segments of the industrialist bloc joined the reactionary, antirepublican "Harzburger Front," with the aim of hastening the fall of the tottering democratic state, and of establishing in its place a national government of nonpartisan experts (on the order of that later embodied by the von Papen cabinet). On October 5, 1931, Wilhelm Cuno of the Hapag shipping firm submitted to President Hindenburg a list of nominees for a new cabinet, which included many industrialists. But only one of them selected by the new Brüning government had close ties with industry.[17]

Industrialist support was also extended to the National Socialist movement. A minority group led by Emil Kirdorf, a director of a Ruhr mining concern, and by Fritz Thyssen, Albert Vögler, and Fritz Springorum, all directors in the steel industry, was in sympathy with its principles of authority and order and its opposition to communism. Still other industrialists, who became interested in the movement after the spectacular showing made by the Nazis in the election of September 1930, formed late in 1931 a "Friendship Circle." They hoped that Hitler would be able to prevent future political crises and to join in their struggle against trade unions.

On January 27, 1932, at the behest of Thyssen, Hitler was invited to address the Industrieklub of Duesseldorf. His famous speech on this occasion lasted two hours and was a polemic against the democratic order. It had a mixed reception.[18] In

[17] Fritz-Ullrich Fack, "Die deutschen Stahlkartelle in der Weltwirtschaftskrise," (Unpublished Ph.D. dissertation, Free University, Berlin, 1957), pp. 178, 180.

[18] Thyssen asserts that he had originally invited the more "liberal" Gregor Strasser to appear, in order to offset an earlier speech by a Social Democrat, but that Hitler showed up instead. Thyssen, *I Paid Hitler* (London, 1941), pp. 100–101. Erich Eyck speaks of enthusiastic applause in *Geschichte der Weimarer Republik* (Erlenbach, 1956), II, 443; Louis P.

general the five hundred employers present were pleased with Hitler's anti-Bolshevik remarks, and many of them were ready to donate more money to the cause. Others, who saw Hitler as an eccentric, and who found his pronunciamentos and his economic schemes muddled or self-contradictory, were contemptuous of him and continued to back the conservative parties. But this public debut before a major audience of industrialists gave Hitler added confidence in his mission, and was the prelude to other appearances before employer groups.

After the national election of November 1932, certain members of industrial circles circulated a petition to President Hindenburg urging that the new cabinet be headed by "the Führer of the largest national group."[19] After General von Schleicher, rather than Hitler, became Chancellor, these same industrialists looked askance at his proposed work program. On January 4, 1933, a secret meeting between former Chancellor von Papen and Hitler was held at the Cologne house of Freiherrn von Schröder, who had close ties with banking and industry, for the purpose of agreeing on a future government. At the end of that same month Hitler became Chancellor.

How much financial support from industry did Hitler actually receive? Before 1932 he had few direct contributions from industry. Most of the money from such individuals as Karl Emil Kirdorf and Thyssen, and from such industrial associations as that of the Ruhr, reached him through General Ludendorff, Hugenberg, and other reactionary channels. In the early 1930's,

---

Lochner characterized the reaction of the listeners as frosty in *Tycoons and Tyrants: German Industry from Hitler to Adenauer* (Chicago, 1954), p. 83. Also see Karl D. Bracher, *Die Auflösung der Weimarer Republik* (Stuttgart, 1957), p. 441.

[19] Karl D. Bracher, Wolfgang Sauer, Gerhard Schulz, *Die Nationalsozialistische Machtergreifung* (Köln u. Opladen, 1960), p. 406. At the end of the war a copy of the petition was found in a safe at a banking house in Cologne. Whether the petition was ever sent has been a point of controversy among historians, but letters with a similar content written by industrialists to Hindenburg were found more recently in Potsdam, according to a report in an East German historical journal. *Ibid.*, p. 406, note 128.

grants from industry amounted to an estimated two million marks per year, in addition to miscellaneous amounts for demonstrations and for other special funds.[20] In late 1931 and early 1932 Hitler began systematically cultivating the friendship of industrialists through the efforts of Thyssen and other sympathizers, and from then on the flow of money into Nazi party coffers increased. These contributions remained insufficient to cover major expenditures, and had to be supplemented by membership dues, street collections, and the sale of Nazi books and pamphlets.

Once he came to power, Hitler intensified his efforts to obtain an industrial slush fund. On February 20, 1933, he met at the presidential office with Göring, the financial expert Hjalmar Schacht, Walter Funk, who served as a liaison officer to business, and about twenty-five leading industrialists and bankers. Hitler spoke of the decadence of democracy, its threat to the free enterprise system, and the necessity for an authoritarian order, promising a "quiet future" once the Marxist forces were eliminated. When Göring appealed for funds for the use of the National Socialists in the next election, on March 5, a reply made by Krupp von Bohlen und Halbach, president of the RDI, expressed hope for a politically strong, independent state, in which industry and commerce could flourish. As a result of this meeting, at least 3 million marks were raised, largely by heavy industry.[21] Hitler was undoubtedly pleased not only by the

[20] Thyssen admits indirectly giving the Nazis an initial donation of 100,000 marks, and a total, over the years, of one million marks. *I Paid Hitler*, pp. 114, 133. Gustav Stolper argues that Thyssen was not as important politically as he claims to have been. *German Realities* (New York, 1948), pp. 179–180. William Shirer, on the other hand, speculates that funds from industry were much larger than the estimates generally cited. *The Rise and Fall of the Third Reich* (New York, 1960), p. 145.

[21] Bracher, Sauer, Schulz, *Die Nationalsozialistische Machtergreifung*, pp. 69–71, 629. Once in power the Nazis received up to 60 million marks per year from the "Adolf Hitler Spende" sponsored officially by the employers' associations. Breitling, "Das Geld in der Deutschen Parteipolitik," *Politische Vierteljahresschrift*, II, No. 4 (Dec. 1961), 349.

actual financial support but also by industry's implicit endorsement of his program.

To what extent industry contributed to the rise of Nazism is a matter that cannot be definitely established. There is no question that without the financial aid of certain powerful Ruhr magnates, the Nazis, who were more than once all but bankrupt, would have been hampered in their propaganda campaigns and in their rise to power. But to say that industry as a whole was responsible for the rise of Nazism would be too sweeping. It would be more accurate to assert that although a minority were responsible for direct aid, the great majority supported conservative and often reactionary forces, with another minority backing liberal forces. It must be recalled that the top leadership of the government proved incapable of meeting the economic crisis, and that Hitler was supported by other strata of the population and would most probably have achieved power even without the financial help of industrialists. Nevertheless, few will disagree with Chancellor Adenauer's assertion in 1949 that "the Ruhr industry—and therein I include coal mining as well as the entire heavy industry—in the years up until 1933 used the great economic power that was concentrated there for political purposes to the detriment of the German people."[22]

[22] Speech to the North Rhine–Westphalia Landtag, in *Stenographischer Bericht über die 4. Vollsitzung des Landtages Nordrhein-Westfalen am 23. und 24. 1. 1947*, p. 10, as quoted in Erich Potthoff, *Der Kampf um die Montan-Mitbestimmung* (Köln, 1957), p. 19. George Hallgarten is more sweeping in his indictment, and blames industry for laying the foundations of Nazism by creating economic concentration and monopolies, and thus squeezing out the small entrepreneurs. *Hitler, Reichswehr und Industrie* (Frankfurt, 1955), p. 119. Since World War II, industry has denounced attempts by trade unions and others to make a blanket indictment of prewar industry. It has argued with some logic that financial contributions to parties alone do not lead to automatic success, since if that had been so the German People's Party, which had the closest ties with industry, would have become strongest. "Hitler und die Unternehmer," *Der Arbeitgeber*, Dec. 1, 1951; Deutsches Industrieinstitut (hereafter referred to as DI), "Die Legende von Hitler und der Industrie" (hectographed, 1962). On the other hand, William Shirer asserts that the businessmen and bank-

In retrospect, one of the tragedies of this epoch may be seen as the lack of political acumen and sophistication on the part of many industrialists, who blindly and unquestioningly accepted Hitler as a man capable of solving their most pressing problems and of bringing about an era of economic recovery in Germany.

It may be asked at this juncture why some leading industrial leaders should on occasion exhibit such extreme naiveté in deciding which political horse to bet on. As will be brought out in the section on ideology, they would seem to have neither an understanding of the democratic process nor a commitment to democratic principles. For them a multiparty system is a sign of division and incoherence. These views may reflect both the conservative tradition in which they were schooled and the authoritarian structure of decision-making in their own enterprises.

THE NAZI ERA

After gaining power in 1933, the Nazis swiftly eradicated every trace of the Weimar order; but they were more cautious toward the powerful industrial associations, at least partly because of the prestige their leaders enjoyed in the nation. Within the RDI, of which Krupp was president at the time, there was no unanimity, although a letter drafted on March 24, 1933, after a meeting of its presidential board, pledging assistance to the new government, was indicative of the sentiments of the majority among the directors.[23] Nevertheless the Nazi press denounced the RDI as "liberalistic, Jew-infested, capitalistic, and reactionary"[24]—obviously for not capitulating quickly enough to Nazi demands for a revamping of the presidential board and the ouster of Jewish directors. On April 3 the Nazis installed a

---

ers contributed proportionately more money to the Nazi party than any other source. *The Rise and Fall of the Third Reich*, p. 143. However, this statement would also be true of contributions by industry to the conservative parties.

[23] For full details on the takeover see Lochner, *Tycoons and Tyrants*, pp. 154 ff.

[24] *Ibid.*, p. 159.

liaison man in the RDI's administrative staff, but further efforts at Nazification by Otto Wagener, the ambitious head of the party's economic section, ended in temporary failure, and he was replaced by Wilhelm Keppler, another Nazi economic boss —who was, however, more trusted by industry.

Krupp, who was soon to become an ardent Nazi, fought a rearguard action to save the organization, but his efforts ended in failure. In June, a last-minute attempt to maintain a modicum of independence led to the merger of the RDI and the VDA as the National Estate of German Industry (Reichsstand der Deutschen Industrie); but even this corporate organization did not fit into the Nazi mold, and consequently succumbed soon afterward.

The Nazis adopted toward business the seemingly contradictory but in fact quite logical policy of pursuing a hard and a soft line at once. On the one hand, they could not tolerate a free and independent business association; on the other, they needed the cooperation of the business community. The hard line therefore insisted on a full control over the economy, and set up the tightly structured and authoritarian Organization of Trade and Economy, which streamlined the network of associations of the Weimar era, and at the same time expanded it to include all businessmen. To assure a monolithic unity and adherence to state principles, the new organization was directly controlled by and responsible to the Minister of Economic Affairs and the National Economic Chamber. Its structure followed the traditional lines—territorial (chambers of industry and commerce, and of handicraft) and functional (industry, trade, banking, insurance, power, tourism, and handicrafts)— with further subdivisions into branch groups and subgroups. Thus the Reichsgruppe Industrie, one of the seven nationwide functional groups, served as the successor organization to the RDI.[25]

[25] For a detailed description and organizational chart see Franz L. Neumann, *Behemoth: The Structure and Practice of National Socialism* (New

The net result of this elaborate bureaucratic machinery was to ensure Nazi control of the economy, and to eliminate almost all opposition. Not surprisingly, businessmen occasionally had to bribe subordinate officials in order to reach those who actually made the decisions. They also had to contend with the far from negligible power of the German Labor Front, some of whose demands on behalf of workers they had to meet. In later years there was some grumbling about the pace and direction of the government's preparations for war, and even such leading Nazi sympathizers as Kirdorf and Thyssen began to have second thoughts about a regime that imposed so many controls and restrictions. Some leading industrialists opposed the war and warned Hitler that it would be lost. Many others, however—especially those who profited greatly from the preparation for war—supported it. At any event, the Allies were not able to prove their postwar charges that top industrial leaders such as Flick, Krupp, and officials at I.G. Farben were guilty of crimes against the peace in planning and waging aggressive wars, even though these men had been adherents of the regime.[26]

While wielding this big stick, the Nazis also dangled more than a few carrots before the business community. Although they had cultivated its support even before 1933, to ensure its continued cooperation they instituted self-administered organs, restored monopolies formerly held or controlled by the state to the private domain, and assured a great measure of freedom

---

York, 1942), pp. 240 ff. See also Ludwig Hamburger, *How Nazi Germany Has Controlled Business* (Washington, 1943); Maxine Y. Sweezy, *The Structure of the Nazi Economy* (Cambridge, Mass., 1941); Brady, *Business as a System of Power*; Erich Welter, *Der Weg der Deutschen Industrie* (Frankfurt, 1943); Josef Winschuh, *Gerüstete Wirtschaft* (Berlin, 1939); and Arthur Schweitzer, *Big Business in the Third Reich* (Bloomington, 1964).

[26] The leaders were found guilty of the charge of using slave labor, but not guilty of the charge of waging aggressive war. See *Trials of War Criminals before the Nuernberg Military Tribunals*, Vol. VI ("The Flick Case") VII and VIII ("The I. G. Farben Case") and IX ("The Krupp Case") (Washington, 1952).

to the individual firm. In later years important concessions were made to the tycoons of defense industries and other large corporations. High profits, high tariffs, and other import restrictions, representation in new state-owned war industries, and permission to engage in consolidations and cartels were all granted. Although few representatives of industry held high government positions, and although the government had few representatives in business, the formation in 1942 of the Institute for Business Leaders in Defense and of the Defense Council made it evident that industry held a significant leverage in both the party and the army.

This alliance of government with industry marked a radical change from the 1920's, when the Nazis—obviously for propaganda purposes—had proclaimed their opposition to the capitalist system. Once in power, they set out to strengthen the central economic powers of the Reich by launching the four-year plans and the policy of economic autarchy. Despite the amount of improvisation, power politics, and party influence to which it was subjected in the process of fulfilling the government's goals, industry had little cause to complain so far as its prosperity was concerned.[27]

Any survey of industrial associations from their infancy in the nineteenth century to the end of World War II must be viewed within the political, economic, and social environment in which they operated and flourished. Needless to say, the Nazi machine could not tolerate an independent employer association, and in the relentless process of *Gleichschaltung* the party set up its own hierarchy of associations. Within this controlled setting, industry nevertheless forged ahead until the Allied bombings began. In the long-range development of the industrial associations, an increasing tendency toward centralization, greater internal cohesion, and a refinement in the use of pressure, were all of importance. Moreover, as in France, the legacy

[27] Friedrich Facius, *Wirtschaft und Staat* (Boppard am Rhein, 1959), p. 129; Stolper, *German Economy 1870-1940* (New York, 1940), pp. 249-253.

of Hitler seems to have touched off an eagerness on the part of businessmen to join economic associations and to submit more or less uncritically to their directives. Not all of these developments are either salutary or desirable, but in the twentieth century they appear to have been inevitable.

II

The Federation of

German Industry

WHEN the Nazi era ended, employers as a group were discredited in the eyes of the Allies and of many Germans. The Allies—understandably reluctant to restore the status quo ante of employer associations, which were blamed for helping to finance the Nazi party and for continued collaboration with the Nazi government—arrested and jailed leading industrialists and put some on trial at Nuremberg for war crimes. They issued a host of regulations and requisitions, and dismantled many business enterprises, thereby making it difficult for the entrepreneurs to launch a program of economic reconstruction. The consequence, a rare one in history, was that employers and workers united in an effort to protect their plants and jobs. There were strikes to interrupt a period of social tranquility, during which the Allies encouraged the formation of trade unions from the local level upward, partly on the theory that organized labor had been little compromised by collaboration with the Nazi state. This imbalance was later redressed, however, as political relations between the Western Allies and the Soviet Union changed.

What had begun as a punitive policy shifted gradually to one of economic reconstruction.[1]

Although initially the allies were agreed on the necessity of restricting the might of economic associations and the concentration of monopolies and cartels, they differed in their approach even from the outset. The Soviets of course took the "hard" line; they jailed two secretaries-general of the RDI, and in their zone during the period of nationalization forbade the formation of economic associations. The Americans, bent on the creation of a decentralized federal state, took the lead in at first restricting organizations to the local or district level, only later permitting them to extend throughout the geographic confines of the American zone. The Americans further insisted that membership in such associations was to be voluntary, and that the associations were not to exercise any of the functions of public authorities or hold any public power, but to be wholly advisory.[2] On the other hand, the British, with their unitary bent, provided the greatest impetus to the formation of industrial associations (*Fachverbände*), which they soon allowed to cover the entire zone. The French policy was patterned like the American.

As regional and industrial groups mushroomed in the three western zones, German businessmen were soon making attempts to establish them on a suprazonal basis. Among these men was Fritz Berg, a successful processor of metals, head of a metal association, and later president of the Federation of German Industry. Having lived in the United States during the 1920's, Berg had—as one observer put it—a clear conception of the

[1] For full details see André Piettre, *L'économie allemande contemporaine 1945-1952* (Paris, 1952), esp. pp. 417 ff.

[2] For a summary of the legal aspects see Walther Herrmann, "Industrielle Organisationen," *Handwörterbuch der Sozialwissenschaften*, ed. Erwin von Beckerath *et al.*, V (Stuttgart, 1956), 268-272; Kaiser, *Die Repräsentation organisierter Interessen*, pp. 111-112, note 42. See also U.S. Military Government Regulation 13-120; British M. G. Regulation 78; French M. G. Regulation 179; Appendix A to Bipartite Control Office, BICO Memo. 48/13 (n.d.); and Bonn Basic Law, Art. 9, par. 3.

"mentality" of the western Allies.[3] As early as August 30, 1946, he invited representatives of twenty-three industrial associations to a conference in Wuppertal for the purpose of forming a national association. Given the Allied mistrust of any suprazonal organization, at that time nothing more was possible than a loose conference among the secretaries of the associations, who set up a center for the exchange of information and opinions. Further pressures led to more Allied concessions; for example, permission was granted for the establishment of numerous committees to deal with specialized problems—first those of industry, then those of regional associations, and finally, in February 1948, those of the Working Group of Iron and Metal. Although the Working Group nominally encompassed only two industrial sectors, among employers it came to be considered as in effect a trustee for industry as a whole.

The setting up of numerous groups, committees, and industrial and regional associations was intended to be a logical stepping stone toward the formation of a national organization. The granting of Allied approval was unexpectedly speeded up by developments from a most unlikely quarter. In 1949, when organized labor set up its national organization, the German Trade Union Federation, it was ready to negotiate with an opposite number which did not exist. Consequently the Allies made a further retreat from their initial position, and granted not only the employers but also the industrialists and the chambers of commerce the right to form national organizations, their statutes to be subject to Allied approval.

The industrialists were not slow to take advantage of this offer; after a preparatory meeting in May 1949, delegates from thirty-five industrial associations, representing 90 per cent of

[3] Herrmann, "Der organisatorische Aufbau und die Zielsetzungen des BDI," *Fünf Jahre BDI* (Bergisch Gladbach, 1954), p. 38. Others active in the organizational efforts were Alexander von Engelberg (gravel industry), F. R. Linsenhoff (construction), W. Alexander Menne (chemicals), Carl Neumann and Otto Vogel (textiles), and Hermann Reusch (steel). Franz Reuter, "Wieder Industriespitze," *Volkswirt*, No. 43 (Oct. 28, 1949), pp. 3-4.

industry, gathered in Cologne on October 19, 1949, to found the Commission for Economic Questions of the Industrial Associations. The new organization was actually the successor to the RDI. Three months later, the awkward camouflage of the original title was dropped in favor of the more realistic "Federation of German Industry" (Bundesverband der Deutschen Industrie, or BDI).[4]

NATIONAL ECONOMIC ASSOCIATIONS

Before going on to discuss the organization and philosophy of the BDI, a brief description of two other major economic associations—set up at the same time and likewise comprising industrialist elements, among others—is in order.

The Diet of German Industry and Commerce (Deutscher Industrie- und Handelstag, or DIHT) has its antecedents in the medieval merchant associations, although it was actually organized in 1861 along contemporary lines. During the Hitler era the DIHT was broken up into several state-controlled federations of trade and industry. It was reconstituted in 1949, and now comprises eighty-one local and district chambers of industry and trade, grouped into *Länder* (state) associations.[5] Since 1956, membership for all enterprises has been made compulsory, as it was before 1945, thus giving the DIHT a semiofficial character. Each enterprise, irrespective of size, has one vote in the general assembly, which usually meets once a year. Policy is

---

[4] For further details see *Die Gründung des Ausschusses für Wirtschaftsfragen der industriellen Verbände* (Bergisch Gladbach, 1949), pp. 5 ff; *Fünf Jahre BDI*; Kurt Pritzkoleit, *Die Neuen Herren: Die Mächtigen in Staat und Wirtschaft* (München, 1955), pp. 156–164. The Allied statutes and regulations which had licensed economic associations terminated on May 30, 1956, whereupon German authorities assumed jurisdiction. For a discussion of the present legal position of associations see Rüdiger Altmann, "Zur Rechtsstellung der öffentlichen Verbände," *Zeitschrift für Politik*, II (new series), No. 3 (1955), 211–227. Most of the associations are set up as legal entities through registration with the local district court.

[5] See its *Liste der Mitglieder und der angeschlossenen Organisationen, Stand vom Oktober 1954* (hectographed, 7 pp.).

made by a professional staff, a central committee of representatives of the local chambers, a board, and a president. The organization primarily serves the regional interests of industry and commerce by analyzing economic developments, making policy recommendations, fostering vocational training in trade and industry, establishing fair-trade practices, and fulfilling advisory duties and also such semiofficial ones as assisting government agencies in dealing with business enterprises. The DIHT engages in lobbying activities on national, state, and local levels, but owing to the broader interests of its members, its policies tend to be more moderate and liberal than those of the BDI. On occasion it has sponsored lectures on political affairs and given unofficial support to candidates of conservative parties. The DIHT might be compared to the United States Chamber of Commerce, and the BDI to the more conservative National Association of Manufacturers.[6]

The Federation of German Employers' Associations (Bundesvereinigung der Deutschen Arbeitgeberverbände, or BDA), dissolved in 1933, was reorganized in 1949. Its primary purpose is to serve employers as a coordinating and advisory center concerning labor and social policies. General economic policy, on the other hand, is the responsibility of the BDI. The BDA itself does not engage in collective bargaining with the trade unions, but it does sometimes recommend basic wage policies to be followed by its forty-one constituent national associations—in which industry, banking, insurance, transportation, trade, crafts, and agriculture are all represented. Occasional conferences have been held with the German Federation of Trade Unions on matters of mutual concern. In addition, the BDA acts as a pres-

[6] For details of the work see DIHT Yearbooks, *e.g., Wirtschaft aufgerufen zur Bewährung: Tätigkeitsbericht für das Geschäftsjahr 1958/59* (Berlin n.d., [1959]); also Taylor Cole, "Functional Representation in the German Federal Republic," *The Midwest Journal of Political Science*, II, No. 3 (Aug. 1958), 271; *Structure and Functions of the Top-Level Organizations of Industry and Trade in the Federal Republic of Germany* (pamphlet issued by DI, Köln, n.d.).

sure group to influence labor and social legislation, participates
with the government in certain aspects of social security and the
labor market, gives financial aid to its constituent associations
during periods of strife, and carries on an extensive public
relations campaign.

In organization the BDA is similar to many other business
associations. A plenary assembly is held once a year, but actual
decision-making is the function of the presidential and executive
boards and the executive office. As a result of a distribution
formula and of a two-thirds preponderance of industrial associations within the BDA, industry is better represented on the
two boards and makes a larger financial contribution to the
organization than does any other branch of the economy.[7]

In its policies the BDA reflects the conservative standpoint
of the average businessman. It opposes collectivization and state
planning, and supports the social market economy. On the other
hand, it has quite realistically accepted the concept of a unified
trade union movement.[8]

In studying this triumvirate of national busines organizations
—the BDI, BDA, and DIHT—two questions may be posed: first,

[7] Ronald F. Bunn, "The Federation of German Employers' Associations:
A Political Interest Group," *The Western Political Quarterly*, XIII, No. 3
(September 1960), 652–669. Some authors translate the name of the association as "German Confederation of Employers' Associations." The BDA
may actually be viewed as a combination of federation and confederation,
since its powers correspond to those of a federation, but its structure to
that of a confederation. In addition to the forty-one national associations, a
single trade association in construction, mining, textiles, and paper manufacturing, affiliated to the BDI and BDA, will handle both economic and
social problems of that industry. In others, separate associations exist. E. G.
Erdmann, Jr., "Organization and Work of Employers' Associations in the
Federal Republic of Germany," *International Labour Review*, LXXVIII,
No. 6 (Dec. 1958), 533–551. Cf. also BDA Yearbooks, *e.g. Jahresbericht
der BDA*, Dec. 1, 1960–Nov. 30, 1961; Ernst Bardey, *Unternehmer-
Organisationen-: Wofür sind sie da?* (Stuttgart, 1959).

[8] Bunn, "The Ideology of the Federation of German Employers' Associations" *The American Journal of Economics and Sociology*, XVIII, No.
4 (July 1959), 369–379.

what is the relative power of each organization? and second, what are the chances of a fusion among them? In a rating of power (although not necessarily of popularity), according to one seasoned observer, the BDI ranks highest, followed by the BDA and then the DIHT. That these three associations will ever be fused is extremely unlikely, given the vested interests involved and the tradition of maintaining separate associations for economic, social, and regional affairs. A merger would certainly offer the advantage of trimming the heavy total outlay, eliminating the duplication of effort and the overlapping of membership, and strengthening the power of the entrepreneur. Some leaders in the BDI and BDA argued along these lines during the early stages, and in the fall of 1950 the managing directors of the three associations studied the problem. A joint report concluded, however, that a merger would not be feasible owing to the specialization of the associations. In 1952 further pleas for a merger led to a joint session of the three presidents at which they listened to the arguments but once again came to a negative conclusion.[9] In recent years some further efforts to achieve unity have been made, for example in 1963, when there was a proposal to fuse the BDI and BDA, or at least to have Berg become president of both federations.

Although the three associations cling to their independence, and feud with each other at times, on many occasions they also cooperate, making use of the few institutional ties between them. The geographical propinquity of their headquarters (all of which are located in the Cologne-Bonn radius), overlapping membership in the respective decision-making organs, and a common ideology and interest facilitate constant exchange on both official and unofficial levels. These ties are further cemented by the practice of having the presidents and general managers of the BDI and BDA sit as observers at one another's presidential board meetings, and by various joint committees.

[9] *Jahresbericht des BDI*, June 1, 1951–April 30, 1952 (Bergisch Gladbach, 1952), p. 118 (hereafter referred to as *JB*, by year).

One of these involves top-level representatives not only of the BDI, BDA, and DIHT, but also of the nonindustrialist associations—banking, wholesale and foreign trade, insurance, retail trade, shipping, transportation, and handicrafts—and is known as the Joint Committee of German Trade and Industry (Gemeinschaftsausschuss der Deutschen Gewerblichen Wirtschaft).[10] Its purpose is to arrive at agreements or compromises on key topics of interest to all associations—a lofty goal which, however, frequently cannot be realized because of the conflicting interests involved. The committee is further weakened by the rule that no public statement can be issued once the veto power has been exercised by any association. It has nevertheless proved useful as a forum for discussion, and the position of committee president—which rotates yearly among all the associations—is one that affords some prestige.

That prestige is still not enough to induce the committee to meet on a regular basis; the associations usually prefer to act on their own, and for some years the committee failed to convene at all. Since 1958 it has met only two or three times a year; however, *ad hoc* working committees meet more often, to discuss such topics as the European Economic Community, and economic aid to Berlin and to underdeveloped countries. Even though formal meetings are rare, personal consultations and exchanges frequently take place among top and lower echelon leaders. The intergroup bargaining process thus becomes most effective as an unofficial rather than an official process.

In addition to the major economic associations, there are smaller ones to serve the specialized needs of employers. The League of Catholic Entrepreneurs (Bund Katholischer Unternehmer, or BKU) attempts to foster an awareness of social problems among its membership, but does not act primarily as a pressure group.[11] The Association of Independent Entre-

---

[10] For a list of business associations, addresses, and names of officials see G. Paulini, *Wirtschafts-Behörden und Organisationen* (Essen, 1956).

[11] See BKU pamphlet series, *e.g. Was will der BKU? Wie arbeitet der BKU? Wie wird man Mitglied des BKU?* (Köln, n.d.).

preneurs (Arbeitsgemeinschaft selbständiger Unternehmer, or AsU) represents the interests of about 1,300 owners who manage their own small or medium-sized business firms.[12] Although the AsU works closely with other employer associations on matters of mutual interest, it is frequently at odds with the BDI concerning its tax, cartel, and social policy, which is regarded as too strongly oriented toward big business. The AsU is an extremely vocal pressure group despite its limited power, resources, and membership.

THE FEDERATION OF GERMAN INDUSTRY

Thus, of the national organizations in the business sphere, the Federation of German Industry may very well rank first in prestige, financial strength, and influence. The BDI restricts its membership to federally structured associations of the various branches of industry (mining, textiles, food processing, and so on), of which there were thirty-nine in 1964. These associations in turn contain seven hundred subsidiary associations with a membership of 94,000 employers (many of whom are members of more than one association). According to a BDI official, 98 per cent of all West German industrialists are represented through the BDI. This index of density is high indeed as compared to the 6 per cent of manufacturing concerns represented in the NAM.[13] But unlike either the NAM or its own predecessor, the

[12] See AsU pamphlet series, *e.g. Jahresberichte, Verzeichnis der Mitglieder, Satzung, Unternehmer und Staatspolitik,* and its monthly journal *Die Aussprache.*

[13] Gustav Stein in *Mitteilungen des BDI,* IX (July 1961), 18 (hereafter referred to as *Mitteilungen,* with date). Stein also said that of the thirty-nine BDI associations, none had less than 80 per cent density. The figure on the NAM was given in a letter from Carleton McVarish, director of its Field Program and Service Department, Dec. 27, 1961. Mr. McVarish writes, however, that the NAM's member firms produce 75 per cent of the total United States manufacturing output, and employ 71 per cent of the industrial work forces representing businesses of every size. The 6 per cent membership is out of a total of approximately 324,000 manufacturing firms. See also R. W. Gable, "N.A.M.: Influential Lobby or Kiss of Death?", *Journal of Politics,* XV (May 1953), 254–273; Alfred S. Cleveland, "NAM:

RDI, the BDI does not enroll individual concerns as members. Since these concerns are members of other organizations, the intensity of their commitment to the BDI tends to be lessened. At one time an effort was made by certain large firms, led by Krupp's general manager, Berthold Beitz, to obtain direct membership in the BDI as a means of increasing their powers; however, Beitz dropped the plan after discovering that he would not be able to count on majority support in the General Assembly of the BDI.

Constituent Associations of the BDI

The role of the federated associations within the BDI may be illustrated by a brief glance at the Association of German Machine Construction (Verein Deutscher Maschinenbau-Anstalten, or VDMA). The organization is subdivided into twenty-nine branch associations (representing turbines, machine tools, and so on) and eight regional groupings. All business firms that become members of the VDMA automatically belong to a branch and a regional group. The branch associations deal directly with the problems of the member firms, to whom they pass along information and advice; the regional groups handle regional problems and ties with the *Länder* (state) governments; and the VDMA's federal headquarters deal with matters of concern to the entire industry, representing the economic interests of the firms to the public authorities in Bonn and to other economic associations. The organization of the VDMA resembles that of the BDI (which will be discussed below) and is highly centralized, cohesive, and bureaucratic. Individual firms play a greater role in the VDMA than in the BDI because their common interests—taxation, tariffs, and so on—are directly

---

Spokesman for Industry?" *Harvard Business Review*, XXVI, No. 3 (May 1948), 353–371. Samuel H. Beer, "Group Representation in Britain and the United States," *The Annals*, vol. 319 (Sept. 1958), p. 135, argues the NAM figure would be more like 20 to 25 per cent if the same base were used as that of the Federation of British Industries, which asserts that 85 per cent of its firms are organized.

at stake, even though they may be highly competitive among themselves.[14]

Thus for the staff members of any association within the BDI, the services to the member firms occupy much more time than does the representation of their interests. The staff must maintain a diplomatic balance in the output of its work. If the member firms receive too many releases and requests, a negative attitude toward the association may easily develop; if too few, they may complain about "not getting their money's worth."[15]

Within each association a distinction must be made between large and small firms. The latter will avail themselves of the services of the association to a greater degree than the large firms, whose own payrolls are staffed with experts. Inherent in this setup is the risk that the large firms may bypass the association in an effort to gain their objectives more quickly or easily. They are inclined to fear that their goals may be compromised by an association that tries to achieve internal unity. This is not to imply that the large firms have no interest whatever in the association. On the contrary, since they provide most of the necessary financial support, they expect the stand taken by the association on any issue to meet with their approval. But the staff experts of all large firms do maintain a direct liaison with the staff of the BDI as well as with that of their own association.

Between the thirty-nine constituent associations and the BDI there is a clear demarcation of function. The former handle matters of interest only to their particular industries, the latter

[14] VDMA, *Geschichte und Aufgaben der deutschen Maschinenbau-Organisation* (pamphlet, Darmstadt, 1959); Breitling, *Die Verbände in der Bundesrepublik*, p. 13.

[15] "Geschäftsbericht 1959/60 des Hauptverbandes der Deutschen Holz-industrie und verwandter Industriezweige e.V.," *Gelbe Holz-Mitteilungen* (München-Wiesbaden), No. 24 (June 16, 1960), p. 9. The Association of the German Rubber Industry which issued 1,497 releases in one year, and made 14,000 photostats, is typical. *Geschäftsbericht des Wirtschaftsver-bandes der deutschen Kautschukindustrie e.V. über das 10. Geschäftsjahr* (1.1.–31.12.1959), p. 31.

those of concern to all the industries represented. Exceptions to this rule may occur on occasion, as when a smaller association, short on staff and money, asks the BDI to take up a specialized problem.

The associations are officially represented in the BDI at all levels from the presidential board down to the committees. In each instance there is both a formal and an informal relation between the associations and the BDI. At meetings of the presidential board, for instance, the president of the association will voice the views of his organization. But he may also communicate these views informally to the BDI president before the meeting takes place; and he may also approach the presidents of other associations to ask for their support. The views of the associations are arrived at either through an elaborate internal process of decision-making, in which compromises must often be patiently worked out, or at times simply by the president's sounding out the top industrialists in his association. Procedural decisions are sometimes made by the managing directors of the associations—who, incidentally, meet several times a year with the managing director of the BDI to coordinate their manifold activities.

So far as the relative power of the associations within the BDI is concerned, those associations made up of the largest number of firms do not necessarily rank first—as the example of the consumer goods industries well illustrates. The Federation of the German Food Processing Industry includes few giant corporations, but consists largely of small, highly competitive firms, which are unwilling to contribute sizable funds to their association, and which have a negligible impact upon industrial policy. These small firms prefer to be consumer-oriented rather than association-oriented. On the other hand, the basic industries—coal, steel, and chemical—along with certain processing industries such as metal, machine construction, and electric machinery, play a not inconsiderable role in the BDI, thanks to their fiscal resources and to their corporate structure, which is typically that of the giant corporation. With rapid technological changes, the relative importance of the associations within this spectrum also changes. Coal declines, for instance, as oil forges ahead. In any event, the spokesman for the big industries will carry a good deal of weight in all organs of the BDI. If the representatives of four major associations—say, electric machinery, chemicals, machine construction, and automobiles—are united on one issue, they can sway other associations or block any unfavorable action.

An idea of the importance of the large corporation in the BDI may be gleaned by checking the membership lists of its various organs. For example, at one time the managers of the Allgemeine Elektrizitätsgesellschaft (AEG), while officially representing the electric manufacturers association in the BDI, were also members of the presidential board, as well as chairmen of the foreign trade committee, the committee for vocational training, and the executive committee of the Berlin regional office, and members of numerous other committees.[16] An executive of a large firm will often hold key offices not only in the BDI but in the BDA, DIHT, and other organizations as well, thus providing a great measure of coordination and ensuring the influence of big business at the same time.[17]

The Structure of the BDI

Given the important role played in the BDI by constituent associations and large firms, the chief policy-making body—under the statute drawn up by a commission of executive officers and staff members—consists of the General or Membership Assembly (*Mitgliederversammlung*).[18] Delegates to the Assembly are chosen by each of the constituent associations according to their strength in proportion to the total payroll of all firms

[16] Pritzkoleit, *Die Neuen Herren*, p. 179.

[17] *Ibid.*, pp. 182–191.

[18] The text of the statute may be found in BDI, *Organisationsplan*, July 1962.

within the industry.[19] Conceivably this weighting of the vote could lead to oligarchic control by the heavy industry of the Rhine-Ruhr complex. The actual votes have not, however, been of primary significance since the Assembly merely ratifies decisions already made on the upper echelons—including the election of the president and five vice presidents, the distribution of budget, and all amendments to the statute. There is remarkably little discussion at the closed meeting attended by the delegates, to which neither the press nor the public is admitted.[20] To what extent this situation reflects lack of interest or an unwillingness to criticize the officials cannot be accurately determined. At the open meeting—a formal affair at which leading officials of the BDI and the government make public speeches—discussions of course do not take place. As one staff worker put it, "It is too public a meeting, and no one wants to air his dirty linen."

In order to understand the internal government of the BDI, to identify the decision-makers and other loci of power, one must look to the effective governing bodies: the executive board (*Vorstand*), the presidential board (*Präsidium*), and the executive office (*Geschäftsführung*).[21] The executive board, headed by the president and up to five vice presidents, consists of about fifty-five members (the exact number varies) who are heads of the constituent associations and of the regional offices. Its func-

[19] Associations with less than 50,000 employees receive two votes. Two votes additional up to a maximum of seven are granted for each multiple of 50,000 up to 200,000 employees. Thereafter one additional vote is granted for each multiple of 50,000. *Ibid.* See also Almond, *The Politics of German Business* (Santa Monica, Cal., Rand Research Memorandum RM-1506-RC, 20 June 1955), p. 38.

[20] This information, as well as the undocumented information that follows, was obtained during personal interviews.

[21] Up until 1955 a central committee (*Hauptausschuss*) also existed coordinating the work of the committees. But since its functions overlapped with those of the executive board, it was disbanded. In turn, the membership of the executive board was considerably expanded to include members of smaller companies and *Länder* affiliates. *JB*, 1954–1955, p. 217.

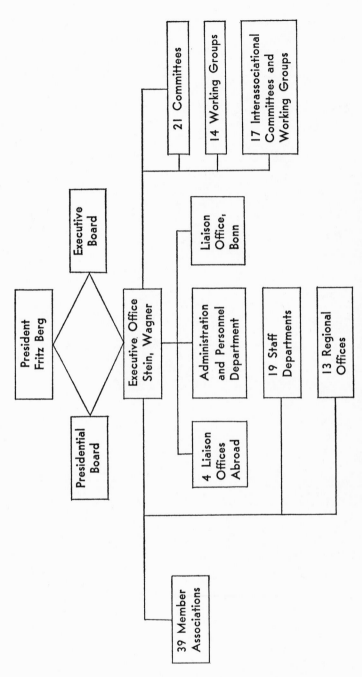

The Organization of the Federation of German Industry*

* Adapted from BDI *Organisationsplan, July 1962.*

tions are to set the general line of the BDI, to coordinate the work throughout the organization, and to elect part of the presidential board. But its importance should not be overestimated. It meets not more than from two to four times a year, on which occasions the members of the presidential board defend their points of view and their decisions, or controversial topics are discussed. Since sixteen members of the presidential board are also members of the executive board, a coordinated policy can usually be achieved without much difficulty. According to one staff official, the two boards have never disagreed on any basic issue, but only on matters of detail. Nevertheless, the policymakers on the presidential board cannot disregard the executive board, and in their determination of policy they will make sure that its approval is assured. In this sense the executive board serves as an effective control organ. Nevertheless, those members who are not on the presidential board would like the executive board to become more important and self-assertive.

The top policymaking organ is the 24-member presidential board. Officially, the General Assembly elects the president and the five vice presidents by secret ballot for a period of two years, and the executive board elects twelve members from its own ranks. The presidential board thus constituted elects four additional members, and the other two members are invariably the heads of the Institute of Germany Industry and of the Berlin regional office. Although the eight most powerful associations always have a seat on the presidential board, a broad industrial and geographic representation is sought by rotating four seats among the smaller associations.[22]

The statute confers upon the presidential board the power to lead the work of the organization, and in an emergency to make decisions, which must subsequently be approved by the other organs. The monthly meetings are not devoid of controversy. There are no ideological clashes between left and right wings;

[22] One or two members from smaller companies have been re-elected continuously in recognition of their share in founding the organization.

but differences of opinion between associations representing big business on the one hand, and small business on the other, or between heavy and consumer goods industries, are frequent. Even this categorization tends to be too rigid, since even within particular industries the unity is not absolute. In the circumstances, the lack of unity on many aspects of policy tends to lessen the potential power of the BDI.

In the procedure of the presidential board, there has emerged the extraconstitutional practice of allowing the president to call together a few of its members for consultation on urgent matters. This gives the president a free hand in critical situations, since he will obviously decide who is to be a member of the inner circle. The president will tend to consult those whom he trusts, and who represent the influential groups. At many meetings of the board, however, there are no urgent matters to be discussed. The president may simply report on talks he has held with government officials concerning, say, the European Economic Community. A prosaic discussion may ensue. The problem of a rival business association publicly taking a stand contrary to that of the BDI might then be debated, and a decision might be reached that in the future such differences are to be settled privately before the public is informed.

Often staff section heads and committee chairmen will report to the board concerning particular objects of study, and will give progress reports on especially controversial topics. At times the president of the BDA or a high government official might discuss legislative matters of concern to the BDI. Or the board might set up a working committee composed of its own members to deal with a special topic and to report on its findings to the entire membership.

More colorful meetings of the board occur when that body serves as the arena in which each of two contending factions within the organization presents its case—especially after an attempt to settle the dispute at lower echelons has failed. The Federation has evolved a style of operations comparable to that in many other organizations. One hallowed principle is not to air an internal controversy unless there has been an agreement to disagree publicly. It is considered tactless and disloyal for any official openly to express dissenting views. Nevertheless, such things have been known to happen—as in 1954, when leading spokesmen for the automobile and steel industries clashed sharply on a policy matter concerning a transportation bill, and when a minority also publicly opposed the BDI's cartel policy.

The executive office of the BDI—headed until 1963 by the executive member of the presidential board, Dr. Wilhelm Beutler, and the general manager, Gustav Stein, and since 1963 by Stein and Dr. Hellmuth Wagner respectively—plays a significant role in the making and execution of policy. Although its primary function is to serve, rather than to direct, it wields, because of the sheer expertise and continuity in office of the top men, a power that should not be underestimated. One informant offered a rough guess that the executive office would be responsible for 40 per cent, the presidential board for 40 per cent, and the executive board for 20 percent of the content of an ordinary statement of policy. However, it is the business of the staff not to give the impression of playing too prominent a role in the decision-making process, and to stress the idea of being "on tap, not on top."

A general trend toward bigness in organizations applies to the BDI along with the rest. The inexorable expansion of its activities has brought the number of its staff to a total of 180, divided into nineteen departments. Here as elsewhere, the bureaucratic apparatus has a tendency to perpetuate itself, and to rationalize its own importance.[23] Much more time is spent by the staff on services to its constituent associations in the form of advice, information, education, and legal briefs, and on preparing reports

[23] Max Weber deals with this theme in *Wirtschaft und Gesellschaft* (4th ed. Tübingen, 1956), I, 204. Seymour M. Lipset, in an analysis of bureacracies, says that large-scale organizations are constrained to develop bureaucratic hierarchies as a result of internal and external pressures. *Political Man: The Social Bases of Politics* (Garden City, N.Y., 1960), p. 359.

and proposals to the committees of the BDI, than in any comparable organization in the United States. Staff sections devoted to economic, legal, foreign trade, tax, and transport matters, and so on, have a cadre of skilled personnel whose work is highly respected by industry and government. The recommendations of these experts cannot be ignored either by the top echelons of the BDI or by the representatives of the constituent associations, whose interests tend to be somewhat parochial. The staff must try to remain as neutral as possible if it is to mediate the differences that arise between the associations.

To carry out these functions, the staff must be constantly aware of all the conflicts of interests involved in any situation, and must feel out the sentiments of the members so as to anticipate the support a proposal is likely to receive. These proposals not only originate in the BDI and the associations, but may also be evoked as countermeasures to ministerial drafts, statements by trade unions and other opponents, or commentaries in the press.

The executive office maintains a close and usually harmonious liaison with the top organs of the BDI, although the presidential board has been known to vote against a proposal recommended by the executive office. Friction may also occur over the minutes of the proceedings of the board, which are sent out after a session to all constituent associations. Even though these minutes give no more than a summary of the discussion, at times an association may object to the handling of some key point.

The agenda worked out by the executive office for meetings of the presidential board is of some importance. There may be a temptation on the part of the office to bypass the board when it fears an adverse decision on some issue which it holds dear, or which directly affects some members of the board. For example, in 1957 an important issue concerned with insurance never appeared on the agenda, presumably because the managers deemed it too touchy a subject for certain members who also belonged to the supervisory boards of insurance companies.[24] On some occasions the office may first assess the strength of contending parties within the board before bringing a matter before it.

With the mushrooming size of the organization, the fiscal needs have risen sharply. The budget of the BDI has expanded steadily—from a million marks in 1950 to 5.5 million marks in 1960—thus far surpassing that of the RDI, which hovered around a million marks.[25] In the BDI a commission of seven or eight members works out the budget estimates, which are then submitted to the top staff, the presidential board, and the General Assembly for approval. The contribution of each constituent association is calculated on the basis of the payroll and total sales of its member firms. The minimum contribution of an association is one per cent of the BDI budget; the most powerful associations, such as steel, machinery, and mining, each contribute from 10 to 14 per cent, thus assuring themselves of some voice in policy-making. As in any organization, there is an undercurrent of complaint against the steep assessments; but the BDI finds it difficult to cut operating expenses. It has been estimated that industry spends as much as 2 per cent of its total sales for the BDI and other associations.[26]

The Committees of the BDI

Although a substantial amount of the preparatory work for the presidential and the executive boards is handled by the executive office, the standing committees of the Federation also have a hand in the preliminaries. More than thirty such committees (including interassociational bodies) have been organized to deal with such subjects as taxes, tariffs, and transportation.

[24] Minutes of an executive board session of a constituent association, Dec. 4, 1957.

[25] RDI, *Mitglieder-Versammlung des RDI am 3. und 4. Sept. 1926 in Dresden*, Heft 32, p. 78; BDI budget: Statement by a BDI staff official, personal interview, Cologne, Sept. 24, 1959. The NAM budget for 1959 was about $6 million. *NAM at Work* (pamphlet, n.p., n.d.), pp. 28–29.

[26] Herrmann, "Industrielle Organisationen," p. 271.

Each committee consists of one delegate and one alternate from each association, chosen by the association—sometimes in consultation with the executive office. These delegates are employers who serve without compensation, although top staff members of their respective associations frequently substitute for them. Internal politics plays a role in the selection not only of the members of each committee, but also of the chairman, who serves for two years. This post is often awarded by the BDI—and merely given official sanction by a vote of the members—to a prominent employer in the association most directly concerned with the committee's primary function. For example, an officer of the Automobile Industry Association may head the BDI committee on transportation. Within his own association the same official is very likely also to head a committee dealing with the same subject.

Each committee has an executive council—membership in which is greatly coveted—to discuss strategy and tactics, and smaller subcommittees, which meet frequently to hear spokesmen of industry and government, and to draft reports for the committee's scrutiny. After discussing these reports, the committee sends them to the top organs of the BDI. But it can be genuinely effective only if a harmony among its members' divergent views is obtained, which is not always possible, despite the manipulative tactics of the chairman.[27] The executive office plays an important role in the work of the committees, since staff officials often provide its members with the documents on which their work is based. A close liaison has been established between the executive office departments and the corresponding committees. However, in certain controversial areas affecting only a segment of the economy—such as small businesses or consumer goods industries—the BDI has often decided to set up new committees. *Ad hoc* and interassociational committees (for example, BDI-BDA) are also frequently organized, adding further to the bureaucratic maze. The consequence is that commit-

[27] *JB, 1958–1959*, p. 11.

tee members are overburdened and fail to show up at meetings, although the constituent associations will, of course, make sure that their delegates are present at any meeting of a committee which may have a vital effect on their interests. To some degree the effectiveness of a committee member depends on his own expertise, but it is also governed by the extent of his preparation for the special work of the committee. Leading employers who serve on too many committees, in the BDI and in other organizations, may come ill prepared and thus fail to exert their potential effectiveness.

Once again the number and influence of managers of large corporations who serve these standing committees is most striking. The BDI argues that their greater competence and specialization compared to others justify their prominence on committees. Nevertheless, the small businessman, who has both less available time and fewer financial resources than the big businessman, is somewhat uneasy over this prevalence of big business in the work of committees. In 1956 the discussion at a meeting of the presidential board of a BDI-affiliated association of finished goods centered on this inequality of representation. There was a decision to approach a number of associations for the purpose of ensuring that the BDI committees, and especially their executive councils, were representative of all interests.

But the small businessman himself must take some of the blame for this situation. Too often he shows no interest in attending committee meetings. Smaller associations tend to complain that they are unsuccessful in attracting industrialists to committees unless the work is of immediate concern to them.

The integration of standing committees into the framework of the BDI has always been of key importance to its officials. As long ago as 1949, Stein, who was then deputy managing director, warned the founders of the BDI that the committees must not lead a separate existence, and that their reports must be submitted to the executive office for distribution to the appropriate organs.[28] Since the executive board is expected to coordinate the work of the committees with general policy, the secretariat of the committees are identical with the parallel departments of the executive office. The influence of the salaried staff is therefore considerable, especially when employer delegates are too busy to devote much time to the work themselves. Of course, on most occasions staff and employers have the same views, and their task will be to persuade others in the Federation to support them. It has been known to happen that the members of the presidential board who are present at a particular committee will be urged to represent the interests of the committee at the next meeting of the board.[29] Generally, the broad policy lines are fixed at the top, and committees are asked to fill in the details. But at times when work submitted from below suggests that the original policy is defective, a change of policy may be made at the top. Once a decision has been reached, the executive office must see to it that appropriate action is taken. Often this action will consist of negotiations with officers of other national associations or with governmental ministries.

Regional Offices of the BDI

The federal character of the West German Republic led the BDI to decide, after some hesitancy, to include regional offices as well as trade associations in its membership. The BDI has a centralist orientation, philosophically speaking, and according to one informant, it was at first opposed to the setting up of any *Länder* units. But more separatist-oriented industrial centers, such as that of Bavaria, made the organization of affiliates in all *Länder* a prerequisite of their joining.[30] After protracted talks a compromise was agreed upon: *Länder* affiliates might be set

[28] *Die Gründung des Ausschusses für Wirtschaftsfragen*, p. 8.

[29] BDI, *Konsumgüter-Rundschreiben*, No. 3/59 (Feb. 3, 1959), p. 5.

[30] According to published sources, the planners of the organization always envisaged the creation of *Länder* affiliates. See, *e.g.*, *Tätigkeitsbericht der Landesvertretung Hessen des BDI, Stand Ende April 1959* (Frankfurt/M., n.d.), p. 8.

up so long as they were financed by local industry rather than by the BDI.[31] Accordingly, in each *Land* a regional office was set up for the purpose of coordinating the specific territorial interests of industry; of representing them in the *Länder* governments, in the Bundesrat (the upper house of parliament), and at BDI headquarters; and of publicizing these to influence public opinion.

The regional offices vary both in attitude and in importance. Some—as in Bavaria, where there is an impressive staff and suite of offices—still regard themselves as semiautonomous organizations with every right to assert their regional interests in outspoken terms; others, which may have only a part-time official as staff, act as mere subsidiaries of the BDI. If one adds to these structural differences the obvious lack of interest in the regional offices on the part of the parent organization, it is no wonder that disputes occur within the BDI when regional issues are at stake. The regional offices are also involved in occasional disputes between big and small business. Bavaria and Baden-Wuerttemberg are traditionally hostile to big business, although some large firms are located there. In the BDI executive board and other organs where the *Länder* have an official voice, their representatives tend to support the claims of small business. This is not true of other *Länder,* where representatives of the large corporations may control a sizable majority, or even all, of the seats on the regional executive committees.

The representatives of the regions will seek direct access to the policy-making organ of the Federation. Since they are not represented on the Presidential board, the spokesman for their interests on whom they must rely are primarily those members who sit as delegates of associations, but who also take a more general interest in the affairs of the regions in which their own businesses are located.

To coordinate the regional work the directors of the *Länder*

[31] Hence, industrial firms are faced with double taxation: indirectly by the BDI, and by its *Land* affiliate.

affiliates meet several times a year with staff members of the executive office. The regional officers are kept abreast of current problems of concern to the Federation, and the executive office of current regional problems. This exchange of views is important and useful, even though it ends up as a series of pep talks by Federation officials. The basic difficulty seems to be that only a limited number of important regional issues are simultaneously of concern to a federal organization. To the BDI, national taxation or cartel policies are of greater moment than such matters as air pollution or regional planning. Moreover, the powers of the *Länder* lie primarily in the fields of educational and cultural affairs, which are of secondary importance to industry.

International Activities of the BDI

On the other hand, the international activities of the BDI are becoming increasingly important, as is evident from the number of organizations that are springing up on the supranational level. The Federation is affiliated indirectly with the International Chamber of Commerce and is a member of the Council of European Industrial Associations, established on the initiative of the French industry in 1949 as an adjunct of the Organization for European Economic Cooperation. The Council, with headquarters in Paris, is a loose organization of the fifteen West European industrial associations. Although it has been handicapped in its work by differences in method and goals, it serves the useful purpose of encouraging exchanges of opinion between leading industrialists, and acts as a spur to supranational thinking—a level at which more and more decisions are now being made.

After the European Economic Community was set up, the industrial associations of its member nations (with the BDI representing West Germany) organized the Union of Industries of the European Community (UNICE). The industrial trade associations (*e.g.* chemicals and textiles) of the six nations have in turn established centers for liaison to the EEC in Brussels.

These centers, as will be brought out later, serve primarily as information and lobbying agencies. Executive organs and a staff direct their activities.[32]

There are, in addition, periodic conferences of the managing directors of the national associations; international manufacturing conferences to which the BDI sends representatives; and numerous bilateral talks with industrial and government leaders of other countries. The BDI also maintains liaison headquarters in New York, London, and Paris, but these, according to one official, are used more for making arrangements for visiting dignitaries than for gathering information.

Decision-Makers of the BDI

No survey of organs of the BDI on the national and international levels would be complete without some account of the decision-makers and of the power structure within the Federation. There are two primary groups of leaders who determine policy: the industrialists, family entrepreneurs, and managers of corporations who hold high positions in the constituent associations and who serve the BDI without compensation; and the staff executive officers who serve on a salaried basis.[33]

In a general way it is possible to characterize leaders in the first group. According to one study of the German elite, the president of an association such as might belong to the BDI is typically an older man, well educated, Protestant, with no record of anti-Nazi activities or of military service.[34]

The question now arises as to how these leaders are chosen and whether there is a distinct pattern of recruitment. Many of

[32] Thus, for instance, the chemical industry associations of the EEC countries have organized the Secrétariat International des Groupements Professionels des Industries Chimiques des Pays de la Communauté Economique Européenne (SIIC). *Wirtschaftspolitik im Chemiebereich 1958* (Verband der Chemischen Industrie, e.V.), (Frankfurt/M, 1958), p. 17.

[33] Heinz Hartmann, *Authority and Organization in German Management* (Princeton, 1959), pp. 224–228.

[34] Karl W. Deutsch and Lewis J. Edinger, *Germany Rejoins the Powers* (Stanford, 1959), pp. 127 ff.

the senior posts in the BDI are allotted automatically to top officeholders in the constituent associations. In the associations themselves the choice of a president is the result of the usual multiplicity of factors: personal initiative and ambition, services to the industry, contacts with the "right" people, and sheer chance. Recruitment of other leaders for the top posts is largely on a closed basis. The BDI management will go directly to the highest officials and managers of the constituent associations for suggestions, thus precluding any show of preference on the part of their rank-and-file membership. Less desirable posts, on the other hand, must be filled through open recruitment. The BDI constantly seeks to attract more employers to committee work, but without any marked success.

Differences in the degree of influence among the decision-makers are due to the strength not only of the associations represented but also of individual personalities. One member of the presidential board, the head of a relatively small consumer goods association, told this author that he could expect his views to carry weight only when he had made personal contacts with other board members before a meeting was scheduled. On the other hand, many of the captains of industry who are now advanced in years do not play the role they once did on the Board, despite the importance of the associations they represent. To be sure, some of them retain their posts there simply because of their position as president of an association —a position which is in turn simply a reward for services faithfully rendered over the years.

The chief influence, then, belongs to such men as the BDI president, Fritz Berg; Dr. Richard Freudenberg (leather); Dr. Otto A. Friedrich (rubber); Carl Neumann (textiles); Dr. Heinrich Nordhoff (automobiles); Dr. Hermann Reusch (steel); Dr. Rolf Rodenstock (opticals); Dr. Hans-Günther Sohl (iron and steel); and Dr. Peter Siemens (machinery). These industrialists, who are nearly all members of both the presidential and the executive boards, play a key role in the organization. Their chief common characteristic, with few exceptions, and that of most other members of the two top organs, is that they represent big business. The presidential and the executive boards are largely composed of the managers of giant firms—Hoechst, Phoenix, Volkswagen, Thyssen, Siemens, and so on. This is a matter of some concern to smaller businessmen, even though their views obviously have to be taken into consideration. The views of leading German industrialists who prefer not to be active in the BDI likewise cannot be disregarded. For example, Alfried Krupp, the son of the RDI president Gustav Krupp, and his managing director Berthold Beitz prefer the freedom of working outside an association, partly because the name of Krupp has been so closely identified with the RDI; yet the BDI must try to maintain cordial relations with such men if real unity of policy is to be achieved.

The task is difficult enough, as we have seen, even within the BDI. Among its constituent big businessmen are some who hold progressive views—Friedrich, Kost, and Neumann, among others —along with those who tend to be much more conservative. On the whole the conservative point of view, as enunciated on many occasions by senior officers Berg, Beutler, Stein, Reusch, and others, prevails. In terms of influence Reusch was for some time the *éminence grise*, and he was once considered a leading candidate for the presidency; but his label as spokesman for the Ruhr interests, combined with fear of an Allied veto, led to the selection of Berg as a compromise candidate.

Large organizations rarely see a rapid turnover among their officers, and the BDI is no exception. Indeed, it had an exceptional continuity of command—Berg, Beutler, and Stein having been at the helm from its inception until 1963, when Beutler retired. Among the members of the presidential board, too, there has been an extremely small turnover, aside from that occasioned by death, retirement, or loss of the presidency of a constituent association (which means an automatic loss of office in the BDI).

The General Assembly has re-elected Berg by acclamation for two-year terms—and has done so despite his suggestion at the 1960 assembly that there be a formal vote by secret ballot. In 1964, however, such a formal vote did take place, and it would have been unanimous but for two abstentions. His unanimous re-election does not mean that Berg enjoys total support within the organization, but rather that those who would like to see a change have not found a suitable candidate who would also be willing to assume a responsible and time-consuming position that is the target of continual crossfire from without even more than from within the BDI itself.

Berg is generally regarded as, in many ways, the ideal man for the job. He may have been a member of the Nazi party from 1937 to 1945, but does not appear to have been active in the movement.[35] In any event he was given a clean bill of health by the British immediately after the war, and was appointed mayor of Altona in 1945. After several months in this post he began organizing local and regional industrial associations. From then on he enjoyed a meteoric rise to power.[36] He holds the traditionally conservative—if not rightist—views of the respectable German industrialist. Moreover, Berg is unlike the presidents of the RDI, who were all big businessmen, in that his own metal-processing company is a medium-sized family firm; hence he is generally trusted by the small businessman. As the firm has prospered, so has Berg.

Since he is a millionaire, he remains independent enough not to be beholden to big businessmen. He receives no remuneration from the BDI, but enjoys the power and prestige of

[35] According to *Fortune* magazine, he was a member of the Nazi party. "Eighteen German Businessmen," XLV (March 1952), 155. On the other hand, the *Financial Times* (London) reported he never joined. Feb. 27, 1958.

[36] According to *Der Spiegel*, the rise to power was interrupted by accusations of black market activities and bribery. "Berg; Der Interessen-Bündler," XIV (Nov. 2, 1960), 32. See also "Ein Fabrikant aus dem Sauerland," *Die Welt*, May 3, 1958.

the Federation office. As he put it once, "I have no children, I cannot eat more than one beefsteak, and I have fun in running the Federation."[37] Few deny that he is an efficient chairman, a skillful negotiator, and a man who has excellent connections: with former Chancellor Adenauer, with the presidents of the French and British federations of industries, and with other leading industrialists abroad. As a British correspondent has observed, "It is a moot question whether Herr Berg has been elected and re-elected ever since 1950 because he is known to carry influence with Dr. Adenauer, or whether he has the ear of the Chancellor for having been the trusted spokesman of industry for so long."[38]

Others regard Berg as colorless, humorless, impulsive, self-important, and too closely tied to Adenauer. They assert that what is needed at the top is a more dynamic personality who will inject new ideas into the organization. Otto A. Friedrich, director general of the Phoenix Rubber Corporation, has occasionally been mentioned as a possible successor; however, as an ardent follower of Erhard's neo-liberalism he would receive major support only from light industry.[39] Thus, although there is an undercurrent of dissatisfaction with some of Berg's policies and public statements, and although big business would occasionally prefer to see a stronger exponent of its interests in the presidency, thus far no pro- or anti-Berg bloc has developed, and it seems likely that Berg will stay in office in the years immediately ahead. Whether he will retire in 1966, as rumored, remains to be seen.

There may be more than a coincidence in the remarkable similarities between the president of the BDI and his counterpart, Georges Villiers of the Conseil National du Patronat Français. According to Henry Ehrmann, Villiers also heads a

[37] *Financial Times*, Feb. 27, 1958.

[38] *Ibid.*

[39] A writer for *Fortune* described Friedrich as a man of "exceptional vision and public responsibility," and "the German equivalent of Paul Hoffman." XLV (March 1952), 155.

family-owned metal works which has brought him some afflu-
ence.[40] As president of the CNPF, Villiers over the years has
gained new stature in the employer movement, and he too has
escaped the label of being an all-out proponent of either big
or small business. The two men, who are close personal friends,
would not appear to be intellectual giants, but to have been
attracted to the positions they hold because of the power they
are able to wield over the employer community.

Any generalization that might be based on these limited ob-
servations concerning two leaders can be no more than tentative.
It is safe to say, however, that there is a certain type of ambitious
personality that seeks leadership in employer associations not
for any financial gain but for the power and prestige inherent
in the office. If Berg and Villiers had not attained that kind of
prestige, they would be comparative unknowns in their own
respective countries. They are able to confront the tycoons of
industry with some authority only because during the unsettled
postwar period big business has been content to let others,
including the heads of family firms, take the driver's seat. If
in the future big business assumes a more aggressive stance,
there may no longer be an opportunity for men like Berg and
Villiers. In Great Britain, for instance, the presidency of the
Federation of British Industries (FBI), which is rotated every
two years, is held by "chairmen of multimillionaire corporations," who carry a good deal of moral weight, take a broad view
of the interests of industry, and have excellent contacts with
the industrial community.[41] In the United States, the NAM
likewise had a rotating presidency until 1962; but the office
does not necessarily go to a member of the big business fraternity. (The president chosen in 1960 was R. F. Bannow, head
of Bridgeport Machines, Inc.)

In the internal process of arriving at decisions the gap between theory and practice is often wide. Berg has indicated

[40] *Organized Business in France,* pp. 133–135.
[41] Finer, "The Federation of British Industries," p. 70.

that democratic rules of voting usually cannot be applied in the governing bodies because they so often lead to protracted wrangles and thus exacerbate the differences among the associations. He once remarked at a presidential board meeting that if too many different views were to be aired among the membership, the organization would be paralyzed just where speed is of the essence. In practice the views of the most powerful associations and individuals tend to prevail, even when they are in a minority. Where they are deeply divided among themselves on an issue, the Federation may not take a stand at all.

The problems of voting are illustrated by an executive board meeting held in the fall of 1959, when a national dispute was raging over a government plan to increase the tax on fuel oil in order to help the ailing coal industry. The views expressed by members of the various associations were of course colored by the effect of the tax on their own industries. When a member called for a vote that would have shown just who was for and who against, Berg argued that a vote would only intensify the divisions over this delicate issue.[42]

One annual report of the BDI contains the frank statement that "never in German economic history have crisis developments been overcome through votes or majority decisions, but rather by finding men who were ready, because of their duty vis-à-vis the economy, to take decisive steps, and thereby also carry responsibility."[43]

Occasionally the BDI is forced by pressure from certain of its associations to take a vote on a divisive issue. This happened, for example, to the much debated question of reforming the turnover tax, on which no compromise could be reached. Two-thirds of the associations favored a reform, the other third were opposed, and there were powerful voices in both camps. Berg

[42] Hauptgeschäftsführung (HGF), *Vorstandssitzung vom 4. September 1956* (hereafter referred to as *Vorstandssitzung*, with date). Protocol issued by the Executive Office of the BDI on Sept. 11, 1956.

[43] *JB*, 1953–1954, p. 22.

declared that if as a result of the differences within the Federation no stand were taken, the Federation might find itself not being consulted on the issue in the future. At a meeting of the presidential board in December 1959 he asked for authorization to inform Adenauer that the BDI supported a reform. A minority refused to concur. At the next meeting in January 1960, his proposal was again rejected. Instead there was an agreement —which the executive office considered unsatisfactory—to inform the government of the division within the BDI.[44] This example serves to indicate the power of a minority to block action when its vital interests are directly at stake.

In effect, the Federation's position is such that it cannot alienate either big or small business, either heavy or light industry, for any length of time, for fear that, at worst, a dissident wing may leave. Hence the president and the executive office must constantly work for compromise on issues of a divisive nature.

The Ideology of the BDI

What, it may be asked, is the nature of the decisions made by the elite? Do they rest on a preconceived system of values, with well-defined goals? Has the BDI developed a systematic ideology or merely a pragmatic program of action? Experience to date would seem to indicate that the BDI has stressed the need for an ideology but that in practice it has put more emphasis on tactics and strategy.

At the outset it was clear that the goals of the BDI would correspond to those of other interest groups. Thus, (1) it would defend its interests in order to prevent any unfavorable action by the government in areas of immediate import, such as European integration, foreign trade, and defense; (2) it would educate and indoctrinate its members; (3) it would try for a consensus on policies, which would then be communicated to

44 HGF, *Niederschrift über die Präsidialsitzung vom 14. Januar 1960* (hereafter referred to as *Präsidialsitzung*, with date).

the public, the government, and the legislature; (4) it would carry on intergroup negotiation and bargaining with other national organizations in Germany and abroad.[45] BDI leaders and members realized that it would take time to achieve these goals, but made them the framework for action. To preclude any criticism by skeptics in the nation and beyond, all doctrinaire statements were carefully avoided at the founding of the organization in 1949. As time went on, however, statements on economic and political affairs were released by the Federation or by publicists closely allied with it.

The question of what kind of state is envisaged by the BDI as a model is not easily answered. In the economic realm it has followed an ambiguous policy. In theory it has supported the social market economy (*soziale Marktwirtschaft*) as launched by Ludwig Erhard, a former professor of business economics and Chancellor since 1963. This economic system rests on Catholic social theory and on the neo-liberalist theory propounded by Friedrich Hayek, Wilhelm Röpke, Alexander Rüstow, and others. The latter theory has been described as "liberal conservativism with a streak of social radicalism." It has flourished since World War II primarily as an answer to communist and fascist ideologies, and has been institutionalized in the Liberal International, a movement founded in 1947, which has some political and economic strength in western Europe and especially in Germany. Here its proponents are to be found in all the nonsocialist parties, but primarily in the Free Democratic Party, a successor to the liberal parties of the pre-Nazi era. German neo-liberalism has strong parallels with the American doctrine of free enterprise. The accent is on the freedom of the economy to evolve within the context of some government regulation and interference. It is acknowledged that in order to maintain maximum competition and prevent a concentration of power, the state must assume some controls. Subsidies to the

[45] *Fünf Jahre BDI*, p. 17; Herrmann, "Industrielle Organisationen," pp. 268–269.

economy are generally frowned upon except where they are designed to correct basic weaknesses. There is an emphasis, too, on eliminating the inequities of the nineteenth-century capitalist system. The accent is thus on social benefits for the masses, and lately on their sharing in the entrepreneurial profits by owning stocks. As Carl J. Friedrich observes, "The neo-liberal movement is strongly economic in orientation. The neo-liberals see economics as 'embedded' in politics, and are convinced that economic and political systems are strictly interrelated."[46] On occasion, however, the BDI has assailed such theorists of non-liberalism as Röpke and Rüstow, on whose ideas Erhard has so heavily relied. The BDI believes that the state is establishing too many restraints and controls upon the business fraternity, but that in periods of crisis for some industries it is not generous enough in its subventions. On this problem there are, of course, dissenting views within the BDI. A minority for which O. A. Friedrich is a spokesman, has loyally supported the Erhard line. Friedrich has maintained that there is no more dangerous concentration of power than that produced when the state and the economy join forces, and that if freedom is to be sustained a separation between the two is essential. In any event, all elements in the BDI are opposed to a mammoth state, which they fear would become collectivist and socialist.

Although politically the BDI supports the democratic form of government, the depth of its commitment is hard to gauge. Obviously some industrialists are more favorable to it than others. Many of them interpret democracy as the rule not of the masses but rather of a responsible elite. According to their view, it is the business of an economic elite to share in the governing of the nation and promote its general welfare.[47] To

---

[46] Carl J. Friedrich, "The Political Thought of Neo-Liberalism," *The American Political Science Review*, XLIX, No. 2 (June 1955), 511; Winschuh, *Das neue Unternehmerbild: Grundzüge einer Unternehmerpolitik* (Baden-Baden, 1954), pp. 121, 184–185; *Unternehmerbrief des DI*, No. 21, May 1957, pp. 1–3 (hereafter referred to as *UB*).

[47] *JB*, 1959–1960, p. 36.

avoid giving any impression that it is an interest group with base, selfish, and narrow aims, the BDI constantly identifies its own goals with those of the entire nation. It rationalizes this position by declaring that a one-sided presentation would only weaken its influence on a skeptical public, and that it is already broadening its interests by making compromises among its constituent associations. It pledges its loyalty to the nation so long as the administration and parliament are both willing to consult it on economic matters, asserting that it would not assume a position of power either parallel to the state or as a state within the state—which, the BDI argues, is precisely what the trade unions did when they threatened to call a general strike in order to obtain desired legislation.

In essence, "the employer must regard himself as the bulwark and champion of a political and economic order in which the basic principle is the inviolable freedom of creativity for the individual and the capacity of each individual to develop his own powers."[48] The employer must be ready to defend this traditional order, and to persuade the people of its superiority over any other. As one of the guardians of an important part of the nation's wealth, the argument continues, he must play a corresponding role in politics, because his sense of reality and of responsibility can serve the state most usefully, and can secure a proper social order.[49]

One German publicist cites the example of the United States as a country in which businessmen are regarded as constituting the leadership, and are not bound by the dictates of bureaucrats or politicians. Although the same publicist speaks of other elites in German society as capable of sharing the spotlight with the employers, the inference is that employers ought to form the primary elite at this stage of historical development, especially since economic forces are still so great a determinant in the political sphere. Thus the new elite is envisioned as governing a state

[48] *JB*, 1952–1953, p. 18.
[49] *JB*, 1958–1959, p. 40.

in which a synthesis of economics and politics had been achieved —a goal which, its proponents argue, is the establishment of an industrial society primarily by businessmen.[50]

Running through all these arguments is an irrational belief in managerial superiority, in charismatic leadership based upon a "calling." There is a negative attitude toward the party conflicts of a democratic system, and toward the mass of voters, who are assumed to be politically immature and confused, and to act on the basis of envy, emotionalism, and radicalism.[51]

This kind of thinking may be partially explained by historical and social factors. The social prestige of the entrepreneur in the early nineteenth century had not been high, since his concern appeared to be solely with profits. But since the end of the nineteenth century he has become a pillar of the community. World War II brought the demise of such rival elite groups as the Prussian landed gentry, the officer corps, and the aristocracy. After a few setbacks at the beginning, during the last decade the power of the entrepreneur has risen rapidly, and he can now consider himself an influential person.

Not all entrepreneurs hold this view. As will presently be shown, few are actually interested in direct political activity. Many would question the thesis of the primary importance of the economy. Nevertheless, most of them share, whether consciously or not, the concept of an elite class—a concept that provides the necessary cohesion to the employer community, and that is especially cultivated at the managerial training centers for junior executives which are operated by the BDI and other economic associations. Of course, this sense of belonging to an elite is strengthened by the need to fight for some immediate goal or to defend the status quo.

[50] Herbert Gross, "Die geistigen Grundlagen," *Unternehmer in der Politik*, ed. Gustav Stein (Düsseldorf, 1954), pp. 54, 170, 171, 173.

[51] *Ibid.*, p. 166; Hartmann, *Authority and Organization in German Management*, pp. 22 ff.

CONCLUSION

Who the holders of power really are, how they arrive at their decisions, what checks can be exerted upon them, and what measure of internal democracy exists in practice—these are the questions to be asked of any organization. The thesis of Brady, Berle, and Means, among others, that there is a narrowing de facto control of the business world by very "small, almost entirely self-perpetuating and largely nonowner directorial and managerial cliques,"[52] would seem to hold true for the BDI as well. Although family ownership of enterprises is still romanticized, even all but deified, in Germany its actual significance in the economy would seem to be declining. It is true that some entrepreneurs hold key positions in the BDI, but power is vested primarily in a directorial body of executives from large corporations and in the managerial command. Among these officials who share in the making of decisions, there has been remarkably little "circulation of elites." Rather, as in other countries, they tend to be "self-appointed, self-perpetuating, and autocratic,"[53] and to exert pressures on the executive and legislative branches.

Robert Michels' thesis that mass membership organizations have an oligarchical superstructure and few democratic controls applies as well to the BDI, even though it rests on a small membership base. From a constitutional point of view, the trappings of democracy are there—in the obligation to hold periodic elections of officers and in the power of the General Assembly to decide on the general line of policy. But in actuality the elections merely ratify the choices already agreed upon by the presidential board. To some extent this development is due

[52] Brady, *Business as a System of Power*, p. 13; Adolf A. Berle and Gardiner C. Means, *The Modern Corporation and Private Property* (New York, 1932), and a discussion of this theme by Hartmann, *Authority and Organization in German Management, passim.*

[53] Brady, *Business as a System of Power*, p. 313 (his reference is to business in general). On the BDI presidential board, the average age of the members in 1962 was 63 years.

to apathy among the membership, and to the fact that an individual entrepreneur is far removed from the central locus of power. Since it is structured as a confederation, from which individual corporate membership is excluded, the BDI officially deals only with the representatives of its constituent associations. Thus a centralized hierarchical system has evolved in which the interests of, say, an individual textile firm are represented only indirectly in the BDI, through the Association of the German Textile Industry. In effect, oligarchical control is made possible by a high degree of centralization and bureaucratization in which an active minority hold the seats of power. So long as the members of this group can demonstrate a modicum of success, the membership will give them its support.

Some latent checks upon the freedom of the power-holders do exist. Their decisions can neither be made in a vacuum nor run counter to the interests of the associations, since the latter can always secede. No one has left the BDI so far; but a threat to secede actually carried out would impair the effectiveness and prestige of the Federation. Furthermore, the decisions of the power-holders must take into consideration those made by competing groups and by the government. On several occasions the president of the BDI has been forced to recognize that he could not pose as the sole spokesman for all of industry without being severely criticized. The unity within the BDI is anything but monolithic. Its fabric has been weakened at times by struggles among divergent sub-elites. Such infighting may be harmful to the interests of the organization; but on the other hand it does promote a certain democratic give and take. At any rate, there is enough cohesion based on common interests and a common philosophy to unite the divergent factions in the long run.

A comparison of the BDI with the NAM, its counterpart in the United States, reveals both likenesses and contrasts. Both associations represent a conservative political philosophy and have an extensive national network. But the BDI is much more centrally organized and inclusive than the NAM, despite the fact that both operate in federal, although dissimilar, political systems. The trade associations and state manufacturing associations belonging to the NAM enjoy a degree of independence from the parent organization that tends to weaken its total effectiveness. The BDI by comparison thus wields more power in the body politic than the NAM.[54]

A comparison of the BDI with the Federation of British Industries shows parallels in their power structure. In the FBI, as in the BDI, policy is made by the president and his official advisers, the professional staff, and the committees.[55] The French counterpart of the BDI, the Conseil National du Patronat Français, is structured similarly.[56] Such parallels obviously suggest that employer organizations, by and large, develop a framework for action corresponding to their needs and their historical traditions. The NAM, reflecting the strong federalist tradition of the United States, is an exception to the oligarchical and centralist pattern found in the other organizations.

[54] Gilbert Burck, "The German Business Mind," *Fortune*, IL (May 1954), 114; Truman, *The Governmental Process*, pp. 137 ff; Almond, *The Politics of German Business*, pp. 39–40.

[55] Finer, "The Federation of British Industries," pp. 61–84. See also FBI annual reports and pamphlets.

[56] Ehrmann, *Organized Business in France*; Jean Meynaud, *Les groupes de pression en France* (Paris, 1958).

PART TWO: TACTICS AND TARGETS

III

Public Opinion and

Mass Communications Media

FOR a fuller insight into the way in which the BDI acts as an interest group at all levels of political activity, it is necessary to investigate both its tactical approaches and its targets, public opinion and the mass communications media, parties and their electoral struggles, the legislature, and the executive. The judiciary is omitted from consideration as a target not because its role is insignificant, but because problems of litigation and claims are dealt with by the BDI primarily in the more specialized Finance Courts. The first target to be considered in this survey is public opinion and the media of communication.

New dimensions have been added to the age of advertising in which we live. In the United States the efforts of "Madison Avenue" are still directed mainly toward manipulating the consumer's choice among the myriad goods and services available to him; but it has also played its part in political campaigns. In Europe, especially since World War II, organized groups and parties are also devoting much money and effort to the techniques of advertising. The success of such efforts depends not only on public relations activities but also on the social setting, the type of audience, the political climate, and the degree of consensus or fragmentation in the body politic.

And what of the public relations efforts of the BDI, their magnitude and their impact upon the public and the communications media? Fundamentally, of course, any organization, in whatever country, differs little from any other in its drive to wield optimum power in a political climate that is either favorable or unfavorable to its interests. But less is known of why some interest groups, the French business associations, for example, should be publicity-shy or consider large-scale public relations programs a waste of money, while others, such as the BDI, devote a considerable portion of their budget to publicity. As one study of interest groups has pointed out, the answer may lie in the pattern of communications activity, or the type of political community in which the interest group operates.[1] In any event, no matter what technique a group may use, the ends remain the same: the creation of a favorable climate, in which its demands will be met by the executive and legislative branches of government.

Despite its close ties with the administration and the governing parties, in recent years the BDI has become more aware of the necessity of influencing public opinion. Traditionally German employers have shrouded their business activities in secrecy, and have been excessively shy of publicity. During the last decade the BDI and other business associations have urged them to change their attitude, and this campaign has met with a fair amount of success. For example, although 20 per cent of all firms still refuse to issue to the authorities and the public any but the legal minimum of information concerning their finances, the rest have released an increasing amount of data, and in an increasingly attractive form.[2] The degree of public relations consciousness decreases with the size of the company,

[1] Committee on Comparative Politics, *A Comparative Study of Interest Groups and the Political Process*, pp. 15–18.
[2] *JB*, 1956–1957, p. 50.

so that small firms tend to hold to the tradition of avoiding publicity.

To counter this attitude, the German Public Relations Society was set up with headquarters in Bad Godesberg, near Bonn, and staffed by a group of public relations experts closely identified with industry. The purposes of the society are to promote all aspects of public relations, to refine its techniques, and to provide for the training of specialists—no small assignment, since public relations in Germany is still looked upon with a good deal of apprehension and mistrust.

The BDI itself has had to embark on an intensive public relations campaign in order to change the image of the business leader held by the average German, and to increase the knowledgeability of the public on economic matters. In the early postwar years the German public had little enthusiasm for the traditional values and concepts of the entrepreneurial system. From polls it would appear that several factors may have accounted for this attitude. There were many who blamed industry for collaborating with the Hitler regime, for its part in the preparations for war, and for its failure to bring about economic prosperity. Because of the economic stagnation after the war, a majority declared that they were worse off than in previous years.

On the left there was also the traditional criticism of industry for generally ideological reasons. For instance, of a sampling who were asked the question, "In a dispute between employers and workers would your sympathies in general lie more with the former or the latter?" a majority identified themselves with the worker.[3] The legacy of German class-consciousness was reflected in the fact that 52 percent of the workers questioned replied that employers were only thinking of their own profits and had no social consciousness.[4] Many of these same workers

[3] Unpublished survey, 1957, by DIVO-Institut, Frankfurt/Main.
[4] "Unternehmen und Unternehmer im Spiegel der Meinungsforschung," *UB*, No. 5, Jan. 30, 1958; DI, *Wirtschafts- und Sozialprobleme in der öffentlichen Meinung* (hectographed, 1958).

believed that employers wanted to increase social tensions. On the other hand, the attitude of a worker toward his own boss was more favorable than that toward employers as a class where his own immediate contact with superiors in the plant or shop was friendly.

A postwar poll of youth leaders bore out the same ideological attitude toward industrialists. To the query, "Do you have any reservations about big industrialists holding high positions in the federal government?" 34 per cent answered that they had strong reservations, 36 per cent that they had some reservations, 26 per cent that they had no reservations, and 4 per cent that they had no opinion. The conclusion from this particular study was that leading industrialists in government posts "incur ill will most often from the less educated, as well as from respondents favoring a socialistic economic system, *i.e.* SPD partisans and trade union members."[5]

Thus it is not surprising to discover that in a scale of popularity among several largely unrelated professions, university professors were found to rank first, bishops second, and directors of large corporations third.[6] The results were similar in another poll taken in 1958 on the question of what group was doing the most good for the country. Here statesmen were ranked first, trade union leaders second, the clergy third, and top industrialists fourth.[7] In an international study, also taken in 1958, the attitude toward employers was found to be most favorable in Denmark, followed in descending order by Great Britain,

[5] DIVO, *Basic Orientation and Political Thinking of West German Youth and Their Leaders* (hectographed, 1956), pp. 62–63. See also OMGUS Berlin, "German Opinions on Socialization of Industry," *ICD Opinion Survey*, Report No. 90, Jan. 23, 1948, p. 3.

[6] An EMNID survey of 1956 cited by Alfred Grosser, *Die Bonner Demokratie* (Düsseldorf, 1960), p. 261. Thirty-one per cent ranked professors highest, 27 per cent bishops, 12 per cent directors; the remaining 30 per cent listed other professions or gave no answer. Astonishingly, SPD members ranked directors fairly high.

[7] *Umfragen, Ereignisse und Probleme der Zeit im Urteil der Bevölkerung* (published by DIVO-Institut, II, Frankfurt, 1959), p. 62.

Sweden, and Japan; and was found to be most unfavorable in the Netherlands, West Germany, and Italy.[8] To some degree the extent of social tensions and traditional class hostility would account for the differences in attitude.

Despite such indications of the relative unpopularity of employers in West German society, especially during the years immediately following the war, there is no doubt that they now enjoy more esteem than ever before. The change is due to popular satisfaction with the miracle of economic prosperity, and to a lesser extent to the campaign by industry itself to create a more favorable attitude toward employers. Thus, whereas in 1950 only 7 per cent of a sampling of the population felt that they lived better than before the war, by 1959 the percentage had risen to 40 per cent.[9] Similarly, other surveys reveal a declining support for the nationalization of industries.[10]

Proponents of the free enterprise system are nevertheless still not completely satisfied. They point out that despite growing support for their system the population at large are relatively ignorant of economic matters, and cite public opinion polls to reinforce their arguments. For instance, 56 per cent of the total population (or 59 per cent of the workers) had no understanding of what was meant by "social market economy"; and 27 per cent did not know what "stocks" were.[11] Although 84 per cent could identify the Krupp firm, only 37 per cent had

[8] *Ibid.*, p. 63. The index numbers, based on subtracting the negative from the positive statements, are: Denmark +30; Great Britain +16; Sweden +14; Japan +4; the Netherlands −1; West Germany −4; Italy −6.

[9] "Wie denkt die Bevölkerung über die Wirtschaft?" *UB*, No. 29, July 21, 1960.

[10] Reactions Analysis Staff, Office of Public Affairs, HICOG, Germany, *Trend in German Opinions on Socialization of Industry*, Report No. 27, Serial No. 2, July 27, 1950; *Umfragen 1957* (published by DIVO-Institut, (Frankfurt, 1958), p. 77; *UB*, No. 29, July 21, 1960.

[11] *Die Waage, Ein Bericht über die Tätigkeit in den Jahren 1952–1957*, p. 2; DI, *Wirtschafts- und Sozialprobleme in der öffentlichen Meinung*, pp. 2–3; "Was sagt die Bevölkerung über die Marktwirtschaft?", *UB*, No. 1, Jan. 5, 1961.

heard of Hermann Reusch, a leading steel industrialist and BDI official.[12] As in other countries, there is a strong correlation between interest in and comprehension of political and economic affairs: those who care little about economic affairs care equally little about politics, and vice versa.

Thus when industrial associations embark on multiple efforts at the indoctrination and education of the general public, as well as of their own members, the purpose is to mobilize support for the goals of the BDI and of other national organizations vis-à-vis the executive and legislative branches of the central and state governments. Indoctrination of the public also serves to create a more favorable image of the employer. Accordingly there is a constant emphasis on the achievements of industry, on the way in which it has contributed to the welfare of the nation.[13]

Moreover, for not altogether disinterested reasons the BDI has been active in furthering educational, scientific, and cultural affairs. Despite some grumbling from socially-conscious artists about industry's subsidies to those who are less so, there is no doubt about the BDI's consequent gain in prestige among the general public. It has been able, after all, to raise 50 million DM a year for educational and scientific affairs. From the American point of view such sums appear modest, but in Germany owing to smaller tax incentives, private industry is not over-enthusiastic about such expenditures, and is just beginning to donate sizable funds for purposes not directly related to its immediate functions. It was not until 1959 that the Fritz Thyssen firm set up the first major private foundation in Ger-

[12] *Wirtschafts- und Sozialprobleme,* p. 5. A 1963 poll of workers and salaried employees showed that 36 per cent had heard of the BDI (51 per cent had heard of the BDA), but that of these many had no further knowledge or had the wrong information. *Hannoversche Allgemeine,* as cited in *The German Tribune,* July 27, 1963, p. 13.

[13] See, *e.g.,* Carl Neumann, "Der Unternehmer und die öffentliche Meinung," *Vortragsreihe des DI,* No. 10, March 10, 1958 (hereafter referred to as *VR*).

man history, apparently to facilitate the merger of two companies. On its board of trustees is, *inter alia*, President Berg, thus giving the BDI yet another indirect opportunity to control the awarding of funds. Whether the establishment of the fund in itself demonstrates a greater awareness of corporate responsibility to society remains to be seen.[14] On a number of occasions BDI spokesmen have also urged employers to make a less conspicuous show of their wealth. Instead, they have been told, if the employer wishes to contribute to the betterment of society, then let him donate more money to science and the arts.

The BDI itself engages in relatively modest publicity activities, leaving the bulk of the work to the Institute of German Industry. Among the publications of the former are a yearly report, a monthly news bulletin, and a series of publications on diverse topics. It has also been active in organizing industrial fairs, although its proposed "Week of Industry" failed to arouse any enthusiasm.

The regional offices of the BDI in each of the *Länder* engage in a good deal of public relations work. Contact with the "interested" public—teachers, the clergy, doctors, lawyers, and civil servants, among others—is assiduously cultivated in the hope of instilling an appreciation of the economic system which may in turn be transmitted to the mass public. To this end, public lectures and seminars are held, teachers are provided with informative material and with speakers for their classrooms, factory tours are organized, and university students are invited to meetings of the local industrial associations.

Individual employers have also conducted intensive "human relations" programs in their plants. Many of the larger companies have their own house organs, libraries, sport clubs, kindergarten, and youth groups.[15] Such efforts are aimed at

[14] *JB*, 1958–1959, p. 83; "Zehn Jahre Kulturkreis im BDI," *Bulletin*, No. 178, Sept. 22, 1961, p. 1697; *News from the German Embassy* (Washington), IV, No. 5 (Aug. 5, 1960), 2.

[15] Horst Berger, "Im Spinnennetz der 'Human Relations,'" *Vorwärts*, Sept. 11, 1959.

creating a company spirit, and reflect a degree of paternalism on the part of the firm. Whether they are successful in winning over employers and workers is problematical. Among many of the latter, loyalty to the trade union and the Social Democratic Party has not been affected. But among others an identification with the firm and with the prevailing free enterprise system has been the result. This is especially true among many white-collar employees who are moving up in status, rank, and pay.

INSTITUTE OF GERMAN INDUSTRY

Public relations at the national level are primarily handled by the Institute of German Industry (Deutsches Industrieinstitut, or DI) set up jointly by the BDI and the BDA in January 1951, with its own separate headquarters in Cologne. Among its founders were a small number of industrialists, including Carl Neumann, its board chairman from the beginning, who is head of the textile association and a member of the presidential boards of both the BDI and the BDA. Until 1959 the managing director was Dr. Fritz Hellwig, who was active in the highest CDU councils and was also a deputy in parliament. He left these posts upon being named to the Commission of the European Coal and Steel Community, and was succeeded in the DI office by Dr. Ludwig Losacker, formerly business manager of the Employers' Associations of the German Chemical Industry (BDA). The DI is organized into departments dealing with associations, parties and legal matters, economic and social policy, public relations, and educational services.

To give the point of view of industry to the public and its own members in the most favorable light, the DI engages in costly research and publicity campaigns. In 1959 the payroll budget alone amounted to 1.5 million DM, and at least the same amount was spent for publicity.[16] In that year there were

[16] In 1954, 600,000 DM was spent for the payroll, 400,000 DM for public relations, and between 410,000 and 440,000 DM for other expenses. *Präsidialsitzung*, April 5, 1955.

between thirty-five and forty high-level specialists out of a total staff of 140. American manufacturing associations, however, have even larger staffs and spend more money on publicity than their German counterparts.

The DI sees its primary tasks as supporting the work of the BDI and BDA, helping to make clear the advantages of the free enterprise system, making known the views of industry to the public, attempting to obtain backing for or against particular pieces of legislation, and creating an atmosphere of public good will toward industry.

In carrying on its public relations efforts the DI puts out an impressive array of publications and news releases, many of which are written in a vigorous, readable, and persuasive style. Its clientele ranges from trade associations to government officials and the interested public. The materials issued deal primarily with questions of economics and industrial relations, but political affairs are not entirely omitted. Many articles, for instance, are attacks on the SPD and the trade unions.[17] Much of the material is used by the press, radio, and television, as well as by representatives of industry in speaking to groups throughout the nation. To the charge by its opponents that it fails to live up to its claims of objectivity, the DI replies that it was organized partially to neutralize the efforts of the trade union research institute. At any rate, not a month goes by without some controversy between the two institutes.

Another effort to sell the employer philosophy, although not one directly related to the publicity work of the BDI and the DI, is *Die Waage* (the word *Waage* means "scale" or "balance

[17] The DI issues a semiweekly news sheet (*Schnelldienst*), sent primarily to employers' associations, the government, universities, and the press; a weekly information letter (*UB*), sent primarily to business firms; a weekly reprint of a lecture given by an employer (*VR*); a fortnightly release to the workers (*Mitarbeiterbrief*), with a circulation of 100,000; a daily commentary on radio programs; a weekly "Economic Report from Germany" sent to most countries abroad; and a number of other publications. *Publications of the German Industrial Institute* (mimeographed, n.p., n.d.). See also *Veröffentlichungen des DI 1951–1961* (Köln, 1961).

wheel"), an organization formed by a group of employers, some of them close to the BDI, in September 1952, with the aim of boosting Professor Erhard's version of the free competitive system. Considering such traditional publicity methods as cultivating the press inadequate for this task, the group opted instead for mass advertising. In a systematic saturation coverage, conspicuous advertisements have appeared in newspapers which, as a group, account for 30 per cent of the country's total circulation, as well as on billboards, and have been incorporated into film shorts to be shown in commercial movie houses. The advertisements are merely attributed to the organization, and thus do not reveal the constitution of its membership.

Die Waage goes into high gear when pending legislation threatens the principles of the social market economy; when labor strife is intense; and during election campaigns, when it follows a nonpartisan line, although through its propaganda effort it gives indirect support to all nonsocialist parties that stand for free enterprise. An official of *Die Waage* has revealed that the organization spends an average of 1.2 million DM yearly; of course the figure is considerably higher during an election year.[18] The same official complained of the reluctance of employers to contribute generously or—especially those in heavy industry—to contribute at all. To some extent this situation is due to the presence on supervisory boards of coal and steel firms of trade union representatives who would look unfavorably upon such contributions. For this reason, the bulk of *Die Waage*'s financial support has come from consumer goods industries that have traditionally relied to a large extent on advertising in their public relations work.

[18] The SPD estimated an expenditure of 6–10 million DM for the 1953 election. *Unternehmermillionen kaufen politische Macht!* (Bonn, n.d.). For further details on *Die Waage* see its own releases; also Almond, *The Politics of German Business*, pp. 45–46.

MASS COMMUNICATIONS MEDIA

The BDI uses the most important media of mass communications—the press, radio, television, and films—to carry its message to the public. The techniques it employs, and the degree of its success in persuading its constituent associations, and employers generally, to cultivate these media will now be examined.

The Press

In order to maintain direct contact with newspapers and journals the BDI occasionally holds formal press conferences; however, it prefers to cultivate the friendship of journalists and the representatives of other media on an individual basis at monthly luncheon meetings or through scheduled tours of plants. Confidential, off-the-record information is sometimes fed to certain domestic and foreign journalists, who are expected not to publicize it but to use it merely as background information. The BDI has also set up a working group in which the heads of its own press department as well as those of the individual associations and the large corporations meet occasionally to discuss common problems and to share experiences—such as how to write stories so as to avoid having them land in the editor's wastebasket.

Obviously the goal of the BDI is to provide the reader with maximum exposure to news from industry. The daily avalanche of releases for domestic and foreign consumption that reach the press and the wire services originate not only with the BDI but with the DI, the constituent associations, and individual companies. Although the DI once estimated that at least 50 per cent of the press—which has a total circulation of 13.5 million —used a special news article or commentary sent to it at any one time, industry is still dissatisfied with the extent of the coverage. The highly popular "boulevard" press usually has no separate section for economic and financial news. Such news, if it appears at all, consists of brief items.

One survey has shown that the more responsible newspapers

tend to be more generous, providing a maximum of 25 per cent of their entire coverage to events in the business community. But the depressing fact remains that out of 1,400 daily newspapers only a hundred carry such news in a separate economic and financial section. Moreover, according to another survey, where it does exist that section is one of those least read by the average citizen. Whether this reflects a fundamental lack of interest or the dry and difficult nature of the material is difficult to judge. It is hardly surprising that more men than women are interested in this kind of news, and that among men an interest in economic matters develops with age.[19]

The BDI at one time considered illustrated journals to be the worst offenders in ignoring news of economic and political affairs, to which less than 2 per cent of their articles were devoted. When it came to articles about industry, many of these dealt only with reports on trade fairs or textile showings, such as lend themselves readily to visual presentation. Industry complained that one cause for the paucity of material in these journals as well as in the daily press was a lack of qualified economic journalists.[20] The press retorted that all too many journalists had been lured by attractive salaries into public relations work for industry. In recent years, however, journals have been devoting more space to economic affairs.

The BDI is interested not only in news coverage but also in the editorial policy of the press. Since fewer than 7 per cent of

---

[19] The chief newspapers—*Frankfurter Allgemeine Zeitung* (hereafter referred to as *FAZ*) and *Die Welt*—carry from 20 to 25 per cent; a second group, including the *Frankfurter Rundschau* and *Rheinischen Post*, carry from 1/7 to 1/11; a third group, including the *Hannoverschen Presse* and *Abendpost*, carry economic reports only from 1/13 to 1/50 of their coverage, the average totaling 5.5 per cent for papers with a circulation of over 100,000. Wolfgang Mansfeld, "Wirtschaft und Presse," *VR*, No. 27, July 7, 1958. "Spannungsfeld Wirtschaft und Öffentlichkeit," *Der Volkswirt* (supplement, n.d.), p. 18; *Der Westdeutsche Markt in Zahlen* (published by DIVO-Institut, Frankfurt, 1958), p. 151.

[20] DI, *Die deutschen Illustrierten*, Strukturbericht No. 7 (March 1958), p. 10.

the newspapers reflect the line of the SPD, the BDI attempts to convince the rest that the interests and goals of industry correspond with those of the nation. If after 1945 the Allies had given licenses to the old entrepreneurial families who had once owned many of the newspapers, the task of the BDI might have been relatively easy. Even so, some of the leading dailies and weeklies closely follow the conservative line, for example the now defunct *Die Deutsche Zeitung mit Wirtschaftszeitung,* and also *Das Handelsblatt, Die Frankfurter Allgemeine Zeitung,* and *Der Industriekurier.* The last tends to support medium-sized industry, and is occasionally critical of the BDI. *Die Frankfurter Allgemeine Zeitung* was actually launched by the managers of a number of large corporations, who put up the necessary capital. It tends to support Erhard's neo-liberal policy, and thus has clashed with the BDI on several occasions.[21]

In the matter of editorial policy there is, as in other countries, a subtle relation between the press and advertising. The heavy reliance by the press on income from this source means that a newspaper subsidized by the BDI and industry, such as *Die Deutsche Zeitung mit Wirtschaftszeitung,* will be extremely reluctant to print any stories adverse to the interests of industry. Indeed when BDI officials in 1964 realized the extent of their subsidy to this particular newspaper they cut off all aid entirely, which led to its collapse. In the mass circulation press, according to the estimate given to this writer by one journalist, from 10 to 15 per cent of the stories are either colored by corporate advertising or placed inconspicuously in order not to alienate it.[22] A few cases have actually come to light in which advertising

[21] Hans Münster, *Die Presse in Deutschland,* Vol. I, *Die Moderne Presse* (Bad Kreuznach, 1955), p. 84. In 1957, 24.5 per cent of the newspapers considered themselves independent; 13.5 per cent called themselves nonpartisan; 12.5 per cent were "home town" papers; while 6.6 per cent were sympathetic to the SPD, 4.2 per cent to the CDU, 1.9 per cent to the conservative and liberal parties, and 36.8 per cent were unknown. DI, *Die deutschen Tageszeitungen,* Strukturbericht No. 8 (Aug. 1958), p. 8. See Pritzkoleit, *Wem gehört Deutschland* (München, 1957), p. 228.

[22] Werner Friedmann, *Presse und öffentliche Meinung* (München, 1957)

was withdrawn, or there was a threat to withdraw it, as a result of stories unfavorable to industry. It would appear, from the report of one commentator, that during the protracted legislative struggle over a cartel law some companies made continuing to advertise contingent upon the editorial stand of the newspaper concerning the bill in question.[23]

As a result of such pressures, a few political parties and organizations have advocated the passage of a law guaranteeing freedom of opinion to journalists. Although industry is cool toward legislation of this sort, there is a realization that a favorable public image of itself would be swiftly destroyed by too many reports of coercion or of actual dishonesty. Consequently the BDI and other associations deemed it advisable to work with the press in adopting a code of standards which drew a sharp dividing line between text and advertisements.[24] But in itself the adoption of a code cannot solve the problems that inevitably arise so long as newspapers continue to depend greatly on advertising for their revenue. In small communities, especially, there is a danger to the independence of a newspaper in the often close relationship between a publisher and leading citizens, including businessmen, whom he does not want to alienate.

Nevertheless the concept of the freedom of the press has assumed more meaning in the postwar era than it had, say, in the Weimar years, when the press was often controlled by political parties and interest groups. Alfred Hugenberg is the classic example of a press czar in that he also headed the National People's Party, which was not only strongly oriented

---

makes the same point without giving a statistical estimate. See also Theodor Eschenburg, "Kritische Betrachtungen eines Zeitungslesers," *Der Journalist*, supplement, May 1960.

[23] Carl Guggomos, "Inserate und Pressefreiheit," *Vorwärts*, March 7, 1958; "Ist der Redakteur unabhängig?", *Junge Wirtschaft*, VI, No. 6 (June 1958), 236.

[24] It was worked out by Zentralausschuss der Werbewirtschaft, Bad Godesberg. Münster, *Die Presse in Deutschland*, p. 85.

toward business but largely controlled by it. Many more news-papers now follow an independent, nonpartisan line, which on occasion may be quite critical of the BDI or of its affiliated associations. Thus frictions are bound to occur; for example, a decision by the coal industry to raise prices produced a chorus of protest in editorials throughout the country. During the recent period of economic prosperity, some industries have been reluctant to provide the press with information about their activities and profits, for fear the trade unions would ask for a round of higher wages. An employer is naturally eager not to give a wholly rosy picture, and if the press fails to do so he will object. There is also the problem of those employers who live too ostentatiously and thereby contribute to an occasional bad press.

But despite such instances of strain between industry and the press, on the whole the relationship may be characterized as good. The bulk of the newspapers—excepting, of course, the trade union and socialist press—tend to give generally sympa-thetic treatment to industrial interests.

Radio Broadcasting

The potentialities for industry of radio and television broad-casting are not lost on the BDI. In November 1963 a total of seventeen million radio sets and eight million television sets were to be found in West German and West Berlin house-holds.[25] The broadcasting stations are operated as noncommer-cial, semiautonomous public law corporations administered by the *Länder*. Supervising the decentralized network of stations are broadcasting councils made up of members selected from various cultural, educational, and economic interest groups, including, of course, business associations and trade unions. In theory the members of these councils are to serve the general interest; but in practice the parties represented in the *Land*

[25] German Federal Republic, Presse- und Informationsamt, *The Bulletin,* Nov. 12, 1963 (English ed., hereafter referred to as *The Bulletin*).

legislatures, which have a role in their selection, also exert an influence on the choice of station personnel. As a result, the political complexion of the legislature tends to be mirrored in the makeup of a station's staff. A *Land* where the CDU has a majority will normally have a station manager sympathetic to the CDU and an assistant manager favorable to the SPD. The manager, incidentally, is entirely responsible for the station's programming.[26]

The BDI naturally looks askance at any station run by a pro-SPD manager, even while it realizes that no manager can afford to use the medium to publicize the views of his own party. As a matter of fact, any station will generally pursue a neutral policy for fear of arousing the wrath of the opposition. The BDI is concerned not only with having economic matters appear on news broadcasts (20 per cent in effect on an average) but even more in having weekly programs dealing with economics, and to a lesser extent with industrial relations, beamed to domestic audiences and also to those overseas. The directors of these programs, most of whom are quite sympathetic toward business, are free to choose the topics and speakers; the latter are often recommended to them by the top industrial and business associations, with which they maintain a close relationship.

The number of such weekly programs varies with the station. In 1959 one of the more enterprising stations in this respect, Radio Bavaria, transmitted an average of four program hours per week on economic affairs and industrial relations, and three of these hours were scheduled for the prime evening period. The programs lasted from one-half hour to an hour, and consisted of commentaries, speeches, documentaries, and interviews. But how many people actually listen to such broadcasts? According to one poll, the average program on economic affairs drew 15 per cent of all potential listeners, although occasionally a popu-

[26] See the author's "Federalism in Germany: The Broadcasting Controversy," *The Journal of Politics*, XXIV, No. 3 (Aug. 1962), 545–561. The section on radio and television is based to some extent on this article.

lar documentary might draw as many as one-third.[27] The economic program director of Radio Bavaria believes that interest in economic affairs is increasing among the listening audience. But to find ways of making such programs appealing enough to the mass public, as well as to more sophisticated listeners, is a challenge both to the broadcasters and to the managers of industry. The problem is compounded by the difficulty of locating employers who want to be on the air and who can also speak effectively.[28]

In 1955 the BDI formed a radio and television section within its press department to improve cooperation between the business community and the media. To this end, section and *Land* officials of the BDI have held numerous conferences with station directors and other leading personnel. Moreover, the DI has established a radio monitoring service in order to summarize and check on broadcasts of interest to its immediate clientele.

But industry really cannot put very much pressure on the broadcasters. Since the stations operate primarily on a noncommercial basis (their income is derived from monthly fees paid to the post office by the radio set owners), the impact that advertisers might otherwise have on the nature and contents of broadcast programs is negligible. Stations do allow commercials on some hour-long programs, but not on those during the prime listening time. Actually the stations have done a commendable job of providing equal time to the major interest groups. Despite occasional assertions to the contrary, it cannot be said that

[27] Letter from Rudolf Mühlfenzl, economic program director, Radio Bavaria, April 13, 1960. Ludwig Mellinger, *Wirtschaft und Funk*, No. 16, Schriftenreihe der Pressestelle Hessischer Kammern und Verbände (Frankfurt, 1957), p. 18. Economic news and programs total 6.5 per cent of all programs, which is a better ratio than the newspapers achieve with over 100,000 circulation (5.5 per cent). Mansfeld, "Wirtschaft und Presse," p. 5.

[28] Dieter Schäfer, "Die Türen weit offen halten-Die Wirtschaft in Rundfunk und Fernsehen," *Junge Wirtschaft*, VI, No. 6 (June 1958), 248–252; "Die Aufgaben des Wirtschaftsfunks," in "Spannungsfeld Wirtschaft und Öffentlichkeit," *Volkswirt*, pp. 21–25.

any group has been favored over another by the basically free and politically neutral medium of radio.[29]

Television Broadcasting

The newest communications medium, which in West Germany has been in operation since 1952, offers industry fewer opportunities than its competitor, radio. Association managers have frequently asserted that it is more difficult to present economic questions in an attractive package on television. Thus in the survey year 1958-1959 only 2 per cent of the programs in the afternoon and 5.7 per cent of those in the evening hours dealt with economics and labor relations. (In 1960 the latter figure had risen to 7 per cent.) The programs consisted primarily of reports from industry, such as a brief newsreel on a trade fair, or an outstanding industrial documentary. One such documentary did attract 27 per cent of the potential audience, of whom 70 per cent apparently liked it.[30] Interviews can command a high rating only if they feature the most prominent industrialist. A popular commentator who happens to share the views of business can do more to establish a favorable climate than many an industrialist.

Industry and business have been dissatisfied not only with television programming but also with the advertising aspects of the medium. The existing *Länder*-supervised public television stations carry no commercials except during a brief period before the start of the regularly scheduled program. The BDI and other top associations aware of the power and influence of business on United States television networks and on the Independent Television Authority, the British commercial network, therefore began efforts to establish a commercial network in West Germany to compete with the existing stations.

[29] W. Phillips Davison, "The Mass Media in West German Political Life," *West German Leadership and Foreign Policy*, ed. Hans Speier and Davison (Evanston, Ill., 1957), p. 262.

[30] DIVO-survey (untitled manuscript, 1960); *JB*, 1958–1959, p. 91; *JB*, 1960–1961, p. 33.

In December 1958 the BDI, the Brand Names Association and the publishers of newspapers and periodicals set up a Free Television corporation in which each group had one-fourth of the shares. In order to encourage more public support, agricultural, trade, and banking interests, and various cultural organizations, were promised an opportunity to buy additional shares once a government license had been granted.[31] In effect the BDI played a leading role in organizing the corporation. Heinz Schmidt, who until then had been head of the BDI press department, was one of the two men chosen as its managers, and Fritz Berg was named a member of its supervisory board. At the same time, other private corporations, also with business support, made similar preparations to begin commercial broadcasting, but their weaker capital base gave them little chance of receiving the first license.[32]

The BDI and other business interests looked upon television primarily as an additional medium for advertising, but, despite public statements to the contrary, political motivations were also important. Having no sympathy with certain programs emanating from stations whose directors were Social Democrats, they envisaged a second program slanted toward the interests of business and following the conservative line of the Bonn government.[33] Their model was Britain's ITA, which competes with the British Broadcasting Corporation. Opponents of commercial broadcasting raised a chorus of protest. The Catholic hierarchy and a Protestant group assailed commercialization as cultural leveling. The trade unions and the SPD also opposed

[31] "Wer wird das zweite Fernsehprogramm betreiben?", *FAZ*, Feb. 8, 1960; Markenverband e.V., *Wettbewerb um den Fernsehschirm* (Wiesbaden, 1958); Studiengesellschaft für Funk und Fernsehwerbung e.V., *Möglichkeiten für die Verwirklichung eines zweiten Fernseh-Programms* (n.p., 1958). Two pamphlets urging commercial programming.

[32] *FAZ*, Feb. 8, 1960; one such corporation was the Westdeutsche Fernseh A. G., Wiesbaden-Frankfurt/Main (see its statute, 8 pp., multigraphed). Letter from Dr. H. Schleussner, chairman, March 20, 1961.

[33] Statement by an official of the BDI, personal interview, Cologne, Oct. 6, 1959.

the idea. Even the communications expert of the CDU issued a statement calling for the rejection of party and interest pressures, and for the separation of advertising and programming.[34]

At the same time the federal government also made plans to launch a second and preferably commercial network. When after protracted debates on a broadcasting bill, parliament finally struck out the provision for a new television network, Chancellor Adenauer quickly found another alternative. On July 25, 1960 he set up the privately financed German Television Corporation, which was to have the power to issue licenses to responsible private organizations, such as Free Television, that were capable of producing a full range of television programs. This administrative edict, concerning which parliament and the *Länder* were not officially consulted, but which asked the *Länder* to participate, represented a juridical coup on the part of the Chancellor. It may be surmised that business interests were in close touch with him during this period.

Adenauer's move precipitated a dramatic showdown. Four *Länder* controlled by the SPD took the issue of the establishment of a second program to the Federal Constitutional Court, which on February 28, 1960, ruled against the federal government. The position of the Court was that in broadcasting the *Länder* had the constitutional prerogative.[35] The consequence was that the *Länder,* which for years had been under pressure to establish a second network so as to give the viewer the advantage of variety in programming, in 1962 finally launched a competitive though noncommercial television program. Forced to disband their plans for the projected Free Television Corporation, the BDI and its associates suffered a major defeat in their attempt to establish a commercial network.[36]

---

[34] Bruno Heck, "Unabhängigkeit im Rundfunk," *Die politische Meinung*, IV, Heft 35 (April 1959), 47–58. For an excellent account of the ITA controversy in Great Britain see H. H. Wilson, *Pressure Group: The Campaign for Commercial Television in England* (New Brunswick, N.J., 1961).

[35] Bundesverfassungsgericht, 2 BvG, 1/60, 2/60, pp. 1–82.

[36] On the 66-member council of the new network the BDI is not represented, but the BDA has one representative. *JB,* 1961–1962, p. 43.

As long as German television remains in public hands, industry has less chance of playing a decisive role in programming than does its counterpart in the United States. Nevertheless, it has continued its efforts to make the greatest possible impact upon both television and radio.

Motion Pictures

Film-going, although it is less frequent than before the advent of television, still serves as a popular escape from the daily routines of life. Despite the dip in attendance, in one recent year 660 million tickets were sold to motion picture patrons.[37] Interest groups can hardly manipulate the contents of major motion pictures, whose writers and directors enjoy maximum freedom in determining their content and controlling their production. Hence the BDI was not very happy when during the late 1950's the socially radical films *Rosemarie* and *Wir Wunderkinder*, both containing barbed satire of big business, became overnight hits throughout the Federal Republic.

But industry has a chance at least partially to counteract such motion pictures by producing documentaries of its own and showing them to the public in commercial theaters, clubs, and institutes, as well as to workers in plants, to students, and to audiences abroad. One film produced by a giant electrical firm was seen by as many as 28 million people in one year. From 1950 to 1960 nearly 1,500 films were made for 400 firms and associations. Since 1958 the production has been stepped up to 200 films yearly—which is still far below the United States production of 8,000 industrial films in 1961. In Germany such films are made chiefly by the chemical, petroleum, machine construction, iron and steel, and electric appliance industries. The majority of films are designed to enhance the image of the corporation or the product by providing general information, while a minority are intended to provide economic and technical information

[37] The figure is for 1959. *Facts about Germany* (published by the German Federal Republic, Press and Information Office, Bonn, 3rd ed., Wiesbaden, 1960), p. 234.

about work methods and machines in the plants, or are concerned with progress in research and development, and with workers' training and social problems.[38] Film experts have expressed some dissatisfaction with the contents of the documentaries. They find too many to be overly technical, and to lack human emphasis on the worker in the plant. In any event, industry is provided with a fertile field in which to spread the gospel of free enterprise.

CONCLUSION

The success of the BDI in the public relations field cannot be measured statistically because of the many variable factors involved—for example, the state of the economy, political crises, and the effectiveness of the opposition. As a matter of fact, the Social Democrats strongly believe that the promotional efforts of the employers find a more sympathetic reception by the public than do their own or those of organized labor; there is at least no doubt that in recent years industry has found the public more responsive to its message than in those immediately after the war.

The BDI has the advantage of operating in a favorable environment. The country has been ruled since its inception by a coalition of conservative parties, and has flourished under a free enterprise economy. Hence a majority of the people favor a continuation of the political and economic system under which they have prospered, and may be expected to continue their support of the system. One consequence of prosperity has been an increase in prestige for the business community—aided, of course, by its own promotional campaign. Access to the mass communications media and to the locus of public decision-making in the

[38] "Der deutsche Industriefilm 1961," *Bulletin*, No. 214, Nov. 15, 1961, p. 2007; "Wirtschaft auf der Leinwand," in "Spannungsfeld Wirtschaft und Öffentlichkeit," *Volkswirt*, pp. 25–28. The DI has instituted a film division which serves as a clearing house for industrial films. See its *Films of German Industry* (Köln, 1959) and *Der deutsche Wirtschaftsfilm in Zahlen* (multigraphed, 1959).

government have made that campaign much easier. Although the political left also has means of expressing and publicizing its views, the majority of the media support the prevailing conservative order.

The BDI and other associations bombard the press and other purveyors of information and opinion with a volley of news releases; and even where the climate of opinion is already favorable, the BDI has no intention of slackening this assault. It is well aware that a long-range strategy must be developed in order to counteract the appeal that Marxism still has for many, and in order to win over the new generation to a belief in the free enterprise economy.

IV

Political Parties

IN assessing the politics of the BDI it is essential to examine its influence on a major target, the political parties of West Germany. Since the industrialists are beholden to no single one of these, the BDI must perforce adopt a nonpartisan policy. But this does not deter it from committing its resources to the support of the nonsocialist parties. Through considerable financial donations and personal contact with their leaders, the BDI assures itself of an influence on the economic policies and, as will be brought out in Chapter VI, to a lesser degree on their selection of parliamentary candidates. The parties in their turn are interested in a close collaboration with the BDI, and with other interest groups, in order to obtain financial support to cover not only the year-round expenses and those of periodic elections, but also the services of experts for party and parliamentary work. The parties also seek a heavy vote at election time; but in this respect the BDI cannot oblige since the numbers of its clientele are limited.[1]

One other important obstacle effectively limits the powers of

[1] For a discussion of this topic see the proceedings of the roundtable conference held by German sociologists: "Der Staat der Gegenwart und die wirtschaftlichen und aussenwirtschaftlichen Interessentengruppen," *Kölner Zeitschrift für Soziologie*, V, Nos. 2/3 (1952/1953), 204–229.

the BDI. This is the changing nature of the West German party system. Where a two- or three-party system is still in the process of evolution, the identification of any one party with one ideology or one interest group will be limited. Rather, there will be frequent coalitions in order to screen "authoritative policy-making agencies from the particularistic and disintegrative impact of special interests."[2] As a consequence, each party will adopt a program of general appeal to the bulk of the electorate. The interest groups, in turn, can no longer make extensive use of *Querverbindungen* (the extension of their influence "through divided representation in diverse parties").[3] Thus in each party the power is shared by "multiple elites," rather than held by one powerful ruling class. The BDI, as will shortly appear, encounters this situation notably in the CDU. The RDI, the predecessor of the BDI during the Weimar era, exercised considerable power in a number of conservative parties which were more ideologically oriented, and mirrored the views of only a few interest groups.

Even though parties are now becoming more pluralistic, the BDI maintains that its position could be strengthened if the employers were to take an active interest in party work and politics. It argues that although the BDI can perform certain tasks for employers, for many reasons the latter must enter the political arena directly. First of all, they can help the parties in matters of economics and industrial relations, including the problems of defense and of aid to developing countries, for which the parties need their advice and help. Second, unlike paid party functionaries, they can pursue a truly "independent" policy. Third, they are needed to come to the rescue of the few employers who are serving in politics on their behalf. Fourth, they can exercise a more effective limit upon the ubiquitous

[2] Committee on Comparative Politics, *A Comparative Study of Interest Groups and the Political Process*, p. 20.

[3] Sigmund Neumann at a round table of the International Political Science Association, in *Interest Groups on Four Continents*, ed. Ehrmann, p. 261.

power of the state by taking countermeasures through the parties. Fifth, they can use the experience gained as business leaders in the political sphere, which the BDI regards as merely an extension of the sphere of business. Sixth, they are the men with constructive ideas, with a knowledge of the "limits of the possible," and with the positive sense of values necessary to counter the "crass and confusing" elements in politics.[4]

The BDI has still another reason for wanting its constituents to be political activists. According to one spokesman, during the period 1919-1930 employers continued their fathers' tradition of participating in local and regional party organizations, in which they played an influential role. Thus the employers represented on executive committees at the regional level formed a close liaison with the leaders in politics. In the postwar era this tradition has not been maintained. If employers remain aloof, the same spokesman warns, they cannot expect the parties to put them up as candidates, or to represent them adequately. They should be active not only at the local and regional level but also in the top party organs at the federal level, where they can act as counterweights to a parliamentary group which may not sympathize with their goals. According to the argument, they should either work their way up through the party into the top organs, or be ready to be co-opted into them.[5]

The BDI combines this appeal with another for a reform of the parties, which it sees as too isolated in the public realm, and as being too often regarded by the citizenry as a necessary evil, an attitude that leads to stagnation in their membership rolls. What the parties need, according to the BDI, is new blood and more youth in order to force open their closed system, to re-

[4] See, *inter alia*, "Berg, Der Interessen-Bündler," *Der Spiegel*, XIV, No. 45 (Nov. 2, 1960), 34; BDI *Jahrbücher, passim*; C. Neumann, "Die überbetriebliche Verantwortung des Unternehmers," *Junge Wirtschaft*, VIII, No. 8 (Aug. 1960), 331; Stein, "Unternehmer nach 1945," *Fünf Jahre BDI*, pp. 27 ff; Stein, *Unternehmer in der Politik*, p. 139.

[5] F. A. Pinkerneil, "Die Politische Mission des Unternehmers," *VR*, No. 36, Sept. 8, 1952.

juvenate their leadership, and to prevent a few leaders from holding too many party offices.[6] Why, it may be asked, should the BDI be worried about such internal party matters? It is partly a desire for political and economic stability that leads it to exhort the parties themselves in this manner, since undoubtedly, if they are not attuned to the times, the objectives of the BDI might be endangered.

The BDI sees political activity on the part of the employer as perfectly legitimate. Berg once declared that "as an organization we do not want to make any politics and could not make any politics. But one point is clear: as industrialist and as employer, my friends and I have the right to do that in politics which every other citizen in the state claims for himself."[7]

In speeches and articles on the same theme, BDI and DI officials have repeatedly called on employers to devote time to party affairs. They have argued that the responsibility for political action should not be left to industrial associations whose personnel are not direct participants in the business sphere, but rather that the employer himself must be in politics, and become a "business statesman" on the United States model.[8] To produce such statesmen, the BDI and its associations have sponsored political seminars composed of leading politicians and employers, gathered for the discussion of current political, economic, and social themes.[9] It may be added that such seminars have also been organized for middle-management executives of large corporations in the United States in recent years with the aim of increasing their awareness of politics, as well as of promoting the free enterprise system.[10]

[6] "Der Unternehmer im Staat," *UB*, No. 20, May 16, 1957.

[7] Quoted in Stein, "Unternehmer nach 1945," *Fünf Jahre BDI*, p. 30.

[8] Cf., for instance, Otto A. Friedrich, *Das Leitbild des Unternehmers Wandelt Sich* (Stuttgart-Degerloch, 1959), p. 29.

[9] The seminars were led by BDI staff members Stein and Bernd Tönnessen and now by Günter Triesch of the DI. See their yearly publication *Politisches Seminar* (*supra*, note 5, Ch. I).

[10] "Corporations Make Politics Their Business," *Fortune*, LX, No. 6

One German industrialist has suggested that such employers as are politically motivated might enlighten their fellow employers by forming a loose nonpartisan working group. The idea has evoked no response in industrial quarters even though another executive has asserted that the average man of business could devote 30 per cent of his time to outside activities without harm to his business, a statement that is undoubtedly true of the larger but not the smaller firms.

The many appeals of the BDI to employers to take an active interest in politics have not had the desired result. Most businessmen—estimates run as high as 99 per cent—have remained aloof from politics and party activities. They simply do not want to be involved. Why should this be so? At the root of the problem is a combination of political, economic, and psychological factors. Many executives, who recall all too well their own cooperation with the Nazi regime and the era immediately after the war when they were jailed for their collaboration, do not want to have their fingers burned again for joining a political party. For some of these men the sole political activity is to vote on election day and perhaps to donate money to some of the parties. The manager of a large steel firm in the Ruhr area reported, "Once a month I tried to schedule a political information and discussion session, which all section chiefs in our firm would have to attend. My idea was to have three people give talks of twenty minutes each, to be followed by a general discussion. Nothing came of this plan." That it failed cannot be blamed solely on the past, but must also be attributed to the present intense devotion to work, which leaves little time for anything else. One observer has characterized the Ruhr managers as "industrial fanatics" with few interests outside their work, who are indifferent to politics except when it impinges directly upon their own businesses, in which event they tend to

---

(Dec. 1959), pp. 100 ff. Triesch writes that 80,000 German employers and managers would need to be politically active in order to match the 300,000 Americans who have been participants. *UB*, No. 25, June 22, 1961.

adopt a "narrow, tough" interest in politics with a strong spice of nationalism. According to the same observer, even the more liberal employers in the south, the Rhineland, and the Hanseatic cities are largely apolitical.[11]

The repeated charge that employers tend to have an egocentric business point of view seems justified. If one may be permitted to use a group stereotype, the typical employer seems to be compulsive about making money, and to regard serving in a less well paid political post as a luxury he cannot afford. After the war many of these men had to build up their plants from scratch and were faced with every sort of obstacle, insufficient capital, scarce resources, and intense competition. After the currency reform their opportunities were greatly improved, thanks to a favorable government policy, and there has thus been little cause for them to mount the political barricades. Moreover, management often regards its executives as indispensable, and frowns on their running for political office. The executives in turn fear they may lose their jobs, not be promoted, or be less satisfactorily employed after serving in politics.[12]

Other reasons or rationalizations are advanced to justify the political indifference of employers. Industrial tycoons who are the masters in their corporations may be less successful in politics, where they tend to feel insecure against the opposition. They are uneasy about being labeled or defamed as pressure group deputies, and thus they tend to be withdrawn and introverted when it comes to serving in politics. Indeed, as one student has aptly noted, some of them, in looking at the past, see that business has usually "profited from political abstention and suffered from political involvement." Or they distrust politics as "subversive of good character and individual integrity,"[13]

[11] Almond, *The Politics of German Business*, pp. 53–55. Cf. also an unpublished study by Suzanne Keller, "Attitudes of the French, German, and British Business Elite," MIT, Cambridge, Mass., May 1958.

[12] See, *e.g.*, O. A. Friedrich, *Das Leitbild; Junge Wirtschaft*, III, No. 4, April 1955.

[13] Hartmann, *Authority and Organization in German Management*, p. 231.

since they would have to associate with a "bunch of politicians."[14] Thus the attitude of the average employer toward political involvement is a mixture of inferiority and superiority
feelings, both of which lead to rejection.

On balance, then, there has been relatively little activity by
employers in the political parties. The exceptions include those
employers who are parliamentary deputies or party activists;
and not a few younger employers are especially active in junior
chambers of commerce or in the "Young Entrepreneurs," an
affiliate of the Association of Independent Entrepreneurs
(AsU).[15]

The general aloofness of employers from politics has been
criticized by one American observer who believes that the
growth of German democracy would be fostered by a more general participation by all interest groups in party politics. On the
other hand, a German critic warns against such participation,
especially in parliament, arguing that employers would simply
dictate their own narrowly conceived policy to the parties.[16] An
examination of the BDI's activities in the respective parties may
suggest the degree to which this criticism is justified.

Since German party discipline is relatively strong, there is no
such spectacle as occurs at party conventions in the United
States, where groups openly participate in drafting a platform.
Although a group may have a hand in the final platform, its
basic content is often settled in advance by the policy-makers.
Thus the BDI and other organizations seek direct access to these
men: the party leader, the chairman and members of the parliamentary group, the leading members of the executive board—
some of whom serve as liaison men to the groups—and the
minister-presidents and party chairmen of the *Länder*.[17] The
question must then be posed as to the extent of the BDI's im-

[14] Herbert Gross in *Unternehmer in der Politik*, ed. Stein, pp. 138, 140.

[15] Almond, *The Politics of German Business*, p. 56. The Young Entrepreneurs have an approximate membership of 1,200.

[16] *Ibid.*, pp. 103–110; Pritzkoleit, *Die Neuen Herren*, pp. 194, 280.

[17] *Ibid.*, p. 281.

pact on the party VIP's, and of overlapping membership in the BDI and the party organizations.

THE CHRISTIAN DEMOCRATIC UNION

The Christian Democratic Union/Christian Social Union (CDU/CSU) had its origin after the war, when prominent Catholic and Protestant lay leaders, Catholic trade union officials, and certain conservative businessmen decided to establish an interconfessional "Christian" union, to be restricted to no single social group or class. It was designed to be a broad popular movement, comparable to the Mouvement Républicain Populaire in France, which would appeal to all segments of the population. For this reason it lacks the inner cohesion and ideological solidarity found in its major rival, the Social Democratic Party. The CDU receives the support of conservative farmers and the middle class in the north, and of radical Catholic workers and conservative businessmen in the Ruhr, while the CSU receives the support of Catholic farmers in Bavaria. Although the party can be labeled conservative, it has a strong left wing in the Catholic trade-union bloc. As will be noted, major differences arise between this bloc and the more conservative elements whenever economic policy is discussed within the party.

Between 1945 and 1949 (before the BDI was in existence) there appears to have been no concerted effort on the part of the relatively weak industrial associations to capture the leadership of the *Land* organizations then being formed by the CDU. It is true that in some *Länder* certain individual businessmen and lawyers for employer associations played a key role, but they were a minority.[18]

[18] For example, Eric Köhler of Hesse, who later became first president of the Bundestag, 1949/1950. Gerhard Schulz, "Die CDU-Merkmale ihres Aufbaues," *Parteien in der Bundesrepublik* (Stuttgart, 1955), p. 46. See also, for the early history of CDU, Hans-Georg Wieck, *Die Entstehung der CDU und die Wiedergründung des Zentrums im Jahre 1945* (Düsseldorf, 1953); Wieck, *Christliche und Freie Demokraten in Hessen, Rheinland–*

Since 1949 the CDU/CSU has emerged triumphant on the national scene. As a consequence, a number of groups representing agriculture, the Catholic wing of organized labor, the middle class, and the business community, have applied maximum pressure upon it; and the CDU/CSU has in turn sought their continued support since they all provide important electoral and/or financial backing; and it has thus been obliged to develop a program attractive to them all. The danger inherent in this multiplicity of interests, whose factions are often at odds, is that the leadership may fail to maintain peace or to achieve satisfactory compromises. On the other hand, the existence of factionalism also allows the leadership a certain freedom of action and guarantees that the CDU will not identify itself exclusively with business or any other interest group.[19] Under the leadership of Chancellor Adenauer the CDU was successful in this integrative function. Whether the same cohesion and balance will be maintained under Erhard's administration remains to be seen.

If the party must heed so many interests inimical to the BDI why does it have the support of the latter? Obviously the answer is that the BDI expects to profit from betting on a winning horse, although the dividends and favors it hopes to obtain cannot be exacted on the sole basis of financial support, but must be actively sought through direct influence upon party programs and top party councils.

A look at the economic programs drafted at the periodic party congresses reveals the influence of the BDI and other leading business associations. This was not yet true in 1947, when the first important regional program was adopted by the British zonal committee of the CDU at Ahlen. An economic and social

Pfalz, Baden und Württemberg 1945/46 (Düsseldorf, 1958); Arnold J. Heidenheimer, *Adenauer and the CDU* (The Hague, 1960).

19 S. Neumann, "Germany: Changing Patterns and Lasting Problems," *Modern Political Parties*, ed. S. Neumann (Chicago, 1956), pp. 380–382; Deutsch and Edinger, *Germany Rejoins the Powers*, p. 195.

committee on which Catholic trade unionists were strongly represented spent a year drafting what turned out to be an anticapitalist program for a mixed economy. The committee called for the socialization of the coal and steel industries, controls over big business, aid to small enterprises, and economic codetermination, and criticized the economically mighty who also wielded political power.[20] In 1947 the BDI did not yet exist; the industrial associations were still weak, and their only hope of counteracting a program of this nature was to work hard in the future for a more conservative program. In subsequent years, as the CDU achieved a more cohesive nationwide organization, it tended to become less radical, and the Ahlen program was abandoned. In an effort to minimize its significance, the statement was made that the program "had to be seen in its historical perspective, it had in fact even then been designed to prevent socialization."[21]

Between 1947 and 1949 an emphasis on reviving the economy, including heavy industry, was spurred on by the Bizonal Economic Council and by the pending formation of the federal government. The CDU decision in 1948 to champion a free enterprise system was largely a political one. It was worked out in theory by Ludwig Erhard and a team consisting of Franz Etzel, a former corporation lawyer who was later to be Minister of Finance; Dr. Alfred Müller-Armack, later State Secretary in the Ministry of Economics; and Professor Franz Böhm, a CDU deputy-to-be and exponent of the neo-liberal school. Although segments of industry were dismayed when the team emphasized the necessity of certain limitations upon the free economy, the business community as a whole nevertheless gave the proposal its blessing.

[20] *Politisches Jahrbuch der CDU/CSU,* 1. Jahrgang (Frankfurt, 1950), pp. 226 ff; *Ahlener Programm* (mimeographed, n.d. [1947]); Schulz in *Parteien in der Bundesrepublik,* pp. 90–91; Heidenheimer, *Adenauer and the CDU,* pp. 126–127.

[21] Uwe Kitzinger, *German Electoral Politics: A Study of the 1957 Campaign* (Oxford, 1960), p. 91.

In 1949, as the first federal election drew near, a nucleus of the CDU's Federal Committee for Economic Policy went to work on the economic plank of its platform. The members of the group were Etzel, Böhm, the banker Hugo Scharnberg, Professor Pfister of Munich, and Dr. Fritz Hellwig, future managing director of the DI; and their program, which came to be known as the "Düsseldorfer Leitsätze," received the approval of Adenauer and also of Erhard, who joined the CDU only in the summer of 1949. The Leitsätze, a dilution of the Ahlen program, still had some mention of public ownership and of curbing economic power, but its main emphasis was on the Erhard theory of the social market and the role of the employer in rebuilding the economy.[22]

From then on, to the chagrin of its own left wing, the party committed itself to a conservative policy, which was reflected in the next program offered by its Committee for Economic Policy. Adopted in 1953 at Hamburg, it no longer spoke of socialism or of the dangers of industrial concentration. It did acknowledge the need to control monopolies and cartels, but called for the removal of state controls over industry in general.[23]

For the 1957 congress, the CDU's Executive Committee appointed a small committee of deputies and economists, with Hellwig at its head, to work out an economic program with special emphasis on the measures not enacted in the previous term of parliament. The BDI must have been satisfied with this group of policy formulators, who included not only Hellwig, Etzel, and Scharnberg but also Dr. Wolfgang Pohle, then an

[22] CDU/CSU, *Düsseldorfer Leitsätze über Wirtschaftspolitik, Landwirtschaftspolitik, Sozialpolitik, Wohnungsbau* (Sonderdruck des Deutschland-Union-Dienstes, July 15, 1949); Alois Schardt, *Wohin Steuert die CDU?* (Osnabrück, 1961), pp. 95–98.

[23] *Politisches Jahrbuch der CDU/CSU*, 3. Jahrgang, 1957 (Recklinghausen, n.d. [1957]), pp. 45–46; Wilhelm Mommsen, *Deutsche Parteiprogramme der Gegenwart* (2nd ed.; München, 1954), pp. 8–24. Hans-Heinrich Zimdahl, *Wirtschaftssysteme und Parteiprogramme der wichtigsten Parteien der Bundesrepublik* (Frankfurt, 1955).

official of the Mannesmann steel corporation, and Dr. Günter Henle, a leading manager of the Klöckner firm. At the 1957 congress, with the social market economy booming, the conservatives were in the saddle. Erhard urged the transfer of government-controlled enterprises to private ownership through the issuance of "people's shares," and Dr. Eugen Gerstenmaier, president of the Bundestag, advocated a limitation upon welfare activities by the state.

Beginning in 1957, however, there were strains between representatives of big and small business within the party as the CDU attempted to capture the vote of the latter. Painful compromises between the two had to be made. Similar cleavages had already developed between the business and labor wings. At one party congress Hellwig and two representatives of the labor wing engaged in a public dispute over the phrasing of certain key statements. Compromise was achieved only after Adenauer had enjoined the three to come to some sort of agreement.[24]

In recent years the party held one-day economic meetings at which government and party officials made formal speeches on public policy and the state of the economy. As this chronology would suggest, industry has little cause for complaint against the CDU. The increasingly conservative character of its economic programs reflects the shifts in power within the party from left of center to right of center, and thus of the part taken by the proponents of industry in formulating its programs. It should be emphasized, however, that the realization of those programs is contingent upon the entire political complexion of the CDU and of the nation. In recent years the CDU has had to develop a broad social policy as a result of pressures from the left wing and in order to undercut the demands of socialists. The response of business to all this has not been enthusiastic.

Another way to gauge the influence of industry is to assess the legislative programs initiated by the CDU-led governments.

[24] CDU Deutschlands, *6. Bundesparteitag CDU, Stuttgart, 26–29.4.1956* (Hamburg, n.d. [1956]), pp. 154–157.

That influence will be treated in Part Three; but it may be noted here that it is extensive. Of course the BDI is not alone in its influence on the CDU program. Other business groups, the church hierarchies, the peasant associations, individual labor leaders, and the military elite are all extremely active. Since the conservative values reflected in the program are those of the bulk of the party leaders, it is impossible to gauge the exact degree of influence of the BDI or any other group. Certainly the BDI has had differences of opinion with the CDU on many matters of economic and social policy. At the time of the 1961 election, for example, it was far from pleased when the Chancellor veered slightly to the left in order to capture the vote of the masses.

The BDI also attempts to exert an influence on the top policy-making organs. Originally the party was decentralized in structure, but in recent years the federal headquarters in Bonn have wielded an increasing authority over the *Länder* organizations. Thus the party has tended more and more to identify itself with national rather than with regional interests. Such a trend is welcomed by the BDI, whose own interests center primarily on national affairs. Until 1963 the BDI's chief means of direct access was through the party and government boss, Chancellor Adenauer (a matter to be discussed in Chapter IX). Since he was not the sole policymaker in the CDU, other organs with far fewer actual powers had to be approached as well. The Federal Committee *(Ausschuss)* was one of these. Heterogeneous in composition, it includes a strong provincial representation, together with that of both Protestants and Catholics, members of the government and the legislature, labor and business. Its sizable membership makes it a less effective policy-making organ than the Federal Executive Committee *(Vorstand)*, an inner circle of ministers and of parliamentary and regional leaders. This circle, to which several men close to industry belong, is exposed to a variety of pressures from interest groups.

In order to take some of the pressure away from the center,

the CDU has organized committees to deal with the interests of youth, women, the middle class, labor, business, and municipalities. The divergences of opinion between some of the groups are so wide that, as one FDP leader put it, "these wings can only find each other with radar."[25] As economic reconstruction gains momentum, the power of the labor-dominated autonomous Social Affairs Committees has declined. Christian trade-unionists are in an uncomfortable position. They are considered too "red" by the CDU, and too "black" (*i.e.*, clerical) by the unified but socialist-oriented trade union federation (DGB). They are still extremely active in the CDU, however, and continue to call for a more radical economic course, including the breakup of corporate concentration.

Such a course of action is not supported by the Committee for Economic Policy, which since its inception in 1951 has been headed by Franz Etzel,[26] and which represents the business community. Of a membership of about sixty, three-fourths are big businessmen or bankers, and one-fourth are managers of associations. Its functions are purely advisory, and although its recommendations may carry some weight with the Federal Executive Committee, it is regarded in many circles as a mere figurehead. Moreover, Erhard was by no means pleased to have Etzel at the head of such a committee, and has made his own economic recommendations to the cabinet and the party. Even so, the BDI regards it as another means of entry into the party,

[25] *Die Zeit*, April 7, 1961.

[26] Bundesausschuss für Wirtschaftspolitik der CDU, *Niederschrift über die konstituierende Sitzung*, Bonn, June 5, 1951 (mimeographed); *Entwurf eines CDU-Wirtschaftsprogrammes* (Arbeitsergebnis der Sitzung des Bundesausschusses für Wirtschaftspolitik der CDU vom 30. u. 31. März 1953 in Bonn). Late in 1963 a semiautonomous CDU Economic Council was set up to deal with economic and industrial problems. The impetus for its formation came from economists, CDU members, and small business leaders who were dissatisfied with the big business orientation of the Committee for Economic Policy. *Handelsblatt*, Oct. 30, 1963, and personal interviews.

especially since Hellwig has been one of the key members and has been responsible for many draft recommendations.

Although the economic programs of the CDU to a great extent reflect the thinking of the committee members, the CDU must be careful not to favor their views above those of the Social Affairs Committees. It will either seek a compromise between the two when discord arises or promise one law to one committee and a second law to the other.

The Committee for Economic Policy has its counterparts in some of the *Länder*. Many BDI officials and industrialists have sat on the executive board or have held membership in that for the Rhineland, one of the most noted of these committees. For the BDI it serves as another channel of access to the CDU and to the deputies from the region. Moreover, the BDI profits from the fact that many of the members of its executive board are in close touch with ministers and top civil servants in Bonn.

A different setup is found in Hesse where the CDU established the ostensibly nonpartisan Economic Forum, chaired by Ernst Leitz, a Wetzlar industrial executive. The Forum sponsors four or five meetings a year at which leading ministers explain government policy for the purpose of bringing businessmen into contact with the government.

The industrial associations take a certain amount of interest in party organs at the district and local level since these do make some decisions in economic matters.[27] At higher party levels there is hardly any overlap of officers of the BDI and the CDU. If the BDI cannot identify itself too closely with the party, one reason may be the number of FDP sympathizers in its midst. At any rate, no BDI official sits in the top CDU party organs,

[27] See protocols of the Committee for Economic Policy, CDU Rheinland, Köln. In an apparently atypical study of the Berlin CDU, one observer reported that associations exerted no influence on the district committee. As a matter of fact, only a few employers (2 and 1 per cent respectively) sat on the district and local executive organs. Renate Mayntz, *Parteigruppen in der Gross-Stadt: Untersuchungen in einem Berliner Kreisverband der CDU* (Köln, 1957), pp. 61, 110, 116.

even though the membership of the latter includes a number who are sympathetic to industry. The situation is due not only to the reluctance of the BDI but also to the feeling within the party itself that representation must be granted to groups with a larger membership and stronger electoral support than business can provide.

Indeed, relatively few employers are members of the CDU. On the basis of one regional survey, it appears doubtful whether the number amounts to more than 2 per cent.[28] If the BDI could persuade more industrialists to be active in party politics, its position within the party would be strengthened. In the actual determination of policy, however, the members play only an insignificant role, since policy is made primarily by the Chancellor and by an inner circle of parliamentary and regional leaders with whom the BDI maintains direct contact. All in all, the BDI cannot complain that its interests are totally neglected by the CDU.

THE FREE DEMOCRATIC PARTY

In considering its relations with the second most important nonsocialist party, that of the Free Democrats, it might seem at first glance as though the BDI would find it advantageous to give full support to the FDP. A conservative party committed to the interests of business in its economic policy statements (drafted in part by Dr. Martin Blank, a director of a large steel firm) it makes copious reference to the safeguarding of private property, adherence to the free enterprise system, and aid to the middle class, and it is implicitly opposed to the trade union movement. In short, the FDP takes the antisocialist, anticlerical position of the traditional Manchester liberal. Immediately after the establishment of the Federal Republic in 1949, when the CDU was still somewhat oriented toward the left, there was in

[28] Ossip K. Flechtheim, *Die Deutschen Parteien seit 1945: Quellen und Auszüge* (Berlin, 1957), p. 56, citing a survey of the North Rhine area in Wieck, *Die Entstehung der CDU*, pp. 220–222.

fact a good deal of support for the FDP within the BDI. Originally Berg, Beutler, and Reusch were all supporters of the FDP, and Fritz Berg's brother, a doctor, sat as FDP deputy in the Bundestag. But the realities of the political situation caused the BDI leaders soon to transfer their allegiance to the CDU. The FDP, after all, remained a minor coalition partner in the CDU-dominated cabinets. As economic policy was being determined more and more by the CDU, top officials in the BDI, along with other conservative industrialists, swung their support to the CDU. Consequently the FDP became mainly a party of the Protestant middle class, although retaining some support from the conservative upper class.

This trend was accentuated during the period from 1956 to 1961, when the FDP could no longer remain in the coalition on the national level, and on the *Länder* level proceeded to ally from time to time, for opportunistic reasons, with the SPD—especially in North Rhine–Westphalia, the heart of the industrial Ruhr. Many industrialists could not stomach such an alliance, and accordingly cut off funds to the party. There was a prolonged strain between the BDI and the FDP after the 1956 break between Adenauer and the latter. The BDI began to ignore the FDP. One employer, an FDP deputy, accused Berg of having publicly indicated that German industry identified itself with the policies of Adenauer, whereas the FDP represented the business community in economic, financial, and social questions more vigorously than the CDU. Thus, the critic declared, Berg had violated the political neutrality of his own organization.[29] When the BDI failed to accept the invitation to send a representative to its 1958 convention, the bitterness within the FDP was increased, despite Berg's assertion that the BDI did not generally participate at party conventions. In an effort to restore harmony, Berg did, however, invite a leading FDP official to the 1958 General Assembly.[30]

[29] *Freie Demokratische Korrespondenz*, VIII/44, June 25, 1957.
[30] *Das freie Wort* (FDP weekly), May 10, 1958.

In 1958, when there was to be a *Land* election, the FDP sought to restore close connections with industry by scheduling conferences with groups of industrialists. Some of these, including Dr. Hermann Winkhaus, director general of Mannesmann, Alfried Krupp, and Dr. Alexander Menne, a BDI vice president who was then president of the Association of the Chemical Industry, had been supporters of the party all along. (Menne in 1961 became a party deputy.) Liberal businessmen in Wuerttemberg-Baden, Hamburg, and Bremen, and conservative businessmen in other areas, also maintained their allegiance. Within the BDI some of these men expressed opposition to policies that were at variance with those of the FDP. Backing for the latter also came from some elements of the business community which mistrusted the government's fixed pro-Western orientation, and were loath to burn all bridges to the east. These elements were partially responsible for the foreign policy planks of the FDP platform which from 1956 on has emphasized a more flexible conduct in foreign affairs, calling for direct government negotiations with the Soviets and for a program of withdrawal of military forces from central Europe.

Despite such support, however, the party was still not satisfied. In 1959 its treasurer declared that the party leaders must develop more direct contacts with business leaders interested in politics, not only in order to raise funds but also to urge their participation in party affairs.[31] Such a plea would hardly have needed to be made in the earlier years of the coalition with the CDU, when the BDI and other top associations were attempting to capture key party positions in a majority of the *Länder*, especially in Hesse, Lower Saxony, and North Rhine–Westphalia, which represented the stronghold of the nationalist wing of the party. There was a danger in the formative years that the party would be eaten up by interest associations.[32]

[31] Hans W. Rubin, *Bundesparteitag der FDP in Berlin v. 21.–23.5.59* (mimeographed).

[32] See the author's "The Free Democratic Party in West German Poli-

Although to some extent this danger has evaporated, business still plays a role in the FDP. The party treasurer is Hans Wolfgang Rubin of North Rhine–Westphalia, who is director of a steel company. Of the eleven *Land* chairmen in 1962, two were from industry and three were industrial lawyers or advisers. On its executive committee the same ratio prevailed.[33] The business wing is thus obviously in a position to affect party actions. In 1961, according to one report, it pressed for an alliance with the CDU in order to augment its influence on the economic and social policies of the government.[34]

However, the decentralized structure of the party, and its heterogeneous clientele, prevent any one interest from dominating the party exclusively. For membership and for electoral support the party must rely not only on businessmen but also on salaried employees, on the self-employed, and on professional people and farmers. As a typical conservative party it has little appeal to manual workers. Even though in practice, despite this conservative backing, the BDI has maintained a closer liaison with the CDU than with the FDP, since the 1961 election brought about participation of the FDP in the government, the attitude of many industrialists in the BDI has become more favorable.[35]

THE GERMAN PARTY

The third nonsocialist party to receive a modicum of support from the business community has been the German Party (DP), whose primary strength is in Lower Saxony and Bremen, especially among middle class groups and farmers. Arguing that the CDU has allied itself with the SPD in a number of *Länder*, in

---

tics," *The Western Political Quarterly*, XIII, No. 2 (June 1960), 332–348; Rudolf Wildenmann, *Partei und Fraktion* (Meisenheim am Glan, 1954), pp. 90–92.

[33] Bundesvorstand der Freien Demokratischen Partei, 1960, revised 1962.

[34] *Vorwärts*, Aug. 30, 1961, p. 5.

[35] Letter of Managing Director of FDP, Karl-Hermann Flach, March 16, 1962; Bundesgeschäftsführung, memorandum WK 1/60, dated Aug. 25, 1960.

its own program it makes a bid for support from business by urging lower taxes, the simplification of tax laws, and fiscal encouragement for the accumulation of private capital.

The DP has been a faithful coalition partner of the CDU, but has lost its role as a minor national party since the 1961 election, when it failed to garner the necessary 5 per cent of the votes.[36] Business has supported the party financially, especially since 1957, when a wing of the FDP loyal to Adenauer merged with the DP.

THE BLOC OF EXPELLEES

The All-German Bloc of Expellees (GB/BHE) must finally be cited, even though the BDI has shown no great interest in it owing to the special nature of its constituents. The latter consist of expellees and refugees from former German centers, primarily territories now under Polish and Soviet administration. The party has received some financial backing from industry, but it withered on the political vine in 1961, when it failed to obtain a single parliamentary seat.

The BDI does not favor the existence of a large number of conservative parties because of the way businessmen scatter their votes among them. Although there is no statistical breakdown for the business community as a whole—which is covered in censuses by the more general category of "self-employed and professionals"—a survey after one typical national election showed that 58 per cent of the category had voted for the CDU, 8 per cent for the FDP, 5 per cent for the DP, and 7 per cent for the SPD.[37] The high figure for the SPD obviously represents many small businessmen engaged in retail trade.

[36] For details of the electoral system, see pp. 135–136.

[37] The rest apparently did not vote, or gave no reply. Evaluation Staff, Office of Public Affairs, Office of the U. S. High Commissioner for Germany, *A Survey Analysis of the Factors Underlying the Outcome of the 1953 German Federal Elections*, Dec. 11, 1953; cited by Almond, *The Politics of German Business*, p. 27, note 10. According to another survey, the category of "self-employed and professionals" was most heavily represented

In the top BDI organs, one informant has estimated that 80 percent of the members support the CDU and 20 per cent the FDP, although only a few are party members. There is no evidence to suggest that conflicts between the conservative parties have often led to serious splits within the BDI. Obviously there are several points of view within the BDI as to the political course it ought to pursue. There are those who feel that the FDP is not to be trusted, in view of its six-year split with Adenauer, its warring factions, and the strength of its right wing. There are others who feel that the CDU is too far to the left and that the FDP is the only party of industry. And finally there are those who believe that the BDI should work with both parties. At times when the CDU and FDP are in a governing coalition, as they have been once more since late in 1961, the BDI, pragmatically, will choose the latter course. It will only be when the FDP is in opposition that the debate can be expected to flare up anew.

Unquestionably, the BDI would welcome a little less enmity among the conservative parties. It has repeatedly called for increased political solidarity among employers, arguing that political fratricide must end if the freedom of the employer, the free market economy, and private property are to be maintained.[38] If a conservative coalition is to have any meaning, according to the leaders of the BDI, the differences among its parties—above all, differences concerning foreign policy—must be settled privately and not in the full glare of publicity.

THE SOCIAL DEMOCRATIC PARTY

The BDI's primary purpose in calling for less infighting among the conservative parties is to present a united front

---

in the FDP—33 per cent of its voters being in this category. For the CDU the figure was 15 per cent; for the BHE 9 per cent; for the SPD 6 per cent. In the population at large, 13 out of 100 belonged to the category. "Wie setzt sich die Anhängerschaft der Parteien zusammen?," *UB*, No. 24, June 13, 1957.

[38] See, *e.g.*, Otto Mejer, "Politische Solidarität des Unternehmertums," *VR*, No. 22, Nov. 19, 1951.

against their chief opponent, the Social Democratic Party. In former years Berg has vigorously assailed the SPD, asserting that 30 to 45 per cent of its members were camouflaged communists, and decrying its lack of national consciousness.[39] These statements brought sharp replies from the SPD, which did not prevent the DI from once again assailing the SPD for its attempts to burden industry with "false historical reminiscences and current poisonous slanders."[40] This was a reference to the controversy surrounding the financing of Hitler by industry, and the arrest by British authorities in January 1953 of a circle of former Nazis to whom, according to SPD sources, industry was giving financial aid. According to the DI, there was no proof for this charge; all that had happened was that certain industrialists, through this circle, had offered to buy the newspaper *Die Welt* which was then for sale.[41]

The DI kept up a barrage of criticism of the SPD over the years, but more recently, since the adoption by the SPD of the 1959 Godesberg program, its tone has moderated. This reformist document reflects the more moderate economic doctrine common to socialist parties in all industrial countries, and is the means by which the SPD hopes to attract voters not only from among its traditional supporters in the working class, but also from the growing middle class. The Godesberg program regards nationalization as no longer the fundamental principle of a socialist economy, but rather as the last of several possible means of counteracting the power and concentration of wealth. The DI has warned its clientele that in such a program economic democracy would eventually lead to full-blown socialization, thereby making the economy dependent on a handful of bureaucratic functionaries.[42]

[39] "Berg, Der Interessen-Bündler," *Der Spiegel*, XIV, No. 45 (Nov. 2, 1960), 33.
[40] "Die Brunnenvergiftung muss aufhören," *UB*, No. 3, Jan. 22, 1953.
[41] *Ibid.*
[42] *UB*, No. 48, Dec. 3, 1959.

CONCLUSION

This survey of the influence of the BDI on the conservative parties at least suggests the extent to which a few key people in the BDI and the DI may take part in shaping their economic programs. To make their voices heard, neither the BDI nor industry as a whole needs occupy many top posts in the party hierarchy since they provide the necessary expertise and money —both of which are in short supply.

Of course, the pluralism of the German parties and the trend toward a two-party system both mean that each party must reconcile a host of demands from interest groups within its own organization. No group can hope to have all of its demands fulfilled, and each must expect to make some compromises. Thus in any country the extent to which such groups make the parties their primary vehicle for seeking satisfaction will depend on the nature of the party system. It is well known that political parties in the United States are decentralized and undisciplined, and consequently lack the kind of effectiveness that is found in other countries. Accordingly, interest groups tend to approach individual legislators, legislative committees, and the executive instead. Although the parties in Great Britain and Germany play a more important role, they are still circumscribed in their powers to the extent that the BDI and similar associations also seek access to other centers of power—an access that can be facilitated by the financial resources an organization is willing to commit to the parties themselves.

V

Party Financing

THE financing of parties can be of critical importance in a country where the party membership figures are relatively low in proportion to the electoral vote, and where the parties are thus obliged to seek funds not only from membership dues and special contributions but also from the business community.[1] Such is especially true of the cadre-type conservative party whose total enrollment is low. This pattern of financing is prevalent in many countries and is not new in Germany, where business made large subsidies during the regimes both of the Empire and of the Weimar Republic.

In 1949 a committee was founded by the banker Robert Pferdmenges and a number of businessmen to help finance the

---

[1]

	Estimated Membership	Vote	Ratio
CDU	320,000	14,298,372	2.24%
SPD	650,000	11,427,355	5.95%
FDP	80,000	4,028,766	1.98%

Sources for membership: CDU, letter, H. Wirzbach, Bonn central office, March 9, 1962; SPD, letter, Herta Wolf, SPD central office, March 22, 1962; FDP, letter, Karl-Hermann Flach, March 16, 1962. Other sources give lower membership figures for the CDU and FDP—e.g., CDU 250,000, *Der Spiegel*, XVI, No. 1/2 (Jan. 10, 1962), 38. Source for electoral vote, DI, "Der 17. September 1961 unter der Lupe," *Material zum Zeitgeschehen*, No. 10, Oct. 26, 1961.

conservative parties in the first federal election. Pferdmenges, an old and trusted personal friend of Adenauer and a partner in the Oppenheim bank at Cologne, also helped to organize the CDU in the Rhineland. As a leading Protestant layman and a banker trusted by heavy industry, and as a man whose extensive contacts in the business world included "fifteen chairmanships or deputy chairmanships in industrial and insurance corporations, and a total of more than twenty directorships," he became invaluable to Adenauer.[2] Industry relied on him in its turn because he had the ear of Adenauer at all times, was a leading though unobtrusive deputy of the CDU in the Bundestag, and had excellent contacts with other parties and with the ministries. He held no office in the BDI, but up until Pferdmenges' death in 1962 Berg was in close and continuous touch with him, and deposited the funds of the BDI in the Oppenheim bank.

The aim of Pferdmenges' committee was to raise from 2 to 4 million DM from industry, trade, banking, and other quarters. It asked for a specific amount from each branch; the assessment from industrial associations was based on the number of employees on the payrolls of the member firms. The funds were distributed to the parties on a formula prorated in advance: for example, the CDU might receive 65 per cent, the FDP 25 per cent, and the DP 10 per cent.[3] It may further be surmised that August Heinrichsbauer, the first press chief in the BDI, took part in the distribution of funds, since it was alleged during a legislative inquiry that he had maintained an office for this purpose in the name of an industry consortium.[4] But since the BDI itself was then only in the process of organization, it did not participate to any very notable degree in the financing operations. The SPD, which was less dependent on outside sources for help than the conservative parties, naturally charged

[2] Almond, *The Politics of German Business,* p. 31.

[3] *Ibid.,* pp. 32–33. See also *Unternehmermillionen kaufen politische Macht!*

[4] Hirsch-Weber and Klaus Schütz, *Wähler und Gewählte* (Berlin, 1957), p. 58.

that the financing of such parties by industry was comparable to the support given to Hitler, that it represented a threat to the democratic order, and that it tied the deputies to the apron strings of business.[5] The general public showed hardly any reaction to this charge.

The pattern of financing during the first federal elections and subsequent *Länder* contests was regarded as not altogether satisfactory by the business donors and the conservative parties because it lacked uniformity and varied from region to region. In some instances where the executive committees of the parties wanted more funds than they had been allotted, they turned directly to the industrial and trade associations; in others a single firm might be approached by several representatives of the same party. To forestall further embarrassments of this sort, behind-the-scenes preparations were made to systematize assessments not only for elections but also for year-round operating expenses. It is difficult to trace the origin of this practice. The CDU, the BDI, and other business associations were all weighing various possibilities. According to some reports, Pferdmenges suggested the final plan to Adenauer and received his approval; then, in the spring of 1952, business leaders met with Adenauer and the treasurers of the conservative parties at Pferdmenges' apartment to discuss it. Adenauer is presumed to have emphasized the need of strengthening the Federal Republic against communism abroad, and of helping the conservative parties as a counter-weight to the growing power of the SPD.[6]

Subsequently the managing directors of the BDI regional offices were called to BDI headquarters to be apprised of the details of the plan. It called for the organization in each *Land* of promotional or sponsors' associations, to be set up under different names, for the primary purpose of financing *Länder* elections. In most instances the managing directors of the BDI's

[5] *Unternehmermillionen*, p. 7.

[6] Flechtheim, "Politische Entwicklung und Finanzierung der CDU," *Die Neue Gesellschaft*, V, No. 3 (May–June 1958), 186.

regional offices, or staff officials of the BDI trade associations, were to serve as directors, assisted by an executive board composed of leaders from industry, trade, banking, and other branches of business, who would also represent the various parties that were to receive aid. In 1954 the Civic Association (Staatsbürgerliche Vereinigung)—a sponsors' group that had been informally in existence for some time—was incorporated. Its major goal was to help finance the federal election campaigns and national headquarters of the nonsocialist parties. To this end, Adenauer reportedly asked the directors of fifty or sixty leading industrial and commercial firms, insurance companies, and banks, for generous contributions, and asked some of the same firms, plus other smaller ones, to sustain the *Länder* associations.[7]

It may be noted parenthetically that as managing director of the Civic Association, Gustav Stein, a top staff officer of the BDI, probably wielded as much power in making crucial decisions in the organization as did the presidents of the national associations who sit on its executive board, including Fritz Berg. Stein, a lawyer and former staff member of the Association of the Chemical Industry, was politically active in center and right-wing parties during the period before World War II and was a member of the Nazi party from 1933 on. He supported the Adenauer coalition after the war, and became a CDU deputy in 1961. The BDI exercises further power in the civic and the *Länder* associations by holding coordination meetings several times a year.[8]

For the business community the establishment of the associations held several advantages. By pooling its resources the community acquired a lever within the parties, and could prevent them from playing off one firm against another. In addition, the parties were forced to account more exactly for their expendi-

7 Flechtheim, "Gewerkschaften und Parteifinanzierung," *Gewerkschaftliche Monatshefte*, X (Oct. 1959), 584.

8 Kitzinger, *German Electoral Politics*, pp. 213–214.

tures. And finally, donations to the sponsors' associations were partially tax-exempt up to 1955, and generally so from 1955 to 1958.[9] The SPD opposed exemption from taxes on the ground that it represented an indirect state subsidy to the conservative parties. In 1957 it petitioned the Federal Constitutional Court to void an amendment to the 1955 income tax law which exempted donations for political purposes from taxation. In June 1958 the Court upheld the SPD and voided the amendment, finding that there had been a discrimination between citizens, "since those with large incomes save a larger absolute and relative amount of tax as a result of their political donations." The Court also found that the equality clause in the Basic Law had been injured by those parties that had been materially strengthened by donations from the wealthy.[10] Since then business has been more reluctant than ever before about financing the parties, although loopholes have been found that permit the plowing of money into such revenue-producing party activities as the publication of business journals.

Before dealing with recent developments, however, it will be useful to note how the sponsors' associations have raised and distributed the money and apparently still do at the *Land* level.

[9] According to an interpretation of the 1952 tax laws, money spent by the sponsors' associations in turn was tax-exempt if up to one-third of the funds was given directly to the parties, and the rest for more general purposes, such as political seminars, lectures, and information services. On November 16, 1954, a slim Bundestag majority passed an amendment to the tax laws, incorporated in the Income Tax Law of 1955, which added political to charitable, scientific, religious, and similar donations having a tax-exempt status. For details see Kitzinger, *German Electoral Politics*, pp. 210–211; Heidenheimer, "German Party Finance: The CDU," *The American Political Science Review*, LI, No. 2 (June 1957), 376, 381.

[10] Bundesverfassungsgericht, 2 BvF 1/57, June 24, 1958, p. 24. While Germany has moved to tighten the tax-exempt status, the United States is moving the other way. See U.S. Government, President's Commission on Campaign Costs, *Financing Presidential Campaigns* (Washington, 1962) and a White House press release, May 29, 1962, dealing with draft bills concerning campaign contributions—both of which advocate providing tax incentives for contributors.

The amount to be collected from industrial firms was customarily determined on the basis of payroll figures and turnover, and often came to one or two DM per worker per month. In election years, of course, the amount had to be increased drastically. The firms apparently had the option of designating a specific party to which their contributions should go,[11] but most of them were satisfied to put the money into the common pool.

The distribution of the funds gave a key position in German politics to the managers of the sponsors' associations, to whom the party treasurers were obliged to justify their requests in direct negotiations. The funds were distributed on the basis of the needs and relative strength of the parties, as measured by membership figures, by the vote in the last national or state election, or by seats in the parliaments. Also taken into consideration were such matters as whether the party's electoral program had an appeal to the sponsors; whether the party would or would not enter into a coalition with other conservative parties; whether it would help in attempts to oust an SPD-led government at the *Land* level; and the extent of its debts, if any.[12] One high official of the Civic Association told this author that support was provided the smaller parties out of a sense of loyalty, and to give them a chance to gain strength in two consecutive campaigns. Parties that failed in this effort would then find their funds cut off.

Decisions have tended to be made by the top managers and the executive committee of the sponsors' associations. In one *Land*, the three managers have met several times a year with the committee, consisting of sixteen men representing eight districts. A membership assembly has no substantial say in this process. The primary decisions to be made are how much money is to be raised and which party is to get it. There must

11 Kitzinger, *German Electoral Politics*, p. 208. The top management in a firm, and not the shareholders, decided whether money would be given, and how much. Stein interview with *Spiegel* editors, reported in "Das demokratische Wirtschaftsgeld," *Der Spiegel*, XIII (Nov. 4, 1959), 24.

12 Kitzinger, *German Electoral Politics*, p. 208.

also be discussion of how contact between the firms and the parties is to be made, and how the political seminars are to be conducted.

The distribution of funds, as allocated for the national level by the Civic Association, tends to vary from year to year or election to election. According to Stein, up until 1953 the CDU received 50 per cent, the FDP 35 per cent, and the DP 15 per cent. When the All-German Bloc of Expellees (GB/BHE) entered the coalition, and the FDP was split, further changes in the formula were necessary. Of money raised specifically for the elections, the CDU received 53 per cent, the FDP 29.2 per cent, the DP/FVP (a splinter wing of the FDP) 13 per cent, and the BHE 4.8 per cent.[13] After 1957 the BHE received no further subsidies—except during a transition period of fifteen months in which its debts were paid—because it failed to receive any representation in the Bundestag.[14] On the *Länder* level the formula differs sharply in accordance with the strength of each party. In Lower Saxony, for instance, it was set at one-third each for the CDU, the FDP, and the DP. In Hamburg the CDU received 60 per cent, the FDP 30 per cent, and the DP 10 per cent.[15]

It may be asked how much money the parties actually received for their electoral expenses. In the 1953 federal election, according to Stein, the sponsors' association gave a total of 5.7 million DM, of which the CDU received 2.5 million, the FDP 2.2 million, and the DP a million DM.[16] It must be borne in

[13] *Der Spiegel*, XIII (Nov. 4, 1959), 22.

[14] Kitzinger, *German Electoral Politics*, p. 216.

[15] *Der Spiegel*, XIII (Nov. 4, 1959), 22; Heinz Josef Varain, "Das Geld der Parteien," *Geschichte in Wissenschaft und Unterricht*, No. 8/1961, p. 496.

[16] *Der Spiegel*, XIII (Nov. 4, 1959), 22. For general commentaries on party financing see, in addition to articles already cited, Erwin Hielscher, "Die Finanzierung der politischen Parteien," *Politische Studien*, V, No. 64 (Aug. 1955), pp. 6–19; Werner Grundmann, "Die Finanzierung der politischen Parteien," *Zeitschrift für die gesamte Staatswirtschaft*, Vol. 115, No. 1 (1959), 113–130; Eschenburg, "Das Geld der Parteien," *Der Monat*, XII,

mind that the money represented a substantial income for the parties, but that it included neither direct business support for individual candidates or parties—which in some *Länder* was quite high—nor other subsidies to be discussed below. One BDI staff officer estimated that the total business donations to the parties for 1953 ranged between 20 and 25 million DM.

After the 1953 election there was some talk of dissolving the associations, but their importance in helping to finance the parties assured their survival. Early in 1957 Adenauer conferred with representatives of the BDI and of industry concerning the financing of that year's election, and was promised twice as much financial support as in 1953.[17] The promise was made good, although highly conflicting claims and counterclaims have made it impossible to determine precisely how much the parties received and spent. In an objective study of the 1957 election Uwe Kitzinger arrived at a total expenditure by all parties of 55 to 60 million DM, of which the CDU spent 35, the SPD 8, the FDP 6, the DP 3, and the BHE 2 million DM. These figures exclude indirect government propaganda expenditures for the sponsorship, for instance, of so-called "non-partisan" organizations, which runs into the millions, but include private parallel financing campaigns.[18] According to the CDU, the total spent

---

No. 140 (May 1960), 31–37; and Ulrich Dübber, *Parteifinanzierung in Deutschland* (Köln, 1962). The estimates of expenditures for the 1953 election vary widely, with a top of 30 million DM, according to various sources cited by Flechtheim, "Politische Entwicklung der CDU," pp. 185–186.

[17] *Der Spiegel*, Feb. 27, 1957, p. 13. See also *Die Finanzierung des Wahlkampfes 1957* (Hannover, n.d. [1957]).

[18] *German Electoral Politics*, pp. 309–314. However, a nonsocialist informant closely connected with the financing of the campaign asserts that the conservative parties spent between 80 and 100 million DM, exclusive of government propaganda. The SPD charged the opposition with having spent between 90 and 120 million DM, of which the CDU/CSU and the DP were said to have spent 46 million DM, the government and its auxiliary public relations organizations 40 million DM, and *Die Waage* and other private publicity organizations 30 million DM. *SPD Pressemitteil-*

by all parties was not more than 50 million DM.[19] Stein has revealed that the national sponsors' association contributed 19.4 million DM to the conservative parties, of which the CDU/CSU received 11 million, the FDP 4.6 million, the DP 3.3 million, and the BHE 0.5 million DM.[20] Moreover, to these sums must be added direct business donations to candidates or individual parties—which, one BDI official asserted, would bring the total of business contributions to an estimated 25 or 30 million DM.[21] A high FDP administrator confirmed that his party had received 4.6 million DM, of which 3 million came from the national sponsors' association (spent half on the national level and half on the *Länder* level by the FDP), and about 1.6 million from the *Länder* sponsors' associations and other donors.[22]

Few deny that the 1961 election was costly. As in earlier elections no exact data is available—not only because of the usual attempts to shroud expenditures in secrecy but also because the federal headquarters of parties often do not receive adequate or reliable financial information from their satellite organs in the *Länder*. Most observers agree that during the 1961 election more money flowed into and out of party coffers than in the 1957 election. One report put the figure as high as from 120 to 150 million DM; others, more conservative but seemingly reliable, estimated the amount spent by the parties at from 70 to 80 million DM, of which 10 million DM was said to have been raised by the candidates themselves.[23]

Presumably the CDU/CSU spent not less than 30 or 35

ungen und Informationen, Sept. 13, 1957, quoted in Kitzinger, *German Electoral Politics*, p. 304. See also *Süddeutsche Zeitung*, June 22, 1961.

[19] CDU Deutschlands, *9. Bundesparteitag CDU, Karlsruhe, 26.–29.4. 1960* (Hamburg, n.d. [1960]), p. 84.

[20] *Der Spiegel*, XIII (Nov. 4, 1959), 22.

[21] Statement of BDI official, personal interview. In an unpublished survey, Breitling estimates the *Länder* associations' contributions in 1957 at 6.3 million DM.

[22] See the author's "The Free Democratic Party in West German Politics," p. 338.

[23] *FAZ*, Sept. 21, 1961; *Süddeutsche Zeitung*, June 16, 1961.

million DM, of which 17 or 18 million DM came from business through the sponsors' associations. The SPD reportedly spent the equivalent of from 28 to 30 million DM—some of it provided in cash but a good deal in the form of services rendered by SPD-owned publishing and other enterprises. The election cost the FDP anywhere from 9 to 13 million DM. Before the campaign picked up momentum, FDP federal headquarters and the *Länder* hoped to receive 7.2 million DM from the sponsors' associations and 5 million DM from its own fund-raising campaigns. Large business concerns, including that of Krupp, again made generous donations to the party. The DP, in alliance with the BHE, reportedly received 1.5 million DM from the sponsors' associations and 1 million DM from the BHE.[24]

That the conservative parties were able to raise these amounts is quite remarkable in the light of the court decision of 1958, and the consequent inability of the Civic Association to continue its role as the rich uncle. Other ways and means had to be found to loosen the purse strings of businessmen for campaign expenses, which seem to increase by geometric progression with each election. According to the cited interpretation of the tax laws, anywhere from 20 to 30 per cent of money which associations have at their disposal may be donated tax free to political parties. A complicated manipulation permitting money to be raised from associations at various levels, meant that in the end the parties were able to obtain as much money on a

[24] According to one report, the sum for the CDU did not include 8 million DM which the CDU *Länder* received from the sponsors' associations. Dieter Schröder, "SPD hat fast so viel Geld wie die CDU," *Kölner Stadt-Anzeiger*, June 20, 1961. Schröder wrote a series of articles on election finances, which appeared in that newspaper from June 16 to 23, 1961 and in the *Süddeutsche Zeitung* from June 15 to 22, 1961. Figures for the SPD are from Walter Gong, "Goldene Kugeln rollen für den Sieg," *Die Zeit*, June 6, 1961. For the FDP the figures are contradictory; Chairman Mende spoke of 9 million DM (*Die Welt*, Nov. 10, 1961), but another party spokesman acknowledged an expenditure of 13 million DM (*FAZ*, Sept. 21, 1961). Figures for the DP are from *Süddeutsche Zeitung*, June 16, 1961.

tax-free basis in 1961 as they had during the 1957 campaign. The BDI, and most of its associations, gave no money at all to the parties, according to a BDI lieutenant, but in a majority of cases the *Länder* sponsors' associations were regarded as "professional associations" and could thus continue their financing activities. Other indirect ways of financing the parties employed in order to bypass the restrictions imposed by the Court included the launching by donors of parallel propaganda actions which tended to identify the parties with them, the printing of campaign literature without charge to the parties, and paying the wages of party secretaries under the designation of "association secretaries."

The attempt by the parties to obtain direct contributions from the business fraternity appears to have been more successful than ever before. In view of earlier denunciations by the SPD of such donations, it is remarkable that the party sought to raise a million DM from 12,000 businessmen in the same manner as its more conservative rivals. These saw in the SPD action a clever propaganda move designed to give the SPD a conservative image or at least one of friendliness rather than hostility to business.[25] The SPD did not publicize this new revenue-producing technique, but one of its spokesmen acknowledged that the party no longer wanted to be identified as the "poor people's party."[26] Despite these similarities in approach, the SPD still relied more heavily on its membership for dues and voluntary services during the campaign than did its rivals.

A further means of revenue, consisting of public appropriations received by all parties out of central and state treasuries, will be discussed presently.

The sponsors' associations not only contribute funds for national and state elections, but also subsidize the yearly overhead costs of party headquarters and personnel in Bonn and

[25] *Ibid., Deutsche Zeitung,* Aug. 2, 1961.
[26] Franz Barsig as quoted in *Süddeutsche Zeitung,* June 16, 1961.

in the *Länder*. According to Stein, from 1952 to 1958 the four conservative parties were given an average total of 7 million DM per year.[27] These sums were then allocated to each party, presumably on the same prorated basis as during the election campaigns. The parties often complain of insufficient funds, or of their failure to be disbursed when promised. One CDU *Land* agent reported in March 1957, "There is a tendency within the Federation of German Industry to have a large political fund constantly at its disposal, but to make available to the parties, especially the CDU, only the means needed to meet current expenses."[28]

It is doubtful whether this state of affairs exists to the same extent since the 1958 decision on tax exemption. The sponsors' associations have been unable to collect as much money as before. It is known, for instance, that for some years the CDU has had difficulty in meeting minimum operational expenditures. In Schleswig-Holstein, the income of *Land* and of many district headquarters has been 50 per cent less between 1958 and 1961 than it was before. The central headquarters of the CDU/CSU is known to receive 100,000 DM per month, and that of the FDP 50,000 DM per month, from business to defray part of their operating expenses.[29] But additional money is

[27] *Der Spiegel*, XIII (Nov. 4, 1959), 22. Stein revealed at a BDI General Assembly that the CDU received 1,000 DM, and each of the smaller parties from 500 to 750 DM per month for every one of the 252 election districts. *Mitteilungen*, VII, No. 7 (July 1959), p. 9. This would mean a yearly subsidy for the CDU of 3 million DM, presumably 2.25 million DM for the FDP, and 1.5 million DM for the DP. Since 1958 the funds apparently have been cut. A FDP official told this author in December 1959 that the FDP received only about 600,000 DM per year from the Civic Association.

[28] Heidenheimer, "German Party Finance: The CDU," p. 377, note 19. The author reports on one dispute in December 1952, in which a "CDU Land secretary wrote to the Sponsors' executive secretary to complain that although the agreement had entailed a payment of DM 150,000 over the ten pre-election months, the check for November had in fact been only for 'the usual DM 3,000.'" *Ibid.*, p. 379.

[29] Letter from Dr. Rudolf Wildenmann, University of Cologne, April 27, 1962; Schröder, "Wer bezahlt den Wahlkampf?" *Kölner Stadt-Anzeiger*, June 23, 1961.

needed so that party treasurers have been forced to develop both finesse and perseverance in this thankless and time-consuming task. One technique, both before and since 1958, has been to approach firms with a direct plea for further loosening of the purse strings. After the heat of a campaign, however, the response is usually cool, and the consequence may be a drastic reduction of party personnel. Raising more money from membership dues has proved equally unsatisfactory. In the CDU, for instance, the dues remain mostly on the local level if they can be collected in the first place. Since this source accounts for only a fraction of the necessary outlay, the CDU must depend on the sponsors' associations, individual donors, deputies, and firms for millions of DM per year more.[30] The CDU and FDP treasurers have urged firms to purchase some party services, such as the weekly economic journals published by these parties, whose subscription rates are extremely high and thus amount to a concealed form of subsidy—especially if a firm places a bulk subscription. When it was revealed that the Volkswagen Works had subscribed for 100 copies of the CDU journal at a rate of 60,000 DM per year, the SPD launched a parliamentary protest—but in vain.[31] Party treasurers may also ask firms to buy advertising space in party journals; in another instance firms were asked by Berg to contribute a minimum of 1,000 DM—tax exempt—in honor of Adenauer's seventy-fifth birthday, ostensibly for "scientific and cultural" purposes. Other organizations, such as *Die Waage*, have approached business for funds to advertise the benefits of Erhard's free enterprise system, especially during an election campaign. *Die Waage* receives

[30] Heidenheimer quotes a total income of between 5 and 7 million DM at all levels; "German Party Finance: The CDU," p. 384. The CDU treasurer, Professor Burgbacher, revealed that his party had received, presumably in 1963, approximately 4 million DM from membership dues. *Hannoversche Allgemeine*, April 9, 1964. According to one informant, to this sum must be added about 4.5 million DM in contributions.

[31] For details see Kitzinger, *German Electoral Politics*, pp. 206–207. Reportedly the *Wirtschaftsbild*, the CDU economic journal, has an income of between 2 and 3 million DM a year. *Kölner Stadt-Anzeiger*, June 20, 1961.

support not only from German firms but also from certain foreign enterprises with plants in Germany, which do not want to be involved in domestic politics but are willing to support Erhard personally.

As early as 1949, the FDP employed the technique of setting up its own sponsors' association to reach those employers who shared its conservative ideology. This source of funds became quite important after 1956, when the FDP was no longer in the Bonn governing coalition and found itself in the same camp as its opponent the SPD. As a result of FDP alliances against the CDU in North Rhine–Westphalia, Lower Saxony, and Hesse, the sponsors' associations for a time turned off the financial tap. Since many businessmen in the Ruhr and Wuerttemberg-Baden maintained their support of the party, up until 1958 the financial resources available to it were not unduly jeopardized, once an equalization scheme had been worked out in which the wealthier *Länder* affiliates were to share their bounty with their poorer brethren.[32]

Primary support for the conservative parties from the business community must come, then, either through the sponsors' associations or directly in the form of donations, subscriptions to economic journals, advertisements in the party press, and to a significant extent, from hidden government subsidies. Although from an American point of view the sums expended might be considered modest, they nevertheless have an impact on the party system and on the nature of particular election campaigns.[33] Up until the 1961 election business subsidies to the smaller conservative parties gave them a chance to maintain

[32] FDP, *Bundesparteitag der FDP in Berlin v. 21.–23.5.59. Bericht des Bundesschatzmeisters Hans W. Rubin* (mimeographed). The scheme had to be shelved after the 1958 North Rhine–Westphalia election in which the FDP fared poorly. Breitling, "Das Geld in der Deutschen Parteipolitik," p. 360.

[33] But not from a British point of view. Kitzinger estimates that the CDU in 1957 spent at least three times as much as the British Conservatives in any postwar election. *German Electoral Politics*, p. 202.

their existence and to gain representation in the Bundestag. Moreover, during election campaigns subsidies to all the non-socialist parties provided more money for advertising and billboard space than the SPD was able to raise.

This is not to say that the SPD is poverty-stricken. Most of its 14.5 million DM per year comes from dues, but it also receives income from its own business concerns, which include printing and publishing; from a sponsors' association supported by the cooperatives; and indirectly from the trade unions for the co-sponsorship of certain political actions.[34] Furthermore, it is not averse to accepting election-campaign funds from individual business firms, especially those located in areas under SPD control where contracts may be expected—for example Hamburg—or such firms as breweries and department stores, whose customers may be to a great extent supporters of the SPD.[35] Clearly such firms do not want to identify themselves with any one party, and as a form of insurance have contributed to several. The SPD never asked for money from the sponsors' associations, however, and in any event would not have received

[34] The BDI has publicized the charge that, according to one source, the DGB gave direct, but concealed, financial support to the SPD in the 1953 election. The source is Hans-Georg Hermann (pseud.), *Verraten und Verkauft* (Fulda, 1959), pp. 176–177. The DGB denies the allegation by Hermann, a former trade union editor, and argues that since there are supporters of the CDU in its top ranks (as well as many in the lower ranks) it must remain nonpartisan. A CDU deputy, Wacher, made the same charge in parliament. German Federal Republic, Deuscher Bundestag, *Verhandlungen des Deutschen Bundestages*, Stenographische Berichte, 3rd election period, 104th session, p. 5647 (hereafter referred to as Bundestag, 3rd el. pd., with session). See also Triesch, "Die Finanzierung der SPD," *Die politische Meinung*, Heft 28 (Sept. 1958), pp. 36–51; and SPD yearbooks. The SPD treasurer asserted that party revenue in 1963 was 14.5 million DM, but CDU spokesmen claim that the SPD revenue was 16.7 million DM, of which 14 million DM came from membership dues. To this revenue must be added 10.2 million DM from the federal and *Länder* public treasuries. *Hannoversche Allgemeine*, April 9, 1964.

[35] Kitzinger, *German Electoral Politics*, pp. 217, 219; Schröder, "Die goldene Kugeln finden ihren Weg," *Kölner Stadt-Anzeiger*, June 17–18, 1961.

a penny. In a speech to the 1959 Assembly of the BDI, Stein argued that the existence of an opposition was crucial, but that the SPD already received a sizable income from membership dues, and did not need the support of organized business.[36]

If only a small segment of business supports the SPD, it may be asked, do the rest support the conservative parties, either directly or via the sponsors' associations? The associations are supported by from one-third to one-half of all employers, although an estimated 60 or 70 per cent of the large corporations provide funds.[37] Of course more employers contribute during an election year than in other years. But again there are many, of the rugged-individualist school, who consider the associations' tendencies too strongly collectivist and who prefer to support individual deputies from their own bailiwicks—especially if the latter are personal acquaintances or if their campaign expenses are high. One employer told this author that such contributions would never be publicized—first, because the candidate would receive that much less support from his party at the next election, and second, because the employer would alienate any sponsors' association that felt that funds should be channeled solely through its hands. The BDI has been concerned with the great number of businessmen who give the parties no support, either direct or indirect. Its task has not been made easier by the 1958 court decision. Not only will employers who gave nothing in the past refrain from giving in the future, but those who did give will now give less.

The businessman is also wary of legal attempts to force the parties to reveal the source and amount of their income. Recollections of Nazi party financing led to the stipulation in Article 21 of the Basic Law that political parties must publicly account for the sources of their funds, and that details shall be regulated by federal legislation. But owing to the opposition or apathy of the parties, although the problem has been considered

[36] *Mitteilungen*, VII, No. 7 (July 1959), p. 10.
[37] *Ibid.*, p. 9; and personal interviews by the author.

since 1950, no implementing legislation has ever been passed. A Ministry of the Interior draft bill was rejected by Chancellor Adenauer at a cabinet session in 1952, presumably because the draft called for the naming of individual donors.[38] Late in 1955 the Ministry designated a commission of university professors to advise on the drafting of a new bill (to include the question not only of party financing but also of internal party democracy and the regulation of lobbying activities). The commission made several proposals, one of which was to publish the names of party donors, and another to identify donations by groups—industry, and so on.[39]

The BDI officially opposed the first of these proposals, since businessmen would obviously be most reluctant to publicize the extent of their individual contributions, and thus correspondingly reluctant to make them. It agreed to the latter, not out of love for the proposal itself but simply from the necessity of accepting the regulation that would be least painful to its interests.[40]

In 1959 the Ministry of the Interior finally drafted a new party bill, based less on the recommendations of the university professors than on the wishes of the business community. According to one Ministry official, these wishes were so well known to the Ministry section drafting the bill that there was no need to hold talks with business associations. The provisions of the draft were mild indeed: no listing of donors was required, either individually or by groups, but simply a breakdown of party income by such loose categories as membership dues, contributions of deputies, profits from party enterprises and activities, other donations, and credits.[41] Support from industry would

---

[38] Kitzinger, *German Electoral Politics*, p. 198; Dübber, "Die Geldgeber müssen genannt werden," *Vorwärts*, July 25, 1958.

[39] See German Federal Republic, *Rechtliche Ordnung des Parteiwesens: Bericht der vom Bundesminister des Innern eingesetzten Parteienrechtskommission* (Frankfurt/M., 1958).

[40] *Mitteilungen*, VII, No. 7 (July 1959), pp. 9–10.

[41] Bundestag Drucksache 1509, Dec. 22, 1959, p. 6. See also Hans-

thus be subsumed under "other donations." Furthermore, all such donations would once again be tax free. In short, the bill represented a triumph for the views of the BDI. But widespread opposition by the parties prevented action upon it by the Third Bundestag, although at the time of writing it appeared possible that a revised bill would be passed by the Fourth Bundestag. Indeed, in 1964 the party treasurers arrived at an agreement to put a ceiling on campaign expenses.

The parties have also sought funds from the state treasuries. As a result of such pressure the Bundestag and the *Länder* have voted them funds—initially for the sole purpose of "political education," but now without any restriction. On the *Länder* level, in 1964, they received 10 million DM. On the federal level, the original allotment of 5 million DM a year was increased to 20 million DM a year in 1962, and to 38 million DM a year in 1964. The money is allocated to the parties on the basis of their strength in the Bundestag—thereby provoking much critical discussion, since the present system is manifestly unfair to new parties and to small parties unable to surmount the 5 per cent barrier.[42]

The CDU claims to be opposed to a complete state subsidy, but late in 1960 Adenauer was reported to have abandoned his

Eberhard Roesch, "Die öffentliche Rechenschaftspflicht der politischen Parteien über die Herkunft ihrer Mittel," *Deutsches Verwaltungsblatt,* Sept. 1, 1958, pp. 597–602; Ludwig Bergsträsser, "Der Entwurf des Parteiengesetzes," *Politische Studien,* X, Heft 113 (Sept. 1959), 596–605; Dübber, "Aufgaben und Grenzen eines Parteiengesetzes," *Die Neue Gesellschaft,* V, No. 2 (March-April 1958), 118–126.

[42] *Die Zeit,* May 4, 1962. See also World Political Science Congress, *Report on Proceedings, Meetings on Research in Party and Campaign Finance,* Paris, Sept. 27–29, 1961 (mimeographed), pp. 8–9; Eschenburg, "Staatsgelder für die Parteien," *Die Zeit,* April 21, 1961. In April 1964 in a Bundestag debate on party financing, the CDU treasurer stated that the parties represented in the Bundestag needed 85 million DM a year, inclusive of campaigns, so that public subsidies of 48 million DM still would leave a gap of over 35 million DM to be covered by dues and donations. *Bulletin,* No. 66, April 18, 1964, p. 577.

previous stand and to be willing to consider some state financing —possibly as a warning to industry to be more generous in its donations or less insistent in its demands.[43] The SPD has supported a limited state subsidy, but has officially denounced the substantial increase in 1964, fearing that the parties will become overly dependent on the state. The FDP, according to one of its spokesmen, prefers a heavy dose of government financing because it regards too much dependence on support from industry as unhealthy. Along with the other small parties, it would welcome a limit on expenditures, such as is imposed in Great Britain. The BDI declares that the party bureaucracies favor state financing which frees them from having to seek more members—the very reason why the BDI itself opposes the scheme.[44] The BDI would of course prefer to see the conservative parties recruit more members; but its chief concern is obviously with the important lever of influence within the parties, of which it would be deprived if the present system of heavy business subsidies were drastically altered.

Evidently industry is not willing to aid the conservative parties out of pure altruism. Explicitly or implicitly it wants the assurance, first of all, that they will pursue economic and social policies in harmony with its own goals; second, that they will support the candidacy of Bundestag deputies who are sympathetic to the BDI. The way in which industry has attached strings to its financing activities may readily be seen from several cases which have been publicized by the press or by the opposition, and of which there has been no official denial.

In February 1952, at a meeting in Frankfurt of representatives of industry, banks, and the CDU and FDP, the industrialists accused the governing parties of giving in to the trade-union drive for codetermination, and reportedly threatened to cut off

[43] Eschenburg, *Probleme der mordernen Parteifinanzierung* (Tübingen, 1961), p. 33; Heidenheimer, "Campaign Finance Outside the United States" (mimeographed, 1962), p. 15.

[44] *Mitteilungen*, VII, No. 7 (July 1959), p. 9.

their funds.[45] In 1960, according to one news story, the Chancellor yielded to strong pressure from steel executives who threatened to reduce their contributions to the CDU and to increase those to the FDP unless he reversed himself on the question of prohibiting Sunday work in the steel mills.[46] Another report has it that in 1961 the monthly check for 100,000 DM which organized business sent to the CDU for operating expenses was suddenly withheld because of Berg's annoyance at Adenauer for having gone back on a promise not to revalue the currency.[47] In addition to such financial pressures in relation to legislative and executive policy, there have been other cases involving party coalitions and internal party affairs.

According to the SPD, in August 1954 the chairman of the Bavarian Party, Josef Baumgartner, wrote the directors of several firms a letter suggesting that further contributions to the sponsors' association should be made only on condition that the association distributed funds on the basis of the percentage of votes received by the various parties in the previous Landtag election. If this procedure were not adopted, the chairman's letter went on, the Bavarian party would turn directly to the firms for funds.[48]

As has already been indicated, the sponsors' associations and the FDP have often been at loggerheads over the question of the FDP's joining a *Land* coalition with the SPD or allying itself with the opposition SPD at the national level. In January 1956 Berg and the Civic Association urged FDP representatives to support Adenauer's attempt to revise the electoral law in order to provide himself with a majority at the next federal election. A revision could have meant the end of the FDP as a national party. The FDP, rejecting the suggestion, allied itself

[45] DGB, *Informationsdienst der Pressestelle beim BV des DGB*, June 3, 1952.

[46] *Stuttgarter Zeitung*, Oct. 19, 20; Nov. 5, 1960; cited by *Labor Headline News* (U. S. Embassy, Bonn), No. 1986, Nov. 7, 1960, p. 4.

[47] Gong, "Goldene Kugeln rollen für den Sieg," *Die Zeit*, June 23, 1961.

[48] *SPD-Pressedienst* W/IX/79, Sept. 30, 1954.

with the SPD in North Rhine–Westphalia, partly in order to gain more votes in the Bundesrat, which could then block Adenauer's proposal.[49]

The predicted consequence of the FDP's break with the CDU in North Rhine–Westphalia was that the *Land* sponsors' association would cut off all funds to the FDP. Industrialists close to the FDP thereupon threatened to cut off funds to the association unless the FDP received its normal share. Eventually it did, but not before another incident had further strained the uneasy relationship. Certain economic associations allegedly tried to coerce three FDP deputies to leave their party by threatening them with a loss of business. Pferdmenges heard of this effort at blackmail, and was able to suppress it.[50]

In 1956 the FDP left the government coalition. A year later the Civic Association told the FDP that generous donations would be made to its federal election campaign in exchange for a promise not to join a coalition cabinet with the SPD. To this Willy Weyer, who was then North Rhine–Westphalia Finance Minister and a high official of the FDP, replied, "We are, after all, not a political shop of the BDI or the employer organizations"[51]—and the FDP made no promise. Moreover, the FDP officers in the Association threatened to leave it unless there were guarantees that contributions to the party would continue. Once again the FDP won the dispute, largely because industry did not want to throw all its support on the national level to the CDU. The FDP provided industry with a useful lever, and its demise would have led to repercussions within the BDI, where there was a circle friendly to the party.

In 1959, once again—this time in Lower Saxony—the executive committee of the sponsors' association debated at length the

---

[49] Breitling, "Das Geld in der Deutschen Parteipolitik," p. 358.

[50] *Süddeutsche Zeitung*, Feb. 20, 1956.

[51] *Frankfurter Rundschau*, June 11, 1957; D. Schwarzkopf, "Die Förderergesellschaften," *Der Tagesspiegel*, May 6, 1956, cited by Flechtheim, "Politische Entwicklung und Finanzierung der CDU," p. 188; Hirsch-Weber in *Interest Groups on Four Continents*, ed. Ehrmann, p. 109.

question of further subsidies to the FDP, in view of its alliance with the SPD and the BHE in the *Land* government—especially since the FDP had earlier made promises not to join such a coalition. As a result of this "treason," a majority threatened to pull out of the association if the FDP received any money. Funds were cut off, and the FDP members on the executive committee promptly resigned.[52] Just before this the association had even asked the executive committee of the *Land* FDP to install a treasurer who would be acceptable to the association.[53]

Disputes arise not only between parties and sponsors' associations but also among the conservative parties themselves. The BDI and the Civic Association may try to arbitrate such disputes, in order to enhance the strength of the parties vis-à-vis the SPD. Or they may urge minor conservative parties to combine, especially for electoral purposes, pointing out that they do not want to sustain parties that merely compete with one another.[54]

All this goes to show that the sponsors' associations quite often bear out the adage that "he who pays the piper calls the tune." This is not to imply that there is any large-scale network of bribery; in fact, few instances have come to light. But it does mean that when the situation seems to demand it, the associations are not averse to applying pressure on the recipients of funds. Officially the BDI refrains from comment on the matter, while vigorously denying any influence on the parties—and insisting that the funds for operating expenses are sufficient only "to cover rent and telephone bills."[55] (Of the funds for electoral campaigns there is no mention.)

[52] Interview with a BDI official.

[53] Josef Schmidt, "Guerillakrieg bei den Freien Demokraten Niedersachsens," *Süddeutsche Zeitung*, March 8, 1960; cited in Varain, "Das Geld der Parteien," p. 503, n. 55.

[54] F. A. Freiherr von der Heydte and Karl Sacherl, *Soziologie der deutschen Parteien* (München, 1955), p. 171; *Manchester Guardian*, Sept. 13, 1957.

[55] *Mitteilungen*, VII, No. 7 (July 1959), p. 9.

It is hard to disagree with the FDP *Land* chairman who, when the FDP was in opposition, publicly criticized the influence of giant corporations and their managers on German politics, and charged some sectors of industry with making assistance contingent upon a promise from the parties to grant them their demands.[56] Another critical power possessed by industry is that of determining whether a small party will continue to exist or perish for lack of funds. Although in the past the sponsors' associations have been generous in their support of minor parties, there have been several exceptions, as has already been noted. Whether the associations are entitled to the power they now wield in the field of financing has been the subject of some discussion in Germany; but so long as no effective alternative system of financing them can be found, the situation will remain basically the same. It would appear unlikely that the conservative parties can ever become mass organizations, with an income primarily from dues. And even should a party law be passed, the sponsors' associations could still make their influence felt. If expenditures for campaigns were ever effectively limited by law, or if the state were to finance all parties even more fully, the situation would naturally be changed. At this stage of West German political development the prospect for such a change is within the realm of possibility.

[56] *Das freie Wort*, Feb. 28, 1958.

VI

Nominations and

Election Campaigns

NOMINATIONS

"The prime function of the political party is the nomination of candidates for public elective office."[1] Although in this statement V. O. Key, Jr., was describing the nominating process within the United States, his statement is no less applicable to the Federal Republic of Germany. There is, however, a difference in the relation of interest groups to parties and to the legislature in the two countries.

Associations in the United States have traditionally avoided exposing their leaders to the political frays of Congress. Not many chiefs of either industry or organized labor have been willing to run the gauntlet of the nomination process, including the primaries. Instead, the associations have preferred to press for the selection of candidates sympathetic to their objectives, to whom access would be easy once they were elected to public office. Thus lobbying is much more extensive in the United States than in Europe.

In West Germany, on the other hand, the associations prefer

[1] *Politics, Parties, and Pressure Groups* (New York, 1946), 360.

to have direct representation in the legislatures on the federal, state, and local levels. They feel that as members of parliamentary groups *(Fraktionen)* and committees, they can influence legislation more effectively than by lobbying from the outside. Hence the BDI seeks to maximize its power in the legislative organs by suggesting names of industrialists and employers willing to run for public office. Accordingly it must try to maintain fraternal relations with the conservative parties who are ultimately responsible for the selection of candidates. Since other interest groups are likewise pressing for the nomination of their own candidates, an intense struggle develops within each party as the slate of candidates is drawn up. With each federal election the intensity has increased. In 1949 many potential candidates preferred to wait and see what kind of system would develop; in 1953 many who had not expected to win were swept into office by the CDU victory. Consequently, in 1957 the competition for seats in the Bundestag—a total of 2,073 list and 1,700 constituency candidatures of all parties—was keen indeed.[2] It may be surmised that in 1961 it was no less so.

A brief description of the complex electoral process is necessary in order to understand the two-way system of gaining seats in the Bundestag. As a result of a compromise between the major parties, the Electoral Laws of 1949, 1953, and 1956 call for a combination of proportional representation and a system of single-member districts. One-half of the seats are allotted to the single-member districts, the other half to parties which draw up slates of candidates in each *Land*. A voter accordingly casts two votes—one for his district candidate and one for the party slate. In the district a plurality suffices to win the election. At the *Land* level the number of seats allotted to each party is determined on the basis of proportional representation. In order to reduce the number of splinter parties, the law also stipulates

[2] Kitzinger, *German Electoral Politics*, p. 59; Karlheinz Kaufmann, Helmut Kohl, Peter Molt, *Kandidaturen zum Bundestag: Die Auswahl der Bundestags–Kandidaten 1957 in zwei Bundesländern* (Köln, 1961), p. 200.

that a party must either receive a minimum of 5 per cent of the total federal vote on the second ballot, or win three seats in the districts. A candidate may stand for election both in a constituency and on a party list as added insurance of gaining a seat. But if a candidate is not placed high on the list his chance of election is slight, unless he has won in the constituency, or unless the party itself has received an overwhelming victory. Many candidates prefer to stand in a constituency where the challenges are greater and where contact with the constituents is more personal. Some of those who have run only on a *Land* list believe that "they were suspected of having had their seats bought for them by organized interests: 'With all my industrial connections,' one member was heard to say, 'I simply must have a constituency seat.' "[3]

A look at the 1961 election results shows that of the 33 CDU/CSU deputies who were elected from the business community, 23 were elected in districts and 10 on *Land* lists.[4] Usually the names of experts appear high on the latter. These men are important to the party but may not have the forensic ability or personal popularity to capture a seat in a district.

Practices in selecting candidates vary among and even within the parties; but in none can the average dues-paying member be said to have a large part. Rather, the choices are made by the national and state leaders. In some *Länder,* for instance, it is the relatively decentralized CDU *Land* Executive Committee or

[3] Kitzinger, *German Electoral Politics*, p. 60.

[4] See Appendix C for the names of the Bundestag deputies who are from the business community. Compilation made by the DI, Fraktion der CDU/ CSU (FDP) im IV. Deutschen Bundestag (mimeographed; names of deputies close to business are underlined). These lists, containing the names of 33 CDU/CSU and 16 FDP business deputies, do not tally with another total of 76 deputies issued by the DI (see Chapter VII, Table IV), in which a different classification system obviously was used. The list of deputies elected by *Land* list or constituency appears in German Federal Republic, *Amtliches Handbuch des Deutschen Bundestages, 4. Wahlperiode* (Darmstadt, n.d. [c. 1962]), pp. 175–193. All FDP deputies were elected on the *Land* lists.

Board that has the decisive say; in others it is the *Land* party congress or the district organs; in still others it is a combination.[5] Candidates must be approved in secret ballot by the delegates of the party at the district level. In this process neither the BDI nor any other associations find it possible to control a majority of the delegates. Federal headquarters have little effect on the autonomy of the districts, although one speaker at a CDU convention pleaded for at least a minimum of coordination and "sounding out" before the nominations were made, in order to have a balanced parliamentary representation.[6] Another speaker was troubled by the failure of the bulk of CDU members—not to mention the average voter—to participate in the selection process. His prescription was a more active membership, or primary elections on the United States model.[7]

National leaders in the CDU and FDP, upon prodding by the BDI and other associations, may occasionally recommend certain candidates to the state chairmen, or propose that incumbents not be selected again. Thus, although they have no coercive or veto power and may have their recommendations blocked by lower party organs, they do have some influence upon the composition of the top echelons of the parliament.

In all this jockeying for seats the associations must, of course, receive consideration, because they provide the party with financial assistance, with votes, and with experts for the legislative committees. In order to maintain the proper balance and to obtain the maximum electoral support, each party must offer carefully prepared slates which would give spokesmen for the various associations—and for regions, women, refugees, and youth groups—an adequate voice. The CDU is faced with the

[5] Schulz, "Die Organisationsstruktur der CDU," *Zeitschrift für Politik*, III, No. 2 (Oct. 1956), 152; Kaufmann, Kohl, Molt, *Kandidaturen zum Bundestag*, p. 230.

[6] CDU Deutschlands, *6. Bundesparteitag, 1956*, p. 115.

[7] CDU Deutschlands, *8. Bundesparteitag CDU, Kiel, 18.–21.9.1958* (Hamburg, n.d. [1958]), p. 61.

additional difficulty of balancing the number of Catholics and Protestants on its slate.

Each party is bombarded with lists of names from every conceivable association. For example, before the 1954 Landtag election in North Rhine–Westphalia, the CDU received the names of a hundred suggested nominees, even though not more than six had a chance of election.[8] Although the associations cannot be ignored, the parties must also appease the hunger of their own functionaries. Hence the safe constituencies and the top places on the lists are filled by the most important party people beginning with potential government ministers, down through parliamentary party leaders, then experts (many donated by the interest groups), and finally, the candidates who will add numerical strength at the lower levels.[9]

No wonder, then, that the BDI on the whole expresses dissatisfaction with the nomination system. The "sterility" of the parties, according to the Federation, means the leadership of the elderly, which precludes the appearance of many new and younger leaders on the party slates. The result is a parliamentary group with an overabundance of veteran party bosses. According to the argument, it is, after all, the responsibility of these bosses, who built up the parties in the post-1945 era, to draw both qualified young politicians and men from industry who are not seasoned politicians into the political arena. Only then will each parliamentary group be well balanced and capable of fulfilling its program. The initiative, however, must come from the party bosses, who must select the right candidates at the right time. Concurrently, the BDI insists, the employer community has an obligation to free for political service those employers or staff members who express an interest in politics; otherwise the willingness of the parties to put up candidates from the business world is simply wasted.[10]

---

[8] Heidenheimer, "Schattierungen im Röntgenbild der Christlichen Demokraten," *Die Neue Gesellschaft*, V, No. 3 (May–June 1958), 179.

[9] Wildenmann, *Partei und Fraktion*, pp. 144–146.

[10] *JB*, 1956–1957, pp. 24–25; *UB*, No. 20, May 16, 1957; No. 42, Oct. 19, 1961.

To be sure, when the BDI speaks of a balanced ticket, it means one having an adequate number of representatives of industry. Officially, of course, it declares that deputies must not act for any selfish interest, but only for the general welfare. On the other hand, it is critical of those who oppose the election of deputies representing business interests to parliament. If such groups were not represented, it argues, they would withdraw from an active interest in politics, and end by plotting against the democratic state through devious and anticonstitutional means.[11]

That such a situation has not arisen is due in part to the parties' actual practice of presenting tickets that are relatively well balanced (though no association ever feels it is represented in sufficient numbers). Moreover, aware of the pluralistic make-up of society, the parties have no wish to be labeled as either a "business" or a "peasant" party. The trend toward a two-party system further reinforces their relative independence vis-à-vis any interest group. In their turn such groups attempt to ensure strength in parliament by distributing their representatives through several parties, so as to have a better chance of making an impact on economic, agricultural, labor, and other policies.

The BDI has never denied taking an active part in the nomination process. At a general assembly of the BDI in 1953, Gustav Stein declared, "I would like to emphasize that . . . a great many individuals have put themselves at our disposal, and that during these days in which parties ask us whether we can supply to them individuals for the coming federal elections, we can supply them with a very long and comprehensive list of individuals."[12] He went on to say that the BDI restricted the list to those employers who had not been in politics before, and whom it had then asked whether they were willing to serve. Stein averred that there had been no scrutiny of the members of the current

[11] Dr. Wolfgang Pohle in Wilhelm Beutler, Gustav Stein, and Hellmuth Wagner, (eds.), *Der Staat und die Verbände* (Heidelberg, 1957), p. 29.
[12] As quoted in Hirsch-Weber and Schütz, *Wähler und Gewählte*, p. 57.

Bundestag to name substitutes for those who were not deemed suitable; if there had been, he said, the BDI would have become embroiled in a hopeless political wrangle. Since the list was long, he went on, the percentage of successful candidates in the next Bundestag would be high, and would satisfactorily represent the business community in the Bundestag and its committees. It was not the task of the BDI, Stein concluded, to make exaggerated political demands, but rather to ensure a continuation of the economic policy.[13]

These remarks have the ring of truth; but they do not tell the whole story. The BDI does not entirely refrain from making demands, and does insist on an adequate representation by the parties to which it has given its financial support. Events in *Land* Schleswig-Holstein may serve as an illustration. In preparation for the 1953 election, according to Heidenheimer and Varain, there were protracted negotiations between the sponsors' association and CDU leaders. In addition to extending a promise not to fight the other conservative parties, in November 1952, the CDU signed an ambiguous written agreement to submit names of leading candidates to the association which "might make use of these names."[14] Twenty-four deputies were to be elected to the Bundestag from Schleswig-Holstein, fourteen of whom were to represent the single-member constituencies and ten the *Land* lists. The association called on the three conservative parties (CDU, FDP, and DP) to divide the fourteen districts among themselves, with all parties agreeing to support one candidate in each district, a scheme that meant the nomination of candidates from the CDU in eight districts, from the FDP in three, from the DP in two, and an independent in one. The association reasoned that a coalition of conservative parties would increase its electoral strength, but the parties could agree

[13] *Ibid.*

[14] Heidenheimer, "German Party Finance: The CDU," p. 378, note 22; Varain, "Kandidaten und Abgeordnete in Schleswig-Holstein, 1947–1958," *Politische Vierteljahresschrift*, II, No. 4 (1961), 363–411.

neither to this proposal, which meant a restriction on their freedom of action, nor to a later list of nineteen suggested candidates. The CDU subsequently nominated some of the men whose names appeared on the list; but these happened to be artisans or farm leaders who had a large electoral following. The sponsors' association was eager to see its favorite candidate, Dr. Wilhelm Jentzsch, who was deputy chairman of the BDI regional office, given a high place on the CDU list; but the CDU ranked him seventh, below several farm leaders. Since Jentzsch had no abiding party loyalty for the CDU, the FDP (to which he consequently transferred his allegiance) placed him at the top of its *Land* list, with the result that he was elected.

The CDU undoubtedly resented the strong interference of the association, which in July 1953 had promised increased financial backing to all conservative parties providing they reached an accord. The CDU *Land* secretary wrote in a report dated August 15 that "the demands of the sponsors' association for the adoption of candidates without regard to their previous political position, and the blackmailing way in which these demands were presented have created . . . an impossible situation. . . . We can no longer give in to the sponsors' association's political demands!"[15]

Thus the CDU was much more cautious in preparing its electoral strategy for the *Land* election of 1954. It was careful not to become involved in any agreement with the FDP that would necessitate supporting the FDP candidates. The CDU *Land* secretary warned the party leaders that the CDU must obtain more influence in the regrouping or enlargement of the sponsors' association executive body.[16]

In many instances the sponsors' association plays no direct role in the nomination procedure, but financial donations may still be a source of conflict. This is especially true in the single-

[15] *Ibid.*, p. 381, note 48; Heidenheimer, "German Party Finance: the CDU," p. 379.

[16] Varain, "Kandidaten und Abgeordnete in Schleswig-Holstein," p. 385.

member districts, where tough negotiations at lower party levels may be needed to resolve the clash of interests, or where the contest may center on the personality or record of competing candidates. For example, the CDU's local executive committee in 1949 in the Kiel district suggested the name of the party secretary as nominee. The expellees objected to him, and insisted on the nomination of a newspaper editor who was obviously in closer agreement with their aims. The party chairman, in backing the secretary, made the revealing comment that representatives of business who had made financial donations to the party wanted the secretary as a candidate. At the *Land* convention a majority of the delegates finally supported the secretary; but obviously such disputes engender at least temporary bitterness and rancor.[17]

A rather different dispute during the 1961 campaign illustrates the thankless difficulties of making up a list. Early in July, according to one account, a nine-man committee of the Rhineland CDU decided not to award seat number 35 (out of 40 that were considered safe) to Hans Dichgans, a prominent iron and steel industrialist, but to give it instead to a leader of commerce —a sector that had complained of insufficient representation. In his turn, Dr. Hans-Günther Sohl, a Thyssen director who was also active in the BDI, regarded this as an affront to his own industry which after all heavily financed the CDU. The banker Robert Pferdmenges, taking up his cause, arranged a meeting

---

[17] *Ibid.*, p. 369. In another case, three men sought the candidacy in a district of Baden-Wuerttemberg in the 1957 election. Two were local party members—one an agricultural expert, the second a merchant—and the third aspirant was Walter Gassmann, a director of Mercedes-Benz of Stuttgart. Even though Gassmann had the support of the sponsors' association and the *Land* Executive committee, he nevertheless sought the seat himself, partly because outside intervention would have reduced rather than enhanced his chances. As a result of a deadlock among the two regions comprising the electoral district and their failure to agree on either of the two local candidates, Gassmann received the nomination and won the Bundestag seat. Kaufmann, Kohl, Molt, *Kandidaturen zum Bundestag,* pp. 77–78.

between Sohl and Wilhelm Johnen, the chief of the Rhineland CDU, at which the latter capitulated when Sohl threatened to cut off all contributions from the steel industry to the CDU. At the CDU delegate assembly soon afterward, Johnen announced that he backed the candidacy of Dichgans because the latter was Adenauer's choice. The representatives of commerce felt betrayed because they had reason to believe that Adenauer had originally supported their candidate. The outcome was that Dichgans received seat number 35 and won the election.[18]

Although in many instances there is no such tie-in between donations and the choice of candidates, in crucial situations it is obvious that money talks. The last instance also reveals the importance of receiving the backing of Adenauer where there is a contest for one seat. Ordinarily, as has been indicated, the conservative parties approach the BDI to ask for the names of competent industrialists or managers who would be available to run for office; the parties then approach the individuals directly, or an individual employer—perhaps unknown to the BDI but locally prominent—may take the initiative of approaching the parties themselves. This happened more frequently in 1961 than in previous elections.

But such procedures are no guarantee of nomination, or of election after being nominated. Representatives of industry have told this author of the many obstacles they must overcome. A Protestant will have no chance in a Catholic district, and vice versa. Anyone who has not been active in the party will find it reluctant to nominate them. Anyone who is placed in a safe position at the top of a *Land* list may then be confronted by party tacticians who fear that he may detract from the image of the party, and proceed to assign him to a lower berth. This is what happened to the manager of a large concern who decided to enter CDU politics. He made barnstorming trips in his constituency, delivered many speeches, and met a number of CDU groups. But because he was identified with industry—or so he

[18] *Der Spiegel*, Aug. 16, 1961, p. 16.

concluded—and despite his intensive party activity, he obtained only twenty-fifth place on a 1957 *Land* list. If the CDU had not made a favorable showing he could not have been elected.

In 1961 Dr. Curt Becker, a well-known employer and long-time deputy in the CDU, who had the support of employer organizations and the CDU Economic Committee of the Rhineland, failed to receive a safe seat in a CDU *Land* list and was not re-elected. In another instance, the firm of Buderus Wetzlar gave one of its managers permission to run for office; but despite his party activity at the local level, he too failed to obtain top billing on a *Land* list.[19] According to one informant, there have even been instances when a party promised to put up some representatives of industry as candidates and then reneged.

The parties complain, on the other hand, of the caliber of many men from industry who volunteer their services. One party leader asserted to the author that if in 1957 the BDI could have submitted the names of ten top-notch industrialists, they would easily have been elected. Moreover, representatives of industry would be given a higher berth if they were capable experts, not simply retired second-string staff men from business associations. But one difficulty is that competent staff men are often reluctant to enter politics for fear of losing their jobs, or of causing disputes within the association if they opt for one party. Another difficulty is that experts are whisked away from the parties and into posts in the executive branch or in international bodies, leaving the conservative parties with a dearth of qualified parliamentary experts in such fields of immediate concern to the BDI as finance, taxes, economic affairs, and industrial relations.

But altogether the industrial community has little cause for complaint. In theory it cannot expect a sizable representation

[19] Letter from Triesch, Feb. 9, 1962. Occasionally the support of the CDU's economic committee and youth branch may be most helpful, as was true in the 1957 candidacy of Dr. Gerhard Fritz, a 36-year-old executive of a chamber of industry and commerce in the Rhineland-Palatinate. Kaufmann, Kohl, Molt, *Kandidaturen zum Bundestag*, pp. 161–162, 168.

because of the low proportion of its members in relation to the total membership of the parties. For instance, a 1955 survey in Westphalia showed that only 3.1 per cent of the CDU's members were employers. Yet because of its financial importance, in practice (as will be shown in Chapter VII) the industrial community has a not insignificant number of representatives in the Bundestag. Thus the same survey in Westphalia showed that 21.8 per cent of the CDU's deputies to the Bundestag from that area were employers—a high proportion indeed.[20] It is the contention of industry, however, that the quality of its deputies is as important as the quantity, and that the only hope for improvement on its own part is in greater activity in the parties, and on the part of the latter in a re-examination of the nomination process with the aim of providing maximum representation to capable representatives from industry.[21]

ELECTION CAMPAIGNS

The heterogeneity of the West German parties means that they are dependent for support on a wide array of interest groups, none of which can commit themselves officially to one party. Although it is clear enough that an interest group that is conservative in ideology, as is the BDI, will back the conservative parties, and vice versa, it is often far less clear why one industrialist should vote for the CDU and another for the FDP. The reason may be a matter of religion, of program, of ideology, or of sheer opportunism. At any rate, the great bulk of the business community as a whole identifies itself with the nonsocialist parties and individual businessmen vote as do individuals everywhere, according to "social pressures and inner feelings of social obligation."[22]

Officially the BDI cannot be a mouthpiece for any party, but according to its spokesmen, there is no reason why it cannot

---

[20] Heidenheimer, "Schattierungen im Röntgenbild der Christlichen Demokraten," pp. 178–179.

[21] Letter from Triesch, Feb. 9, 1962.

[22] Lipset, *Political Man*, p. 200.

support the nonsocialist parties, as it has done in all federal elections since 1953. It had not yet been formed at the time of the first federal election in 1949, but the trade associations at the time gave the nonsocialist parties their financial blessing, even though the legacy of the Nazi era caused employers as a group to shy away from political involvement.

But by 1953, the year of the next federal election, the *Wirtschaftswunder* had made its impact on German politics and society, and the BDI was urging the government to maintain the free enterprise system and the political alliance with the West. The industrial community looked for electoral support among farmers, artisans, homeowners, and other conservative elements, but shunned the idea of a separate "economic" party, since such a move would have isolated industry from the mainstream of German politics, and have prevented it from exercising its influence on the governing parties.[23] It endorsed no party, although there were hints by some employers in the DI organ in favor of the CDU. Simultaneously the DI condemned the alleged violation of political neutrality by the DGB, whose slogan, "Elect a better Bundestag," implied that its trade union members ought to be backing candidates from the SPD.

Industry was elated by the results of the election, which gave the ruling conservative parties an undisputed victory. This was viewed as a mandate to the Adenauer government to anchor the economic system still more firmly in the nation's politics. One BDI publicist warned, however, that only continued political activity of employers could ensure further gains.[24]

As the 1957 election approached, the pace of political activity increased. The BDI became more concerned with the election than ever before, although the DI took direct charge of the propaganda on behalf of industry. Carte blanche was given to none of the conservative parties, which were seen as having

[23] Winschuh, *Das neue Unternehmerbild*, p. 187. See also *JB*, 1952–1953, foreword, p. 17; *UB*, No. 46, Nov. 14, 1957.

[24] Winschuh, *Das neue Unternehmerbild*, p. 198.

committed some errors, and as therefore obliged to mend their ways. For instance, Carl Neumann, board chairman of the DI, asserted that the Federal Republic really only had two parties that were significant (*i.e.*, the CDU and the SPD). Such a statement, even if it were true, would obviously have alienated those adherents of the FDP in the BDI who still hoped that their party, which was then in opposition to Adenauer, would achieve a balance of power in the next legislative period. While giving implicit support to the CDU, Neumann nevertheless remained critical of both major parties for failing to arrive at a fundamental agreement on foreign policy, or to humanize their politics.[25]

Another publicist criticized the government program of the previous two years for having made too many concessions to advocates of the welfare state, and censured Finance Minister Schäffer for having collected high taxes without making the equivalent expenditures. This critic urged all employers to vote intelligently, to the right of the SPD, and for a party which after the election would not make a pact with the socialists (to vote, in plain words, for any conservative party but the FDP).[26]

The DI assailed the SPD's election program as irresponsible and unproductive. Its moderate economic planks, calling no longer for direct public ownership but for public controls over key industries, was considered a façade for socialization. In the area of foreign affairs, the protracted campaign of the SPD and the DGB against atomic rearmament—which had not been restricted to the election period—was denounced as playing into the hands of the Soviets.[27] Wide distribution was given to a pamphlet, *When the Socialists Govern*, and to a letter, beginning "Dear Voter in Perplexity," in which the aims of social democracy were vehemently denounced.[28]

The 1957 election marked a signal triumph for the CDU,

---

[25] *UB*, No. 16, April 19, 1956.

[26] *Ibid.*, No. 21, May 23, 1957.

[27] *Ibid.*, No. 18, May 1, 1958.

[28] As cited by Grosser, *Die Bonner Demokratie*, p. 220; Kitzinger, *German Electoral Politics*, pp. 246–247.

with 50.2 per cent of the voters giving it their support. Even in industrial areas the SPD lagged behind the conservative parties. The BDI regarded the election as a recognition of the contribution made by business to prosperity, as a testimonial of electoral backing for the social market economy, and as a sign of popular opposition to radical experiments.[29] What the BDI did not reveal was that early in 1957 Economics Minister Erhard had successfully extracted a promise from brand-name producers not to raise prices before the election, obviously in order to improve the chances of the CDU. Erhard was far from pleased when his cabinet colleague Schäffer indirectly caused a substantial increase in bus fares.[30]

In 1961 industry assumed basically the same position as in previous elections. While Neumann supported the CDU, despite mistakes and weaknesses, as the "best guarantee for the maintenance of order," other spokesmen did not endorse any specific conservative party, but merely opposed the record and campaign promises of the SPD.[31] One DI staff writer pointed out that since the two major parties were on the way to achieving a *rapprochement* in foreign policy, the differences between them could be expected to center on economic and social affairs. The danger from the point of view of business, he went on, was that in the Fourth Bundestag (1961–1965) priority would be given to social policy at the expense of economic policy; moreover, the SPD was attempting to split the business community by wooing small- and medium-sized establishments and decrying the evils of big business.[32]

Once again, intensive political activity by the DGB was alleged (and denied by the DGB itself). For example, it was reported that Otto Brenner, head of the powerful Metal Workers Union, was planning to follow the practice of the AFL–CIO in

[29] *JB*, 1957–1958, p. 9.
[30] Kitzinger, *German Electoral Politics*, pp. 84–85.
[31] *UB*, No. 48, Dec. 3, 1959.
[32] *Ibid.*, No. 43, Oct. 27, 1960; No. 25, June 22, 1961; Nos. 36 and 37, Sept. 7 and 14, 1961.

supporting candidates who were in sympathy with organized labor. In addition, the DI charged, many labor leaders were identifying the government with the interests of employer organizations, even though the legislative activity of the government could hardly be labeled "friendly" to employers.[33]

After the 1961 election Adenauer made peace with the FDP and brought it into a coalition cabinet. If the CDU and the FDP are able to maintain their rather precarious harmony, there may be more amicable relations among their adherents within the BDI. Moreover, the narrowing of differences between the government and the SPD that became evident during the campaign —notably in the area of foreign affairs—has been welcomed by the BDI as necessary for the forging of greater national unity.[34]

Even though the DI's political appeals during federal elections have been designed to rally support for the conservative parties among its clientele, its effectiveness other than within industry itself remains a matter of conjecture. The BDI, committed to a nonpartisan policy, has not officially participated in election campaigns, although it has been willing to subsidize those of the conservative parties. Its attempt to stir the industrial elements to more activity in party politics will now be examined.

[33] *Ibid.*, No. 43, Oct. 27, 1960; No. 29, July 20, 1961.
[34] *JB*, 1961–1962, p. 9.

VII

The Legislature

SEVERAL years ago Representative Emanuel Celler of New York wrote, "After thirty-six years as a target of messages [from a host of interest groups], I still regard them as the bloodstream of the democratic process and a *sine qua non* of effective legislation." But, he went on, "the elected representative who *wholly* subordinates the selfish requirements of interest groups to the furtherance of abstract principle . . . falls as far short of fulfilling the legislative function as the legislator who sells his vote."[1] Not everyone would agree with these ideas, but they do suggest the importance interest groups attach to the legislative process and the dilemma facing many legislators.

In the Federal Republic a multitude of interest groups makes their views known to parliament, from both inside and outside its chambers. An assessment of the role the BDI plays in parliament must concern itself with such questions as the relation between the executive and legislative branches, the importance of the federalist structure, the type of legislative process, the extent and style of access of the BDI and other interest groups

[1] "Pressure Groups in Congress," *The Annals*, 319 (Sept. 1958), 2–3. Italics in original.

in the legislature, and the nature of the parliamentary party groups.[2]

As in Great Britain, where the executive and legislative branches are likewise closely connected, much of the initiative for legislation stems from the executive. With comfortable voting majorities in the Bundestag (the lower house), the coalition governments led by the Chancellor since 1949 have been able to translate a good deal of their program into law. It is true that the federalist structure of West Germany, plus the political makeup and powers of the Bundesrat (the upper house), lead to occasional difficulties. Nevertheless the CDU/CSU has effectively dominated the executive and legislative arenas for more than a decade.

Concern with legislative activity forces the BDI to pay attention to the political complexion of parliament. The only way the BDI can compensate for the small number of its constituents (less than 100,000 employers) is to send qualified experts to represent its interests in parliament. Recognizing the importance of the legislature even though the executive usually has primacy, the BDI has asserted that " . . . it is simply a matter of vital importance for business whether it is duly represented in parliament by experienced deputies, who are willing and able consistently and convincingly to look after the interests of industry and the rest of business."[3] This is especially important, according to the BDI, because so many party politicians are not sufficiently knowledgeable in economic affairs.

The BDI's relation with the conservative parties, its interest in their financial health, its intense concern with the nomination of candidates and, to a certain degree, with election campaigns, are all aimed toward increasing its influence in the legislative process. To learn the success of the BDI in fulfilling

[2] Ehrmann, "The Comparative Study of Interest Groups," *Interest Groups on Four Continents,* ed. Ehrmann, pp. 5–6; Committee on Comparative Politics, *A Comparative Study of Interest Groups and the Political Process,* pp. 29–34.

[3] *JB,* 1952–1953, p. 18.

this goal, the number of deputies from industry, or closely identified with it, who are actually elected to the Bundestag, and the role they have played in it, will require a look at the composition of the Bundestag from 1949 to the present.

THE DEPUTIES FROM INDUSTRY

It is difficult to arrive at the exact number of deputies from industry in any one legislative period, owing to the reluctance on the part of some to divulge essential biographical data, including the exact nature of their professions. A manager in a corporation may call himself merely a "salaried employee," for example. As a result, estimates of the number of representatives from various interest groups and professions tend to vary widely. Nevertheless we can arrive at some rough answers, even though numbers alone will not measure the influence of any group of deputies.

The number of "interested" deputies from industry remained relatively constant through the 1953, 1957, and 1961 elections after a poor start in 1949, when the industrial associations were not yet strong. At that time the BDI was merely nascent, and many employers bore the taint of collaboration with the Nazis. The DI calculated that out of 410 deputies in the First Bundestag, 37 were industrial and commercial entrepreneurs, and 3 were leading executives in economic associations. (See Table I, lines 5, 6.)[4]

Not surprisingly, industry and other groups found their own representation to be inadequate and that of the "opposition" to be excessive. There were, for example, 115 deputies who at one time or another had been members of trade unions (of these, 41 were on the staffs of trade unions).[5] Most of industry's depu-

[4] See also Otto Kirchheimer, "The Composition of the German Bundestag," *Western Political Quarterly*, III, No. 4 (Dec. 1950), 594–595; Breitling, *Die Verbände in der Bundesrepublik*, p. 101; Almond, *The Politics of German Business*, p. 25.

[5] Kurt Hirche, "Gewerkschafter im Bundestag," *Gewerkschaftliche Monatshefte*, XII, No. 11 (Nov. 1961), 646, cites the 115 total. Breitling, *Die*

ties were overworked because of the multitude of bills in the economic sphere, and asked for support from the BDI and other national organizations in economic legislation.[6]

The coal and steel industries were dissatisfied with their representation in the legislature, where they were losing the battle over codetermination.[7] Yet the BDI and its regional offices were represented by six members, the industrial associations affiliated to the BDI by ten members, and many of the largest firms by their own personnel.[8]

The 1953 federal election saw a spectacular increase in the number of representatives either from industry or closely allied to it (see Table I). To the BDI the election was a source of satisfaction since nearly all the deputies from industry were re-elected, and many more joined their ranks.[9] What was most striking about the composition of the business bloc was the high percentage of functionaries and elected officials of business groups and the low percentage of deputies from large-scale industry and banking, many of whom were only junior executives.[10] Nevertheless, major firms (Klöckner, Honsel, Winters-

---

Verbände in der Bundesrepublik, p. 103, cites the 41 total. As with the employer statistics, the various studies arrive at different totals for the trade-union bloc. For example, Hirche, in an earlier study, "Gewerkschafter im Bundestag," *Gewerkschaftliche Monatshefte*, VIII, No. 12 (Dec. 1957), 707, writes of a total of 89 deputies with some trade-union affiliation.

[6] Thus Deputy Wellhausen at a BDI economic conference. *Niederschrift über die ordentliche Sitzung des Hauptausschusses u. die 1. Wirtschaftspolitische Tagung des BDI* (1950).

[7] *Vo'wi'/Statistik der Vereinigten Stahlwerke*, cited by a private *Korrespondenz*, Jan. 31, 1952.

[8] These firms included Klöckner, Gutehoffnungshütte, MAN, Portland Cement, and Gerling-Konzern. Breitling, *Die Verbände in der Bundesrepublik*, pp. 102–103.

[9] See also *Zusammensetzung des Bundestages, Stand vom 20. Oktober 1953 (ohne Berlin)*, (hectographed). See *Handelsblatt*, Sept. 9 and 21, 1953; *Die Welt*, Sept. 8, 1953; *Bulletin*, Sept. 22, 1953; *Industriekurier*, Sept. 10, 1953.

[10] Almond, *The Politics of German Business*, pp. 25–26.

TABLE I

OCCUPATIONS OF DEPUTIES IN THE FOUR BUNDESTAG PERIODS*

OCCUPATIONS	1949	1953	1957	1961
1. Civil service officials	69	100	100	120
2. Lawyers, notaries, auditors	32	36	42	39
3. Scientists, educators, clergymen, doctors	31	33	36	32
4. Journalists, editors, writers	35	32	34	36
5. *Independent entrepreneurs*	*37*	*60*	*58*	*59*
6. *Executives from the economic associations*	*3*	*16*	*20*	*17*
7. Merchants, craftsmen, and salesmen	22	35	35	32
8. Farmers	52	62	68	62
9. Employees and workers	26	25	28	28
10. Officials and employees of trade unions and the social administration	41	59	51	50
11. Party officials and employees	55	35	33	33
12. Housewives	7	16	14	13
Total	410	509	519	521

* DI, *Material zum Zeitgeschehen,* No. 10, Oct. 26, 1961; also *UB*, No. 43, Oct. 26, 1961. Italics mine.

hall, Portland Cement, Mannesmann, Gutehoffnungshütte Oberhausen, and MAN-Nuremberg) were again represented.[11]

The 1957 federal election produced a smashing victory for the CDU. The business community had cause to rejoice, since most of its representatives were re-elected. An analysis of the strength of the business community in each party (see Tables II and III, lines 6, 11, 14) shows the highest concentration to have been in the FDP, followed by the DP, the CDU, and the SPD. It seems clear that the high representation in the FDP and the DP (about 24 per cent) was due to the conservative

[11] For lists of all members of the Bundestag, cf. Deutscher Bundestag, *Amtliches Handbuch des Deutschen Bundestages,* and Fritz Sänger, *Handbuch des Deutschen Bundestages,* issued for each legislative period. For the 1953 Bundestag, see also Hans Trossmann, *Der Zweite Deutsche Bundestag* (Bonn, 1954). Pritzkoleit, *Die Neuen Herren,* pp. 199 ff, lists 23 leading managers of corporations. The representation of business, agriculture, and organized labor is further analyzed by Gottfried Eisermann, "Parteien und Verbände im neuen Bundestag," *Gewerkschaftliche Monatshefte,* IV, No. 12 (Dec. 1953), 750–755.

TABLE II
OCCUPATIONS IN THE BUNDESTAG, 1957*
BY PARTIES

OCCUPATIONS	CDU	SPD	FDP	DP	TOTAL
1. Civil service officials	60	26	7	4	97
2. Farmers and representatives	51	4	8	3	66
3. Officials and employees of trade unions and the social administration	20	27	—	1	48
4. Lawyers, notaries, auditors	26	11	8	1	46
5. Scientists, educators, clergymen	20	17	1	—	38
6. *Members of management*	*17*	*11*	*3*	*4*	*35*
7. Merchants	17	8	3	2	30
8. Craftsmen and salesmen	14	10	—	1	25
9. Journalists, editors, writers	7	15	1	—	23
10. Party officials	3	14	2	1	20
11. *Independent entrepreneurs*	*13*	*2*	*6*	—	*21*
12. Housewives	9	7	1	—	17
13. Workers	3	8	—	—	11
14. *Executives from the economic associations*	*6*	*4*	*1*	—	*11*
15. Doctors	3	2	—	—	5
16. Other employees	1	2	—	—	3
17. Other professions	—	1	—	—	1
Total	270	169	41	17	497

* *Schnelldienst des DI,* No. 91, Nov. 19, 1957. Italics mine. These figures do not tally with Table I since they are based on a different survey.

character of the two parties, whereas the CDU and especially the SPD (with 13 and 10 per cent respectively) drew much of their support from less conservative elements.

The 1961 election once again produced a victory for the non-socialist parties, but this time the CDU had to seek the support of the FDP in order to form a governing coalition which would have the backing of a majority in the legislature. According to the DI, the business bloc nearly maintained its strength (see Tables I and IV). Some well-known representatives of industry —including Dr. Curt Becker, entrepreneur and former member of the BDI presidential board—were not re-elected; others, including August Neuburger, an expert on taxes, did not stand

TABLE III

OCCUPATIONS IN THE BUNDESTAG, 1957*

BY PARTIES AND PERCENTAGES

OCCUPATIONS	CDU	SPD	FDP	DP
1. Civil service officials	22.2	15.7	17.0	23.7
2. Farmers and representatives	18.9	2.6	19.6	16.8
3. Officials and employees of trade unions and the social administration	7.4	16.4	—	6.0
4. Lawyers, notaries, auditors	9.6	6.9	19.6	6.0
5. Scientists, educators, clergymen	7.3	9.5	2.4	—
6. *Members of management*	*6.3*	*6.3*	*7.3*	*23.7*
7. Merchants	6.3	4.5	7.3	11.8
8. Craftsmen and salesmen	5.2	5.6	—	6.0
9. Journalists, editors, writers	2.6	8.8	2.4	—
10. Party officials	1.2	7.6	4.9	6.0
11. *Independent entrepreneurs*	*4.8*	*1.2*	*14.7*	—
12. Housewives	3.3	4.4	2.4	—
13. Workers	1.1	5.0	—	—
14. *Executives from the economic associations*	*2.3*	*2.5*	*2.4*	—
15. Doctors	1.1	1.2	—	—
16. Other employees	0.4	1.2	—	—
17. Other professions	—	0.6	—	—
Total	100	100	100	100

* *Schnelldienst des DI,* No. 91, Nov. 19, 1957. Italics mine.

for re-election. Nevertheless, as the official government bulletin observed, "Industry and business are heavily represented in the new Bundestag. More than before, men from leading industrial positions have been elected."[12] These new men included Stein of the BDI and Hans Dichgans of the Association of the Iron and Steel Industry, both CDU candidates; Alexander Menne of the BDI and the chemical industry and Albrecht Aschoff of the Ruhr coal-mining employers' association, candidates of the FDP; and Dr. Alex Möller, a director of a large insurance firm, a candidate of the SPD.

Of the 76 deputies in the employer bloc, 59 are industrial entrepreneurs, members of boards of corporations, executives or

[12] Nov. 14, 1961, p. 4 (English ed.).

managers of economic associations, including the chambers of industry and commerce. Of the 59, 32 are members of the CDU/CSU, 18 of the FDP, and 9 of the SPD (one is not classified). This group accounts for 11 per cent of the total number of deputies—a fairly constant ratio since the 1953 election. Furthermore, 17 deputies out of the 76 (3 per cent) are leading managers in business firms.[13]

TABLE IV
OCCUPATIONS IN THE BUNDESTAG, 1961*
(1957 FIGURES IN PARENTHESES)

OCCUPATIONS	CDU/CSU	SPD	FDP	(DP)	TOTAL
1. Civil service officials	60 (59)	48 (31)	12 (8)	— (2)	120 (100)
2. Lawyers, notaries, auditors	19 (25)	12 (9)	8 (7)	— (1)	39 (42)
3. Scientists, educators, clergymen, doctors	15 (23)	16 (13)	1 (—)	— (—)	32 (36)
4. Journalists, editors, writers	9 (11)	24 (22)	3 (1)	— (—)	36 (34)
5. *Independent entrepreneurs*	*32 (32)*	*9 (8)*	*18 (13)*	*— (5)*	*59 (58)*
6. *Executives from the economic associations*	*9 (11)*	*5 (5)*	*3 (1)*	*— (3)*	*17 (20)*
7. Merchants, craftsmen, and salesmen	20 (21)	8 (11)	4 (1)	— (2)	32 (35)
8. Farmers	47 (54)	3 (3)	12 (8)	— (3)	62 (68)
9. Employees and workers	10 (10)	16 (17)	2 (1)	— (—)	28 (28)
10. Officials and employees of trade unions and the social administration	19 (19)	31 (32)	— (—)	— (—)	50 (51)
11. Party officials and employees	5 (5)	25 (25)	3 (2)	— (1)	33 (33)
12. Housewives	6 (8)	6 (5)	1 (1)	— (—)	13 (14)
Total	251 (278)	203 (181)	67 (43)	— (17)	521 (519)

* DI, *Material zum Zeitgeschehen,* No. 10, Oct. 26, 1961, p. 15. These figures tally with Table I, but not with Table II (based on a different survey). Italics mine.

[13] Of the 17, 9 are in the CDU/CSU, 5 in the SPD, and 3 in the FDP (see Table IV). Once again, figures vary. The CDU *Union in Deutschland,* XV, No. 38 (Sept. 22, 1961) lists 9 CDU, 1 SPD, and 5 FDP managers and

For the BDI, representatives from its own ranks and from business are not the only valuable contacts; these latter also include deputies from other segments of the business community scattered throughout the conservative parties—bankers, merchants, artisans, and some of the farmers. In addition, there is a numerically large bloc of 120 civil servants (23 per cent) whose support has to be wooed.[14] It is obvious that deputies of these rather loosely organized blocs, if they belong to the CDU and the FDP, will often support bills backed by the BDI—provided the latter is willing to reciprocate on other measures. Thus it is difficult to measure the support the BDI may receive for any particular bill.

Whether industry has been represented adequately in the respective Bundestag sessions since 1949 is largely a subjective matter. If its numerical strength in the Bundestag is compared to its proportionate strength in the nation, then the industrial bloc of over 10 per cent must be regarded as more than adequate. But if the size of the industrial bloc is compared to that of other economic groups, such as agriculture, and to the number of their experts in the legislature, the proportion is less favorable. Industry has repeatedly pointed out these weaknesses. For instance, in 1961 Günter Triesch of the DI complained of the paucity in the new Bundestag of industrial relations experts

---

industrialists. A sociological classification of the CDU/CSU parliamentary group may be found in *Betriebsrätebrief der Christlich-Demokratischen Arbeitnehmerschaft Deutschlands*, No. 104, Oct. 1961, p. 2. See also *Neue Rhein–Zeitung*, Oct. 17, 1961; *Deutsche Zeitung*, Sept. 30, 1961; *Politische Korrespondenz*, Sept. 1961.

[14] DI, "Der 17. September 1961 Unter der Lupe," p. 16. Hirche in his 1961 study (pp. 646, 650) classifies only 25 deputies of the 222 who hold trade-union membership as officers of unions. Of the 25, 21 are in the SPD and 4 in the CDU. Of the 222, 179 are in the SPD, 41 in the CDU/CSU, and 2 in the FDP. The 222 total represents the highest proportion of trade-union deputies in the four *Bundestage*. According to the DI, the percentage has risen steadily: 21.7 per cent in 1949; 33.79 per cent in 1953; 38.15 per cent in 1957; and 42.23 per cent in 1961. *UB*, No. 43, Oct. 26, 1961.

from industry. Social policy, he wrote, seemed more and more to be regarded by the parties as a preserve of workers' representatives. In areas of finance and taxation, too, there were few experts left—as would be painfully evident, Triesch warned, once the legislative mill started turning.[15]

The BDI is not the only group concerned over "interested" deputies. One observer, Rupert Breitling, has remarked that the number of such deputies in the Bundestag was actually not too high, since if the number were to be reduced, more party bosses and civil servants would invade the lower house.[16] On the other hand, another writer, Kurt Pritzkoleit, has asserted that no other category carries greater weight than the deputies who are managers of heavy industry—back of whom, he writes, "stands the great financial might of numerous firms, which disposes of an army of hundreds of thousands of workers, the control of a large part of our natural resources, excellent connections with high finance, a number of social relations to the political leadership, and invincible means of influencing opinion."[17]

A somewhat different point of view is that of Professor Eschenburg, who has expressed concern over the great number of deputies who are dependent on interest groups not only materially but intellectually, and who would not be in a position to defend the so-called general interest.[18] There is no doubt that the number of truly independent deputies has dwindled, and that the number of those closely tied to parties and associations is high. A study of the 1953 legislature estimated that 60 per cent of the CDU deputies, 62 per cent of the SPD deputies, and 78 per cent of the FDP deputies were "bound" to their respective parties and/or associations.[19] The same trend is evi-

[15] *UB*, No. 42, Oct. 19, 1961.

[16] *Die Verbände in der Bundesrepublik*, p. 138.

[17] *Die Neuen Herren*, p. 217.

[18] At a BDI-sponsored conference on the state and associations; Beutler, Stein, and Wagner (eds.), *Der Staat und die Verbände*, pp. 30–31.

[19] Viola Gräfin von Bethusy-Huc, "Die Soziologische Struktur Deutscher Parlamente" (Unpublished Ph.D. dissertation, University of Bonn, 1958), p. 111.

dent in the legislatures of other countries, and one writer has asserted that such influences have "contributed to the rigidity and unimaginativeness of those institutions."[20]

Although these criticisms have some validity, a high number of interested deputies does not inevitably mean a proportionate influence upon the legislative process, or vice versa. For example, of 35 deputies in the 1957 Bundestag whom the BDI regarded as sympathetic to its aims, a majority—perhaps 24— had little political stature or expertise. The industrial bloc tended to be made up of middle-management executives in large concerns, of small factory owners, and of executive secretaries of economic associations who either had been co-opted by the party or had risen in it and could control a loyal constituency. One BDI staff member characterized many of these deputies as having little political influence in their party groups. Many were too "opportunistic," too "conceited," or too old and lacking in "political appeal." The same spokesman implied that some were more a liability than an asset to the BDI. He regarded any listing and counting of industry representatives as misleading and rather trivial. "Not only is one contact with Pferdmenges worth ten deputies," he said, "but some of the deputies cannot be relied upon to represent BDI interest at all times." Even Hellwig and Pohle, both active in industry councils, did not follow the industrial line 100 per cent. On the other hand, deputies from the banking and legal professions often gave support to industry.

Of course, the BDI makes it clear to the deputies that they must not be tagged as tools of industry if they do not want to commit political suicide. For example, one BDI association now considers its staff executive in an earlier Bundestag to have been a political liability because of certain activities which immediately labeled him. The association and the BDI both consider it more advantageous to support a lawyer or tax expert who is not generally identified with industry but who can give hard

[20] Almond, *The Politics of German Business*, pp. 26–27.

support to its goals. They believe that if deputies from industry are to speak up, they should deliberately give the impression that they are not mere tools by dealing with general topics rather than those of concern to their firm or association. One representative of big business put it to the author this way: "I learned my lesson in the Bundestag in the first few months. I spoke up on some matter involving my company's interests. Since then I do not 'identify' myself. I have not joined the Committee on Economic Affairs, which would have been the logical place for me, but rather two other committees." Another frankly said, "I stress the problems of small business and economic concentration, which is good as a vote-catcher. I come out for higher wages for workers, more purchasing power, and increased welfare."

On occasion a deputy will admit publicly that he is an interested representative. During a debate on gasoline prices one FDP deputy spoke up frankly as a representative of a coal and shipping firm.[21] But in many instances there is no such identification. One parliamentary exchange that illustrates the complex interplay of private and natural interests began when Deputy Kalbitzer (SPD) spoke of the government's plan to reduce tariffs on several products, including wooden flooring blocks and linoleum. He charged that because the flooring industry, a small one, had no spokesman in the Bundestag, the tariff-cutting plan relating to it met no opposition. But the plan relating to linoleum soon met considerable opposition from interested government deputies. Walter Löhr (CDU), associated with the chemical industry, said in defense of those Foreign Trade Committee members who had voted against the linoleum tariff-cutting plan, "I know of no colleague on the committee who represents the point of view of any interest for egotistical or other reasons. All deal with tariffs from general economic interests." To this Kalbitzer retorted, "It would naturally be difficult for us to have received the same inside information in the last weeks concern-

[21] Bundestag, 3rd el. pd., 101st session, Sept. 22, 1955, p. 5635.

ing the situation in the linoleum industry as a managing director of the Association of the Chemical Industry."[22]

An interested deputy will, of course, publicly proclaim his loyalty to the national interest, even when he is defending his own industry on the floor of the Bundestag. Dr. Alexander Elbrächter, an executive in a large food concern, came to a spirited defense of his industry when a pure-food bill was debated in 1956, although on an earlier occasion he had declared it a defamation of character to presume that a deputy supported the interests of a group. After all, he said, "these associations come to us all, and you can see how differently the individual deputies react to the wishes of associations."[23]

Voices are nevertheless raised in the parties against the domination of parliament by interest groups, and even by deputies who have been closely identified with the business world. In June 1957 Dr. Hans Wellhausen, manager of a major steel corporation, declared that he would not become a candidate again, giving, as one reason, the "predominance of interested politicians" in the Bundestag who wanted to take advantage of the economic prosperity.[24]

But the problem is not so simple as these statements would suggest. In actuality the deputy is frequently faced with a dilemma when he is obliged to take a stand and cast a vote on a particular issue. As one asserted, "It is like walking a tightrope over Niagara Falls. If I represent my firm too much, its competitors will complain. If I represent my industry, I am labeled a tool of industry. If I were to represent the 'general interest' only, my firm and industry would be dissatisfied. If I abstain from voting, I demonstrate weakness. I must commit myself." Whatever commitment he makes, such a deputy must expect to meet criticism from some quarter.

22 *Ibid.*, 64th session, Jan. 27, 1955, pp. 3333–3337.
23 *Ibid.*, 149th session, June 8, 1956, p. 7609 ff, 57th session, Nov. 19, 1954, p. 2859.
24 *FAZ*, June 22, 1957.

The result may, indeed, be a crisis of conscience. According to Article 38 of the Basic Law, "The deputies to the German Bundestag are elected in universal, direct, free, equal, and secret elections. They are representatives of the whole people, are not bound by orders and instructions, and are subject only to their conscience." One industry deputy has said, "I would rather abstain than vote against my conscience." Another has asserted, "On three key issues I voted against the industrial point of view. I told my industry friends: 'Listen, it is a question of conscience on every vote.' " Still another commented that "if the BDI had a good case, and I was personally convinced of it, I would go to bat for the BDI." The paradox emerging from these expressions of opinion is that even though a legislator may be "interested," it is not always possible to know whether his vote represents his own conscience, his "interest," or both coincidentally. In any event, allegiance to industry runs all the way from unswerving to marginal.

The relation of the deputy to the party must also be considered. If his interest is not directly affected, a deputy will bow to party leaders; but if there is a collision between party and industry, he must decide whether his ties to the party or to his industry are stronger.[25] Some observers have detected a process of emancipation among interested deputies. At the outset of his career, such a legislator identifies himself closely with his firm or association, but as the legislative term progresses he becomes more self-assertive and develops a sense both of party loyalty and of parliamentary identity. Because he needs the support of fellow legislators he becomes more and more a member of the team.

Although interviews with several industrial deputies revealed a continued identification with and dependence on their firms as they moved up or down the political ladder, they also showed a dependence on the parties for support. One deputy, a manu-

[25] On this subject see the excellent series "Parteien und Verbände," *Neue Zürcher Zeitung*, May 7, 12, 13, 22, 23, 1954.

facturer, had been interested in politics during his college years and had joined a political club at the time of the Weimar republic. In 1946 he helped found a city branch of the CDU, and became immersed in party, association, and BDI affairs. Another deputy, the manager of a major firm, in 1949 became active at the local level in the FDP, rather than in the CDU, which he considered too far left in social policy. In 1957 the FDP asked him to run for the Bundestag, and he obtained a four-year paid leave from his firm, although he still works for it on Saturdays and Mondays. As a consequence, the physical burden is heavy, and he has no time to prepare adequately for his parliamentary work. He considers it a civic duty to hold public office; but he has no desire to remain permanently in politics, and was not sure whether his firm would want him to run again in 1961. (He did run, however, and was elected.) He said that although his firm received all the information it needed from Bonn through the association, his presence in the federal capital nevertheless provided some valuable contacts. Two other corporation managers, both without any political heritage in their family background, were similarly without any wish to make politics a permanent career, since their corporation salaries were too attractive to be relinquished. On the other hand, one corporation executive relished political and association work. He had been in the Bundestag and was either chairman or a member of six CDU political and economic organs and of three BDI committees, in addition to belonging to an advisory committee for the European Economic Community.

These sketches tend to belie the image of the power-hungry businessman in politics. There are some such men, of course. Many are not, however, committed to an extended political career, and would just as soon return to a less dramatic but more profitable milieu—and this feeling is not exactly surprising in view of the lukewarm attitude of most companies toward having their managerial elite participate in public affairs.

Many of these deputies are overburdened with work and

pressed for time—especially those who still work for their companies. Those from big business may seek the assistance of legal and economic divisions of their firms, and those from smaller companies ask their associations and the BDI and BDA for background information and statistical data. To meet such requests, Stein once proposed at a meeting of the BDI presidential board that deputies from industry be freed from all unnecessary burdens of parliamentary work by setting up a working group, presumably within the BDI; but no action was taken on this.[26]

As a result of these negative factors, the DI points out—although the SPD disagrees—that in the CDU, for instance, small business, agriculture, and the trade-union wings have had more and more voice in determining policy in recent years. According to the DI, economic policy is being narrowed down into small-business policy, in part because small business has a sizable representation in the Bundestag, and its interests appeal more to the sentiments of the voters. The DI has declared that the only remedy for this unsatisfactory situation is to intensify political action rather than to limit one's concern to economic affairs; then and only then, its spokesmen believe, will the seasoned party bosses listen attentively to the voice of industry.[27] Those spokesmen of the SPD and DGB who assert that industry has the government in its pocket and determines its laws are mistaken, according to another industrial source, since even if there were more employers in the Bundestag they would still be in a minority and unable to dictate policy to the government.[28] Moreover, the industrial bloc is not cohesive on all bills pertaining to its interests.

Despite these limiting factors, there is no doubt concerning the advantages of having representatives of industry in the Bundestag. First of all, as one Bundestag assistant has said, it

[26] *Präsidialsitzung*, Feb. 7, 1956.

[27] *UB*, No. 25, June 22, 1961.

[28] "Der Unternehmer als MdB," *Das Wirtschaftsbild*, Folge 252, June 6, 1953.

means, "for the large firms, a 'finger in the pie.' " It will presently be shown how some deputies have been exceedingly useful
in the auxiliary function of courier and lobbyist, though one
deputy minimized the advantage, asserting that his firm really
did not need him for this since it could obtain the necessary
material on bills through the association's own lobby.

In the second place, experts in the industrial bloc can serve
as spokesmen for their parties on the floor. An analysis of the
debates during the 1953–1957 legislative session shows that three
deputies who were closely identified with industry represented
the conservative parties in economic affairs, and spoke on topics
ranging from cartels to the Common Market.[29]

This survey of the BDI's interest in the legislature as a tool
for meeting its objectives has centered on the number of its
representatives in the several sessions of the Bundestag, and
their voting behavior under the stress of multiple cross pressures.
Their effectiveness in the legislative sphere will be explored
more fully in the chapters that follow.

[29] The three deputies are Hellwig (CDU), Atzenroth (FDP), and
Elbrächter (DP, later CDU). Other industry-oriented deputies took the
floor only once or twice in four years. Bundestag, 3rd el. pd., *Register 2.
Teil, Sprachregister. Stenographische Berichte der 1.–227. Sitzung.*

VIII

The Legislature (II)

IN the German Republic, as in many other countries, parliamentary party groups and committees are the scene of crucial debates and vital decisions, and are thus the targets of pressure from interest groups. But neither can the upper house, the state parliaments, and the local councils be neglected, nor can interest groups look with indifference upon the proposed establishment of a federal economic council. The BDI's relation to these legislative areas will be the concern of this chapter.

PARLIAMENTARY PARTY GROUPS

In West Germany the deputies of each party frequently meet en masse as a parliamentary group (*Fraktion*) to discuss legislative strategy and to prepare or refine the drafts of bills, most of which have originated with the executive branch. The decision-makers in such a group will be the party leaders, ministers and state secretaries, committee chairmen, and occasionally association officers. In the highly disciplined SPD, a leading role is played by party and trade union chiefs. In the CDU, a heterogeneity of interests makes a common policy more difficult to work out; and the FDP, although it has fewer diverse factions, lacks a binding ideology.[1]

[1] Bruno Dechamps, *Macht und Arbeit der Ausschüsse* (Meisenheim, 1954), p. 152; Breitling, *Die Verbände in der Bundesrepublik*, pp. 122–128.

Each group has set up committees (*Arbeitskreise*) to perform the preliminary spade work and to advise the party deputies on proposed legislation. The CDU/CSU *Fraktion* has a functional division into five standing committees (on legal, economic, budget and finance, labor and social, foreign and all-German affairs), plus a few *ad hoc* bodies, which in turn are divided into numerous subcommittees. The deputies join whatever committees coincide with their interests. Hence deputies associated with the BDI most often serve on those dealing with economic affairs and with budget and finance.

Proposed bills clear the many hurdles of the groups and the complex executive and legislative machinery in any of several ways. Legislation is usually initiated by the government in the form of a draft bill submitted to the Bundesrat, which after being returned to the executive, is then sent to the Bundestag for the conventional three readings. It is assigned to committee after a perfunctory first reading on the floor; but before this stage has been reached the *Fraktion* will already have dissected the bill, submitted it to the appropriate working committee, discussed it, decided on a stand, and appointed deputies to support or oppose it while it is being funneled through the legislature. Or the procedure may be exactly the reverse: an *ad hoc* subcommittee or a small circle of deputies may initiate a draft bill, which it will have considered by the working committee, the *Fraktion*, and the Bundestag. In either event, the *Fraktion* will meet repeatedly when an important bill is receiving legislative scrutiny.

Whatever procedure is followed, interest groups (and representatives of the government) will have a chance to make their views known in the *Fraktion* or more often in the subcommittees, either through "their" deputies or as interested outsiders. Although the groups deliberate in closed session, the BDI usually is informed through "its" deputies of what has taken place. BDI and other associations may also meet officially with the *Fraktion* or its committees to provide information and present their points of view.

Lobbying is also extensive. It may consist of a discreet approach to individual members of the *Fraktion* or one of its committees. According to one informant, the BDI once invited some *Arbeitskreis* members of the CDU to dinner at a fashionable hotel in Bad Godesberg; when the invitation was refused for fear of later obligation to the BDI, the meeting was held instead in the more businesslike Bundestag building.

PARLIAMENTARY COMMITTEES

Another important target consists of the numerous standing committees of the Bundestag (of which there are currently twenty-eight). These bodies are less powerful than their American counterparts, but they play a more critical role in the legislative process than such committees do in Britain. Each committee mirrors the Bundestag in miniature, its chairmen and members having been appointed on the basis of party strength in the legislature. Theoretically the parties allot these posts on the basis of qualifications and regional interests, but in practice the wishes of the associations must also be considered.

Some committees, such as those on agriculture, social affairs, labor, and refugees, have a strong coloration of interests. The Agriculture Committee, for instance, is made up primarily of representatives of agricultural organizations and civil servants from the Ministry of Agriculture. In other committees, such as that in economic affairs, the interest coloration is also high, but there is much diversity among the members. Such committees are thus apt to serve as clearing houses for compromises in order to satisfy as many members as possible.[2]

The BDI is primarily interested in the work of the Economic Affairs, Foreign Trade, and Finance Committees. By and large, it has been successful in "colonizing" these committees with chairmen and members who tend to be responsive to its aims.

[2] Heidenheimer, *The Governments of Germany*, p. 111.

It is not unusual to find industry deputies from several parties converging on these three committees and then uniting on legislative matters.[3]

For the fourth legislative period (1961–1965) the highest proportion of deputies from industry were to be found, as usual, in the 27-member Economic Affairs Committee. Of thirteen CDU members nine were closely allied with industry, two were civil servants, one was a professor, and one headed the "left-wing" social affairs committee of the CDU. The three FDP members all represent industry. The chairman of the committee until December 1962 was Dr. Rolf Dahlgrün (FDP), head of the legal division of Phoenix Rubber, a firm represented in the top councils of the BDI and BDA by its president, O. A. Friedrich. Dahlgrün was succeeded by Dr. Albrecht Aschoff (FDP), a lawyer who has ties with industry. Deputy chairman of the committee is Peter Wilhelm Brand (CDU), who for many years headed a branch association of the BDI-affiliated Association of German Machine Construction (VDMA). Moreover, the BDI is directly represented in the committee by Stein (CDU) and by Menne (FDP).[4] Since all legislation on economic affairs is

[3] According to Pritzkoleit, in the second Bundestag period representatives of business held a total of 63 seats in these three committees and nine others dealing with economic affairs. They captured the chairmanships of four committees and the deputy chairmanships of four others. (Agriculture only had 22 seats and one chairmanship.) *Die Neuen Herren*, p. 252. The BDI had little ground for complaint when at various times its own chairman of the Bavarian regional office, Reinhold Bender, headed the Foreign Trade Committee; Hellwig chaired the Economic Affairs Committee (until his appointment to the European Coal and Steel Community); Wellhausen, of the MAN firm, the Finance and Tax Committee; and Dr. Martin Blank, of the Gutehoffnungshütte the Auditing Committee (also deputy chairman of the Budget Committee). Note that Dr. Ernst Hilbert of the last cited firm chaired the BDI committee on taxation, thus providing his company with an entree into the BDI and the Bundestag when it came to financial questions. *Ibid.*, p. 204.

[4] DI, *Fraktion der CDU/CSU (FDP) im IV. Deutschen Bundestag* (mimeographed, deputies who are close to industry are underlined). For a list of committee members see *Amtliches Handbuch des Deutschen Bundestages, 4. Wahlperiode*, pp. 207–235. In earlier *Bundestage* industry also

channeled through the committee, the BDI of course finds it extremely important to be well represented.

The same is true of other committees that handle economic and fiscal problems. The Committee on Foreign Trade has nine deputies out of a sixteen-member CDU/FDP group who belong to the industrial bloc (of the remainder, six are from agriculture and one from civil service). Its chairman is Dr. Günther Serres (CDU), a business consultant and managing director of several economic associations; its deputy chairman is Ernst Keller (FDP), an entrepreneur. For the BDI another key committee is that of finance, which includes seven deputies out of sixteen in the CDU/FDP group who comprise the industrial element. Since the occupational background of the members is quite diverse, and since the chairman, Dr. Otto Schmidt (CDU), a lawyer and publisher, is not connected with industry, the BDI's hopes for success in this committee are somewhat limited.[5] Industry is also well represented in the Committees on Development Aid and Federally Owned Properties.

Thus in the fourth legislative period the box score adds up to 43 deputies from the industrial community who hold a total of 57 posts on nineteen committees—although it has none on nine others (*e.g.*, defense, family, health, agriculture; see Appendix C).

Besides noting the extent of industrial representation in their memberships, it is important to evaluate the effectiveness of its deputies within the committees, although the meager information available, and the secrecy of committee proceedings, make this a difficult task. The BDI has indicated only that certain deputies who are experts in their field have proved a real asset

---

had a strong representation in the Committee on Economic Affairs; in the First Bundestag, for instance, five members on the Committee held executive positions in economic interest groups and five others were entrepreneurs or managers in industry. Breitling, *Die Verbände in der Bundesrepublik*, p. 129.

[5] For sources see note 4, above.

to industry, whereas others are expendable. There are some deputies, moreover, who though not officially connected with industry may be strongly sympathetic to its objectives and will be found to give them consistent support in the committees. In the final analysis, what counts in any one committee is not so much sheer number as the ability of the chairman and other experts to convince their colleagues of the merit of a particular item in a bill.

In presenting its own specific recommendations on issues of immediate concern, the BDI will eschew lengthy memoranda in favor of sending short position papers to committee members at the appropriate time. It will approach the chairman, who wields a great deal more power than any ordinary member, who determines the agenda and the pace of discussion, and who may ask the government, the associations, and outside experts for data. On occasions when this does not happen, the BDI is quick to complain, especially if it considers the chairman to be less than receptive to its aims.

However, the chairman may either be generally sympathetic to the BDI, or convinced of the merit of its stand on an issue. For example, Dr. Walter Eckhardt, a tax consultant, lawyer, and former CSU deputy, kept the small-business committee of the BDI informed of his work as head of the turnover tax subcommittee of the Bundestag. During the years in which his committee handled the matter, he has said that not a single change was made in any tax law without the assent of the entire business community. Representatives of associations took part in sessions of the committee, and not always to the satisfaction of the civil servants, who saw their theoretical approach countered by men with practical experience. Eckhardt frankly asserted that he himself would favor no bill that was regarded by important segments of industry as too heavy a burden.[6] In a similar vein the BDI has argued that committee members

[6] HGF, Mittelstandausschuss, No. 20/58, Nov. 10, 1958.

would be less dependent on the administrators if only they would listen more to the case presented by the association; or better still, the argument continues, let the businessman become a deputy and make the committee his primary field of activity: "The quality and the resultant effectiveness of the laws are dependent greatly on his participation and his expertise."[7]

The BDI must maintain contacts in the committees not only to influence the content of the bills, but also to be informed of the outcome of committee discussions and of the stands taken by the participants. Even though the work of the committees is by nature confidential, the "contact" deputies are able to inform their association of developments "within the hour," as one committee secretary has asserted. Many deputies and committee secretaries are good contacts; but that there are exceptions is demonstrated by the experience of a BDI-affiliated association staff employee who approached one secretary and asked him confidentially to provide the association with a sequence of bills which the committee was planning to handle. The reasoning of the employee was that it would be easier to obtain the information in this way than from a deputy; but the secretary denied this request.

Another more formal avenue of approach to the committee is the public hearing. Constitutionally this is something of a novelty. According to the by-laws of the Bundestag, committee deliberations must be held in closed sessions, but such sessions may be preceded, if the committee so decides, by sessions for public information. To these, representatives of interest groups, experts, the press, and other listeners may be admitted, so far as seating capacity allows.[8] But, since in Germany the committees merely have the option to hold such hearings, they tend to be infrequent, and some committees, including that on foreign affairs, hold none at all. It is the practice of the BDI, when

---

[7] *JB*, 1952–1953, p. 18; 1956–1957, p. 48.

[8] Hans Lechner and Klaus Hülshoff, *Parlament und Regierung*, 2nd ed. (München & Berlin, 1958), p. 195.

hearings are held, to send the chairman of an important member of one of its own committees to present its views. If the bill meets with its approval, it may not even care to state its views publicly. Indeed, many deputies would rather read the memoranda and policy papers of the associations than schedule hearings, which they consider relatively unproductive, time-consuming, and replete with glittering generalities.

To sum up, it is not to be supposed that business has a monopoly of power in all committees dealing with economic affairs. Both in the committees and throughout the legislative process there are countervailing powers which blunt its influence. To take the Committee on Finance once again as an illustration, even though at one time it included representatives of interest groups, and though the chairman (Wellhausen) was a man from heavy industry, both he and certain members became quite independent of their groups, when the policy of the Ministry of Finance, to which they lent their support, was at variance with group interests. Moreover, a CDU deputy who chairs a committee is bound by instructions from his party, and must also contend with the opposition of the SPD. Under such circumstance it would be difficult for the business deputies to "corner" the committee entirely.

Furthermore, a bill may still be altered as it proceeds along legislative channels, especially if the legislation emerging from the committees is too one-sided and fails to take the mood of the country into consideration, or if there have been contradictory recommendations by two or more committees to whom the bill has been referred. This may be the situation when a party as diverse as the CDU has not been able to agree on a common policy and thus allows its deputies in the committees to vote as they please. On the other hand, in a few isolated cases a committee has successfully held off the assaults of interest groups only to see its recommended bills amended on the floor by interested deputies at a later stage.

Despite these limitations, the BDI and similar associations

have some part in shaping economic legislation as it proceeds through the committee stage. In several key committees deputies friendly to their cause are able to steer the legislation along favorable lines. As one observer points out, it is difficult to say whether business is over-represented in the Bundestag, but there is no doubt of its power in the committees as compared with other interest groups.[9] In France—at least in the Fourth Republic—the same situation prevails to a striking degree.[10] In the United States the pressure of the interests upon Congressional committee members is, of course, intense.

LOBBYING

In the United States, pressure through lobbying is traditional with most economic associations. Karl Schriftgiesser's account of the NAM's lobby during the Wilson administration describes activities typical of what Pendleton Herring has called the "Old Lobby": "Mulhall was shown to be in a class by himself, the lobbyist extraordinary. He had his own private office in the Capitol. He had on his NAM payroll the chief page of the House who, for $50 a month, kept him informed of what was going on in the cloakrooms."[11] One Congressional investigating committee issued sixty volumes of testimony, seconding what was called "an incredible history of intrigue, intimidation, bribery, and solicitation by the NAM's high-pressure lobbyists in the capital."[12] Lobbying since then has generally become more respectable, although an occasional newspaper headline still testifies to the exceptions. In West Germany, since so many associations are directly represented in the Bundestag, lobbying, so far as that chamber is concerned, is less widespread. Yet it

[9] Hartmann, *Authority and Organization in German Management*, pp. 240–241.

[10] Ehrmann, "Pressure Groups in France," *The Annals*, Vol. 319 (Sept. 1958), p. 144.

[11] Karl Schriftgiesser, *The Lobbyists* (Boston, 1951), p. 40.

[12] *Ibid.*, quoting Kenneth G. Crawford, *The Pressure Boys* (New York, 1939), p. 47.

is a fact of life in the capital at Bonn, and ranges from personal contacts (legal) to rare cases of bribery (illegal). Several hundred lobbying offices have been set up in and near Bonn by a few large corporations and a multitude of organizations, with the primary task of providing information on governmental and legislative developments.[13] Some big business corporations have curtailed their lobbying in recent years, however, because the results did not justify the operating expenses and also because the governmental economic policy no longer was in the formative stage. The Krupp firm maintains a sumptuous office building in a former villa on the main thoroughfare of Bonn, but its chief purpose is to impress visiting foreign potentates and to drum up more business for the firm.

The BDI frequently approaches deputies either directly from its headquarters in Cologne or through its office in Bonn. The former chief lobbyist, Bernd Tönnessen, who shuttled back and forth from Cologne to Bonn and other sections of the country, had only one full-time assistant in Bonn, and felt that to do an effective job four or five staff members would be necessary. Unsuccessful requests for additional funds and staff have been made in the past, but it appears that since the 1961 election the pace of activity in the Bonn office has quickened, possibly as a result of Stein's election to the Bundestag. On the whole, there is less need for the BDI to have a large lobbying machine than for some other organizations with headquarters further away from Bonn. BDI staff specialists in Cologne can reach the capital in one hour to see a deputy or a civil servant, or to attend a hearing. Better still, a deputy close to the BDI can buttonhole other deputies. One such deputy often invites eight or ten deputies from the conservative parties (he excludes the CDU's left wing) to his comfortable residence in Bonn where, over a glass of wine,

[13] The figure was at least 270 in 1952, but no later count has been made. Breitling, *Die Verbände in der Bundesrepublik*, p. 5; Samuel L. Wahrhaftig, "The Development of German Foreign Policy Institutions," in *West German Leadership and Foreign Policy*, ed. Speier and Davison, p. 46.

they discuss matters of concern to the business community.[14]

In addition, once or twice a year the BDI organizes a "parliamentary evening" at which businessmen and specially invited Bundestag deputies from the conservative parties gather to discuss economic problems under consideration by the legislature. Usually these are short speeches followed by a general discussion. As one author observes, "Much depends on the stage management of such an evening. Someone must be there who understands these things and in the right moment calls on the right man to give the right answer."[15]

Typically, a lobbyist for the BDI, or one of its associations, spends much of his day digesting official releases of the parties and the government which are of course made public anyway, but of which he can notify his chief beforehand, so that the latter may act with the least possible delay when intervention is called for. The lobbyist must provide his chief with the views of leading deputies on specific bills, and must gauge their chances of passage. He will approach key deputies or those who have ties with his own particular industry, in order to inform them of the views he represents and, in some instances, may counsel them on tactics and techniques. The number of dinner invitations received by deputies and even by committee secretaries indicates the vigor with which lobbyists work to cement potentially valuable bonds. The reaction may be negative, however. One deputy said, "If I wanted to, I could dine out every night as the guest of this or that firm or association, I receive so many invitations; but obviously I must decline most of them."

---

[14] Association executives and deputies also are in contact at board meetings of corporations. The number of deputies serving on boards cannot be determined with accuracy, but of the forty-three CDU and FDP business deputies in the Fourth Bundestag (1961–1965), thirteen were listed in the latest available edition of *Leitende Männer der Wirtschaft* (Darmstadt, 1955).

[15] Rolf Krengel in *Der Politische Standort des Deutschen Unternehmers* (Schriftenreihe der Pressestelle Hessischer Kammern und Verbände, No. 6; Frankfurt, n.d.), p. 12.

The experienced lobbyist will exhibit a degree of moderation, finesse, and tact not easily emulated by his less practiced brethren.

A letter sent in 1954 by a BDI association manager to "his" Bundestag deputy, an association chairman, might serve to illustrate the complexities of lobbying. The letter was full of queries on the best ways to deal with a pending bill. What circle of deputies would it be best to approach? Should contacts be restricted to members of the Bundestag or to members of coalition parties, or should all deputies be approached? Should the approach be made while the bill was on the floor or while it was in committee? Did the deputy believe he ought to act as go-between in approaching other deputies, and if so when? In justification of these queries the letter went on to say that the bill was vital to the association, and that no opportunity must be overlooked in the Bundestag, the last body to deal fully with it. The association manager did not want to leave any room for the complaint, whether legitimate or not, that the association had done less than everything possible to influence the outcome of the bill. Success was important; and the deputy, as an association chairman, must know how critical of the work of an association some of its members could be. Thus, the letter concluded, the deputy would be performing a fine service if he were to give full support to the manager.

The requests made in the letter were of course entirely permissible and are an accurate reflection of the demands made upon deputies linked to interest groups.[16] But it is sometimes difficult to draw the line between this legitimate kind of lobbying and certain other, more or less apparently improper activities. If the association to which a deputy belongs pays the rent and the secretaries' salaries in his Bonn office, there is an increas-

---

[16] The deputy's answer could not be found in the files. In addition to such requests, the deputies receive an avalanche of mail every week, much of it reflecting organized letter-writing campaigns. The BDI has not been interested in this form of pressure.

ing danger that he may be beholden so completely to his association that he will lose all independence. The same thing may occur if a deputy is paid a monthly salary by his own firm, which expects to be kept up to date on all important developments in Bonn that may affect its interests.

A serious but perhaps atypical occurrence, which was not made public, involved a Bundestag committee secretary who found in the CDU caucus room a briefcase belonging to a business deputy with close ties to the BDI, and containing photostatic copies of confidential Bundestag material. In a much publicized case, Committee 44 of the Bundestag (known as the *Spiegel* Committee after the weekly journal that first broke the story) examined a rumor that a hundred deputies had accepted a total of 2 million DM in bribes. The accusation proved groundless; but it was discovered that in 1949 and 1950 Deputy Hermann Aumer of the Bavarian Party, a key member of a committee that dealt with the controversial issue of the price of gasoline, had received money and a car from Theodor Telle, chairman of a petroleum firm and of the BDI-affiliated petroleum association. Afterward Aumer had several times spoken for the industry in the Bundestag. (The donors had been under the impression that the money was to be distributed to the Bavarian Party, but apparently Aumer kept most of it for himself.)[17]

Such known cases of outright bribery and corruption have been few, but it may easily be assumed that others have simply never been unearthed. Many government officials and deputies are unhappy not only about them but even about the strenuous "legitimate" lobbying by the associations—which they colorfully label as "plagues," "locusts," and "ulcers."[18] Hans Wellhausen, a steel magnate who had been a CSU deputy, refused to run again for the Bundestag in 1957 "partly because of his disgust with the

[17] Bundestag, 1st el. pd., Drucksache No. 2274; Pritzkoleit, *Die Neuen Herren*, pp. 218–220.
[18] *FAZ*, March 3, 1956.

growing influence of pressure groups."[19] His indictment must obviously have included the industrial lobby. Others have called for the regulation of lobbyists, for the control of their expenditures, for maximum publicity of their work, and for the listing of association affiliations of deputies.[20] But it is doubtful whether the government will take any action, even though—as will be seen—the lobbyists are extremely active in the executive branch as well.

The BDI's lobbying efforts in the legislative realm are not as intensive and widespread as those of many less well-known organizations, since excellent contacts with key officials in the executive branch provide it with a leverage on the legislative policies initiated there. For the BDI, lobbying in the Bundestag is mainly to provide insurance against sabotage by rebellious legislators.

THE BUNDESRAT

West Germany's upper house, the Bundesrat, is secondary to the popularly elected lower house in most fields. Nevertheless, its forty-one voting representatives of the states have the function of protecting the interests of the *Länder* and of upholding the federal system; and it must give its approval to all legislation affecting the *Länder*, although in other fields it has only a suspensive veto. Each *Land* delegation to the Bundesrat consists of from three to five ministers (depending on population). They are appointed by their state governments whose executive branches dictate their votes.

Since this procedure makes pointless any direct approach by interest groups to members of the Bundesrat, the source of decision-making—in this case the executive authorities of the *Länder*—are sought out instead. The proceedings of the Bundes-

---

[19] Hirsch-Weber in *Interest Groups on Four Continents*, ed. Ehrmann, p. 111.

[20] See *e.g.*, the discussion in Beutler, Stein, Wagner (eds.), *Der Staat und die Verbände, passim.*

rat are followed carefully at BDI headquarters and its regional offices are notified when legislation is pending on matters affecting industry. The regional offices in their turn approach the appropriate *Land* ministries. The case of a pure food bill may serve as an illustration. Unable to persuade federal authorities to remove certain objectionable provisions from the bill during its passage through the Bundesrat, the BDI asked the regional offices to put pressure on the *Land* ministries. After the chairman of one BDI regional office had gone to the minister and the ranking civil servants, the delegation of that state voted according to the BDI's recommendations.

On other occasions a BDI official may attempt to see the minister-president of the *Land*, especially if he represents a conservative party. When a coalition is in power, however, and there is more latitude for playing off one party against another, the BDI may, for example, approach a sympathetic *Land* minister of economic affairs (CDU), who may then attempt to convince a less sympathetic minister-president (SPD) of the merits or demerits of a particular bill or portion thereof.

In the wake of these initial contacts with the *Länder* executives interest groups may still send memoranda to members of Bundesrat committees. However, these are likely to have little effect on the members—who usually are the same *Land* ministers who have already been approached—and by the time the bill reaches the committee there is little time left to change it drastically.

Interest groups shy away from the plenary sessions, since formal ratification of the committee decisions tends to be automatic.[21] There is, however, a final stage at which interest groups can make their voices heard. From the Bundesrat all bills go to the lower house and are then returned for final approval or, if necessary, for referral to a joint mediation committee. Here is the last hope of killing a "bad" bill or sustaining a "good" one.

[21] Karlheinz Neunreither, *Der Bundesrat zwischen Politik und Verwaltung* (Heidelberg, 1959), pp. 112–114.

For instance, the BDI's committee on cartels in a 1957 memorandum wrote that the Bundesrat would soon deal with the cartel bill, and that it would probably accept the Bundestag draft. To make sure that there were no changes, it would be important for BDI officers to contact the members of the Bundesrat Commission on Economic Affairs in the *Land* ministry offices. The memorandum concluded that there was no use talking with the cartel specialists in the ministries, who were hostile to the bill; it was rather their department chiefs who should be approached—or better still, the *Land* minister of economic affairs and minister-president.[22]

But these efforts with the Bundesrat by BDI liaison officers are the exception rather than the rule. In the legislative arena their energies are directed primarily toward the lower house.

STATE PARLIAMENTS AND LOCAL COUNCILS

Two other levels of activity on which the BDI must set its sights are the state and local legislative bodies. For many years, however, it has had difficulty in arousing the interest of employers in these levels since most employers believe that the important decisions are made at Bonn—whose politics and party feuds are, after all, more exciting than, say, local health problems, and where they believe the powers of the *Länder* have been steadily whittled down to the point that the *Länder* are concerned mostly with education and a few financial and cultural affairs. Thus, according to those employers, any party activity at the local level is a waste of time and beneath their dignity.

The BDI counters this apathy with the plea that democracy cannot flourish unless there is more interest in state and local problems, and that the latter are more important than the employer imagines since they involve fiscal matters and thus affect both the economy of the *Land* and the welfare of the individual enterprise. It argues that employers should show more in-

[22] Committee on competition, Circular (*Rundschreiben*), June 25, 1957.

terest in elections at the state level because of the impact these will have on West German politics and on the composition of the Bundesrat. Moreover, the BDI is concerned with the traditional strength shown by the SPD in urban areas. The DI cites the 1956 local elections in North Rhine–Westphalia, where the SPD won a smashing victory in thirty out of the thirty-eight larger cities—a ratio that applies to the entire country, since between 70 and 80 per cent of the larger cities are usually controlled by the SPD.[23]

One consequence of the absence of political activity on the part of businessmen, among others, is the high percentage of local civil servants, county executives, and mayors who serve as members of the *Landtage*—and whose interests, the BDI warns, may be inimical to industry. Employers are therefore urged to be active in the local party units responsible for selecting the delegates who in turn choose the party candidates for state and national elections. Berg has declared:

The basis of the political substructure is the election district. Here one must find a footing. Here one must solidify the influence of the employer in terms of his importance. . . . It is bad when we are surpassed in political activity and in the readiness to make sacrifices in time and effort in election districts by every lawyer, by every grammar school teacher, by every craftsman, by every civil servant.[24]

By comparison, employers in the United States are deemed to be more active at the community level than in Germany—where spokesmen for industry especially urge younger employers to volunteer to run for local office. It is argued that the experience will be a valuable basis for future political careers, as well as a contribution of expertise toward sounder public fiscal policies. Moreover, at the local level a candidate need not join a party, but may run on any number of nonpartisan or independent

[23] *UB*, No. 11, March 16, 1961; Hans L. Merkle, "Der Unternehmer und die gegenwärtige Politik," *Politisches Seminar, May 1960*, p. 133.

[24] Speech made June 23, 1952 at Bad Godesberg, quoted in *JB*, 1952–1953, p. 18.

tickets. As long as the issues taken up in public debates are local rather than national, no threat to democracy is seen where well-established parties have to meet their competition.[25]

For all its pessimism, the BDI acknowledges that some employers have taken the plunge at local and state levels. Of these, few have national renown or are connected with large corporations; and some have fallen by the wayside out of inability to surmount the roadblock posed by their own lack of previous political activity.[26] In Bavaria the only province where a sociological study of the membership of town and city councils has been made from 20 to 30 per cent of the membership are identified with the business community as a whole. But here industry is much less well represented than commerce and trade.[27]

In other *Länder*, the picture is no more satisfactory so far as industry is concerned. In 1957, Duesseldorf, a bastion of the Ruhr, numbered not one industrialist among its sixty-six councilors, and Cologne had only two out of the same number.[28] It is significant that the occupation of manufacturer is all but unknown in the membership of these bodies; and when it does

25 *UB*, No. 25, June 24, 1954; No. 11, March 16, 1961. See also issue of *Junge Wirtschaft*, VIII, No. 4 (April 1960), which deals with this range of questions.

26 In citing his own experience one employer, Hans Klepper, reports that he had not been active enough politically, and thus did not receive a top post on a party list when he ran for city council in his community; whereupon he set up a nonpartisan ticket, won the seat, and was subsequently re-elected. "Der Unternehmer in der Kommunalpolitik," *Der Volkswirt*, Beilage zu Nr. 23 (June 11, 1955), pp. 48–51.

27 In the Bavarian town councils, independent merchants and entrepreneurs were represented by less than 3 per cent, whereas artisans and tradesmen accounted for 15 per cent. On the city councils the proportion was higher—10 and 19 per cent respectively. And yet of Munich's fifty-eight city councilors only four were merchants and one an engineer (close to industry)—and this, the DI complained, in a city with 864 industrial firms with more than ten employees. *UB*, No. 40, Oct. 4, 1956; No. 51/52, Dec. 19, 1957.

28 Other cities showed equally low ratios: Stuttgart, 2 merchants out of 60; Frankfurt, one merchant and one head of a construction firm out of 80. *UB*, No. 51/52, Dec. 19, 1957.

appear, one is likely to discover a man who still spends most of the day in his firm.

At the Landtag level the proportion of employers and businessmen is not much higher.[29] A DI survey in 1962 revealed that 10.2 per cent of the deputies in the eleven *Landtage* were employers, managers, or staff executives of business associations (the CDU/CSU had 13 per cent, the SPD 6.7 per cent, the FDP 16 per cent, and other parties 10.6 per cent)—which compares unfavorably to their total of 15.5 per cent in the Bundestag (where the CDU/CSU had 16.7 per cent; the SPD 8.4 per cent, and the FDP 32.9 per cent).[30]

Although the BDI is the loser in this kind of numbers game, its policy recommendations cannot be entirely disregarded. Through its regional offices it will attempt to sway the legislators by means of the same techniques as on the national level, a task that is made much easier if the BDI is represented directly in the committees of the *Landtage*. In the Hamburg legislature, one of its representatives (a member of the CDU) was chairman of the tax committee, and another (from the FDP) chaired the economic affairs committee. If there is no direct representation, memoranda will be sent, experts will appear at *Fraktion* and committee meetings, and there will be parliamentary evenings

[29] In 1960, in *Land* Hesse the proportion of those from business was ten out of 110 Landtag members, and of those ten, only three were from industry; but in Bavaria, according to one Bavarian association executive, the CSU was most reluctant to put up any industralist because it feared that he would not attract enough votes, even though representatives from industry were willing to run for office. Consequently there was only one employer among the 100 CSU deputies in the Bavarian Landtag. Even in the highly industrialized *Land* of North Rhine–Westphalia, the 104 CDU deputies contained only 11 from the business community, and these were primarily small businessmen. Merkle, "Der Unternehmer und die gegenwärtige Politik," p. 134. These figures are further evidence that in industrial areas it is the representatives of labor rather than of industry who receive the first nod from the CDU.

[30] DI, "Die Soziologische Struktur der deutschen Landtage," *Material zum Zeitgeschehen*, No. 7, July 3, 1962, p. 14. The percentages represent the totals of the top three categories.

to which not only Landtag deputies but also Bundestag deputies and executive officials will be invited.

In the absence of extensive studies, it is difficult to say just how successful industry has been in putting across its program in the towns, cities, and *Länder*. Although the SPD is in control of a majority of the cities and some of the *Länder*, it must be cautious in its economic and financial policies because it cannot afford to alienate the local businessmen of whose tax support it would be deprived if they were to move to a more hospitable area. Furthermore, these same policies are so interwoven with those on the national level, where the SPD is not in control, that the latter is a good deal restricted in its freedom. There is no doubt that industry has been successful in changing or delaying some *Land* legislation—for example, that on water and air pollution, over which the Bund does not have full jurisdiction. There is no doubt, moreover, that even though business representation at the local level may be small, cities and towns that are heavily dependent on industry must pursue policies in harmony with it if they expect to remain economically viable. This is especially true of those dominated by one major company, as Leverkusen is by Bayer chemicals. In such cases, pressure on the local governments and councils will be more effective than the efforts of the few councilors who represent industry.[31]

Again it must be emphasized that the BDI is much more concerned with Bund legislation, which affects its interests generally, than with *Land* and local legislation, whose effect is indirect and sporadic.

THE PROPOSED FEDERAL ECONOMIC COUNCIL

For decades the idea of functional or occupational representation, in the form of an ancillary legislative organ, a federal economic council, has been repeatedly proposed in Germany. The BDI and other economic associations have been interested

[31] See Staatsbürgerliche Vereinigung, *Wirtschaft und Kommunalpolitik* (Bergisch Gladbach [c. 1962]).

in this kind of representation, since it would provide additional leverage for pressure upon the legislative process.

The first attempt to set up a council was made by Bismarck for Prussia in 1880; but parliament, fearing a rival, refused to assign it any funds, and the council met only three times. During the Weimar era a series of councils ranging from the local to the national level were set up. The National Economic Council—albeit only provisional—had the function of advising parliament concerning business regulation, finance, and social welfare legislation which the government was to submit to it. This procedure meant a slowing down in the legislative process, but was welcomed by the groups concerned. The council was to provide representation for all sectors of business (industry, agriculture, commerce, and so on)—with employers and employees receiving an equal number of seats—as well as for a so-called third bloc made up of consumers, officials, the free professions, and appointees of the government. Since in effect employers were pitted against the employees, it became the function of the third bloc to break the numerous stalemates.[32] The frequent squabbles among the clashing interest groups reduced the council's effectiveness and what little prestige it had.

After World War II, the Basic Law provided for parliamentary democracy at the federal level, but without economic councils—although bodies were set up in the states of Rhineland–Palatinate and Bremen. Both of the latter are merely advisory; the Bremen chamber can, however, submit draft proposals to the legislature. In Bavaria a bicameral state legislature, with a senate as the second chamber, was established for the purpose of minimizing political feuds and of giving more substance to parliamentary debate. The 60-member second body includes representatives of economic, social, cultural, and local interests; but

[32] See Ralph H. Bowen, *German Theories of the Corporative State* (New York, 1947); Herman Finer, *Representative Government and a Parliament of Industry* (London, 1923); Carl J. Friedrich, *Constitutional Government and Democracy* (Boston, 1950), pp. 474–477.

its powers are once again limited to advising the lower house, where its proposals can be rejected by a simple majority. Despite the requirements in the Bavarian constitution that the senate must be consulted in all important matters, during the first four-year period the government submitted only five draft bills for its consideration.[33]

The national trade-union and employer associations were not hostile, however, to re-establishing a series of economic councils based on the Weimar model. In April 1950 a memorandum issued by the DGB advocated the formation of such councils—on a parity basis with employers—in the belief that they might help improve relations between the social partners, bring about greater social justice, and extend the workers' right of codetermination in management from the level of the individual corporation to that of the nation. The position of the DGB is to be understood as a desire to see the trade unions given a more decisive role in the legislative process.[34]

At the outset the BDI and BDA were receptive to the idea of a federal economic council, and along with similar national associations they formed a study group under the auspices of the Joint Committee of German Trade and Industry. A report issued by the latter in May 1950 backed the formation of such a council, with the recommendations that it have merely an advisory function; that the cabinet be required to decide whether the ministries were to request advisory opinions from the council; that the council not have the right to initiate draft legislation (to this a minority dissented); that the council be made up of three groups—employers, employees, and neutrals; and that the Joint Committee have the right to nominate the business

[33] Helmut Weber, "Der Moderne Staat und die Interessengruppen" (unpublished Ph.D. dissertation, Marburg University, 1954), pp. 80–81; Taylor Cole, "Functional Representation in the German Federal Republic," *The Midwest Journal of Political Science*, II, No. 3 (Aug. 1958), pp. 259–266 especially.

[34] This theme is illustrated in Hirsch-Weber, *Gewerkschaften in der Politik.*

members. The council's membership proved the most controversial issue. At first the Committee supported the concept of parity between the two social forces; but then a majority advocated the inclusion of a neutral, third bloc, presumably in the hope that it would tend to side with the employers and that it would favor the social market economy.[35]

The BDI publicly welcomed the proposed council, for the reasons that it would (1) make the legislature more aware of the point of view of business; (2) work out compromises among divergent interests, thus lightening the burden upon the legislature; and (3) facilitate understanding among social groups. The BDI repeatedly emphasized, however, that the council should have a purely advisory function, not equal status with the legislature.[36]

It is doubtful whether these were the only reasons for the BDI's initial endorsement of a federal economic council. Very probably there was also the hope that in such an organ industry might expect to receive more support than it could in the Bundestag, where the deputies were expected to reflect the desires of the masses of voters. It was further likely that a draft law recommended by the council would carry more weight and prestige than any number of memoranda from economic pressure groups, and that the council could serve as a publicly financed platform for the point of view of those groups, thereby reducing (although not, of course, eliminating) the need for expensive lobbying activities. Finally, the council would give the associations greater legitimacy both in the public eye and vis-à-vis the executive and the legislature.[37]

But in the years that followed, the proposal for a federal economic council failed to gain momentum. There was dissension

[35] As reported in BDI, *Memorandum zur Frage des Bundeswirtschaftsrates,* Feb. 6, 1952 (mimeographed).

[36] *JB,* 1951–1952, pp. 10, 102; 1952–1953, p. 134; 1953–1954, pp. 138–139; *Fünf Jahre BDI,* p. 22.

[37] Hans Edgar Jahn, *Gesellschaft und Demokratie in der Zeitwende* (Köln, 1955), p. 159.

within and outside the government:[38] Adenauer favored it, while Erhard and most academicians were opposed. After a few years, for reasons that have never been entirely clear, the BDI publicly reversed its stand. Possibly, like the trade unions, it had become fearful of inadequate representation and an inability to carry sufficient weight. For the record the BDI merely cited the unsatisfactory experience and general weakness of economic councils in other European Economic Community countries— although it did admit that so long as the council's powers were only advisory, pressure would still be directed at parliament by the associations. It had also begun to doubt whether such a council would really diminish the tensions between the partners in the economy. It now argued that a better solution would be to provide the interest groups with more access to the executive through consultations while drafts were still in the working stage, and to the legislature through public hearings, as is guaranteed in the Swiss constitution—measures which would help to dissipate the ill-feeling against economic associations.[39]

Whatever conviction this negative stand by the BDI might have carried was somewhat lessened by juxtaposition with its earlier statements in support of a federal economic council. The trade unions have been no less inconsistent. Recently the DGB has once again appeared to favor the idea of a council, since from its own point of view the councils in other EEC countries

[38] Professors Ulrich Scheuner and Werner Weber emphasized the ineffectiveness of economic councils, the difficulty in the distribution of seats, and the danger of institutionalization of pressure groups. Beutler, Stein, Wagner (eds.), *Der Staat und die Verbände*, pp. 16, 25. Others warned of the danger to parliamentary democracy, especially if the bureaucracy teamed up with the council. Still another critic, a nonacademician, wrote that the council would be made up only of second-string officials of economic associations or old-timers who would be "kicked upstairs." Günther Ohlbrecht, "Grenzen der Verbandsmacht," *Kölner Rundschau*, Dec. 31, 1957.

[39] Beutler, "Die Aufgaben des Spitzenverbandes der Industrie," *Fünf Jahre BDI*, p. 22; Stein, "Der Staat und die Verbände," *Industriekurier*, May 16, 1957.

are performing useful preparatory work. As the only country in EEC without such a council, West Germany is at a disadvantage, according to the reasoning of the DGB.[40] It is interesting to note how the arguments pro and con have been shifting from the national to the international realm, a development that may cause the German government to be more receptive to the establishment of a council in the future.

CONCLUSION

In the legislative process the BDI takes a moderately active role through deputies strategically located in the parliamentary groups and the committees of the Bundestag, and through direct lobbying in other centers of legislative activity—the Bundesrat, the state parliaments, and the local councils—where its interests are also directly at stake. It employs the same techniques and tactics as other economic associations, but its main emphasis is on maintaining close ties with various members of the executive branch. These ties will be examined in the chapters that follow.

[40] *Stuttgarter Zeitung*, April 20, 1961.

IX

The Executive

THE BDI seeks access to the centers of executive authority, from the Chancellor on down to the lowest ranks of the civil servants. The person to be approached will vary with the nature of the problem. A major economic policy decision will call for discussion with the Chancellor or the Minister of Economics, whereas a routine administrative ruling will be discussed with the civil servant in charge. This chapter will be concerned with the relation of the BDI to the high echelons, and the following chapter with its relation to the civil service.

With the President of the Federal Republic few ties are maintained except those of a social nature, since as chief of state he has small political power. Occasionally the incumbent may appear in a ceremonial capacity at one of the yearly BDI congresses, but hardly ever to give a major address. Rather, it will be the Chancellor or some member of the cabinet, especially the Minister of Economics, who presents the government point of view to the assembled delegates. On occasion the Ministers of Economics and Finance have been invited to the sessions of the BDI presidential and executive boards, and several members of the cabinet have spoken to BDI committees whose work falls into their area of specialization.[1]

[1] *JB*, 1958–1959, p. 10.

THE CHANCELLOR

There have been other approaches, more informal and also more productive, of which the most important has been the one with former Chancellor Adenauer. Berg cultivated this relationship so assiduously and with such success that as president of the BDI he had an entrée to the former Chancellor at any time he chose, either directly or through Pferdmenges and others of Adenauer's advisers. Unlike Pferdmenges, Berg did not become a close personal friend of Adenauer's. Rather, a mutually profitable entente developed between the two: the one received financial assistance for his party, and the other frequently received support for the policies of his association. The accord had political repercussions, since whenever necessary Adenauer capitalized on it as a means of opposing Erhard. The bond was of course strengthened by the common views held by Adenauer and Berg on domestic and foreign policies.

Between Adenauer and Erhard, and between Berg and Erhard as well, the discord that had simmered for many years reached the boiling point in the mid-1950's. Between Adenauer and Erhard, personal differences were accentuated by policy differences; Adenauer had little esteem for Erhard as a politician and administrator, and feared his popularity with the electorate. On the other hand, relations between Berg and Erhard were initially quite cordial, at a time when industry needed help from the government and received it with Erhard's blessing, in the form of incentives to investment, depreciation allowances, and so on. But as the economic boom led to the danger of inflation and to social inequalities, and as the protracted struggle over cartel legislation reached its zenith, the two came at times into bitter opposition.

Caught in the middle, the Chancellor refused to support Erhard down the line, and relied increasingly on the advice of Berg—with the consequence that Erhard and Berg were often on equal footing when major economic policy decisions had to be reached. One explanation for this remarkable state of affairs lay in Adenauer's preference for the pragmatic approach of Berg over Erhard's more ideological attitude toward economic problems. Of course Berg relished his advisory ties with the top policy-maker. He once said of Adenauer: "He has a sound understanding of human nature. He simply believes me."[2] His notorious lack of interest in economic matters caused Adenauer to rely as well on such other members of the "kitchen cabinet" as the bankers Pferdmenges and Abs and a few leading industrialists for an exposition of the business and industrial points of view.[3] Their recommendations would be weighed along with those of Erhard and other government ministers in order to arrive at a decision, which might take the form of a compromise when the recommendations were contradictory.

Although in many instances there was agreement among all the parties, in several widely publicized disputes no compromise could be achieved, and there were some in which Adenauer sided with Berg against Erhard (or, very occasionally, vice versa). One such instance occurred in late 1955 and early 1956, when in three successive moves President Wilhelm Vocke of the semi-autonomous Federal Bank—with the support of Schäffer and Erhard—raised the discount rate from 3.5 to 5.5 per cent, so as to curb the business boom and stem the tide of investment. Berg protested sharply not only against the move by the bank, but also against the two ministers for their failure to consult industry, and against Erhard's simultaneous proposal to cut tariffs by 30 per cent. For several months Berg repeatedly urged Adenauer to reverse the fiscal policy, but Adenauer delayed his response until May 1956. Then, at the yearly assembly of the BDI in Cologne, he dramatically disavowed the actions of his two cabinet ministers by announcing his support for the position of Berg. He told his astonished but delighted audience of his

[2] *Der Spiegel*, XIV, No. 5 (Nov. 2, 1960), 36.

[3] Abs, holding twenty-five posts on the boards of directors of corporations, has close ties with industry. *Der Spiegel*, XV, No. 46 (Nov. 8, 1961), 60.

plans to call the ministers to account for their support of the bank's policy at a cabinet meeting the next day.[4] Several months later the bank lowered the discount rate by 0.5 per cent—possibly, however, for no other reason than that the boom had already begun to subside.

One can do no more than speculate on why Adenauer chose the BDI podium to denounce his ministers; but it may be surmised that a need for the financial backing of industry in the 1957 election may have been one factor in his mind. Incidentally, no official invitation had gone to Adenauer, Erhard, or Schäffer; Adenauer had simply announced that he would come and address the assembly.[5] The dust stirred up by this controversy was a good while in settling. Opponents of the Chancellor accused him of capitulating to the association, and even his friends considered his public spanking of Erhard and Schäffer a major blunder. Within the BDI the attempt of a pro-Erhard faction headed by Friedrich and Fritz Könecke to bring about a reconciliation between Berg and Erhard led to a conference between the two for the discussion of pressing economic problems.

What is most remarkable about the entire episode is Adenauer's failure to bring about an effective coordination of economic policies within the executive branch. If this had been done in the first place, the fracas would never have occurred. And even if Adenauer had become convinced by the BDI's arguments that the bank's policy was detrimental to industry, and therefore resolved to alter that policy, he could perfectly

[4] *FAZ*, May 24, 25, 28, 1956; *Handelsblatt*, May 25, 1956; *Deutsche Zeitung und Wirtschaftszeitung*, May 26, 1956, June 2, 1956; *Der Spiegel*, XIV, No. 45 (Nov. 2, 1960), 36–37; Deist (SPD) addressing the Bundestag, 2nd el. pd., 152nd session, June 22, 1956, pp. 8154–8155.

[5] One informant asserted that the BDI did not want to become embroiled in the Adenauer-Erhard feud, did not invite either one, and was most embarrassed when Adenauer appeared. The credibility of this last statement may be doubted, since Berg was desirous of Adenauer's support all along, and may have invited him to the assembly. Another informant said that Berg saw Adenauer's speech before it was delivered, another that only its general import was transmitted to him.

well have done so on the basis of secret cabinet negotiations.

A second major crisis erupted in 1959, with Adenauer and Erhard as the main protagonists, and Berg playing a secondary role. It began as a game of musical chairs when the presidency of the Federal Republic was vacated by Theodor Heuss, who had been in office for two consecutive terms and thus could not be re-elected again. Adenauer urged Erhard to become a candidate, but after some indecision, Erhard refused to be thrust into a post that would have taken him out of the running for the more coveted chancellorship. Adenauer thereupon declared himself a candidate for the presidency, leaving Erhard with the expectation of becoming chancellor. Then without warning Adenauer changed his mind—ostensibly because at that moment he believed himself indispensable in the realm of foreign affairs, but really because he did not want to hand over the reins to Erhard. Heinrich Lübke, the former Minister of Agriculture, subsequently became the CDU presidential candidate and was elected.

The role played by the BDI in the game for these high stakes is of interest. At the outset, a meeting of the BDI presidential board decided to give strong support to Adenauer in his attempt to persuade Erhard to run for the presidency, in the hope of depriving the latter of the opportunity of shaping economic policy, in which he was often at variance with the BDI. It is reported that the BDI suggested Hellwig as his successor.[6] In February, at an official press conference, the BDI sugar-coated its stand by declaring that Erhard would be missed as Minister of Economics, but that it saw in him the best candidate for the presidency, a man with the prestige and authority to meet the high standards set by Heuss.[7]

Nevertheless, the impression was given currency in the press and in the CDU that the BDI supported Erhard's candidacy—and had perhaps even been responsible for launching it—because

[6] *Der Spiegel*, XIV, No. 45 (Nov. 2, 1960), 38.
[7] *FAZ*, Feb. 26, 1959; *Industriekurier*, Feb. 26, 1959.

it wanted him removed from the Ministry. At a meeting of the BDI presidential board on March 5, it was decided to issue a strong public denial, and to declare that Erhard's proposed candidacy was as much a surprise to its members as it had been to the populace. The denial, coming after Erhard had withdrawn from the race on March 3, was not altogether convincing; spokesmen for small business went on insisting that big business had wanted Erhard "kicked upstairs." Erhard's own adherents remained loyal, fearing that his successor might be unacceptable to them. Some, including Friedrich and Könecke, even advocated CDU support for Carlo Schmid of the SPD.

Although Erhard's decision to stay on as head of his Ministry was a defeat for Adenauer and the BDI, it drew attention once again to the BDI's involvement in affairs of state whenever there was a direct or potential threat to its economic interests. It also highlighted the importance of maintaining close contact with the Chancellor, who remained master of the nation's destiny.

A third episode, illustrating the closeness of the relations between the BDI and Adenauer, began in March 1960 at the Leipzig trade fair, where the East German boss, Walter Ulbricht, engaged in a lively and well-publicized political dialogue with representatives of West German steel companies. Berg immediately sent a letter to Hans-Günther Sohl, chairman of the Association of the Iron and Steel Industry, criticizing the attempt of the industrialists to increase their business by making politically naïve and compromising statements, and with Adenauer he issued a joint communiqué deploring the incident for its injurious effects on the interests of the Federal Republic as a whole.[8] When Berg later confronted some of the industrialists at the residence of Pferdmenges, who was attempting to conciliate, according to one news story, he was told by Beitz of Krupp, "If you think, Herr Berg, that you can be the Chancellor's commissar for industry, you have another think coming"—

[8] *FAZ*, March 12, 1960.

to which Berg retorted, "Well, Herr Beitz, you always were insolent to me." Afterward Berg yielded to the directors of Krupp and Mannesmann—who were reported to have threatened to pull out of the BDI-affiliated industrial associations, and thus indirectly out of the BDI—to the extent of canceling any further talks with the industrialists who had been involved in the Leipzig incident.[9]

What is astonishing about this episode is not Adenauer's rebuke to the industrialists, whom he saw as having trespassed upon the realm of foreign policy, but his issuing a joint communiqué with the president of a private industrial federation. It is no wonder that in some sectors of industry Berg's reputation sank to a new low; at a German industrial fair in Teheran, certain German industrialists told Erhard, "Berg is not the German industry, he is only the president of an industrial association."[10]

A fourth notable crisis occurred in September 1960, several months after the curtain had fallen on the Leipzig affair. As in 1956, Adenauer, Erhard, and Berg were once again the leading actors. Erhard, concerned about a new industrial boom and rising prices, proposed to the CDU parliamentary group that— in order to limit exports and increase imports—a trade tax on imports and certain subsidies on exports be repealed in order to bring about what would in effect be a technical revaluation of the mark and a cut in the trade surplus. Berg, when he heard of the proposal, called it a "catastrophe for the entire economy" as well as a "crime," and promptly lodged a vigorous protest with Adenauer. While Erhard was traveling in Afghanistan, he also called a well-timed press conference to announce the BDI's point of view—namely that the economic situation need not be dramatized, but that stability could be achieved, rather, if industry were asked to hold the price line, if the government and the construction industry were to arrive at a gentleman's agree-

[9] *Der Spiegel*, XIV, No. 45 (Nov. 2, 1960), 38.
[10] *Ibid.*, pp. 40–41.

ment not to build unless necessary, and if industry were to provide a billion DM for aid to underdeveloped nations. With these relatively modest counterproposals Berg hoped to bury Erhard's more drastic plan, which would have meant a measurable cut in industrial expansion. During the press conference, Berg made a more ominous suggestion to the effect that he "need only go to Dr. Adenauer to sweep revaluation and its tax substitutes off the table," or that "a nod from him would suffice to bring Erhard's program down in defeat."[11] When Adenauer brought the crisis to a climax by refusing to accept Erhard's proposals, Berg was able to register another victory.

Why Adenauer once again supported Berg rather than Erhard is necessarily a matter of conjecture. It is possible that Adenauer was constrained to do so by his financial benefactors; or it may be that he was convinced by Berg's arguments; or possibly his decision involved both factors. At any rate, it raised a storm of protest. Most of the newspapers backed Erhard in his feud with industry, criticized Adenauer for dabbling in economic affairs he did not understand, and chided Berg for his sweeping and arrogant claims concerning Adenauer. One columnist asserted that at his press conference Herr Berg had given the impression of deciding German economic policy single-handed—an impression "dangerous for democracy, dangerous for the governing party, dangerous for our industry, its legitimate interest representation, and not least for Fritz Berg himself."[12] The same columnist wrote of a growing mistrust in the ministries and in the CDU of a policy built on the Chancellor's conversations with people who were without political responsibility.

Another columnist, under the title, "The Lobbies Must Not Govern," denied Berg the right to interfere in a draft proposal before it had received full discussion in the ministries or the cabinet. It was proper, he said, for interest groups to tender

[11] *New York Times*, Oct. 8, 1960; *FAZ*, Oct. 4, 1960; *Der Spiegel*, **XIV**, No. 45 (Nov. 2, 1960), 26.
[12] Jürgen Eyck, "Erhard oder Berg?" *FAZ*, Oct. 4, 1960.

their advice but not to nip a proposal in the bud as Berg had done. If interest groups were to have such massive financial power that they could dictate economic policy to the government, he concluded, then the only remedy was for the legislature to pass a law which would regulate private donations to parties.[13]

These criticisms brought no rebuttal by Berg or Adenauer, although not long afterward Erhard and Berg appeared jointly at a public ceremony, at which Erhard declared charitably that he regarded anyone who disagreed with him not as an enemy but rather as a partner with whom he discussed policy differences. Thus ended another controversy with the by now familiar alignment of Adenauer and Berg against Erhard.

But this time Berg could claim no more than a pyrrhic victory. During a fifth crisis Erhard, Finance Minister Etzel, and Federal Bank president Karl Blessing launched a counterassault. In March 1961 they were able to convince Adenauer of the danger of economic crisis in West Germany unless drastic measures were taken to slow down the boom. In order to strengthen the purchasing power of the mark, stabilize prices, and reduce the surplus in the international balance of payments, the government leaders secretly made preparations to revalue the mark; and on March 5 their decision was announced without previous notice to Berg or any other association leaders.

The heads of industries dependent on such exports as coal and steel, which would now cost more, were understandably upset by the news. Berg was angered by what he saw as a betrayal by Adenauer, who had assured him a few days earlier that no thought was being given to a revaluation, and who some time before that had assured him—Berg recalled—that if industry delivered a promised sum for development aid there would be no revaluation. It is of interest to note the characteristic manner in which Berg expressed his initial displeasure. He immediately ordered payment stopped on a 100,000-DM check

[13] Eschenburg in *Die Zeit*, Oct. 28, 1960.

which the CDU Federal Office had been receiving monthly out of funds from industry for operating expenses.[14] Publicly, he denounced the government move in strong terms; but in the face of a rather rare unity in government ranks, there was little else he could do.

The dispute over the currency revaluation is convincing proof that there has been an occasional coolness between Adenauer and Berg. Adenauer could not be expected to veto consistently economic proposals made by Erhard which might be distasteful to industry. If this had been so, Erhard would have resigned long ago. It must be recalled, too, that Adenauer could not afford to be beholden to a single major interest group and still hope to win the crucial federal elections. In economic and social policies he has had to weigh the advantages of giving support to industry, which has provided him with financial ammunition at election time, against the disadvantages—which might have included the loss of workers' votes and nationwide exposure to opposition propaganda portraying him as a pawn of big business. His emphasis in recent years on social policies that were at times inimical to industry has demonstrated his ability to withstand the pressures of industry, or follow a line of opposition if he chose. His stand on any given issue often could not be predicted, thanks to his penchant for authoritarian decisions. He once told the Bundestag, "I am a democrat, ladies and gentlemen." Roars of laughter came from the House, whereupon he amended himself: "Well, let's put it this way, ladies and gentlemen, I am approximately a democrat."[15]

There is no doubt of Adenauer's relative immunity from the relentless pressures by a myriad of associations, although the crises already cited entitled one to question the validity of the assertion by one observer that "if [Adenauer] does anything which coincides with industry's thinking it is because he has

[14] Schröder, "Fritz Berg sperrte der CDU das Konto," *Kölner Stadt-Anzeiger*, June 16, 1961; *Bulletin*, No. 46 (March 8, 1961), pp. 417–422.
[15] As quoted in the *New York Times*, March 18, 1962, Section IV.

arrived independently at the same conclusion."[16] Naturally no political figure will ever admit that he depends on any group, and Adenauer, with all the rest, sees himself as standing aloof from the perennial group strife. He once said, "I do not have the feeling that I have ever been handed over to the power of an association."[17]

Thus it would be an error to speak of complete dependence by the former Chancellor on the president of the BDI, despite the unmistakable ties, including a financial one. Actually it worked the other way too: Berg was even more dependent on Adenauer, who in the final analysis determined the government's economic policy. Adenauer was accordingly able to use his ties with Berg in order to enforce the occasional requests he has made of industry. At one time, for example, he urged the BDI to work out a program of help for medium-sized and small businesses in order to forestall more drastic government action. Critics of the BDI president expressed the view that Berg's dependence was too great, and that once Adenauer stepped down from his post, all contact at that level might very well be lost. Berg may one day be obliged to resign or adopt a different style of negotiation.

On the whole, however, the relationship with the Adenauer administration appears to have been a good and mutually profitable one. On the part of the BDI, it was built up over a number of years, and meant cultivating the friendship of the Chancellor's trusted advisers in the Office of the Federal Chancellor—such as the influential head of the economic affairs department, and State Secretary Globke, the *éminence grise* behind Adenauer.

The BDI staff had to spend much time making procedural and tactical decisions whether these advisers were to be con-

[16] Wahrhaftig, in *West German Leadership and Foreign Policy*, ed. Speier and Davison, p. 45.

[17] As cited by Ferdinand Fried, "Die Verpflichtung der Industrie," *Die Welt*, Oct. 22, 1959.

tacted to arrange a meeting with Adenauer, whether a telephone call be made to his office, a letter written, or a memorandum sent. If the decision called for a meeting, Stein might see Globke in order to arrange a private conference between Berg and Adenauer, or with a small staff retinue. In the latter event, BDI presidential board members and Beutler and Stein might accompany Berg, and Adenauer would be flanked by senior government officials.

Perhaps there was no need to approach Adenauer at all if there was a chance that the matter could be solved at a lower level. The minutes of BDI meetings reveal that on several occasions there was a decision to exhaust all remedies before arranging a conference with Adenauer. There was obviously a wish to keep meetings with the chief executive to a minimum in order to avoid overexposure and to increase the effectiveness of such conversations as were necessary.[18]

THE MINISTER OF ECONOMICS

The BDI maintains close contact not only with the Chancellor but also with his ministers, since decisions are commonly made at this level. For the BDI the Ministry of Economics is the primary target, but others, such as those concerned with finance and foreign affairs, also have a part in economic policy.

In Berg's relations with Adenauer, former Minister Erhard has usually appeared as a foe of Berg. More than once, however, Erhard acknowledged the cooperation of the national industrial organizations in a unified economic policy, where differences between government and industry were concerned merely with details. He has expressed opposition to the concept of an all-encompassing welfare state, and to undue interference by the state in economic affairs. On these fundamental aspects of eco-

[18] The minutes of a presidential board meeting of one BDI association reveal a lengthy discussion on whether Adenauer or Erhard should be approached directly concerning a Common Market problem. It was finally decided that a talk with Adenauer would be impossible to arrange, so a letter was written to him instead.

nomic policy, as well as on European economic integration, Erhard and Berg have common views; and Erhard has needed the support of industry in order to reach the objectives of the social market economy, just as Berg has needed the aid and support of the Ministry of Economics. To meet his own needs Erhard organized a circle of industrialists, including some from the BDI, on whom he could rely for advice.

But despite an initial period of harmony, a host of differences between the Ministry and the BDI arose soon after the German economy hit full stride. As will be shown,[19] disputes broke out over cartel, trade, tax, business cycle, wage, and price policies, adding up to a spirited attack by the BDI against Erhard for attempting to limit the freedom of the employers, and a counterattack by Erhard against organized industry.

As early as 1949–1950 the employer community had begun to complain against Erhard. In a letter to the Minister, Otto Friedrich criticized him for failing to listen to spokesmen for industry, for not consulting them when drafting economic measures, for doubting the good will of industrialists, and for calling them lobbyists. The Minister replied merely that not all employers were in love with the competitive system, but implied that he was obliged to consider the interests of other sectors of the economy.[20]

Like Adenauer, Erhard found himself subjected to a good deal of pressures from interested associations—to whose tactics, like other ministers, he responded with some vehemence—and also to accusations by elements of the opposition, including trade unions, that he was too soft toward industry. In his book *Prosperity Through Competition* Erhard entitled one chapter "Minister for Economic Affairs not the Representative of Private Interests"; in it he insisted that he did not regard himself as the representative of special interests, "and certainly not as the representative of the interests of industry or trade."[21] Vested

[19] See Chapters XI and XII.
[20] Friedrich, *Gehen wir aufeinander zu* (München, 1958), pp. 14 ff.
[21] *Prosperity through Competition* (New York, 1958), p. 101.

interests, he argued, "must not be allowed to determine economic policy, and no useful synthesis can be derived from a conflict between these interests. Any fragmentation of the national economy into vested interests cannot therefore be allowed."[22] In another passage Erhard asserted, "It is a question of striking a balance between those interests which brings about a general well-being."[23] And, more colorfully:

In this connection I have on a former occasion pointed to the role of the State as supreme judge. I should like here to use the perhaps somewhat banal picture of a game of football, if I may. I believe that, as the referee is not allowed to take part in the game, so the State must not participate. In a good game of football it is to be noted that the game follows definite rules; these are decided in advance. What I am aiming at with a market economic policy is—to continue with the same illustration—to lay down the order and the rules of the game.[24]

As the BDI and other associations have done, Erhard emphasizes the national interest and the striving for the common good. The difficulty, of course, is in defining these concepts precisely. Erhard's own idea of the common good differs, for example, from that of the trade union chiefs, who with some justification accuse him of identifying the common good with that of the business community. Indeed, he is sympathetic with its general goals, and if the BDI really had been dissatisfied with his basic policies it would have put more pressure on Adenauer to replace him. So far as is known, this pressure was applied only at the time the post of the presidency was open. Moreover, Erhard's friends within the BDI have stood up for him, asking what other popular national leader would have so staunchly defended the free enterprise system as Erhard had done.[25]

[22] *Ibid.*
[23] *Ibid.*, p. 102.
[24] *Ibid.*
[25] The *Handelsblatt*, May 25, 1956, listed the following members of the presidential board in that year as Erhard supporters: Curt Becker, Otto Friedrich, Fritz Könecke, and Carl Neumann.

THE CABINET

Since the Ministry of Economics is not the only one of immediate interest to the BDI, the formation of a cabinet after a federal election is watched with apprehensive eyes. Nor has the BDI hesitated to inform Adenauer of its likes and dislikes. This was especially true during the shuffle of cabinet posts in 1957 and 1961. In 1957 the BDI's distaste for Fritz Schäffer as Minister of Finance was well known, and so was the attempt by it and other business associations to prevent his reappointment. Objecting to Schäffer's fiscal policies (which consisted of levying high taxes in order to build up a reserve fund, and of holding government expenditures to a minimum), they accused him of sabotaging major tax reforms, and called for lower taxes so that industry would be able to accumulate its own reserves for investment purposes. No doubt their objections were quite understandable. The tax system was extremely complicated, capital reserves had declined, and the solvency of many small businesses was threatened. From the point of view of the Ministry, on the other hand, at no period of history had big business been able to make such profits as in the years from 1950 to 1955, or been able to make such profits so easily, thanks to the complexity of the tax laws. Aided by subsidies and liberal depreciation allowances, the basic industries were faring well.[26] In 1956, over Radio Bavaria, Schäffer assailed the associations that were demanding an across-the-board tax reduction and other favors, and simultaneously complaining of the avarice of the state. He argued with some justice that any association will artificially build up a feeling of dissatisfaction, and then attempt to outdo its rivals in its catalogue of requests to the Ministry of Finance; if the Ministry were to honor all those requests, financial chaos would ensue.[27]

In view of its differences with Schäffer, the BDI's attempt to block his reappointment in 1957 came as no surprise. Immedi-

[26] See *Der Spiegel*, XI, No. 44 (Oct. 30, 1957), 14–16.
[27] *FAZ*, Feb. 16, 1956.

ately after the election, the powerful agricultural associations hastened to Adenauer to propose one of their officials as Minister of Agriculture in place of Heinrich Lübke (who in 1959 was elected President of the Federal Republic). While their efforts were unsuccessful, those of the BDI and the banking interests were conducted unobtrusively behind the scenes. Apparently through the mediation of Pferdmenges, they had already obtained the agreement of Adenauer that Schäffer was not to retain his cabinet post.[28] In the Bundestag, Deist (SPD) accused the economic associations of forcing the ouster of the Minister of Finance—presumably in return for their financial support at election time.[29] At any rate, the arguments of the BDI fell on receptive ears, since because of personal and policy differences, both Adenauer and Erhard shared negative sentiments concerning Schäffer, and no one was surprised when Adenauer shifted him from Finance to Justice.

It was a victory for industrial and banking interests when Adenauer appointed their favorite candidate, Franz Etzel, a high official in the European Coal and Steel Community, as the new Minister of Finance. Originally as an industrial lawyer, and then as chairman of the CDU Committee for Economic Policy, Etzel had been associated with these interests for many years. Critics were quick to publicize a family tie between Etzel and the banking fraternity—namely that Etzel's wife was the sister-in-law of the banker Scharnberg. To a limited extent the BDI's hopes that Etzel would be more receptive to its tax and fiscal proposals were realized. Etzel's hand was strengthened by Adenauer's government declaration following the election, in which he turned sharply away from the policy of Schäffer and toward genuine tax and fiscal reforms.

In the other cabinet appointments industry again had no cause to complain. Hermann Lindrath, Minister for Federally

28 *Echo der Zeit*, Oct. 27, 1957; *Stuttgarter Zeitung*, Oct. 28, 1957.

29 Bundestag, 3rd el. pd., 5th session, Nov. 28, 1957, p. 146. He quoted statements in *Deutsche Bauernzeitung*, Oct. 31, 1957.

Owned Properties, represented its interests directly, as head of the Portland Cement Corporation in Heidelberg, and was expected to turn over several federal properties to private or mixed ownership. Siegfried Balke, the Minister for Atomic Energy, had been an industrial manager in an electrochemical firm formerly tied to I. G. Farben, and might thus be expected to be sympathetic. (In 1963 Balke was not reappointed, and in 1964 he became president of the BDA.) From Christian Seebohm, Minister of Transport, some concessions were obtained as a price for continued support: the top officers of the Automobile Industry Association, a BDI affiliate, had discussed at length the possibility of attempting to have Seebohm replaced by a man more amenable to their interests, but after their president and the head of a transport association had met with Seebohm, at the insistence of the Chancellor, in order to resolve certain differences between the Ministry and the private associations, they agreed to back his reappointment.[30] Finally, the BDI could expect from Erhard—who not only was again Minister of Economics but had also been newly appointed Vice Chancellor and chairman of the cabinet-level Committee on Economics—measures more or less to its liking.

It must be recalled that in forming the 1957 cabinet Adenauer had to take into consideration not only the BDI's views but also those of a host of other associations, many of which were at cross purposes. The pressure from these various associations led Adenauer, not surprisingly, publicly to decry their tactics.[31] Four years later, when Adenauer and the CDU chieftains were once again faced with the problem of forming a cabinet, they

[30] *Frankfurter Rundschau*, Oct. 12, 1957.

[31] That the BDI also has an interest in the formation of cabinets on the *Länder* level for the same reasons as on the national level is self-evident. According to one account, Stein met with FDP leaders before the pending North Rhine–Westphalia election in 1958 to inform them of industry's interest in again having the FDP join a cabinet on the federal level, in which one of its then chief leaders, Erich Mende, was to receive a post. *Der Spiegel*, XII, No. 29 (July 16, 1958), 14.

found it even more trying, since in the absence of an operating majority in the new Bundestag, they had the further task of deciding on the nature of the coalition to be formed. Industry once again played an important though inconspicuous role in deciding the composition of the cabinet, although this was officially denied by the BDI.[32] As leaders of the SPD saw it, industry was strenuously opposed to a major coalition with that party, but favored a minor coalition with the FDP.[33] Indeed, in the spring of 1961, months before the election, two newspapers closely identified with industry were already urging the inclusion of the FDP in a future coalition cabinet—even if the CDU were to gain an absolute majority—in order to counter the influence of the CDU's labor wing.[34] After extended negotiations the FDP was included in the cabinet—a step the CDU regarded with misgivings, but to which it became resigned when the FDP promised support for some of its social welfare programs.

The CDU also was faced with the task of choosing a Chancellor, since even though Adenauer had expressed a readiness to run again, he had considerable opposition both within and outside the party. The FDP would have preferred Erhard to Adenauer for reasons of foreign and domestic policy. The industrial and business interests financing the FDP, which have been traditionally close to Erhard, appear to have been largely responsible for this decision, some of them having contributed funds on condition that the party would not support Adenauer after the election. But they were unsuccessful in the end, even though party boss Erich Mende had initially opposed having Adenauer continue as Chancellor.[35]

There was, however, still a pro-Adenauer faction. Berg and Stein are reported to have met with Adenauer to assure him of their opposition to Erhard's nomination. The bulk of industry

[32] *Mitteilungen*, X, No. 1 (Jan. 1962), 1.
[33] *Vorwärts*, Oct. 25, 1961.
[34] *Industriekurier*, Feb. 28, March 4, 1961; *Deutsche Zeitung und Wirtschaftszeitung*, Feb. 28, 1961.
[35] *Der Spiegel*, XV, No. 41 (Oct. 4, 1961), 23; *Die Zeit*, Nov. 17, 1961.

was not, of course, Adenauer's only support, but it unquestionably strengthened his hand. After Adenauer finally formed a coalition cabinet, the SPD asserted that it did not have the confidence of the people, but would be "a government of the BDI."[36] Whether or not the BDI considered this a compliment, it was surely an exaggeration. At any rate, the BDI's official reaction to the nomination of Adenauer was positive: "In view of the difficult problems of an international nature with which the cabinet will have to deal, we consider it right for the helm to remain in the hands of the Federal Chancellor."[37]

A dispute arose over another post in the 1961 cabinet when ill health caused Etzel to decide to retire from public life (he became a banker in Duesseldorf). Among the candidates for his post as Minister of Finance were two men associated with industry—Heinz Starke (FDP), who since 1950 had been general manager of the Chamber of Industry and Commerce in Bayreuth, and Rolf Dahlgrün (FDP), an official of the Phoenix Rubber Corporation. Starke was eventually selected over the opposition of the BDI, by whom he was considered an exponent of small business likely to tamper with the tax privileges of big business. Within the FDP he received the support of the spokesmen for small business and from many Erhard adherents—although not this time from Friedrich, head of Phoenix Rubber, who in a conference with Adenauer made it known that he supported the candidate from his own company.

In view of the BDI's stand, why did Adenauer select Starke and not Dahlgrün? One explanation may be that Adenauer felt constrained to satisfy the small business community; another may be that he saw Dahlgrün's affiliation with a big business concern as too heavy a liability—especially since the massive highway construction program then pending might have led to a conflict of interest. The labor wing of the CDU was naturally hostile to both candidates, but could not persuade Adenauer to

[36] *Vorwärts*, Oct. 25, 1961.

[37] *Mitteilungen*, X, No. 1 (Jan. 1962), p. 1.

consider anyone else.[38] By December 1962, along with Franz-Josef Strauss, who resigned as Minister of Defense, Starke was already out—having irritated Adenauer by maintaining an independent position in cabinet meetings—and Dahlgrün received the appointment—which must have been welcome to the BDI since he had been a member of its legal committee.

Restless over the usual squabbling among parties and personalities during the 1962 negotiations concerning a new cabinet, Berg, Paulssen and Alwin Münchmeyer, then the DIHT's president, called for a speedy conclusion in the interests of political and business stability. It is significant that when the possibility arose of a CDU–SPD coalition, industry did not demonstrate its former intense hostility, even though it naturally preferred another CDU–FDP coalition—which was the eventual outcome. One reason for its greater toleration of the SPD was that the latter's more moderate economic program offered less of a threat to business. Another reason, but of less significance, was that some SPD leaders had established good contacts with the business world. This was true of Dr. Deist, a former steel trustee and chairman of the supervisory board of Bochumer Verein, of Professor Schiller, the West Berlin Minister of Economics, and of Dr. Alex Möller, one of the party's financial experts and director general of one of the largest life insurance companies. A meeting between industrial leaders and prominent Social Democrats was actually scheduled during the crisis, although it was called off. Despite these mild rapprochements, the rumor of Möller's possible appointment as Minister of Finance in a CDU–SPD coalition cabinet no doubt dismayed many a business tycoon, since Möller, although friendly to business, might be expected to impose higher taxes on large properties and incomes.[39]

When Erhard became Chancellor in 1963, the BDI urged him to appoint his former State Secretary Ludger Westrick, who had come from the aluminum industry, as Minister of Economics.

[38] *Der Spiegel*, XV, No. 48 (Nov. 22, 1961).
[39] *Die Welt*, Dec. 27, 1962.

Erhard chose instead to appoint Westrick as State Secretary of the office of the Federal Chancellor to succeed Globke, and to appoint Kurt Schmücker, a CDU deputy and an exponent of small business, as Minister of Economics. Whether the BDI may expect to receive a more sympathetic hearing of its views from Westrick than from Schmücker remains to be seen.

From all this the importance attached by associations to having the right man at the top policy-making level is evident. The national popularity of the Minister of Economics made it inadvisable for the BDI to oppose his "permanent tenure" in that office; but matters were different when it came to the selection of other cabinet members, notably the Minister of Finance. Unless it applies pressure at the launching stage of any government, an association often may find itself saddled for four or more years with a minister whose views and policies are inimical. When this happens, woe to the manager of that association.

X

The Civil Service

ALONG with the executive level the civil service is also a major target of pressure by German interest groups. This chapter will deal with the kinds of pressure employed, and with the degree to which the bureaucracy is vulnerable to them or is able to remain neutral in the face of such pressures. It must be recalled at the outset that traditionally, up until just before World War I, the nobility and the upper strata of the bourgeoisie were well represented in the civil service, giving it a marked tendency toward conservatism. Even during the Weimar era, when it was infused with new blood, the civil service was still more conservative than many of the short-lived coalition governments. Since there has been no period of history when all social classes, including the workers, were equitably represented in the higher levels of the bureaucracy, business has long had an affinity with its views.

This has been less true in the period since World War II— not so much because of any exhortations concerning the civil servant's obligation to represent the public interest and to uphold the ethical character of the profession, but rather, as John Herz suggests, because the civil servant has suffered a loss of prestige and is now plagued by material worries hitherto unknown to his class. As he tends to "conform to lower middle-class standards and views,"[1] he is less often identified with the businessman. Herz observes that "there is much invidious comparison between the lot of an official and that of those who live 'conspicuously': industrialists, small independents, and all those who have expense accounts."[2]

But although he has undergone a distinct loss of status, the average civil servant is still looked upon rather more favorably by the industrial tycoon than by members of the lower income groups. As in many other countries, ranking civil servants maintain a larger number of official and social contacts with industrialists than they do with trade union officials. Nevertheless, the trade unions have achieved one breakthrough: the complaint that their interests were being neglected by the Ministry of Economics has led to the appointment of trade union liaison officials in several ministries.[3] Some ministries—such as those of Interior, Defense, and Finance—naturally tend to be quite neutral toward interest groups; but others, especially Economics, Labor, and Transport, are so closely associated with their constituent groups as to be considered by the latter as a kind of private fiefdom.

Where the BDI is concerned, relations with the civil servants in the Ministry of Economics are regarded as excellent, and those in the Ministries of Justice and Finance as good. In the Ministry of Labor a predisposition toward the trade unions and the left wing of the CDU is to be expected. On the other hand, it is surprising to find that the BDI's relations with the Ministry of Foreign Affairs are not considered satisfactory. The BDI has

[1] "Political Views of the West German Civil Service," *West German Leadership and Foreign Policy*, ed. Speier and Davison, p. 114. For a comparative approach see Ehrmann, "Les groupes d'intérêt et la bureaucratie dans les démocraties occidentale," *Revue Française de Science Politique*, XI, No. 3 (Sept. 1961), 541–568.

[2] *Ibid.*, p. 115.

[3] Hirsch-Weber, *Gewerkschaften in der Politik*, p. 115; Breitling, "Ressort Politik der Verbände," paper given at a Heidelberg University political science seminar, Dec. 4, 1959 (unpublished).

complained not only of being ignored, but also of the inadequate staffing of the Ministry's economics division, primarily as a result of competition from the more ably staffed division of foreign trade in the Ministry of Economics. As Samuel Wahrhaftig has remarked, in international trade and economic negotiations, the Ministry of Foreign Affairs is "nominally in charge, but it has to lean heavily on the Ministry of Economics, which has a number of experienced officials who came originally from the old Wilhelmstrasse Foreign Office. The influence of these people on the economic side of foreign policy is understandably considerable."[4]

On the other side of the ledger, the BDI does have an opportunity to influence trade and commercial agreements made by the Ministry of Foreign Affairs precisely because of this shortage of qualified personnel. The Ministry has asked the BDI repeatedly to supplement its negotiating teams with experts from industry and banking. Moreover, as Wahrhaftig points out, "Some members of the Foreign Office who went over to private industry before 1945 and represented leading German firms abroad—usually chemical, machinery, or electrical firms—have now found their way back into the Foreign Office and hold leading diplomatic positions."[5]

Access to other ministries, too, may be facilitated by an influx of personnel from the associations, or vice versa. An ex-official of an industrial association who has become a ministerial civil servant is likely to be more receptive toward the problems of industry than one whose background is merely academic. This is not always true, however. Many section chiefs in the Ministry of Economics develop sympathy with the industrial or business sector with which they deal, and are consequently friendly toward association officials on whom they depend for statistical

[4] Wahrhaftig, in *West German Leadership and Foreign Policy*, ed. Speier and Davison, p. 31.

[5] *Ibid.*, p. 32. To cite but one example, the top diplomat Heinz Krekeler was formerly an industrialist in the chemical industry.

and other information, as well as for reactions to new drafts of legislation. A positive reaction to one of the latter may enhance the likelihood of its passage by the Bundestag. Because of these close bonds, it may become difficult for a civil servant to say no to an association official whom he has known for a number of years.

For example, a staff official of the Association of the Chemical Industry asserted that with one exception the civil servants who dealt with his branch did not come from the chemical industry, and that whether they did or not was not really important. What mattered was their attitude, and there he had no cause for complaint.

In 1949, when the ministries were originally constituted, industry did supply many experts who became civil servants. But this influx did not continue. Rather there has been a significant exodus of senior civil servants from government to industry, primarily because of the difference in salary. In a recent two-year period eleven state secretaries and ministerial directors made the change, with an adverse effect on the morale of the remaining civil servants.[6] Naturally a former government employee will be of service to his new employer in dealing with the government. In order to prevent any favoritism or collusion from developing out of such connections, the FDP once drafted a bill that would have prohibited civil servants from accepting positions in private industry for a certain number of years after their departure from the government. The draft was prompted by the case of Josef Rust, a former state secretary, who soon after his resignation from the Ministry of Defense had accepted a post on the board of directors of a major fuel corporation.[7] But the bill never became law.

The BDI and its associations are eager to receive favorable consideration not only from the civil servants in one division of

[6] Winfried Martini, "Die Bundesrepublik: Provisorium oder Staat?" *Politisches Seminar*, 1959, p. 130.

[7] *Der Spiegel*, XIV, No. 10 (March 2, 1960).

a ministry, but also from other divisions within the same ministry and from other ministries—all of whom may be dealing with the same draft legislation. Here the BDI is confronted with the oath of impartiality taken by civil servants. Granted that the precise limits of impartiality in any situation are subjective and thus extremely difficult to define, so that civil servants actually have a good deal of leeway; and granted, further, that in order to maintain amicable relations a civil servant may "capitulate" to the views of the association with whom he deals; nevertheless the divisions of his ministry may override his recommendations and suggest alterations in the draft. Likewise, if two rival divisions—say coal and oil—have made contradictory recommendations, the upper echelons will have the final word. Moreover, any minister may issue policy directives which every employee is then obliged to follow, regardless of his sympathies. So far as Erhard is concerned, however, since he is said not to be the most capable administrator, there are many charges of his being "taken in tow" by the ministerial bureaucracy.[8]

The BDI and its associations have encountered numerous difficulties in the ministries. For example, the Association of the Chemical Industry at one time complained of the failure of the iron and steel division of the Ministry of Economics to give full support to its stand on an export problem, despite the backing of the chemical and foreign trade divisions.[9] In 1959 a confidential publication by another association contained the statement that the division of the Ministry of Economics handling its industrial sphere, despite expressions of good will and understanding concerning its trade in the Common Market, could not

[8] Eschenburg, "Last und Leid der Bürokratie," *Volkswirt*, July 17, 1954. Among others, the SPD and the DGB hold this point of view; *Die Welt*, Aug. 11, 1958. One BDI association staff member claims of having learned his lesson, which was to begin with the lowest level in the Ministry of Economics, since Erhard may say yes to a proposal, but the civil servant may say no later on. This case would seem, however, to be exceptional.

[9] Verband der Chemischen Industrie, *Bericht über die Tätigkeit im Jahre 1951* (n.p., n.d.), p. 23.

convince other divisions within the Ministry that it merited special consideration. But the association was instrumental in setting up a joint committee of civil servants and association representatives for solving its complex problems. Another favorite device used by the same association was to have sympathetic Bundestag deputies plead its cause. When direct negotiations failed to obtain a tariff waiver on several of its products, it asked its deputies to intercede with unspecified ministry officials— again to no avail. Finally the Ministry of Economics, which had originally been divided on the issue, supported the association, only to be blocked by the Ministry of Finance.

This case history illustrates the difficulties encountered by associations in dealing with ministries. Asking a deputy to intercede does not necessarily lead to success, since many civil servants resent such high-powered interference and may act negatively as a result of it. Second, to deal with one's "own" ministry also may not lead to success if other more hostile ministries are involved.[10] And so far as one's "own" ministry is concerned, the BDI has learned that it cannot at all times expect to receive favored treatment there either.[11]

But such restraints do not keep any interest group from presenting its case officially to a ministry. On the contrary, the participation of associations (and of *Länder*) in the drafting of bills is legitimately provided for in the ministerial standing orders. According to Article 23, national associations may be brought

[10] Helmut Wormer, "Wirtschaft verlangt klare Kompetenzen," *Volkswirt*, March 31, 1950.

[11] For instance, one would expect a state secretary in the Ministry of Economics who came from the aluminum industry to remain a friend of industry, especially since he was not so inclined to favor the free market as his boss Erhard. Nevertheless Ludger Westrick showed some degree of independence, although he may have been bound by a directive from Erhard or by clashing policies of foreign governments. One deputy told this author that he once saw Westrick in an effort to alter a draft and found that Westrick would not budge from his position—not because he had no sympathy with the deputy's point of view but because of the French attitude on that particular matter.

in for consultation and may submit documentary evidence, although on important bills this occurs only after there has been an agreement on fundamentals among the cabinet members. The article further stipulates that under no circumstances are consultations to render a cabinet agreement more difficult; nor are all bills to be made public to the associations.[12] Article 25 grants the ministers—or, when politically vital legislation is involved, the chancellor—the right to determine whether their contents are to be made known to Bundestag deputies and the press.[13]

The two articles clearly give a consultative priority to the associations, and have been the cause of understandable dissatisfaction among members of the legislature and of the press. It may occur that a deputy, unless he happens to be associated with certain interest groups, knows less about the content of the government's legislative program than certain association officials. As a consequence a civil servant may develop a feeling of superiority over the deputies, or there may be an unhealthy dependence by the deputy on the interest groups, except where the party acts as a transmission belt for information.[14] In defense of the ministerial standing orders it may be said that there would be little sense in having the legislators participate in the drafting of bills; their part in the legislative process will come in due time. The press, however, could be informed of developments in the drafting process—and in fact it often is.

There is a formal machinery for hearings. A ministry may schedule official conferences, which often last for several days, with representatives of national associations, in which the draft

[12] Lechner and Hülshoff, *Parlament und Regierung*, pp. 410–411. Article 23 refers to Part II of the standing orders.

[13] *Ibid.*, p. 411. This article before its revision was even more negative toward the two groups, and in effect prohibited submitting drafts to them, other than when exceptions were made by the ministries.

[14] One industry deputy frankly told this author that he always inquires of his organization what the ministry was planning in the legislative field, and what steps he should undertake in the Bundestag.

will be discussed point by point, and the associations are given an opportunity to make their arguments for changing it.

Correspondence in ministry and association files reveals that many associations interpret the ministerial orders as giving them a right to be heard, and object strenuously when they are not consulted—especially concerning tariff bills, on which the ministries may be secretive so as to avoid having a swarm of lobbyists descend on them. In 1956 a letter to Erhard from the BDI complained that the two previous tariff reductions had been carried out without consulting the industrial circles affected, and expressed hope that in the future there would be consultations before the government took action.[15]

Normally, during the process of drafting legislation, the BDI's professional staff are in constant touch, informally, with the staffs in the ministries. Attempts to obtain confidential information or to change the substance of the draft will be directed toward those civil servants known to be trustworthy and to be friendly to their cause. (The state secretary, or the minister himself, may even be approached.) The number of telephone calls or letters will vary, but there will be efforts to keep them to a minimum in order not to alienate anyone on the ministerial staff. Any preliminary draft that the BDI succeeds in obtaining will be circulated among the member associations for comment, and a memorandum will then be sent, or further meetings will be arranged with the appropriate civil servants. In other instances, the BDI may receive an oral summary from a friendly civil servant if a secret stamp on the draft precludes circulation.

It is not at all unusual for a ministry to be in close touch with the BDI—all unknown to the public. Secrecy may be invoked in order to establish a favorable climate between the two forces, or

[15] BDI, Bericht über den Aussenhandel, Feb. 20, 1956. Dissatisfaction also arises in the BDI if at other times the ministries submit draft bills to it requiring such a swift reply that there is no time to prepare adequate counterproposals.

perhaps to put association officials under obligation so as to extract some concessions from them in return.[16]

There are other tactical considerations. In instances when legislation is pending that appears to threaten the BDI, its representatives may agree (however reluctantly) to accept a modified version which will hurt its interests less. On occasion the national business associations may settle among themselves who is to represent the business point of view, and what stand is to be taken on any particular bill. The DIHT, for example, may assume the offensive in attempting to emasculate the bill, with the understanding that the BDI will hold its fire until that battle is lost, and then step forward with a compromise proposal—or vice versa.

The BDI must also take care not to appear to oppose a bill—for example one favoring the consumer—that may have strong public support. This means that its public relations call for a high degree of finesse and of sensitivity to the mood of the public.[17]

Another possible point of contact for the BDI and similar associations is through ministerial advisory councils responsible for drafting policy papers on fundamental questions—although since these are composed mostly of academicians who are not (with some exceptions) influenced by association executives, and since their recommendations often are not accepted by senior ministry officials, the BDI makes relatively little use of this approach. However, a built-in influence is available in those pro-

---

[16] That the initiative may occasionally be taken by the ministry rather than the interest groups is evident from the call made by a civil servant at work in the Ministry of Transport on the draft of a transportation bill (1960) to a staff member in the Automobile Industry Association in order to obtain its views. The staff member in turn went to the BDI for documentary materials, consulted one or two colleagues in his office, and then wrote a memorandum to the civil servant, who found the information and recommendations most useful. Occasionally the BDI or one of its associations will be responsible for an initial draft, which will then be transmitted to parliament via the government or via a deputy friendly to industry.

[17] See p. 263 for a case history of a stock-corporation law.

fessors who have an ideological affinity to the industrial point of view. It is of interest that in 1963 Chancellor Erhard, after receiving parliamentary approval, made plans to set up a governmental advisory council on economic and social problems, which would issue an annual economic report.

The BDI uses substantially the same tactics in attempting to influence the drafts of bills as it does to influence administrative decrees. Concerning the latter, such groups have no legal right to be consulted, but in practice they are often granted the opportunity. Likewise, there are no substantive differences in the tactics used by the BDI from those of its affiliated associations, except that the BDI has more prestige and will generally have easier access to top policymakers. Still, an association head may bypass the BDI and see a minister when issues directly affecting his own industry are at stake. When business is booming, contacts at all levels are less frequent; but when some industries face an economic crisis, the ministries swarm with visiting industrialists and association executives.

Individual firms hoping to influence legislation will normally channel their requests through their association and thus indirectly through the BDI. Major firms, on the other hand, have an entrée to ministerial offices through their directors or lobbyists—a direct activity they justify on the ground that they cannot wait for a published draft of a bill when important decisions are at stake. Their main concern is to obtain a copy of the draft bill at the initial stage. Occasionally a national association may disapprove of firms that maintain such contacts because they may give rise to jurisdictional conflicts harmful to the entire industry, and because the burden upon the ministries is lightened if they are not obliged to deal with individual firms.

The BDI, its constituent associations, and their member firms seek access not only to the executive branch at the national level, but also to that at the *Länder* level. If the governments of the latter are under the control of conservative parties, access is facilitated; where the SPD is in power, there may be stiff obstacles. In either event the key man is the *Land* minister of economics, who largely determines the fate of economic legislation passing through the Bundesrat. As on the national level, there is a system of informal and formal consultations between ministries and interest groups. Informal meetings will be sought mainly with the civil servants responsible for the drafting of bills on the *Land* level, and for advising the Bonn ministries on national legislation affecting the *Länder*. When such legislation is pending, the BDI will mobilize its apparatus both at Bonn and at *Länder* headquarters. Formal consultations may be made through economic and social advisory councils to the ministries —such as in Hesse, where sixty-four members represent business and labor on a parity basis. But in practice the effectiveness of such councils has been limited.

A BDI regional officer told of his efforts to lobby for a pending bill to bring about a change from public to semiprivate ownership of the Volkswagen firm. To create adequate support for a bill which was in tune with the BDI objective of limiting government ownership of industry, he launched an extensive publicity campaign that included the publication of unsigned articles written by his office staff. To win over an uncommitted *Land* cabinet, he also held several talks with the *Land* finance minister, whom he knew quite well, and who subsequently pressed for executive approval of the draft. When the cabinet gave its approval, the regional officer felt that he had been partly instrumental in seeing the bill clear the first hurdle. (Later it received legislative approval and was enacted into law.)

Other instances of success for the BDI and its affiliates include the dissolution of the Bavarian Ministry of Transport and its incorporation into the Ministry of Economics, for which the Bavarian regional office could take partial credit. The North Rhine–Westphalian chemical affiliate boasted of success in negotiating with the *Land* government to strike out certain clauses adverse to industry in a draft bill on water usage. On the other hand, the Bavarian regional office lost out in its negotiations with Bavarian civil servants over a question of fees for new building construction.[18] These are, of course, no more than isolated instances, and are in no way a gauge of the total effect of BDI activities at the *Land* executive and administrative levels—an effect obviously impossible to quantify with any degree of accuracy.

PATRONAGE AND LOBBYING

The BDI succeeds best both at Bonn and in the *Länder* ministries if there are civil servants whose political bosses hold views attuned to its own. A patronage or spoils system, more extensive than in the time of the Weimar Republic, is in effect and has facilitated some identity of views. After World War II the Allies attempted to make the civil service nonpartisan; but they were hampered by the influence of interest groups, including the churches, and the government parties, on the personnel policies of the ministries. Many posts were filled on the basis of the applicant's party or association affiliations.[19] The result is that a majority of civil servants in Bonn reportedly are in sympathy with the aims of the CDU.[20] Hence even in the matter of promotions, merit may be less important than loyalty to party or association. This is most unfortunate, for as a consequence civil servants are timid or reluctant to make decisions unpopular with their bosses. Theoretically, the state secretary protects his ministry from undue pressure by parties and interest groups, but his own uncertain tenure puts him in a weak bargaining position.[21]

[18] On Bavaria see Landesverband der Bayrischen Industrie, *Jahresbericht 1952* and *Geschäftsbericht 1956* (mimeographed), pp. 33–34. On North Rhine–Westphalia, see Verband der Chemischen Industrie, *Wirtschaftspolitik im Chemieberich 1959/60* (n.p., n.d.), p. 53.

[19] Herz, in *West German Leadership and Foreign Policy*, ed. Speier and Davison, p. 107.

[20] According to a confidential report issued by a national party, the highest number is found in Interior, followed in decreasing order by Foreign Affairs, Labor, Defense, Economics, All-German Affairs, and Finance.

[21] See Kaiser, *Die Repräsentation organisierter Interessen*, p. 273; Eschen-

The extent to which the BDI has been involved in patronage cannot be determined; but resistance to it on the part of many civil servants remains a fact. No wonder, then, that the BDI has criticized the civil service on a number of occasions. The Federation has objected to the general coolness toward employers on the part of civil servants, and in its anxiety over rising taxes has warned about a burgeoning bureaucratic establishment.[22] Some BDI officials, however, have told its critics in industry not to be constantly denouncing the bureaucracy if they hope to see the caliber of the service maintained and governmental planning to be held to a minimum.[23]

That the caliber of the civil service is not at an optimum high is evident to any reader of German newspapers. One problem is that civil servants in the executive branch have been exposed to frequent *démarches* by deputies currying favors with their constituents. In several cases deputies have appeared in the Koblenz headquarters of the Defense Ministry's Office of Procurement, or at the Ministry itself—where lavish defense contracts have been awarded to thousands of firms—in order to obtain details of those contracts, and to provide the names of firms seeking them, for the information of civil servants. But such visits in themselves are not evidence of collusion or payoff.

Occasionally a more serious scandal, involving civil servants, deputies, and industrialists, has rocked the placid Bonn community, testifying to the ubiquity of corruption in most political systems. Here once again much of the excitement has centered around the Ministry of Defense. Several civil servants at the Koblenz headquarters implicated themselves by accepting gifts from firms to which, for example, they had revealed certain

---

burg, *Herrschaft der Verbände* (Stuttgart, 1955), *Der Beamte in Partei und Parlament* (Frankfurt/M., 1952), "Ämterpatronage im Parteienstaat," *Politische Studien*, V, No. 61 (May 1955), 23–27, *Ämterpatronage* (Stuttgart, 1961), pp. 66–70.

[22] *UB*, No. 10, March 12, 1959; *JB*, 1956–1957, p. 19.

[23] Thus, O. A. Friedrich in *Gehen wir aufeinander zu*, pp. 42–43.

contract specifications. On the floor of the Bundestag, Defense Minister Strauss was less vehement concerning the behavior of the civil servants than concerning that of the firms, whose lobbying activities were far in excess of those evident during the Weimar period. At that time, he said, respect for the integrity of the civil servant had been higher; but after World War II, in part as an outgrowth of the American occupation, lobbying had greatly expanded. The morality of civil servants was undermined by industrialists who took them out to dinner and who showered them with opera tickets, furniture, baby presents, whisky, cars, and refrigerators. In conclusion, Strauss called on industry to stop this practice immediately, before the state found itself obliged to take action.[24] Although—as will be seen—the state did take action, industry was surely not alone in being at fault. The alacrity shown by some civil servants in accepting presents in exchange for favors cannot be entirely passed over.

In 1957 the Bundestag dealt with the case of three deputies, members of its Defense Committee, who had been accused of misconduct. It entirely cleared Martin Blank (the director of a steel firm) and Hasso von Manteuffel (a former general), both members of the FDP. The third deputy, Fritz Berendsen (CDU), a former officer and an official of the Klöckner-Humboldt-Deutz steel firm, was accused of misusing his mandate in order to obtain a contract for his firm to build armored tanks. He denied any wrongdoing, asserting that he had not passed secret information or obtained any defense orders for his firm, and insisted that a meeting with Beutler of the BDI had concerned only the decision of a subcommittee of the Bundestag Defense Committee to produce tanks in Germany rather than in France.[25] Whether or not he was guilty, Berendsen's position was compromised, and in 1959 he gave up his Bundestag seat to re-enter the army.

Automobile manufacturing concerns also have been involved

---

[24] As cited in *Handelsblatt*, July 5, 1957.
[25] *Der Spiegel*, VI, No. 43 (Oct. 23, 1957); No. 45 (Nov. 6, 1957).

in scandals at Bonn concerning their practice of lending expensive automobiles to members of the administration for good will and political purposes. In 1958 it led to the arrest of Hans Kilb, a personal assistant to the Chancellor, on suspicion of bribery. Similar charges were lodged against Dr. Fritz Könecke and Rolf Staelin, directors of the Mercedes-Benz Company; Friedrich Hummelsheim, the company's Bonn lobbyist; and Werner Brombach, a government counselor and assistant to the Bundestag Transport Committee. Kilb was judged not guilty after he proved that he had used two cars consecutively (he had wrecked the first one) with the tacit assent of the Chancellor. Hummelsheim had given a car to Brombach, but Brombach apparently had not passed on any of the committee's secrets to the company.[26] In still another case, Colonel Löffelholz of the Ministry of Defense was sentenced to three months in jail because he allowed automobile firms interested in obtaining government contracts to pay his traveling expenses and to put cars at his disposal while he was on official visits to their factories.[27]

Although several industrial managers active in the BDI figured in these scandals, the BDI was not directly involved. Berg, speaking for German industry as a whole, deplored the Koblenz scandals, and declared that industry was not running after defense contracts. The SPD called his answer unsatisfactory, and suggested that the BDI establish a committee of censure. The BDI retorted that as a federation of federations it could neither exclude individuals nor try them, pointing out that it had established an advisory defense committee which had been consulted by the Ministry.[28]

The SPD and DGB then urged the government to take action

[26] The SPD was bitter about the entire case, and charged the government with handing over the case to a judge who was deemed friendly to itself. *FAZ*, Nov. 7, 1958. See also *New York Times*, Nov. 14, 1958; *Die Zeit*, Jan. 20, 1958.

[27] *Die Welt*, July 30, 1959.

[28] *Industriekurier*, June 1, 1957; *Die Welt*, July 27, 1957; *Vorwärts*, Aug. 2, 1957.

to prevent further scandals. When in 1958 they demanded that the names of lobbyists be kept on file, the government pointed out the extreme difficulty of defining a lobbyist. One of its spokesmen inquired whether all persons, including deputies, who had ever visited or written to the Ministry of Defense to ask consideration for a firm, were to be included. The SPD retorted by declaring that the majority of Bundestag deputies had failed to support its position out of fear that not one but a number of deputies would be listed as lobbyists.[29]

Yet pressures from the SPD and from the public forced the Ministry of Defense to take action. In 1959 the Ministry laid down several guidelines: civil servants were not to accept presents from firms; they were to restrict official contacts with firms to a minimum, and were to hold talks in ministerial offices, not in restaurants, canteens, or private lodgings.[30] Further regulations drafted by the Ministry had real teeth in them. They would have subjected lobbyists to a fine amounting to 10 per cent of the initial bid on contracts extending up to ten years if any collusion were uncovered. The BDI and other associations put pressure on the Ministry to reduce this stiff penalty. The Ministry, yielding, stipulated that the fine would amount only to the equivalent of two months' salary for the lobbyist involved, but that the lobbyist would have to be discharged by the company if the charge of bribery were proved.[31]

In 1962 orders issued by the Minister of the Interior outlined categories for bribes: no federal civil servant might accept automobiles, free holidays, low-interest loans, or other major gifts and favors, but he might accept simple gifts such as writing pads and calendars, as well as "meals and drinks if he thinks his duties require participation in social events."[32] The Minister

[29] Strauss (CDU) vs. Schmidt (SPD), Bundestag, 3rd el. pd., 24th session, April 23, 1958, pp. 1297 ff.

[30] *Süddeutsche Zeitung*, Aug. 14, 1959.

[31] *Der Spiegel*, XV (July 19, 1961), 18–19; *Vorwärts*, Sept. 27, 1961.

[32] *New York Times*, Feb. 2, 1962; *Bulletin*, No. 23, Feb. 2, 1962, p. 193.

emphasized that the proportion of civil servants involved in the scandals of previous years had been very small in relation to the total number.

Regardless of the small number involved, the scandals are possibly symptomatic of the prevailing mores in German society, in which a drive for material gains and rapid professional advancement has become paramount.[33] If a high standard of living becomes more widespread, perhaps the prestige and morale of the civil servants will improve, and illegal acts will decrease.

CONCLUSION

The study of the BDI in relation to the executive and the civil service leads to the question of which it considers more important—the executive or the legislature. Will it be the executive officer or civil servant, or will it be the deputy, who is consulted more often? To which will the industrial association address the greater number of memoranda and reports? There can be no doubt of the answer. The executive is clearly the primary target of the BDI, as it is of most other economic associations, even though the legislature is important as a secondary target (and now and then even a primary one). It may be asked why, if the content of legislation is the most important concern to the BDI, it should not concentrate its fire on the Bundestag. However, since in West Germany as in many other countries, the formulation of bills falls increasingly into the lap of the executive, it is no wonder that parliament tends more and more to become simply an organ of "approbation and reprobation."[34] As laws become more general in character, they must be filled in by numerous administrative edicts, whose necessarily specialized content calls for the expertise at the disposal of the interest

---

[33] Eschenburg touches on this theme in *Der Sold des Politikers* (Stuttgart, 1959).

[34] Erich Kaufman, *Zur Problematik des Volkswillens* (Berlin-Leipzig, 1931), p. 13, cited by Kaiser, *Die Repräsentation organisierter Interessen*, p. 268.

groups. Thus not only the nature and content of bills, but also a political balance between the two branches of government, is now at stake. In the postwar period the executive has been more sympathetic to the aspirations of industry than the legislature, which "is sometimes forced to seek popular support by measures pleasing to the political left."[35]

The importance of the executive has led the BDI, as has been seen, to maintain a close bond with it. Thus the number of memoranda sent to administration officials far exceeds the number of those addressed to the legislators. In the period from 1949 to 1958 nearly 83 per cent of the official memoranda sent by the BDI were to executive organs, and only 7 per cent were to legislative organs (the remainder went to the Federal Bank and other autonomous bodies).[36] Unofficial contacts and conferences have been arranged by the BDI with members of both branches, in accord with the progress of particular legislation. The ratio is more nearly equal if the number of visits and telephone calls rather than of official messages is counted.[37]

To measure the success of the BDI in influencing legislation during the drafting process in the executive branch is a difficult task. The BDI itself, however, publicly acknowledges in its yearbooks not only its successes but also what are designated as partial successes, and failures. An assessment of these will be made in later chapters.[38] In order to improve its chances of success, the BDI has urged the adoption of the Swiss system, calling for obligatory consultation of interest groups at every stage in the

[35] Wahrhaftig, in *West German Leadership and Foreign Policy*, ed. Speier and Davison, p. 45.

[36] Wilhelm Hennis, "Verfassungsordnung und Verbandseinfluss," *Politische Vierteljahresschrift*, II, No. 1 (March 1961), 25. In one 12-month period (1961–1962) 98 memoranda were sent. Of these 90 went to the ministries, 4 to Bundestag committees, and 4 to UNICE. *JB*, 1961–1962, pp. 170–174.

[37] No BDI staff member was able to estimate what the ratio then would be.

[38] See Chapters XI–XIV.

drafting of a bill or ordinance.[39] However, some leading German political scientists, and other experts, are already critical of the pressures exerted upon the executive branch by the associations. Professor Theodor Eschenburg speaks of a dominion of the government by the associations, with the government serving merely as a regulatory agency.[40] Professor Joseph Kaiser warns of the inability of associations to reconcile their special interests with the interests of the nation.[41] Professor Werner Weber decries the weakening of state authority and the power of oligarchical groups.[42] All are wary of the limited "colonization" of the civil service by interest groups. A CDU deputy complains that the associations have gone too far in clogging up the ministerial channels with minutiae.[43] Other deputies assail what they consider an unholy alliance between interest groups and the administration, which together make the decisions and then merely ask for parliamentary ratification. Similarly, trade-union spokesmen are critical of what they see as the influence exerted by employer associations on the executive; of the identity of interests between the two; and of the failure of the government to take the point of view of labor sufficiently into consideration.[44]

There is a good deal of validity in these charges. The employer community undoubtedly has a significant influence on the executive branch, and parliament is often subordinate to the executive. This kind of power structure exists in many other countries. But in West Germany, as elsewhere, there are also countervailing forces which limit the power of the business community and even of the executive branch over the legislative branch—not to mention the internal checks within the executive branch itself.

[39] *JB*, 1958–1959, p. 21.
[40] *Herrschaft der Verbände, passim.*
[41] *Die Repräsentation organisierter Interessen*, p. 273.
[42] *Staats- und Selbstverwaltung in der Gegenwart* (Göttingen, 1953).
[43] Kleindinst in Bundestag, 2nd el. pd., 110th session, Oct. 28, 1955.
[44] *DGB News Letter*, No. 9, Oct. 10, 1958.

PART THREE: IMPACT ON
POLICY AND LEGISLATION

XI

Economic Policy at Home

THE attitude of the BDI toward the West German state is of course contingent upon the economic policies of the latter. The Federation decries the general tendency of government to encroach upon industry with regulations made by a "ubiquitous bureaucracy which seeks perfectionism," and likewise deplores the growth of the welfare state.[1] It contends that in a period of prosperity there ought to be less interference in the economy, with more freedoms allowed to the employer, and that the government should concern itself with maintaining order rather than with reshaping the existing society. If the government fails to limit its activities, the BDI asserts, then the employers must be the alert guardians of their interests.[2] Only in a period of economic crisis would the BDI be likely to abandon this neo-liberal stance and to seek government aid in the form of subsidies and of favorable tax, credit, and currency regulations. This theoretical position, however, does not quite correspond to re-

[1] JB, 1955–1956, p. 19; Winschuh, Das neue Unternehmerbild, p. 219.

[2] In this view the BDI officials differ from those neo-liberals who support the creation of a strong state capable of guarding the public interest and keeping the multitude of special interests in check. Cf. JB, 1956–1957, p. 21; O. A. Friedrich, Das Leitbild, p. 27.

ality. Although there has been no major crisis, the BDI has in fact sought help on a number of occasions. Minister Erhard once told the BDI, "You don't have to call the fire brigade just because the milk boils over—the fire department should be called only if the whole house is ablaze."[3]

So far this study has investigated the techniques used by the BDI to influence public opinion, the political parties, and the legislative and executive branches. It is now time to relate the use of these techniques to specific cases in the realm of domestic economy, beginning with one of the bitterest and most protracted struggles of the BDI with the government—the seven-year debate over cartel legislation.

CARTEL LEGISLATION

The BDI was the staunchest opponent of the government's effort to bring about an effective anticartel statute. It used all available resources and pressures first to delay legislation and then to modify its chief provisions. A detailed study of the struggle will reveal the array of techniques at the disposal of each protagonist and the measure of success each was able to achieve.

In the antitrust field, several decartelization and deconcentration laws were promulgated after World War II by British, French, and United States occupation authorities. In the period before the war, between two and three hundred trusts, forming thousands of cartels, had been increasingly controlled by a few wealthy and powerful families. A 1923 statute aimed at cartel abuses had not been effective in curbing these trusts.[4] The post-1945 occupation laws, intended as a temporary measure, were

---

[3] In a speech to the 1958 annual convention; *The Bulletin*, May 20, 1958. See also Scheuner, *Die staatliche Intervention im Bereich der Wirtschaft, Rechtsformen und Rechtsschutz*, Heft 11, Veröffentlichungen der Vereinigung der Deutschen Staatsrechtslehrer (Berlin, 1954), pp. 1–66.

[4] Piettre, *L'économie allemande contemporaine 1945–1952*, p. 136; Brady, "Manufacturing Spitzenverbände," *Political Science Quarterly*, LVI, No. 2 (June 1941), 199–225.

designed to prohibit excessive concentration of economic power by breaking up large combines and prohibiting cartels. The regulations sounded impressive on paper and were instituted with much fanfare, but in the long run they proved to be ineffective.[5]

The German government's failure to enact comparable legislation immediately after it assumed sovereignty, together with opposition by business, led to the obstruction of Allied aims. As early as March 1949 the Bipartite Control Office asked the German Bizonal Economic Council to submit a draft law which would prohibit cartels and other restrictions on competition. In accordance with this request Erhard, who was then director of the economic administration of the western zones, appointed a committee of specialists to prepare the draft, and by July 1949 it was ready.[6] But by that time the formation of the Federal Government was pending, and the draft was simply filed away. In 1950, shortly after the new government had been installed, Dr. Eberhard Günther, then head of the cartel section in the Ministry of Economics, prepared a new draft, again aimed at the outright prohibition of cartels. Its submission to the cabinet in May 1951 received further prolonged discussion in the executive branch and led to demands for changes by the Allies. In March 1952 the cabinet finally agreed upon a new and tougher bill, and submitted it to parliament for approval. Embodying the same concepts as the Sherman and Clayton acts, the bill outlawed horizontal cartel agreements and called for an administrative agency with the right to exercise controls.

Upon learning the details of the bill, the BDI launched a massive counterattack. Its own position, then and later, was as follows: it favored a bill incorporating the principle of cartel controls, registration, and publicity, and the right of the gov-

[5] United States trust-busters envisaged the breakup of 11 steel combines into 26 separate steel units and 20 independent coal companies. On this subject see Henry C. Wallich, *Mainsprings of the German Revival* (New Haven, 1955), pp. 133–135, 382–384.

[6] Erhard, *Prosperity through Competition*, pp. 117–118.

ernment to take action against any firm abusing the principles of a free economy—but not the right of the government to prohibit cartels outright, which would amount to discrimination against industry. The BDI defended cartels for their moderating effect on business cycles, and for their preservation of small business. It took note of the exigencies of increasing economic integration in western Europe—which, it argued, could be achieved only if there were less competition between enterprises. It cited other western European nations where cartels were regulated but not prohibited, and the United States, where the prohibition of cartels was considered to be ineffective.[7]

The BDI's attitude can be understood only if the strongly entrenched cartel movement in German history is recalled, and if the desire of the average businessman to avoid extreme competition, to the extent of forming trusts, is kept in mind. The Ministry of Economics, committed as it was to the neo-liberal doctrine, remained unconvinced by the BDI's reasoning, and held fast to its view of cartels as smothering the free market economy through price and market manipulations. Erhard and Berg each set about organizing groups of employers sympathetic to their respective positions, and commissioned leading professors to prepare studies supporting them. The outcome was a complete deadlock, and the controversy was carried to the summit level. According to one report, BDI officers complained to Adenauer in a private meeting that Erhard was too inflexible, and that unless changes were made in the bill employers might be reluctant to make campaign contributions in the coming election. But Adenauer, confronted by the threatened resignation of Erhard if no support were tendered him, did not then bow to the pressure of the BDI.[8]

While its merits were being fiercely debated outside the legis-

[7] Many of these arguments were cited by Berg in an exchange of letters with Erhard in October 1952. See *UB*, No. 33, Aug. 14, 1952; *JB*, 1951–1952, pp. 103-104.

[8] Interview with a well-informed Bundestag deputy. It was not possible to ascertain the date of this meeting.

lative chambers, the bill landed in the lap of the Bundestag's Economic Affairs Committee. But Erhard's inability to rally the unqualified support of the CDU or of public opinion, the view that the measure represented a heritage of Allied policy designed to weaken German industry, and the pending adjournment of the first Bundestag before the 1953 election, all contributed to the failure of the bill to reach the floor and to be voted upon.

After the election the government made efforts to persuade the new legislature to enact a basically unchanged bill. It was approved by the cabinet on February 17, 1954; three months later it was approved by the Bundesrat, but only after some stormy sessions whose result was a host of amendments that weakened the bill's stringent provisions. Ironically, many of these amendments were introduced by *Land* governments dominated by the CDU. While the Bundesrat in effect allowed five or six major exemptions to the cartel prohibition, the cabinet, on reconsidering the bill after the Bundesrat had voted on it, allowed three exemptions as compared to none before, thus for the first time weakening its own bill. The BDI had in fact proposed fourteen exemptions while the bill was still in the executive branch. The cabinet's normal procedure would have been to submit the bill immediately to the Bundestag; but it delayed the move for nearly a year, until March 1955.

During this interval Erhard deliberately postponed having the Bundestag consider the bill, partly because he wished parliament to give priority to one on tax reform, and even more because he wanted a full discussion of the cartel measure with those concerned, especially the BDI. As early as October 1953, in an effort to resolve some of industry's differences with the government, Berg suggested to Erhard that he set up a mixed commission consisting of officials of the Ministries of Economics and Justice and of the BDI. The government agreed, even though to do so had the rather unorthodox effect of putting the BDI on an equal level with itself in the formulation of policy.

In February 1954, without much publicity, the group began meetings that lasted until October, when Erhard and Berg issued a joint statement to the press announcing a significant *rapprochement*. What had happened was that Erhard had yielded to the BDI to the extent of recognizing industry's plea for more exemptions to the prohibition clause.[9]

The SPD was displeased. A proponent of a tough bill, it stood by Erhard's original opposition to cartels of any kind. This was a reversal of the party's historic position; a few decades before, its neo-Marxist stance had led it to view cartels and trusts as ripe for a socialist take-over, and therefore to be given whatever rope they needed to hang themselves. The downfall of the Weimar governments, partly as a result of the antidemocratic attitude of many cartel industrialists, had caused it to re-examine its position.

In March 1955 the Bundestag finally had its first chance to discuss the bill. The SPD promptly attacked the manner in which the BDI and the government had arrived at a compromise, asserting that although it was proper for associations to be heard by the ministries, it had been improper for the two sides to reach an accord and meanwhile to keep the Bundestag waiting for ten months.[10]

In reply, Erhard denied that the result of the talks had been a binding formal agreement, asserting that they simply indicated the limits within which an understanding with industry could be reached. Since this defense was not altogether convincing, the BDI, which was also sensitive to the SPD's charges, came to Erhard's rescue and at the same time, paradoxically, attacked him. It now declared that it should have been consulted by the government at an earlier stage; that on a number of occasions when it had desired to negotiate with the government it had been rebuffed; that the talks were merely advisory; that it regarded submitting to parliament a bill that had been discussed

9 *JB*, 1954–1955, p. 173.
10 Bundestag, 2nd el. pd., 76th session, March 24, 1955, pp. 4199–4207.

with an outside association as a completely democratic procedure, and not as a bypassing of the legislature; and finally that
it was to the advantage of the Bundestag to know the position
of those who would be affected by the law.[11]

During the negotiations between the BDI and the government, other talks had taken place. Erhard wanted not only to
convince his opponents but to obtain the full support of his own
followers, of whom some were in the camp of the BDI. On July
12, 1954, he called a meeting at Petersberg with a group of
twenty-two employers, primarily representing BDI consumer
goods industries that opposed cartels, to discuss the bill. After
the meeting the employers sent Berg a well-publicized communication in which, claiming to speak for a substantial number
of employers within the BDI, they rejected its position on cartels. Sustained by the presidential board, Berg replied publicly
that the BDI had received the support of the various branches
of industry, and would continue to maintain a policy formulated
under democratic principles.[12]

Naturally, the BDI was enraged at Erhard's attempts to drive
a wedge into the ranks of industry and to publicize its differences, especially while negotiations with his ministry officials
were in progress. The BDI presidential board asked the member
associations not to discuss differences publicly for fear of jeop-
ardizing any agreement.[13] It may be asked whether Erhard did
not deliberately convene the Petersberg group in order to force
concessions from the BDI during the negotiations. During this
same time, according to one deputy, the managers of large firms
who supported Erhard wrote indignantly to Berg, accusing him
of pretending to speak for the entire industry when all he spoke
for was the association management's point of view.[14] The split
in its ranks made the BDI extremely sensitive to this kind of

[11] *JB*, 1954–1955, pp. 173–174; *FAZ*, Nov. 13, 1954.
[12] *Mitteilungen*, No. 8/9, Sept. 10, 1954, pp. 3–4.
[13] *Präsidialsitzung*, Sept. 3, 1954.
[14] Interview with a Bundestag deputy.

criticism. Later it admitted that some industrialists had opted for the prohibition of cartels, but argued that an "overwhelming majority" were opposed, and that after consulting their membership, "nearly all" the constituent associations had approved the principle of prohibiting cartel abuses only.[15]

From the moment the government had forwarded the cartel bill to the Bundestag, the BDI carried on an intensive effort to force through major amendments to the bill. It prepared material to be used by two deputies in the parliamentary debate that followed the first reading; it met with numerous ministry officials who were to appear at committee hearings; and it held conferences with officers of other national business organizations, and with sympathetic deputies in the Bundestag Economic Affairs Committee.

This committee, which had primary responsibility for the bill—although other committees also dealt with it—began its deliberations in May 1955. Along with the government's bill, it also considered another introduced by Deputy Franz Böhm (CDU), calling for a prohibition of cartels with no significant exceptions, and a third introduced by Deputy Hermann Höcherl (CSU), calling for the control of cartel abuses. The BDI of course stood squarely behind Höcherl's draft; but it soon realized that the opposition of a constellation of political forces made its passage extremely unlikely. These consisted of a non-parliamentary bloc made up of AsU, the wholesale and retail trade, and the cooperatives, and of a parliamentary bloc composed of the SPD, the CDU's left wing, and a majority of the FDP, which favored the theory of free competition. The BDI could hope to receive support only from some national business organizations, and in parliament from the conservative wing of the CDU and a few minor parties.

Its strategy was therefore to put pressure on the Bundestag for swift passage of a revised government bill. It had the satisfaction, in 1956, of seeing Hellwig, who was then head of the

[15] *JB*, 1954–1955, pp. 172–173.

DI, made chairman of the Economic Affairs Committee, while the bill was under discussion by that body. Hellwig made some effort to dissociate himself from the industrial point of view, but his identification with organized industry made this difficult. Naturally the BDI benefited from Hellwig's chairmanship, for he had given valuable advice to the BDI presidential board on questions of strategy and tactics even before he became chairman. But despite this advantage, the BDI's hope of achieving victory in the committee came to an end with the first ballot, in which the vote was 24 to 7 for the prohibition of cartels. Thereupon its attention was concentrated on key deputies in the major parties. Among various CDU organs, it attempted to work through an *ad hoc* committee on cartels, formed to achieve a compromise within the party, and through the standing committee on economics and agriculture. A deputy sympathetic toward industry, who headed the latter, urged the BDI officials concerned with the cartel question to make certain concessions for the sake of promoting unity within the CDU. Another deputy urged them not to issue any further memoranda to Bundestag deputies, whose response had become increasingly negative as a result of a flood of publicity releases from various pressure groups.[16]

Three members of the BDI's committee on competition (which deals with cartels) were asked to present their views to the executive board of the CDU Committee for Economic Policy, chaired by Etzel, a majority of whose members supported the position of industry. On the other hand, the Social Affairs Committees of the Christian-Democratic Working Force called for a strong prohibition of cartels. Adenauer continued to give somewhat wavering support to Erhard in spite of several attempts by industry to dissuade him from it. The CDU's lack of unity on a key economic issue delayed a vote on the measure. BDI officials also had a chance to be heard by the FDP parliamentary group, but were uncertain how effective they had been.

[16] Protocol of plenary session, BDI committee on competition, held on June 14, 1955.

While these pressures were being exerted at the national level, deputies from industry at the state level worked diligently to rally support for the BDI position.[17]

Not less important than the backing of parties was the achievement of unity within the business world itself. This proved a vain hope, since the AsU stood firm for the prohibition of cartels and for a stronger bill. It accused Erhard of yielding to the BDI in modifying one section, dealing with market-dominating companies, to the degree that the bill had practically no effect in prohibiting or regulating them. The impression was inescapable, according to the AsU, that Erhard lent his ear only to big business, and ignored the small independent employer. It urged that the proposed cartel agency should have the power to interfere in cases where large corporations tended to squeeze out smaller ones.[18]

Although the AsU remained a rebel, after a series of negotiations the BDI was able to arrive at a compromise with the other national business organizations that had originally called for the prohibition of cartels. On September 1, 1956, they signed a joint declaration upholding the principle of free competition and at the same time asking the Bundestag to grant a number of exceptions to the prohibition of cartels.[19] In effect the BDI had abandoned its opposition to the prohibition of cartels; it now declared itself ready to support a less stringent government bill, not from any change in conviction but as a matter of political realism. Its opposition had after all been formidable, ranging all the way from the major political parties to a section of its own ranks, including some member associations not affected by the cartel legislation, which had urged it to abandon its extremist position.[20]

[17] Such as C. Becker, in the Committee for Economic Policy of the CDU-Rhineland branch.

[18] *Volkswirt*, May 21, 1955.

[19] *Mitteilungen*, No. 8/9, Aug.-Sept. 1956.

[20] Speech by Stein in Hagen, as reported in BDI committee on competition; Circular, Dec. 7, 1956, pp. 7–8.

The arrival, after a long delay, at a compromise among nearly all the factions of the business community, amounting to acceptance of the government bill, made it easier for Erhard to gain parliamentary approval. He was reported once again to have threatened to resign unless Adenauer threw his full support behind the emasculated bill.[21] On July 27, 1957, after seven years of deliberations, the Bundestag finally gave its consent, and on January 1, 1958, the bill went into effect. The voting on the bill found the CDU and FDP in favor, the SPD and GB/BHE opposed.[22] Of course many CDU and FDP deputies voted only reluctantly for so watered-down a version of the bill. The SPD, in explaining its negative position, denounced Erhard for failing to stand by the original government bill, which it had supported. Its spokesman complained that without serious resistance he had allowed the industrial wing of the CDU to dominate cartel policy and to riddle the prohibition with exceptions.

There was much truth in the SPD's accusation. In the final Bundestag debate Erhard put on a brave front and acknowledged the changes from the original bill.[23] It may be surmised that he was dissatisfied with the bill as it had been approved, since the original version corresponded with his own economic philosophy. But he had at least succeeded in obtaining parliamentary support for a minimum of prohibition and regulation of cartels, in the knowledge that some success was better than no success at all. And the bill did provide "that any agreements made by business concerns or associations of business enter-

[21] *New York Times*, March 25, 1958.

[22] During this debate Hellwig, speaking for the CDU parliamentary group, declared that in some respects the bill had been made more stringent. He also accused an SPD deputy of an attempt to defame his name by implying that he (Hellwig) was a lobbyist for the industrial wing of the party. The SPD denied this accusation. Three deputies, including the entrepreneur Raestrup, voted against the bill. Raestrup, true to his principles, rejected any type of prohibition principle. Bundestag, 2nd el. pd., 222nd session, July 3, 1957, pp. 13128–13175; 223rd session, July 4, 1957, pp. 13242–13253.

[23] *Ibid.*

prises shall be invalid if their effect is to limit or reduce free competition." It also authorized the government to set up federal and state agencies to administer the law. On the other hand, the BDI had achieved victory to the extent of forcing through eight significant exceptions to the prohibition clause—thus giving authorization to cartels for common standards in production, for the promotion of exports, for industries in distress, and, with the assent of the Cartel Agency, for price adjustments and agreements.[24]

In the opinion of many observers, these exceptions rendered the law pitifully weak. The *Economist* actually called it "useless."[25] The BDI was also somewhat dissatisfied, because there were not enough exceptions. Aware that a stringent administration of the law might cancel some of the gains it had been able to make, the BDI saw its next task as ensuring a "realistic" administration by the Cartel Agency, under a sympathetic director.[26]

When the government quietly made known its intention to nominate Eberhard Günther, head of the cartel section in the Ministry of Economics, to the post, the BDI used political pressure to block his appointment. Since he had been involved in the preparation of the law, the BDI regarded Günther as an enemy of cartels, from whom little sympathy for industry could be expected. BDI executives, working through Hellwig and State Secretary Westrick in an attempt to force Erhard to nomi-

[24] *New York Times*, July 5, 1957. For the full text in English translation, see W. Friedmann (ed.), *Anti-Trust Laws, A Comparative Symposium*, U. of Toronto Faculty of Law Symposium, III (1956), 191–229. For a painstaking commentary see Ivo E. Schwartz, "Antitrust Legislation and Policy in Germany—A Comparative Study," *U. of Pennsylvania Law Review*, 105, No. 5 (March 1957), 617–690; and Viola Gräfin von Bethusy-Huc, *Demokratie und Interessenpolitik* (Wiesbaden, 1962), pp. 36–81.

[25] "Bonn's Elastic Cartel Law," July 20, 1957.

[26] *JB*, 1957–1958, p. 152; HGF, Circular, No. 2/58, Jan. 31, 1958, pp. 25, 29. According to a BDI cartel expert, the Law represents a 70 per cent contribution by Erhard and Günther, 20 per cent by the BDI, and 10 per cent by others.

nate someone else, were able to achieve a delay. They saw
Adenauer, who remained adamant since he did not want to give
the impression he was a tool of industry, and who was becoming
annoyed by the repeated attempts of interest groups to influence
his personnel policy.[27] One BDI cartel staff member admitted
that in retrospect it may have been a tactical mistake to fight
Günther's candidacy since Erhard was set on his nomination,
and since Günther really was the most capable man available
with a knowledge of the law that was second to none.

At any rate, although the BDI was successful in forcing a
year's delay, it could not prevent Günther's eventual appointment. After the Cartel Agency had been established, the BDI
kept up a relentless pressure for a "realistic" administration of
the law. First it sought to circumvent the agency by setting up
a conciliation board for the quiet settlement of disputes between
firms on the question of cartels. But this board has had little to
do since the conflicts have been less often between firms than
between a firm and the government. In the second place, the
BDI has sought to staff the agency with competent and experienced civil servants who would make "elastic" decisions based
on "due reflection" and not on a "narrow bureaucratic interpretation" of the law. To this pressure the government was not
very responsive.

The BDI's views of the agency's record are mixed. It welcomed Günther's attempt to gain the confidence of industry by
creating a healthy climate for conciliation. But it does not care
for the slow pace of decision-making. The quick—and favorable
—decisions the BDI would like to see are difficult to achieve,
since the agency is obliged to keep under review some 205,000
items whose prices have been fixed by the producer. But the
BDI would not appear to have very much cause for complaint.
In four years, only four of the decisions handed down—all in

[27] Personal interview with a deputy; *FAZ*, Dec. 5, 1957.

relatively unimportant fields—have outlawed cartel agreements; the rest were favorable to industry.[28]

The persistent dissatisfaction that continues to be expressed in BDI literature, somewhat inflated for public consumption, takes the following line: At the beginning, the BDI desired to let the agency "work itself in"; but it can no longer repress its critical views, for it now appears that the forces in the agency who want to extend the principle of prohibition are in the ascendant. This may be an accurate statement, since in a commentary appended to the first report of the agency, the government advocated a toughening of the law in order to prevent further concentration in industry. What the BDI wants is a loose interpretation of the law, not based on neo-liberal doctrines, since 75 per cent of German industry is subject to regulations of one kind or another. One BDI spokesman has said, "Industry has the impression that the cartel authorities, faced by two possibilities, always choose the one unfavorable to industry"—largely because of their doctrinal position. The BDI has called on the Ministry of Economics to review the agency's cartel policy.[29] There is little chance, however, should such a review occur, that the Ministry and the agency would differ in their views.

To sum up, it is clear that the fierce dispute between the BDI and the government issued in no clear-cut victory for either side. It demonstrated the power of an organization successfully to delay and alter legislation, especially when that organization

---

[28] Herz, "The Government of Germany," *Major Foreign Powers*, ed. by Gwendolen M. Carter and Herz (4th ed.; New York, 1962), p. 457; *Der Spiegel*, XIV, No. 45 (Nov. 2, 1960), 37.

[29] The impression should not be gained that industry presents a united front in regard to the agency; the ranks even within some of the BDI's constituent associations are divided on the cartel issue. Moreover, an association may assent to one cartel regulation but not to another. *Handelsblatt*, Oct. 20, 1959; Paul Riffel, "Die Einstellung der Industrie zum neuen Kartellrecht," *VR*, No. 41, Oct. 12, 1959; *JB*, 1957–1958, p. 155; 1958–1959, p. 221. The agency report appeared in Bundestag, 3rd el. pd., Drucksache 1,000, April 15, 1959. Also, letter from agency chief Günther, Aug. 10, 1962.

has strong financial resources that may be needed by the governing party at election time. The BDI applied pressure at appropriate times and places; but Erhard and his supporters also had their resources, which they were able to marshall against the BDI. The result was a legislative compromise, which has been followed by continual sparring over the execution and administration of the law.

SMALL BUSINESS

Another dispute in which the BDI has been involved concerns the role of small business in the German economy. The stand of small business generally, against cartels and in favor of free competition, has already been mentioned. Other problems vital to its very existence—such as the accelerated trend toward bigness in industry, and the proposed reform of the tax structure—will be discussed presently. Within the BDI, these problems have been the subject of never-ending discussion. Those elements of small business that consider themselves to be in an inferior position in the BDI have demanded the setting up of a committee to tackle these questions seriously. In 1957, after prodding from Adenauer—who enjoined industry to renounce its passivity, take the initiative, and submit proposals before the government was forced to take action—the BDI high command decided to establish a small business committee.[30] In order to establish a basis for a *rapprochement*, each BDI association was empowered to send two delegates to the committee—one to represent big business and the other to represent small business. This arrangement caused some raised eyebrows, but the BDI maintained that big business could not stand aloof if the problems of small concerns were to be solved.[31]

[30] *Vorstandssitzung*, Nov. 25, 1958.

[31] *JB*, 1958–1959, p. 16. The committee sought to establish close contacts with the corresponding committees or working groups in parliament, the CDU, the Ministry of Economics, and two research institutes in Cologne and Bonn. One of the chief problems discussed at an early stage was a working definition of small business. The committee found this difficult

The setting up of the committee can also be attributed to the BDI's desire to alter the widespread public impression that it was dominated by big business. Typical of the general attitude was the view expressed in a Christian journal, that although a majority of the firms belonging to the BDI were small or medium-sized, their voices could hardly be heard when important economic decisions were to be made; only big business seemed to have enough resources, energy, or interest in public affairs to produce an influence in politics.[32] Most of these sentiments were shared by the AsU. It charged that organizing the committee did not really redress the balance within the BDI since its only function was to serve as a front for big business. "The big 'tubs' will continue sailing under protection, even if many of the small escort ships must pay for their being pressed into service by sinking," sternly warned the AsU's President Flender.[33] Even while he hoped the work of the committee might strengthen the position of small business, he remained skeptical.

That to some extent his skepticism was justified can be seen from the failure of the BDI to settle differences among business establishments of varying sizes on cartels, taxes, and other issues. Berg himself warned that factions within the BDI could only weaken the organization—an outcome its opponents desired. He called on all forces within the BDI to unite on basic principles and to seek solutions acceptable to all.[34] Whether, as the AsU alleged, the committee was intended merely to serve as a smoke screen for the continued dominance of big business, or whether, as Berg claimed, it was a genuine attempt to resolve the schism in employer ranks, is difficult to determine. Berg's own foes did not accuse him of being personally hostile to small business, but

---

because it could not agree on a numerical concept of "small." Committee on competition, Circular 4/59, session of Jan. 28, 1959.

[32] *Christ und Welt*, May 30, 1955.

[33] *Die Aussprache*, VIII (June 1958), 5.

[34] Berg, "Die Wirtschaft an der Jahreswende," *VR*, Dec. 22, 1958.

rather of being the captive of big business. To counter this accusation, Berg was among the first to express agreement with the position of the government that small business in Germany must be kept alive. An examination of the questions of concentration of industry and of tax reform may shed further light on the basic attitude of the BDI toward small business.

CONCENTRATION OF INDUSTRY

No sooner had the furor over the antitrust legislation died down than a heated discussion arose over a related topic, the steady movement of West German industry toward concentration. Before World War II, oligopolies in many branches of industry, notably coal and steel in the Ruhr, had cornered the markets. After the war the Allies, with the aim of removing one threat to peace, launched a deconcentration process, breaking up large trusts into competing firms. But from 1952 on a reconcentration movement has become evident, as mergers, the expansion of large firms, and the elimination of smaller ones have taken place. This development was the result of pressure by industrial groups, such as the Iron and Steel Association, upon German public authorities and upon the European Coal and Steel Community to reverse Allied policy. Thus, to cite but one example, the ECSC granted permission to the Mannesmann concern to reconstitute itself by bringing six subsidiary firms into its corporate structure. Krupp, Thyssen, and Rheinische Stahlwerke are among the giants in coal, steel, and other domains that followed a similar path. The mushrooming of consolidations and trusts has led to the rise of about three hundred industrial moguls, typified by Friedrich Flick, whose empire includes holdings in foundries, steel, paper, chemicals, and the automobile industry.[35]

The industries' own justification has been, first, that Allied deconcentration and decartelization had been damaging to the German economy, and that concentration was a way of repair-

35 *Der Spiegel*, XII, No. 29 (July 16, 1958), 22–24.

ing the damage. (In any event, that the Allies themselves were no longer objecting strenuously to the consolidation movement was clear from their failure to halt Krupp's acquisition of an important steel firm.) In the second place, the Common Market was encouraging businessmen to enlarge their firms in order to meet new competition. In the third place, technical progress and structural changes could only be sustained by large economic units. Krupp spoke of such units as an inevitable process necessary for competition.[36] In the fourth place, concentration was not restricted to Germany, but was part of a worldwide movement. Finally, German legislation encouraged concentration by granting tax benefits to firms that merged their subsidiaries, provided the parent company had a minimum holding of 75 per cent. (The law expired at the end of 1959.)[37]

Among the political parties, reactions to the concentration movement were varied. Within the CDU there was no unity on this controversial question. The big-business wing regarded the problem as nonexistent; the small-business and trade-union wings found it alarming. Adenauer, to satisfy the majority of CDU supporters, could not but side with the latter. Hence, in a government declaration on October 27, 1957, the CDU went on record as saying, "We do not want our nation to consist of a small group of economic rulers and a large majority of dependents."[38] In a reaffirmation of this Marxist-tinged statement, Adenauer told the 1958 CDU congress: "One must make sure that no economic concentrations develop which will rule over the economic and thereby the political life. Economic concentrations can be as dangerous in the hands of employers as those in the hands of workers' organizations."[39]

The first part of this statement was echoed by the SPD. It considered the legislature to have been undermined by anony-

---

[36] *New York Times*, Jan. 18, 1959.
[37] *Financial Times*, March 28, 1960.
[38] *New York Times*, Jan. 17, 1959.
[39] CDU Deutschlands, *8. Bundesparteitag, 1958*, p. 23.

mous economic forces with enormous capital resources whose political power was steadily growing.[40] The FDP saw a danger to the free economy in the concentration movement if too many small business concerns failed to survive and if there was an increased demand for socialization.[41] The trade unions of course vigorously denounced concentration, fearing that it would lead to conservative political policies, the undermining of democracy, and a social dismantling process comparable to that of the pre-Hitler era.[42]

In the employer camp there were clashing points of view. President Flender of the AsU, as the spokesman for the independent entrepreneur, sharply denounced the concentration movement with its market-dominating firms.[43] Similar complaints were made by tradesmen and artisans. The BDI was caught in an anomalous position. Although on the one hand it could not deny the existence of concentration, neither could it denounce the tendency, since its own leading policy-makers represented firms enmeshed in the concentration process. Berg was of course aware of the necessity of balancing the interests of big and small firms, but he was not sufficiently aware of the political dynamite of the concentration movement until the initiative taken by Adenauer made him realize its seriousness. At a conference following the 1958 CDU congress, Adenauer asked Berg, Beutler, and Stein whether industry would settle the problem itself through voluntary action, or whether the Ministries of Economics and Finance would have to prepare legislation limiting its freedom of action, thereby compounding its difficulties. Although the BDI could not have been happy about the threat of government interference, Berg merely reminded the Chancellor that industry had already taken meas-

[40] *Vorwärts*, May 9, 1958.

[41] *Das freie Wort*, Nov. 8, 1958.

[42] Resolutions of DGB executive committee; *DGB News service*, Sept. 3, Oct. 27, 1958; *DGB Newsletter*, Dec. 1958.

[43] See, *e.g.*, his address to the AsU yearly assembly, May 1959, in *Die Aussprache*, IX (June 1959), 205–214.

ures, and would take others in the near future, concerning the problem.[44]

One of these measures consisted in the establishment, in July 1958, of an arbitration commission for the settlement of disputes between industrial firms over the question of concentration. It had some success in dealing with disputes involving the expansion of basic industries into processing industries. Berg also appealed to industry to supply the BDI with detailed examples of the peaceful coexistence of big and small industries, so as to allay the fears of those who saw a rapid evolution of the German economy toward concentration. What had already taken place was difficult to undo, Berg admitted, but he pointed out that the political situation demanded some restraint upon further attempts at concentration—and that industry not only must act but must talk with restraint if it hoped to prevent legislative action.[45]

Although it was evident that the BDI management was ready to meet Adenauer halfway, the BDI associations were not able to reach a consensus on the question. The Association of the Chemical Industry at least had the courage to denounce bitterly any attempt at state control over the concentration process. It asked the government to maintain a hands-off policy and to let business take any appropriate steps.[46] But Berg, in another speech to industrialists, sustained the government declaration of 1957, pleading for unity within the industrial community and for the preservation of all sizes of business.[47] The BDI yearbook also took a moderate position. It warned that too much concentration would lead to the danger of socialization, but added that some concentration was desirable if the standard of living was to be raised. It underlined the importance of small industry in

[44] Committee on competition, Circular 20/58, Nov. 10, 1958.
[45] *Ibid.*
[46] *Wirtschaftspolitik im Chemiebereich 1959/60*, p. 43.
[47] Speech made in Hagen, Dec. 1958; *Mitteilungen*, VII, No. 1 (Jan. 1959).

acting as a supplier and processor for big business, and called for a reform of the tax system to eliminate the inequities suffered by small business.[48]

Finally, in May 1959, on the basis of a suggestion by Adenauer and in order to counter the alleged public dread of big concerns, the BDI presidential board issued a declaration on the relation of heavy to light industry and on economic concentration. This was obviously the result of a compromise within BDI councils. Attempting to satisfy all elements, it played down the danger of concentration by pointing to big business' awareness of the problem, and by justifying concentration on the basis of the competition German industry faced in the Common Market and throughout the world. On the other hand it admitted that there were inequities of the turnover tax, as well as occasional encroachments by one firm into a field of operation far removed from its own, to which it called on industry to put a stop.[49]

In the meantime civil servants from forty different departments had been at work for nearly a year on a draft bill and the reply to a parliamentary question posed by the government parties concerning economic concentration. It is noteworthy that the present Minister of Economics, Kurt Schmücker, who was then the representative of the small-business element in the CDU, as well as chairman of the Bundestag Economic Affairs Committee, had been instrumental in drafting the question. The Ministry of Economics confidentially asked the BDI's small business committee (and presumably other organizations) to prepare a statement of its position and to supply data, while a committee of the CDU parliamentary group asked the economic associations to present their views.[50] The BDI cooperated fully in the hope that any ensuing legislation would be mild.

In its reply to the parliamentary question, and in a bill introduced in 1960, the government promised to launch a full-scale

[48] *Jahresbericht* 1958–1959, p. 48.
[49] Grundsatzerklärung des Präsidiums des BDI (mimeographed).
[50] Committee on consumer goods, Circular 3/59, Feb. 3, 1959.

inquiry into the concentration movement. Confidential data was to be gathered from the business community in order to determine the most effective measures for curbing or eliminating its undesirable features. On May 1, 1961, the bill became law.[51] To aid in the inquiry an advisory commission has been set up, including members of the business fraternity and of other economic, social, and political organizations. In 1964 the government issued a statistical report on concentration in the various industries, which indicated only that the extent varied considerably.[52] Obviously this report will be followed up by further studies.

This chapter has dealt with three major economic problems—cartel legislation, the role of small business, and economic concentration—in relation to the BDI. In all three instances, the Federation has had to take a position, despite internal schisms that rendered commitment difficult. Although these schisms have reduced effectiveness in the public realm, it managed not only to forestall unfavorable action but to achieve some success.

[51] *Bulletin*, No. 191, Oct. 11, 1960, p. 1850; No. 84, May 5, 1961, p. 804.
[52] *Der Volkswirt*, June 12, 1964.

XII

Economic Policy at Home (II)

AMONG the several economic issues confronting BDI policy-makers, those of fiscal policy (especially tax reforms), the distribution of wealth (people's capitalism), competition among industries (the fuel crisis), and industrial relations (codetermination, price and wage policies), have been singled out for study in this chapter. On all of these the BDI has to take a public and controversial position, and has used varied means in attempting to uphold it.

FISCAL POLICY—TAX REFORMS

All elements in the BDI are directly concerned over government fiscal policy. In the early years of the Federal Republic big business reaped large dividends from a policy geared to put industry back on its feet. The government gave priority to an investment aid law that provided generous financial assistance to basic industries, in the form of relatively low corporate and turnover taxes and of ample depreciation allowances.

But few taxpayers are ever happy about taxes. Organized industry has attempted over the years to reduce the tax burden upon its firms, and to expand depreciation allowances. However, it had no success in the first years of Allied supervision, 1945–1948, when what it considered a high tax rate prevailed.

From the currency reform of 1948 to the outbreak of the Korean war in 1950, partly as a result of industry's own efforts, the tax rate was lowered. But higher taxes were levied during the Korean war, and at its conclusion they were not reduced. Moreover, a tax reform in January 1955 did not live up to expectations, after talks with federal and state authorities had led industrial representatives to believe they would score a success.[1] From then on, they repeatedly accused Minister of Finance Schäffer of resisting any tax cuts and of accumulating enormous reserves. The government also made attempts to cut depreciation allowances, but the BDI exerted pressure to keep the level unchanged, and was successful to that extent.

While the big business element in the BDI was concerned with reducing taxes generally and with increasing depreciation allowances, the concern of small business was mainly with the turnover tax, which had been in existence since July 1951. This cumulative all-phase tax (*Allphasensteuer*), regarded by many as the chief villain in the tax system, imposed a 4 per cent levy at each stage of manufacturing a particular product. Its cumulative effect had led to a vertical concentration among the bigger firms in order to escape part of the burden. In 1955 the Finance and Tax Committee of the Bundestag and the small-business bloc in the CDU/CSU urged the government to study ways and means of changing the system. In April 1955, knowing that it would be asked to give its views on a change, the BDI's tax committee set up a group of experts who understood and sympathized with the complaints of small business. Unable to agree on a satisfactory substitute, they made no immediate recommendation, but left the door open for further studies and proposals, especially if there appeared to be no prospect of appreciably lowering the 4 per cent rate. The BDI in turn communicated this conclusion to the Ministry of Finance.

During the next few years, several draft bills introduced into the Bundestag by deputies called for the abandonment of the

[1] *JB*, 1952–1953, pp. 94–96.

cumulative turnover tax and the substitution of a surplus value tax *(Mehrwertsteuer)*. The BDI experts called on the member associations and regional offices to give their opinions of these bills, to initiate studies within their own industries, and to make recommendations. The response revealed a wide divergence of views, as each association was primarily concerned with how a change would affect the prices of goods and profits of its firms. The task of the associations was not made any easier by the failure of many to reach a consensus. In May 1959 the group submitted a summary of these recommendations to the tax committee, and in turn to the presidential board. It was obvious that the group could not reach a consensus either, owing to the divergent views within the BDI. A compromise formula was worked out which it was hoped all industry would sanction, calling for a competitively neutral surplus tax. Ganser, head of the BDI's tax department, urged the organization to agree on this proposal in order to arrive at an accord with the Ministry of Finance by the end of 1959.[2]

The difficulty, however, was that the Ministry itself could not make up its mind on what was the best tax system, and so went on dragging its feet for a number of years. It feared that any change in the existing system would produce a loss of revenue; and when the government does not seize the initiative in offering a specific proposal, the result can only be confusion worse compounded. If the BDI could have agreed on a proposal, a bill could at least have been introduced into the Bundestag by a friendly deputy and been subjected to debate; but there had been no agreement. Confronted by indecision on all sides, the Chancellor put pressure on Minister Etzel to offer his proposal for a tax reform not later than the end of 1959.[3] It was obvious that political considerations were playing a role in all this: busi-

[2] HGF, Circular to member associations and regional offices on a reform of the turnover tax, Feb. 17, 1960.

[3] Small business committee, Circular 10/59, July 15, 1959 (session of June 25).

ness and government alike realized the urgency of placating the small business community, but they still could not decide how it should be done.

On December 14, 1959, the BDI presidential board met, and although tax reform did not appear on the agenda, Berg asked for authorization to inform Adenauer that the BDI favored the imposition of a surplus value tax. Berg was clearly hoping to railroad the proposal through without much discussion and over the opposition of some powerful associations. But the representatives of the chemical, optical, and electrical associations spoke up against Berg's proposal and demanded that the existing system remain unaltered. As a matter of fact, Ganser revealed to the members that not only these three but a total of nine associations wanted no change; thirteen wanted a change; and seven had not yet taken a definite position. Berg, who was to confer privately with Adenauer the next day, was counseled by the minority to avoid giving the Chancellor the impression that all of industry wanted a new tax.[4]

On January 14, 1960, the board met again. Ganser this time reported that thirty-one associations had expressed an opinion since the summer of 1959, and that of these, two-thirds agreed on a reform of the tax system. In a heated discussion, Berg insisted that the BDI must pledge its support for a more competitive tax even though such a change would mean hardships on some industries. He wanted to be able to report an unequivocal decision if in the future the BDI were again consulted by the government. In support of Berg, Sohl revealed that there had

[4] Protocol of a presidential board meeting of a BDI association reporting on the BDI presidential board meeting. The 9 associations against a change were chemicals, electrical machinery, stone and gravel, mineral oil, ceramics, glass, rubber, optics, and one unidentified; the 13 for a change were automobiles, leather, cellulose, iron and steel, artificial fabrics, shoes, steel finishing, clothing, sawmills, machine construction, steel works and rolling mills; ironwares, tinwares and metalwares; paper and cardboard; the 7 undecided were steel and iron construction, brewers, foundries, nonferrous metals, construction, bicycles and motorcycles, textiles. Others had not yet responded.

originally been a schism in the iron and steel industries, which had been healed only after those who wanted to retain the existing tax system gave way to their opponents. Why, Sohl asked, could this not happen in the BDI too? Let the board authorize a committee, in which all points of view were represented, to negotiate with the Ministry of Finance on the principle of adopting a competitive tax system. On the other hand, those who opposed a change either pleaded for a go-slow policy (*e.g.*, Rodenstock, representing optics) or argued that smaller firms in their associations feared a greater burden if a new system were introduced (*e.g.*, Menne, representing chemicals, and Thörner, representing electrical machinery). The constant fear that a surplus value tax would drive the rates up to 10 to 15 per cent may have motivated the bloc of industries that were against any change. When Berg realized once again that he could not obtain the support of all the member associations, he suggested a compromise: he would tell government authorities the true nature of the division within the BDI—namely that two-thirds favored a change, and one-third were opposed.[5] To the press the BDI announced that Berg would negotiate with the Ministry of Finance concerning a possible surplus value tax in which the minority point of view would not be ignored. Moreover, in BDI committees further efforts to heal the schism would be made.

In 1959, while the BDI attempted to work out a position, the Ministry of Finance asked three commissions to study tax changes. Of these the most important was the so-called Hartmann Commission, on which there were many representatives from the political, academic, and business communities. In 1960, after a lengthy study of the problem, the commission advocated an immediate tax-system reform, consisting of several minor tax adjustments. The BDI presidential board rejected this recommendation, arguing that a minor reform would delay a major reform. The Ministry was of the opinion, however, that time was precious, and that a major reform bill would mean too

[5] *Präsidialsitzung*, Jan. 14, 1960.

long a delay. The power that could be wielded at election time by small businessmen, artisans, and the small retailers, was clearly what the Ministry had in mind. Its spokesman in the Bundestag asked for an immediate reform to free the small businessmen from some of the burdens of the tax, pending a major reform, which would not be put into effect before 1965. Ironically, there was disappointment among small businessmen, who felt that the government proposal was not radical enough, and that the situation had not much altered.[6] A new tax bill was introduced by the government in 1963; in 1964 it remained to be seen whether the Fourth Bundestag (1961–1965) would be more inclined than its predecessors toward a drastic overhaul of the turnover tax.

The violent discussions within the BDI during this long struggle reflect the strains and stresses between basic industries and finishing works, and between big and small firms. The lack of a clear-cut position weakened the BDI considerably in negotiating with government authorities. In the dispute over the turnover tax, primary decisions were made by the executive and legislative branches, and the BDI could not influence them to any marked degree. In other areas of tax policy, however, there has been a marked though not explicitly expressed satisfaction among all elements of the business community.

PEOPLE'S CAPITALISM

Prodded by the SPD and by the labor wing of the CDU, which insisted that it was pursuing a policy too favorable to business, the government in the late 1950's studied ways and means of making the social market economy more social. Under a system of people's capitalism there would be greater social and economic equality among all strata of the population. The govern-

---

6 See *Finanzpolitische Mitteilungen*, No. 158, Aug. 25, 1960, pp. 1551–1552; *Bulletin*, No. 204, Oct. 28, 1960, pp. 203–204; *Die Zeit*, Dec. 9, 1960. The DIHT and the wholesale trade association also opposed the minor reform. The SPD advocated a lower rate to help the consumer. Walter Seuffert, "Das Problem der Umsatzsteuer," *Vorwärts*, July 3, 1959.

ment hoped to encourage employers to introduce profit-sharing schemes for their workers; to facilitate the purchase of property, and especially of corporate shares; to encourage savings and to issue people's shares in public undertakings, or in those that were returned to private hands.[7] Fearful of lowered profits, the business fraternity was cool toward the government's proposals, and offered some criticism of the means it intended to employ. But once again it was on the defensive.

One of the means used by the government was a simplification of the stock-corporation laws in order to encourage the public to buy more corporate shares. Unlike those of the United States, few German corporations have as many as 50,000 shareholders. To augment their numbers, the Ministry of Justice drafted bills intended to make the activities of management more widely known, to give the private shareholder an additional voice in company management, and to restrict the voting rights of banks, which hold a substantial portion of the total issue of securities.[8]

Despite the BDI's calls for less secrecy in business, in 1958 the BDI, the DIHT, and the Federation of Private Banking issued a statement critical of the plan for increased publicity, especially of a provision in the government bill requiring German firms to issue more extensive balance sheets. As ground for their objection, they pointed out that foreign companies did not publish such data. A BDI staff official nevertheless urged his organization not to take a merely negative stand, which would be misunderstood by the public, but to suggest constructive alternatives. The presidential board instructed Berg to talk with Adenauer and with other leading administra-

---

[7] The SPD criticized the measures as not being far-reaching enough. Although Deist, the SPD economic theoretician, said, "It is a legitimate ambition to acquire property and not to have to live from hand to mouth," he also called, *inter alia,* for a wider distribution of big business assets, a progressive wage policy which could result in more savings for workers, and a tax policy that would accelerate an increase in low incomes. *News from Germany,* March 1961.

[8] *The Bulletin,* Nov. 7, 1961.

tion officials, and asked Pohle to form a working committee of specialists from the BDI and other national associations, which was to draft a compromise proposal that would then be the basis for un-publicized negotiations with the Ministry of Justice.[9]

The difficulties of the business community in coming to an agreement were underscored by the efforts of this working committee—as a heated exchange of letters in late 1958 between the then president of the DIHT, Münchmeyer, and Pohle of the BDI makes clear. The differences centered on the kinds of steps to be taken in modifying the draft bill of the Ministry of Justice.[10] President Flender of the AsU took vigorous exception to the stand of the BDI and DIHT, accusing big business of leading an obstinate fight against decisive reforms or, failing that, of making the reforms as ineffective as possible.[11] But the government bill passed the Bundestag in December 1959, with the BDI maintaining its critical attitude toward some of its provisions.

[9] *Der Spiegel*, XII, No. 22 (May 28, 1958), 18; *Präsidialsitzung*, July 9, 1958; Gold, credit and currency committee, Circular 21/58; also see Roland Schupp, "Der Referentenentwurf des Bundesjustizministeriums für ein Aktiengesetz im Urteil der Spitzenverbände der Wirtschaft, der Länder-Wirtschaftsminister und der Deutschen Angestellten-Gewerkschaft," *Die Aktiengesellschaft*, No. 9/1959, pp. 242–249.

[10] It appears that the BDI and DIHT had planned to issue a joint declaration based upon an accord between them before the draft bill was issued by the Ministry. When Münchmeyer heard that the BDI was not ready to issue such a declaration, in the hope of obtaining a postponement of the bill, he saw Berg and Professor Herrmann (of the BDI staff), who urged him to wait until Berg had seen Adenauer. But the Ministry released details of the bill before the projected Berg-Adenauer conference; whereupon the DIHT hastily issued its release. Pohle was angry at the DIHT's unilateral action before the joint BDI–DIHT committee had had a chance to act. Pohle decided to dissolve the committee; but Münchmeyer was able to convince him of the importance of continuing its work. Finally an amicable agreement was reached to issue a joint statement, and to perpetuate the committee under Pohle's leadership even after the Ministry published its draft bill in October 1958. This incident sounds like a tempest in a teacup, but it was something more for the principals involved, since their prestige was at stake. HGF Circular, Jan. 15, 1959, contains the exchange of letters.

[11] *Die Aussprache*, X, No. 6 (June 1960), 202.

Yet it may be that the BDI did wring a concession from Adenauer. According to the SPD, it was in order to satisfy business that the government promised to make available to low-income groups shares of only some, rather than all, of the public companies that had been returned to private ownership. Moreover, while 60 per cent of the Volkswagen shares sold by the government went to 1.5 million persons of limited income, many of the shares of Preussag, a denationalized mining and processing company, eventually landed in business portfolios. Although only 20 per cent of the 2.5 million Germans who own stocks and bonds are businessmen, they own much more than one-fifth of the total capital stock.[12] But even if more shares were sold to small investors, the SPD and DGB would oppose on principle any further efforts to denationalize more enterprises, while the BDI would of course support such efforts just as vigorously.

THE FUEL CRISIS

An economic crisis that adversely affects one major branch of the industrial sector, and results in a boom in another branch, becomes a matter of concern for the BDI. In the late 1950's a change in the pattern of consumption and in consumer preference led to a depression in the coal industry and to prosperity in the fuel oil industry. Since 1958 coal production has stagnated and sales have fallen slightly, while fuel oil sales have risen dramatically.[13]

[12] *DGB News Letter*, No. IX/10 (Oct. 1958). The Volkswagen shares went to single persons earning less than 8,000 DM and to married couples earning less than 16,000 DM. Of the 2.5 million stockholders, 33 per cent are salaried employees, 24 per cent wage earners (but only 3 per cent workers), 11 per cent civil servants, 6 per cent professional people, and 5 per cent farmers. *The Bulletin*, June 12, 1962. See also *UB*, XII, No. 29, July 19, 1962.

[13] By about 275 per cent, from 4.9 million tons (hard coal equivalent) in 1957 to 18.2 million tons in 1961. *The Bulletin*, July 17, 1962. *The Bulletin* also reports: "In 1955 . . . hard coal still held a 69 per cent share in the nation's consumption of primary energy, while oil had only a 10 per cent

Since coal was regarded as the country's number one source of energy, the government and the coal association agreed on measures to bail out the industry. Mechanization was pushed, unprofitable mines were shut down, retraining programs for miners were instituted, and imports of coal from other countries were subjected to a high import duty. The government's most important proposal was to levy a special tax on fuel oil sold in West Germany, amounting to 30 DM per ton for heavy and 10 DM per ton for light fuel oil. All these measures were intended to prevent not only economic but also social and political upheavals.

Obviously the fuel oil industry could not be expected to accept a tax intended to discourage the use of its products without at least putting up a good fight. In 1958 it had fought a skirmish with Bonn, which reluctantly put pressure on major oil companies to sign a cartel preventing any cut in prices (which were fixed at the world market level) and outlawing any advertising. But cheaper oil flowed into Germany from neighboring countries, and led to a breakup of the cartel in the summer of 1959.

At the time the cartel was set up, the BDI's presidential board formed an *ad hoc* committee on fuel policy, under the chairmanship of Reusch (steel)—which, however, did not meet for a year owing to uncertainty over industrial and government policies. The BDI was faced with basically the same question as the government—namely, whether it should support the coal or the fuel oil industry, or whether it could take a neutral stand. It had also to mediate among its fuel-supplying and fuel-consuming industries.[14] In a policy declaration at the end of 1958, which safely kept to a middle course, Berg called on the government

---

share. By 1961, however, the share of hard coal had decreased to 55.8 per cent while that of oil had risen to a full fourth." In 1961 there was a consumption of 121.2 million tons of hard coal and 55.6 million tons of fuel oil. *Ibid.*

[14] *JB*, 1956–1957, p. 50.

to support the coal industry as the basic, and the safest, supplier
of fuel, but not to impose higher tariffs or new taxes on fuel oil
imports, because the latter might then become permanent. (So
far, on this point Berg has been proved right.) He advocated an
accord between the two industries on a flexible price policy en-
abling both to compete on the open market, and ensuring the
miners a full work week.[15]

In 1959 the failure of the fuel oil cartel aggravated the coal
crisis. At a BDI presidential board meeting in March, Helmuth
Burckhardt, a director of the Mining Association and president
of its Ruhr affiliate, warned of the swift expansion of his fuel
oil competitors and their ability to lower prices, which his industry could not match.[16] In early September the Ministry of
Economics was busy drafting a bill to impose a tax on fuel oil.
At a meeting on September 4 the BDI presidential board debated the merit of the tax and explored other ways of resolving
the crisis. Berg opened the session by deploring both the coal-oil
discord and the government's proposal. The representatives of
the rival industries then spoke up. Burckhardt once again cited
the woes of the coal industry, pointing out that the oil industry
could easily undercut coal prices because under ECSC regulations these had to be made public. He denied that his industry
had proposed the tax, placing the blame on the government;
he said he had heard about the proposal himself only a few days
before. Thereupon Erwin Bockelmann, president of the Mineral Oil Association, set forth the position of his own industry.
He assailed the government proposal as too one-sided, arguing
that it would not help the coal industry; affirmed the importance of fuel oil in the economy; denied that there had been
any great increase in oil consumption in the Federal Republic,
and declared that his industry had been most reluctant to accept
the earlier cartel arrangement. In the discussion that followed
these conflicting statements, some members argued that the

15 "Die Wirtschaft an der Jahreswende," *VR*, No. 51, Dec. 22, 1958.
16 *Präsidialsitzung*, March 5, 1959.

problem had become so enmeshed in political considerations that only government and parliament could handle it. Presidential board members representing fuel oil-consuming industries were of course against the tax proposal, but for want of a better alternative could do nothing but suggest a new cartel agreement, even though they were aware of the difficulty of convincing the public and the press of its advantages.[17]

Later the same day the executive board met, and once again Burckhardt and Bockelmann voiced their clashing views. Then the representatives of the various industries spoke up: those primarily making use of coal (*e.g.,* iron and steel) in favor of the tax, those that used fuel oil (*e.g.,* chemicals, wood, cellulose, and leather) against it. An official of the Association of the German Leather Industry asserted that no one had helped the leather or textile industries when they faced a slump, and that therefore coal should receive no help either. Berg expressed some sympathy for the coal industry, asserting that aid to coal had become a political problem. If the BDI were to make a decision against the tax, he pointed out, then it must present an alternative—such as the cartel, which he favored. But—and he recalled that he had said the same on other occasions—if the BDI took no stand, it would lose the right to express its views on future important economic issues. Berg asked for authorization to inform Adenauer and the chairman of the CDU parliamentary group of the executive board's decision to support a cartel. Coal, iron, and steel would of course have preferred a BDI endorsement of a tax; but finding themselves in the minority, they did not press the matter further, since in principle they were not opposed to a cartel. The official of another industry urged a vote be taken, but Berg opposed the suggestion because a vote would only widen the gulf within industry.[18]

[17] *Präsidialsitzung,* Sept. 4, 1959.

[18] *Vorstandssitzung,* Sept. 4, 1959. *Die Welt* (Sept. 8) carried a story entitled "BDI wishes protection for coal," based on a memorandum submitted to the presidential board and the executive committee by experts and the

On September 12, at the Berlin industrial fair, Berg outlined the position of the BDI, which consisted of six points: (1) The security of the fuel supply rested on coal; hence, coal must be aided; (2) the coal industry rejected subsidies, as did other industries; (3) a majority of BDI associations objected to the tax on fuel oil; (4) at a technical conference, representatives of coal, fuel oil, and other industries ought to tackle the problem of improving the competitive position of coal; (5) the industry must improve its own position by closing marginal pits if necessary; and (6) miners and employees of the pits must be aided if they lost their jobs. In his speech Berg also advocated a compulsory cartel among fuel oil firms.

Next on the rostrum was Erhard, who defended the government proposal. He asserted a tax of 30 DM per ton on fuel oil would make the price not prohibitive but rather competitive with the world price scale; suggested that the coal industry be freed from the requirement of maintaining fixed prices in order to compete more effectively with its rival; and assailed the BDI's proposal to create another cartel, since the first one had been destroyed not simply by outsiders' undercutting the domestic distributors but also by industrial consumers who started to import oil themselves.[19]

The government had little difficulty in receiving parliamentary endorsement for its bill, in which the tax was finally reduced from 30 to 25 DM per ton. The tax went into effect in May 1960, and is still in force. But in the years since then the

secretariat in the BDI. Significantly, *Die Welt* printed a BDI denial on the following day, indicating that the memorandum did not represent the opinion of the BDI.

[19] *Die Welt*, Sept. 14, 1959. The press likewise showed no enthusiasm for a new cartel. The *Industriekurier* (Sept. 15), normally friendly to the BDI, regarded the cartel as impractical and supported a tax instead; *Rheinischer Merkur* (Sept. 18) opined that the Berg speech would not influence the cabinet decision, and that the mineral oil industry would fight the cartel proposal; and *Neue Zürcher Zeitung* (Sept. 17) described the generally cool reaction to Berg's proposal.

government has been studying other ways of achieving a balance between the two competing industries, while it goes on helping the ailing coal industry. For instance, in 1962 it helped work out a long-range program to limit the building of new refineries. The oil interests were not happy about the proposed regulation, but they realized that it could have been more stringent and thus more harmful to them. On the other hand, some leaders in the Miners' Union and the Mining Association have charged the government with capitulating to the oil interests in not restricting the level of their imports. However, in 1962 the government also introduced a new bill proposing to raise the tax on oil; to extend the tariff on coal imports; to set up a corporation for modernization of the coal industry; to grant financial assistance to those affected by the closing down of mines; and to study the problem of how Eastern Bloc imports of oil into West Germany, channeled via other countries, could be controlled.[20]

Among the conclusions to be drawn from the controversy between the coal and oil industries is the one drawn by the BDI itself, that internal discords have hampered its effectiveness even more than might have been expected. If, caught on the horns of its dilemma, it had opted for the oil tax, it would have offended some of its powerful constituents, and if it had opted against the tax, it would have offended others equally powerful. Its counterproposal amounted to a weak compromise, lacking in popular appeal, and thus had no chance of scoring a victory against the government.

INDUSTRIAL RELATIONS: CODETERMINATION

In the area of industrial relations the BDA has the primary responsibility, but the interdependence between industrial relations and economic policies is such that the BDA and BDI have been obliged to coordinate their work whenever a problem falls into both areas. The two organizations also are confronted with the power of the DGB, and cannot afford to pursue diver-

[20] *Christian Science Monitor,* June 16, 1962; *The Bulletin,* July 17, 1962.

gent policies. This was the situation in the battle against co-determination, and in periodic skirmishes on the price and wage fronts, which will be discussed presently. The BDI has regularly taken a conservative attitude toward the trade unions, and a negative position in regard to their demands. A former vice president of the BDI, Otto A. H. Vogel, was especially well known for his ultraconservative views, but to a lesser extent the same is true of Berg, who on a number of occasions has called on trade unions to refrain from political and partisan activities and to limit themselves to wage and social questions. The DGB has counseled him to abandon his attempts to sow mistrust between the workers and their unions. The relation between the BDI and BDA on one side and the DGB on the other still shows strong evidence of class conflict, although the BDA on occasion has taken a more liberal position toward the demands of the DGB than has the BDI.

The hostility of employers to unions was notably manifest in the battle for codetermination. Encouraged by the Allies, who authorized the creation of work councils throughout Germany and labor participation in the steel industry soon after the end of the war, the unions have attempted to gain a greater participation in management.[21] Other impulses came from the unions and the Christian social movement; the Ahlen and Duesseldorf CDU platforms, for example, spoke of codetermination. The next logical step was for the Ministry of Labor to draft a comprehensive bill. During the process it attempted to bring the unions and the employer associations together at a series of meetings; but six months of negotiations, from January to June 1950, widened rather than narrowed the differences concerning the extent to which labor might be represented in management, and the extent of codetermination to be allowed in German industry generally.

During the negotiations the DGB pressed for codetermination

[21] Allied Law 22, April 10, 1946, as cited by Piettre, *L'économie allemande contemporaine 1945-1952*, pp. 446-448.

in all industries and at all levels of business enterprise, as well as for a pyramid of economic councils from the shop to the national levels. The BDI and other key employer associations were basically opposed to any "outside" interference in their traditional prerogatives of corporation management. They feared that labor representatives on boards of directors would not limit their discussion to social and labor questions, and also that the trade unions might obtain a monopoly of power, especially since trade-unionists rather than workers from the shops would occupy these seats. But political realities eventually forced their consent to codetermination—provided that it was restricted to heavy industries, and that the representatives of workers on the supervisory boards not exceed one-third of the total membership.[22] In the latter demand, they lost out.

In the confrontation between the two social forces, the trade unions appear to have had the upper hand. The employers, for a variety of reasons that have already been mentioned, were just beginning to gather strength (although they had the support of most of the press). Deputy Wellhausen told a BDI meeting in June 1950 that the organization should concern itself more with the codetermination issue, since up until then the Bundestag committees and the public had received only a one-sided presentation.[23] On November 8, 1950, Berg, Menne, and Vogel presented the views of the BDI officialdom on codetermination to a mass rally of employers, in order to elicit their support.

Meanwhile, in the summer of 1950 parliament began a debate on the codetermination bills introduced by the government, the SPD, and the CDU. The DGB threatened the government with a general strike unless a bill providing for codetermination, especially in heavy industries, was passed before February 1951. The powerful Miners and Metal Workers Unions sustained the DGB, and in January 1951 authorized a strike. BDI and other

[22] *JB*, 1951–1952, p. 10.
[23] *Niederschrift über die ordentliche Sitzung des Hauptausschusses u. die 1. Wirtschaftspolitische Tagung des BDI, June 1950.*

employers associations, as well as the FDP and the right wing of the CDU, denounced the trade union threat as a highly improper and illegal intimidation of parliament.[24] In an exchange of letters during January 1951, Berg wrote to Adenauer of his fear that Adenauer would yield to the union threat, which would be an undermining of state authority and of democracy. Adenauer replied that in the negotiations between the two "social partners" he would merely offer his good offices if no agreement were reached. He had told DGB officers that the government was prepared to include only the coal and iron industries in the bill. Still dissatisfied, the BDI's central committee sent a telegram to Adenauer supporting the position of its presidential board and exhorting him once again not to yield to the pressure of the unions.[25] An additional voice of warning was heard from the United States, where the NAM asserted that passage of the bill would adversely affect American investments in Germany.[26] The warning did not appear to have much effect, since many legislators saw it as an interference in domestic affairs. In any event, investments did not slacken after passage of the law. Conversely, at the 1951 International Industrial Congress Berg sounded a warning that codetermination would be a threat to other industrial countries if it were not stopped at the German border.[27]

In Germany the political scene was charged with excitement. Late in January in order to forestall a strike, Adenauer called five labor leaders and five industrialists, including Kost of the Mining Association, to a series of conferences, and appealed to the latter to come to an agreement with the unions in order to uphold his policy—which incidentally had the tacit support of

[24] Spiro, *The Politics of German Codetermination*, p. 78.

[25] *JB*, 1950–1951, pp. 38–40. Seventy employers for the iron industry also sent a separate telegram, since they had no representation in the BDI at the time. Hirsch-Weber, *Gewerkschaften in der Politik*, p. 94, note 377.

[26] H. G. Gary, "Germans debate Codetermination, Decartelization," *Foreign Policy Bulletin*, XXX, No. 22 (March 9, 1951).

[27] *JB*, 1951–1952, pp. 92–93.

the Allies.[28] Four days before a strike deadline, the representatives of both sides agreed to the government bill. In the meantime, on January 25, Adenauer personally appeared before the Bundestag and called for its support. He had the backing of President Boeckler of the DGB, who had agreed to call off the threatened general strike. A rare joint CDU–SPD vote ensured passage of the bill, and codetermination became a legal reality on May 21.

The law provided for parity representation of, in most cases, five labor and five management representatives on the eleven-man supervisory board of coal and steel corporations, with the eleventh man to represent the public. Furthermore, a manager from the ranks of organized labor was to have a seat on the governing board of each of these corporations.[29]

The employers had lost the first round—a fact the DI exploited in order to refute the charge that the big corporations were powerful in government and parliament. If they had so much influence, the DI asked rhetorically, why could they not prevent codetermination? It went on to blame the power of the unions, which had threatened a general strike and thereby endangered free society.[30] The DI was correct in its assessment of employer strength at the time; but in the ensuing months and years, as businessmen increased their power and received the support of a majority in parliament, they were successful in heading off the attempts of the DGB and SPD to extend full codetermination to other industries. In 1952 the CDU was responsible for a mild labor-management law *(Betriebsverfassungsgesetz)*, which granted labor no managerial positions, but simply the right to provide one-third of the supervisory board members in plants with more than 500 employees. Labor succeeded, however, in getting the Bundestag to vote in June 1956 for an extension of codetermination to holding companies.

[28] *Der Spiegel*, IX, No. 6 (Feb. 2, 1955).
[29] Piettre, *L'économie allemande contemporaine 1945–1952*, pp. 446–452; Spiro, *The Politics of German Codetermination*, pp. 69–70.
[30] *UB*, No. 22, May 30, 1957.

This account of the struggle for codetermination has been concerned with the role of the BDI. But the spearhead of the fight on the management side was wielded by the BDA, with the BDI lending full support whenever direct representations to the government appeared necessary. The united front presented by the employers, and a "restorative" trend in Germany, eventually blunted the force of the trade unions. On balance, although the employers lost the first engagement, they won other battles in this area of industrial relations.

PRICE AND WAGE POLICIES

In the sphere of prices and wages the BDI has had further encounters with the trade unions and the government. The BDI readily admits it has no competence in collective bargaining, a field reserved to the BDA's constituent associations, but asserts its right to take a basic position on wage policy, since it has a direct effect on prices and credit.[31] Unlike the codetermination issue, where BDI and BDA worked together in harmony, price and wage questions tend to produce jurisdictional conflicts, which both federations through their institutional links attempt to avoid—especially when the government enters the scene. Then the BDI and BDA, placed on the defensive, seek to present a united front to government and the trade unions.

There have been several confrontations between Erhard and the "social partners." Having no predilection for price and wage controls, he pleaded with management and labor for self-restraint on prices and wages. In this he was only moderately successful. In 1955, for instance, he informed Berg that price increases could be prevented even though wages had risen, and despite a BDI statement to the contrary.[32] In 1957, an election year, new price controversies flared up. Government leaders attempted to stem an inflationary tide—and perhaps gain more votes—by asking for commitments from several major firms not

[31] *JB*, 1958–1959, p. 19.
[32] *FAZ*, Oct. 6, 1955.

to boost prices until the end of the year. The DGB, in a letter to Adenauer dated August 23, charged that a secret agreement had been concluded between government ministries and industry that price increases would not become effective until after the election. It cited various industries which were planning to boost prices as a result of what they considered an "intolerable" cost situation. It denied that wage increases were responsible for the alleged increase in costs, and instead blamed employers who wanted to reap higher profits. The government in turn denied that any secret agreement had been concluded, and pledged itself to make every possible effort to keep prices stable, both before and after the September 15 election. Adenauer charged that the DGB's letter was merely ammunition for the campaign of the SPD.[33]

It is doubtful that a secret agreement was concluded, but likely that there was some truth behind the DGB's accusation. Deputy Leber of the SPD announced in the Bundestag that he was in possession of a memorandum from an association lobbyist informing his regional branches of a statement by the Ministry of Economics to some lobbyists on the need for sacrifices by industry before the election—such as renunciation of excessive profits—if they expected the Ministry to take a more sympathetic attitude to their demands after the election. Erhard categorically denied this accusation.[34]

In any event, despite repeated efforts by the government to hold the price line after the election, there were numerous breakthroughs. Adenauer, Erhard, Pferdmenges, and Berg were all unsuccessful in persuading the steel manufacturers, headed by Sohl, to hold off on price increases. They were instrumental, however, in heading off a proposed raise to 6 per cent, instead of which the manufacturers announced one of from 3 to 5 per cent for December 1. Berg was said to be interested in low steel

[33] *Labor Headline News*, No. 1658, Aug. 26, 1957; *Economist*, April 27, 1957, p. 317.
[34] Bundestag, 3rd el. pd., 24th session, April 23, 1958, p. 1351.

prices partly because the members of the metal finishing association, which he heads, would be hit directly by higher steel prices.[35]

The coal industry also announced a price rise, to be effective October 1, two weeks after the election. Adenauer deplored the timing of the action, since the new cabinet—which would be obliged to study the economic situation—had not yet been formed. When Erhard urged the industry to postpone any action until November 1, the Mining Association replied that he ought not to complain about the date of the increase, but instead should study the reasons why the increase was necessary. They added that he should pay attention to wage negotiations in other industries, which would have an impact on the economic wellbeing of the miner.[36] A year later, according to Deist (SPD), in talks with Adenauer the coal industry threatened to close mines and lay off workers unless the government came to its rescue. This was too much for Erhard, who publicly warned the Mining Association not to put the government under such heavy pressure.[37]

After these occurrences the BDI presidential board decided to tell the public that wage increases were to blame for price increases. It maintained a laissez-faire policy toward prices, and did not attempt to persuade the member associations to hold them down. It even shied away from any concerted agreement with the BDA on wage policy, although President Paullsen of the BDA urged the BDI board to weigh such a move. One of the few moves, none of them publicized, taken by the BDI was to have its board members talk about the wage problem with the President of the Federal Republic.[38] However, when the gov-

[35] *Der Spiegel*, XI, No. 48 (Nov. 27, 1957).

[36] *Der Volkswirt*, XI, No. 39, Sept. 28, 1957, pp. 2161 ff; Grosser, *Die Bonner Demokratie*, p. 194; *Die Welt* and *FAZ*, Sept. 25, 1957.

[37] Speech to Industrie- und Handelskammer, Augsburg, Nov. 15, 1958, cited by Deist in Bundestag, 3rd el. pd., 59th session, Jan. 29, 1959, pp. 3227–3241.

[38] *Präsidialsitzung*, Oct. 24, 1957; minutes of BDI association presidential board meeting, Dec. 14, 1959.

ernment was reported to be ready to take countermeasures to restrain industry from boosting prices, the BDI swung into action. In January 1960, for example, Beutler told board members that industry must not increase prices appreciably if it intended to avoid a showdown with the government. BDI chiefs also asked the Ministry of Economics not to dramatize the price situation or make public accusations against industry[39]—an implicit plea for bilateral negotiations away from the glare of publicity.

However, the BDI became embroiled in a public squabble several months later, after Berg had committed a *faux pas* in apparently failing to clear a statement on wage policy with the BDA. On March 8 he told Karl Blessing, president of the Federal Bank, that an over-all increase in wage rates by 6 per cent would be possible in 1960 without a price rise on industrial products—the increase to be absorbed by production growth, modernization and automation. Since this statement sounded rather as if it should have come from a trade-union president, some BDI associations were greatly annoyed, arguing the inability of their industries to absorb a boost of such magnitude. Moreover, they said, only the BDA was competent to issue such a statement. A BDA spokesman, not eager to take public issue with the BDI, merely told newsmen that a pay increase of 6 per cent might perhaps be possible in industry, but not in other branches of the economy.[40] In order to undo the damage, a delegation of BDI industrialists informed Adenauer that the Berg statement referred to a 6 per cent top limit, and did not imply that all wages should be raised by that much. In May, at the BDI General Assembly, Berg returned to a traditional theme —that wage demands jeopardized price stability, and that shorter hours impaired economic output and German competition in foreign markets. In its simultaneously published annual report,

39 *Präsidialsitzung*, Jan. 14, 1960

40 *Labor Headline News*, No. 1956, March 14, 1960; minutes of BDI association executive committee meeting, March 29, 1960.

the BDI also warned that labor's attempt to obtain a higher proportion of the gross national product would lead to a curtailment of investments, and to a loss of jobs.[41]

Over the years, organized labor was highly critical of the arguments of organized business and government concerning wages. It did not appear receptive to government pronouncements on maintaining their stability, in view of what it regarded as the modesty of its own demands. Otto Brenner, the head of the Metal Workers Union, accused Erhard of "dancing to the employers' tune" when he requested a wage freeze that would have guaranteed the employers huge profits. When it came to prices, Erhard's opponents contended that he should not have yielded to the Ruhr coal magnates in 1957, since the concept of democracy did not allow for mighty economic groups dictating to the Minister what his job should be. Two years later, Brenner predicted that Erhard would be unlikely to fight industry despite his pleas for price stabilization.[42]

Not withstanding such vehement criticisms from labor, and occasionally from business, in 1962 Erhard resumed his double-barreled assault upon both camps. He publicly called on them to maintain self-discipline and restraint in price and wage policies to prevent German goods from being priced out of the market. In Germany wage expenditures had risen by 21 per cent in two years, as compared to between 6 and 13 per cent in other EEC countries. Trade unions, he asserted, should not attempt to redistribute the nation's wealth by incessant new wage demands.[43] Before the industrialists at the 1962 BDI Assembly, Erhard made an implicit denial of the trade unions' charge that he had singled out labor as the culprit, and said that business was to be blamed too: "Those who believe they can save their necks by

---

[41] *Süddeutsche Zeitung*, April 30, 1960; *Stuttgarter Zeitung*, May 5, 1960.

[42] *Metall Pressedienst*, March 23, 1959; *UB*, No. 19, May 9, 1957; Deist (SPD) in Bundestag, 3rd el. pd., 5th session, Nov. 28, 1957, p. 128.

[43] In a radio address on March 21. Text in *Bulletin*, No. 57, March 23, 1962, pp. 477 ff; *Welt am Sonntag*, March 25, 1962.

increasing prices betray themselves. . . . Price increases in West German business are reaching the limit. We are hitting the ceiling with them." He called on the industrialists to hold a competitive position within the framework of the Common Market: "The German market lies open, defenseless, so to speak."[44] His prime concern was a drop in the German export trade, with serious consequences to the social benefits of workers and to the employment situation. But despite Erhard's denial of having singled out the trade unions, his statement that "the German employers have their backs to the wall" seemed to indicate he regarded labor as more responsible than management for the clouds on the horizon.[45] He may have changed his mind as the weeks went by, for in no uncertain terms he denounced the automobile manufacturers' intention to raise prices in expectation of higher wage demands. When Volkswagen raised its prices by 5 per cent, he asked for a rescindment, threatening to lower import duties on cars manufactured in the other Common Market countries. Although shortly before this, in a similar situation, American steel manufacturers had bowed to pressure from the United States executive, the German automobile manufacturers stood their ground in conference with the Ministry of Economics, where they explained that higher labor and material costs had forced them to increase prices by from 3 to 10 per cent.

Erhard's failure to pull them into line brought the SPD to his support, as in the cartel dispute. The party called the price rises "shocking" and "a slap in the face" to Erhard and the Bundestag, which had supported the denationalization of the Volkswagen company. Neither the government nor Erhard, according to the SPD, but "anonymous managers" were dictating economic policy. The party lent its full support to a government bill to lower import duties on foreign cars, assuring the

[44] *New York Times*, April 4, 1962.
[45] See *Manchester Guardian Weekly*, April 5, 1962.

bill overwhelming passage.[46] The reaction of the business community to this minor political explosion was the claim that
American and German price rises could not be compared, since
the steel workers in the United States had moderated their wage
demands, whereas the German auto workers had not. Consequently, the argument went, German auto manufactures had no
choice but to raise prices—a perfectly permissible act in a free
economy.[47]

CONSUMER GOODS

Wage and price policies are both of significance to the BDI.
The quality of consumer goods, though perhaps of less dramatic
import—but of great interest to the average housewife—is likewise a problem the BDI cannot shrug off. Placed on the defensive, it cannot ignore either the argument by industry that
quality control ought to remain its own prerogative, or the
demands of consumer organizations for some right to exert
controls too. When a privately run Society of Consumer Associations started to test consumer goods, the BDI's consumer
goods committee, deciding to counter the impression that industry had been negligent in this area, issued a booklet calling
attention to the existence of quality controls in twenty industrial
branches, and asserting that a central consumer testing agency
could not possibly conduct widely varying tests for each consumer product. The society criticized the booklet, and called on
Erhard to mediate the dispute. In the fall of 1958 Erhard judi-
ciously took a middle position. He declared that quality controls
did vary widely and that consumer organizations ought not to
become the censors of business; but he also called on industry to
accept the complaints and suggestions of the consumers. To both
sides he recommended further negotiations. These have been
held, and in 1963 reached an accord on a federally financed
institute, to be set up under the auspices of the Ministry of

[46] *New York Times*, April 22, 1962; *The Bulletin*, May 29, 1962.
[47] *UB*, No. 19, May 10, 1962.

Economics, for testing consumer goods, with representatives of both industry and consumers on its advisory boards.[48] Since then a private consumers research and products testing magazine (*DM*) aimed at the mass market has been launched with much publicity, and has already been subject to court suits for alleged misstatements concerning some industrial products.

CONCLUSION

In the important economic problems arising in the Federal Republic the BDI frequently has had to commit its resources and energies to fighting a defensive action to block, delay, or weaken a government initiative. In some instances, such as that of industrial concentration, the government took action only after warning the BDI to exercise corrective self-restraint. The Federation acceded to these warnings, but the action was either too late or too little. Economic associations often find themselves on the defensive in situations where a large section of the populace or the public policy-makers see the "national interest" as threatened by economic developments. This is true not only in Germany but in other countries as well. In the United States, the steel industry's fight against government interference in steel pricing is one illustration. Of course on other occasions economic associations may take the offensive in pressing for favorable legislative action, but this has been less necessary for the BDI since the government has been in accord with most of its objectives.

The relative number of failures and successes registered by the BDI in domestic economic policies add up to a mixed record in nearly every area. Excessively injurious legislation has been warded off, and there have been some positive gains. This is true of cartels, concentration, tax reforms, codetermination,

[48] *JB*, 1958–1959, pp. 136–137. The BDI was somewhat wary of too many confrontations with the society, according to a BDI staff member, because the latter could then regard itself as recognized by the BDI. Consumer goods committee, Circular 3/59, Feb. 3, 1959; *The Bulletin*, March 17, 1964; *Welt am Sonntag*, April 26, 1964.

people's capitalism, fuel, and prices and wages. The balance sheet would not be complete without an assessment of losses and gains for the components of the BDI—the basic as compared to the finishing industries, the big as compared with the small. Here again the record is mixed, with losses and gains on both sides. The complexity of the situation may be illustrated by the tax reform struggle. If there had been no tax reform, big business would have profited; whereas a significant reform would have benefited small business; but the enactment of a minor reform leaves the question of who was the gainer still unresolved.

XIII

Foreign Policy

GERMAN economic associations have always been involved in matters of foreign policy whenever their interests were directly affected. Nowadays a political confrontation between East and West, a government crisis in a Latin American country, or the recognition of a new state in Africa are often matters of direct concern. Indeed, political and economic questions are now so interwoven that organizations elsewhere, for instance the NAM or the AFL–CIO in the United States, can likewise no longer afford to view them with detachment.

Most BDI officials would concur with the statement of former Minister for Foreign Affairs Heinrich von Brentano that political and economic foreign policy should not be viewed as rivaling one another, that neither should be given priority, since they are interdependent.[1] So far as strictly political issues are concerned, BDI officials have been placing trust in the government's formulation and execution of that policy, and rarely voice any criticism. For over a decade they have been staunch adherents of Adenauer's pro-Western course, and have viewed the results of every election post-mortem as expressions of popular confidence in his foreign policy and in the free market economy.

[1] *Bulletin*, No. 92, May 19, 1961, pp. 881-883.

Its own interest in foreign policy, however, remains economic rather than political or ideological.[2]

Also, the BDI has been content to put its faith in Adenauer's policy out of a desire to overcome the mistrust abroad of German industry because of its role during earlier regimes. If public opinion surveys are an accurate barometer, however, a decade or so ago there were still grounds for that mistrust. A poll in May 1951 revealed that 28 per cent of West German businessmen saw National Socialism as more good than evil, primarily because of its economic and social welfare programs, while 38 per cent held the opposite view, and 34 per cent had no opinion. The poll also revealed that 3 per cent would welcome and support a party similar to the NSDAP if it should come into power, and 8 per cent would welcome but not necessarily support it.[3] Nowadays the figures would perhaps be different; but there is every reason to believe that a hard core of Nazis still exists in all strata of the population. As Gabriel Almond points out concerning the 1951 survey, "The business respondents did not display patterns that were consistently different from those of most of the other occupational groups."[4]

Of course, the ordinary harried and overworked businessman or the average German citizen is not inclined to reflect on the past, but would just as soon forget it. The extent to which he reflects on Germany's position in the contemporary world situation, and is informed of political developments abroad, is not

[2] Deutsch and Edinger, *Germany Rejoins the Powers,* p. 101.

[3] Poll taken by the Office of the High Commissioner of Germany (HICOG), as cited by Almond, *The Politics of German Business,* pp. 61, 65. By Dec. 1952 the number finding "more good than evil" had risen to 44 per cent, while 41 per cent saw "more evil than good," and 15 per cent were undecided. The withdrawal of Allied controls may have led to this shift in expressed opinion. On the question of supporting another NSDAP, of the nonbusiness respondents 29 per cent said they would do everything possible to prevent it from coming into power; 25 per cent said they would not like it but would do nothing to prevent it; and 26 per cent said they would not care. *Ibid.*

[4] *Ibid.,* pp. 66–67.

easily determined. According to one survey of the business elite, the leading German businessmen have a considerable interest in international affairs, about which they inform themselves primarily through personal contacts, but also extensively through foreign travel and the press. Indeed, 61 per cent were reported to read at least one foreign newspaper or journal. Among French businessmen the proportion who do so is even higher—73 per cent—but among the insular British the figure is a mere 33 per cent.[5] Among the average German businessman the BDI admits a lack of interest in foreign developments, and also an occasional division of sentiment on issues directly affecting them, or even outright opposition to the government's course.[6]

Some of the key issues in recent years, and the position taken by the BDI concerning them, will now be examined.

GERMAN REUNIFICATION

On the vital political and economic question of the reunification of Germany, BDI leaders have publicly voiced sentiments parallel to those of the government. Several industrial leaders are active in the semi-public organization, *Kuratorium Unteilbares Deutschland*, which publicizes government efforts at reunification. But surprisingly, few thoughtful discussions of the subject have appeared in BDI or DI publications. Few employers have advocated a critical examination of Adenauer's position on reunification. In one DI journal an unidentified author warned that free elections should be scheduled only if the Soviets ended their aggressive tactics and their infiltration of agents into West Germany.[7] In another article, an entrepreneur called on the business community to draft plans for reunification, and

[5] The French businessman prefers foreign travel above all, the British the press of his own country. Keller, "Attitudes of the French, German, and British Business Elite," p. 16.

[6] Deutsch and Edinger, *Germany Rejoins the Powers*, pp. 198–199; "Angelpunkt Aussenpolitik," *VR*, No. 42, Oct. 16, 1952.

[7] "Freie Wahlen zu Deutschlands Wiedervereinigung," *UB*, No. 35, Sept. 2, 1954.

on the government to organize a group of employers who would be attached to the Ministry of Economics and whose job would be to estimate future production capacity, sales, and other aspects of a nationwide industrial complex built upon progressive economic and social foundations.[8] That nothing of the sort has been done may be simply because reunification remains a remote dream, or perhaps because there is a certain coolness among some businessmen toward the idea of reunification. After all, according to the private reasoning of the latter, a reunited country might rock the boat of West German prosperity, or involve large increases in investment under the direction of the government.

Most businessmen, however, take a less jaundiced view. They see in reunification a chance to regain property or to reassert economic control in the Eastern Zone. They are not greatly concerned over Ulbricht's statement to the effect that East German workers will never submit to their control, and that continued nationalization must be a condition of reunification.[9] According to one survey, although most West German businessmen believed in 1957 that more should be done to speed up reunification, and seemed genuinely concerned about the problem, they were resigned to the continued split and saw no likelihood of an early settlement. While a minority advocated continuous negotiation with the Soviet Union, the majority supported the Adenauer policy of dealing from strength through diplomatic pressures.[10] Berg asserted in 1956 that the Soviets were not even thinking about yielding the Eastern Zone, since they viewed it as an outpost of the Bolshevik revolution, and that it was impossible to discuss their price for German reunification, which was nothing less than the bolshevization of all Germany.[11]

[8] Heinrich Krumm, "Probleme der Wiedervereinigung," *UB*, No. 21, May 26, 1952.

[9] John P. Nettl, "Economic Checks on German Unity," *Foreign Affairs*, XXX, No. 4 (July 1952), 554; "Backing for Herr Ulbricht," *Economist*, CLXXV, No. 5829 (May 14, 1955), 554.

[10] Almond, *The Politics of German Business*, pp. 69–75.

[11] *Mitteilungen*, IV, No. 1 (Jan. 10, 1956), 8–9.

After Khrushchev's 1958 ultimatum on Berlin, Berg took the initiative in developing an "economic bridge" with that city. He called on German industry to declare its solidarity with the former German capital by increased purchases and investments in West Berlin. By ensuring the freedom of Berlin, he said employers would be helping the cause of the freedom of Europe and the world.[12] This appeal brought a positive response, and the Berlin economy has been appreciably strengthened even since the erection of the wall.

WEST EUROPEAN INTEGRATION

The BDI is much more urgently in favor of West European integration than it is of German reunification. Many businessmen evidently support integration because they favor the economic and political strengthening of the European continent and the doing away with the narrow focus on nationalism. Others apparently see integration as giving Germany a dominant role in a supranational union.[13] Whatever the motivation, industrialists have unquestionably broadened their horizons. In November 1952 the BDI held a widely publicized "Europe Day" at Trier, where Paul-Henri Spaak, an outspoken advocate of European integration, was invited to give the keynote address. Berg, who also spoke, asserted that one potential threat to European unity, the Saar, must not be an obstacle.[14]

Occasionally, as in 1954, the BDI has warned the government, à propos of certain unattractive economic policies, that it could not always expect to receive the support of industry for its foreign policy, and that on the question of European union "we are determined in the future to be more reserved in order not to be misunderstood"; but such statements remain an exception to the rule.[15] Normally the BDI, through its spokesmen Berg and

[12] "Die Wirtschaft an der Jahreswende," *VR*, No. 51, Dec. 22, 1958.
[13] Almond, *The Politics of German Business*, pp. 83–87.
[14] *Europatag des BDI in Trier am 30. und 31. Oktober 1952* (BDI publication No. 18, 1953).
[15] *Welt der Arbeit*, May 21, 1954.

Beutler, has backed Adenauer's moves to tie West Germany closer to France and other West European powers. A number of industrialists and bankers closely allied to the BDI have been active financially in promoting the movement for European union.[16] Moreover, among the deputies of the German Bundestag who sit in the Consultative Assembly of the Council of Europe at Strasbourg are many with close ties to business.[17] But the role of the Assembly is modest and does not give the deputies much leverage in European politics. The European Economic Community, which will be considered shortly, is another and far more important matter.

THE ATLANTIC COMMUNITY AND THE UNITED STATES

Looking beyond European integration, BDI leaders have declared in an annual report, "Not only does there exist for us no better system of peace than the Atlantic Community—there is no peace and no liberty at all outside this union of the nations of the free world."[18] In June 1959 a privately sponsored Atlantic congress was organized to prepare the foundations of an Atlantic community. Thirty leading German industrialists took part. Berg presided over the key economic committee, and Beutler was the coordinator of a committee studying western commercial relations with the Soviet bloc.[19] In addition, the industrial and banking fraternity is heavily represented in the top council of the Atlantic Bridge, an organization founded in 1951 to promote better understanding between Germany and the United States, and in the German Society for Foreign Policy.

[16] Wahrhaftig, in *West German Leadership and Foreign Policy*, ed. Speier and Davison, p. 45.

[17] For instance, in 1960 Birrenbach, Burgbacher, Illerhaus, Leverkühn, A. Lenz, Müller-Hermann, Löhr, Scheel, Starke. German Federal Republic. *Die Bundesrepublik*, Sammelband 1960/61 (Köln, c. 1961), pp. 372–373.

[18] BDI, *Review of the Annual Report 1957/1958 of the Federation of German Industries*, p. 11.

[19] JB, 1958–1959, p. 57.

For the BDI the main objective of an Atlantic community is to enhance good will and mutual economic benefit between the United States and Western Europe. Among business leaders the reservoir of good will toward Americans is already considerable. A study by Suzanne Keller of MIT shows a positive image of Americans among the German business elite, whose judgment finds the former typically "democratic, unprejudiced, vigorous, vital, business-oriented." The French business elite, incidentally, do not share these favorable views, but consider Americans to be obsessed with business or with money or to be naive.[20]

On a number of occasions the BDI has taken the initiative in promoting American good will toward Germany and especially toward its business community, and in establishing closer contacts with United States leaders for business purposes. In late 1954 Berg and Beutler met with John Foster Dulles, Charles E. Wilson, and other leading government and business officials in the United States. A number of bilateral conferences between United States and German business leaders have led to the evolution of the Petersberg Group, consisting of industrialists from both nations who discuss economic and other problems of mutual interest, and who follow up their discussions with memoranda to their governments and to international organizations.

The BDI has also tackled the problem of the United States government's seizure of German assets held in the United States, which both the BDI and the German government have made strenuous efforts to have returned to their country. In July 1955, for instance, the BDI presidential board discussed the problem in the presence of two members of the Ministry of Foreign Affairs and interested bankers and industrialists. At that time a German delegation headed by the banker Abs was planning a trip to the United States, and the discussion centered

[20] Surprisingly, the French business elite (but not all French elites) expressed a liking for the Germans, and less surprisingly the German business elite did not like the French but liked the British. The judgments on the whole reflected national and not business attitudes. Keller, "Attitudes of the French, German, and British Business Elite," pp. 26 ff.

on a propaganda campaign there, for which the Ministry of Finance was ready to provide 150,000 DM, and German industry anywhere from 350,000 to 850,000 DM. The industrialist Hugo Stinnes suggested that an office be set up in Washington for the purpose of influencing congressmen who would be voting on the return of the assets. The discussion then turned to the question of just how this kind of lobbying could be effective without being too obvious.[21] Two years later in 1957, in response to various pressures from Germany, the United States government submitted to Congress a proposal that two-thirds of the assets be returned—a move that the London *Economist* suggested was timed to strengthen Adenauer's position with business in the coming West German election.[22]

Another effort to influence government and public opinion in the United States involved the BDI only indirectly. Berthold Beitz, managing director of the mammoth firm of Krupp, journeyed to Washington to obtain financial support, both United States and international, for the the so-called "Krupp Point Four-and-a-Half Program," under which the plan was to build steel mills and other major plants in underdeveloped countries. Although Beitz could not rally much support in Washington, the firm eventually was able to tap other sources and to launch some of the proposed projects. On another occasion, Beitz sought backing from the United States government for a reversal of an Allied policy under which his firm would have had to divest itself of the important subsidiary works Rheinhausen. In this undertaking he approached State Department officials and members of Congress (as well as German government officials) whose response was positive.[23] The Krupp firm, incidentally, is again so powerful that it has not needed the support of the BDI.

Indeed, according to the British journalist Terence Prittie,

---

[21] *Präsidialsitzung*, July 20, 1955.

[22] Aug. 10, 1957, p. 467.

[23] Norbert Muhlen, *The Incredible Krupps* (New York, 1959), pp. 248–249; Terence Prittie, *Germany Divided: The Legacy of the Nazi Era* (Boston, 1960), pp. 289–290.

Alfried Krupp has become West Germany's unofficial industrial ambassador, entertaining leading statesmen at the Villa Hügel near Essen in the heart of the Ruhr. "Even members of the hierarchy of France's Fourth Republic," Prittie wrote, "were able to find their taste in ladies' fashions a suitable excuse for ingratiating themselves with the most powerful family of the old German industrial oligarchy."[24]

EDC AND NATO

As the BDI looks to the West, the economic aspects of military and political problems are both of direct concern. In the protracted negotiations to establish the European Defense Community the BDI proffered support, but only on condition that complete sovereignty be restored to Germany and that there be no discrimination against the German people.[25] It privately deplored the failure of the German and French governments sufficiently to consult their industrial associations or to take the business point of view into consideration.[26]

But there was actually no unanimity in business ranks on the question of EDC. According to one survey, from 64 to 68 per cent of the German business elite supported EDC and from 22 to 25 per cent opposed it—a proportion that corresponded closely to the 64 per cent support from the German elites as a whole.[27] Another survey indicated that the EDC was favored either because it was the only way of having Germany rearmed or because it would lead to Germany's reintegration with the European community. The opponents of EDC either saw it as restricting German freedom of action or, at the other extreme, feared that a remilitarized Germany would jeopardize the development of

[24] *Ibid.*, p. 291.

[25] *Deutsche Zeitung*, May 16, 1952.

[26] *Präsidialsitzung*, Oct. 25, 1954.

[27] The rest of the business elite had no opinion. Keller, "Attitudes toward European Integration of the German Elite," (multigraphed, Oct. 1957), pp. 2, 26.

European unity, and accordingly favored economic integration first.[28]

The defeat of EDC came as a shock to many German business-men who had high hopes that it would promote European integration. According to Almond,

One of the most prominent supporters of Adenauer in the business community, a man known for his good nerves and prudence, reflected the strongest anxiety and self-doubt. He spoke as though the EDC had meant a burial, once and for all, of German aggressiveness and of the chance to have it harnessed into a European system where those energies might be used for constructive purposes. The collapse of EDC left him full of doubt. He could not be quite easy in his own mind about the reliability of a separate German army so far as the security of Europe was concerned.[29]

Of other businessmen, says Almond, only a minority were opposed to any kind of rearmament, while the rest supported it to varying degrees and with various qualifications. Many had not given much thought to the alternative presented by NATO. They did affirm that since the Germans had had their fill of militarism, a German army integrated into NATO would not pose a threat to other nations. They again demanded complete equality of treatment for Germany, and especially when it came to any restrictions on trade with the Soviet bloc. The internationalists saw the Paris Agreements of October 1954 as a bond with the West. Other businessmen, more nationalist in outlook, viewed Germany's joining of NATO under those agreements as giving it maximum freedom to rearm.[30]

The Keller survey showed that the main support for the Paris Agreements came from the owners of medium-sized businesses (81 per cent being for and 12 per cent against, with 7 per cent expressing no opinion) and from big business (with 80 per cent for, 6 per cent against, and 14 per cent expressing no opinion).

28 Almond, *The Politics of German Business*, pp. 75–83.
29 *Ibid.*, p. 80.
30 *Ibid.*, pp. 68, 75–83.

It had less support from the small business community (with 61 per cent for, 21 per cent against, and 18 per cent expressing no opinion). Among all German elites (with 74 per cent for, 17 per cent against, and 9 per cent undecided), the medium-sized and big business communities were the most strongly in favor of the agreements. Miss Keller surmises that the position of small businessmen was due to the narrow political outlook and a lack of interest in international affairs stemming in part from the prevailing low level of education as compared with other businessmen. Then, too, a greater number are members of the SPD, which did not favor the agreements.[31]

Although the BDI could not rally the unanimous support of businessmen for the Paris Agreements, its officers felt confident enough of a majority backing to take a stand. During the preliminary diplomatic negotiations they called on the government to give greater heed to the voice of industry than it had done during the EDC imbroglio if it hoped to avoid future difficulties. Once Germany became a member of NATO they set up close ties with it in order to influence any economic decisions that might ensue from the joint defense effort. In 1958, when the government advocated atomic arms for its own forces, and the SPD demanded a national referendum, the BDI, in its yearbook, voiced strong opposition on constitutional grounds: "A referendum organized by opposition parties, amounting to a mobilization of the masses against the constitutionally competent authorities, would deprive Parliament of its powers, run counter to the spirit of our Basic Law, and destroy the very foundations of democracy as representative institutions."[32]

The BDI's attitude toward West European integration and an Atlantic community, its close ties to the United States and to NATO, are consistent with its negative attitude toward the Soviet Union. But although Berg has taken a consistently tough

[31] Keller, "Attitudes toward European Integration of the German Elite," pp. 26–28.
[32] BDI, *Review of the Annual Report 1957/1958*, pp. 10–11.

position toward the Soviet Union, many industrialists who trade with the Soviets do not support him entirely; some of these favor the proposals made in 1954 by former Chancellor Bruening and by FDP deputy Pfleiderer, calling for a return to the diplomacy of Rapallo. At a press conference Berg declared that he had not heard of the proposals, but that if they contravened Adenauer's policy he would oppose them. This answer, so characteristic of Berg's loyalty to the Chancellor, evoked critical comment from several sources. The FDP, a party with some business support, asserted that Berg had no right to set himself up as the business community's spokesman on foreign policy. The DGB also entered the fray, partly in retaliation against the previous charges that it had violated party neutrality. The DGB journal asked its readers whether it was the task of an association to commit itself to a party line and a foreign policy or whether it should remain politically neutral. The reply, of course, was that it should do the latter.[33]

But Adenauer has never hesitated to call on the industrialists to fight against communism. At the 1952 BDI Assembly he asserted that it was the mission of industry to develop a sound economy, hold the domestic peace, and avoid social tensions that might endanger the struggle against the Soviet Union. "You are the ones," he said, "who must be in the forefront in the cold war against Russia." Berg in his reply praised Adenauer and pledged that industry would support his foreign policy "with all of its power."[34]

The Adenauer regime was able to count on almost unqualified support from the BDI in major foreign policy questions, although a minority of industry, especially in the FDP, had serious reservations about the Chancellor's inflexible attitude toward the Soviet bloc. A survey of West German elites in

[33] *Welt der Arbeit*, July 2, 1954; also see *Die Welt*, June 24 and 25, 1954; Almond, *The Politics of German Business*, p. 18.

[34] *Kundgebung und Mitgliederversammlung des BDI am 5. und 6. Mai 1952 in Hamburg*, pp. 10, 13 ff.

regard to sixteen foreign policy issues in the period 1952–1958 found that while the government's policy was usually acceptable to big business, the trade unions rarely registered satisfaction with it.[35] This is hardly surprising, given the affinity of views between government and industry, coupled with a certain opportunism on the part of the latter. There was no reason not to go along with Adenauer on foreign policy matters which did not adversely affect its own interest.

DEFENSE POLICY

When it comes to foreign and domestic policy matters closely related to the interests of industry, such as defense and trade, the BDI can no longer be expected to provide automatic support to the government. Rather, it cautiously assesses every aspect of policy before making any commitment. When late in 1954 the Western Allies invited the German federal government to join NATO, and Germany's rearmament had become a reality, all through the negotiations in Paris the BDI maintained contact with the government delegation there—as well as with the German Ministries of Foreign Affairs and Economics, the Office of Defense, and other European industrial associations—in order to make sure that all economic tasks related to defense be put into the hands of the Ministry of Economics, which it obviously viewed as the ministry most sympathetic to its aims. Upon communicating these views to the government, the BDI received an unexpected invitation to send its experts to the negotiations in Paris.[36]

The BDI viewed the launching of a defense program with mixed feelings so far as its political implications were concerned. It said that German industry was ready to assume a defense burden for the sake of peace and freedom, although the wide-

[35] In the period up to 1955 the response of business was also quite negative, but since 1955 it has been much more positive. Survey based on elite inventory and public opinion polls. Deutsch and Edinger, *Germany Rejoins the Powers*, p. 212.

[36] *Präsidialsitzung*, Oct. 25, 1954; Jan. 26, 1955.

spread "slanders and degradations" and "shameful" punitive measures which industrial leaders were subjected to after the War had by no means been forgotten. The BDI in fact offered its support to Adenauer only on condition that such defamations were not to be revived.[37]

All imputations of eagerness to accept defense orders were vehemently denied by the BDI; on the contrary, it asked for assurances that a policy of business as usual would be maintained along with any defense buildup. It emphasized: (1) that no business boom would follow in the wake of defense production, since existing plant facilities could meet the new orders without expansion; (2) that military programs must be so planned as not to hamper free economic competition; (3) that defense orders should not cut into exports or the domestic civilian market; (4) that all economic aspects of the defense program should be handled by the Ministry of Economics, and all contracts for military hardware by the Ministry of Defense; (5) that there must be close collaboration between the ministries and the business world; and (6) that questions of investment, capacity, and raw materials ought to be discussed jointly by business and an organ representing the ministries.[38]

Translating these six points into action was difficult—especially the one calling for satisfactory relationships with the ministries. As often happens, unanimity of approach between the economic associations was not to be achieved with ease. The SPD's defense expert noted that industry lacked unity—for which, he added, "God be thanked."[39] The BDI was indeed at loggerheads with some of its associations, with the DIHT, and with Defense Minister Blank. At one time Berg complained of the Ministry's failure to give a satisfactory reply to its inquiry on how much hardware German industry was expected to pro-

[37] *JB*, 1954–1955, p. 197; 1955–1956, p. 178.
[38] *JB*, 1954–1955, p. 198.
[39] Helmut Schmidt in Bundestag, 2nd el. pd., 88th session, June 16, 1955, pp. 4936–4937.

duce for defense, so that whatever long-range plans might be necessary to meet the demand for consumer goods could also be made.[40]

In 1958, two years later, industry showed less reluctance to produce defense materials. Krupp was alone in publicly announcing that "military production is not profitable,"[41] and that his firm would restrict itself to producing nonmilitary goods —obviously because the name of his firm was linked throughout the world with war production. But the BDI went to bat for the rest of German industry as it became more interested in defense contracts. Berg asked the new Minister of Defense, Franz-Josef Strauss, to ascertain the number of contracts signed by the Federal Government with suppliers in other countries, and to find out whether German industry could supply the items more cheaply. Although Strauss promised such a survey, Erhard was opposed to having more contracts, especially for heavy weapons, awarded to German manufacturers, since the required expansion of plant capacity simply for defense production would then lead to a dangerous boom and to "first-class" waste in the economy.[42]

The SPD was opposed not only to industry's part in defense production but also in principle to rearmament, although in more recent years the position of most of the party's membership has changed. But in 1958 it assailed the BDI for reversing the original policy of industry favoring a total renunciation of arms production, to one of fervent cooperation with the "dangerous, atom-hungry Franz-Josef Strauss." It asserted that "trucks, tents, buildings, uniforms, and food for the Bundeswehr

[40] Die Welt, June 14, 1956.

[41] Muhlen, The Incredible Krupps, p. 262.

[42] Die Welt, April 17 and 24, 1958; Handelsblatt, April 25, 1958. Berg used another argument to justify giving priority to German manufacturers over their foreign competitors: if Germany produced more military hardware, the technological impact on civilian goods would be enhanced—for instance in the aircraft field. Speech to convention of Iron-, Tin-, and Metal-Finishing Industry, April 9, 1959 (mimeographed).

would have been produced in Germany in any case. The industrialists are beginning to think about the Devil's tools (*i.e.*, missiles, tanks, and atomic artillery) as well."

The SPD stated its position as follows:

It is of course economically unsound to give away industrial contracts and means of investment to foreign companies, when the economy of a country can fulfill these contracts just as well. But these contracts are for armaments, and armament production was "renounced" by German industry. We cannot believe that the Federation of German Industry, and its president, Fritz Berg, can possibly be supported by all West German industry, that they have all forgotten the horrible effects of the past war and the unforeseeable effects of a next one.[43]

The SPD's argument that German industry had "renounced" armament production does not seem quite accurate, at least so far as the BDI was concerned, for no statement to that effect seems ever to have been made by the latter.

In 1955 the business community agreed to designate the BDI as the primary channel of communication with the government, while the DIHT and the artisans' and wholesale trade organizations were to participate in a secondary role. The BDI organized a department of defense affairs and a defense committee with Berg as chairman. The latter established a host of subcommittees representing various branches of industry engaged in defense production, in which representatives of other business organizations were to be included.[44] Government ministries were asked by the BDI to make use of its defense committee in an advisory capacity, especially concerning the kinds and specifications of products industry was to provide. Since then the Ministry of Defense has accepted many of the committee's recommendations.

The committee established a close liaison with the Procurement Office of the Ministry of Defense at Koblenz—but not, the

[43] SPD, *News from Germany*, May 1958.
[44] *JB*, 1958–1959, p. 253.

BDI has insisted, so as to influence the awarding of contracts. After the Koblenz defense scandals had implicated certain industrial firms, the BDI saw the committee's work as more important than ever because it could be free of the unfortunate influence of some company representatives.[45] The scandals nevertheless led to strained relations between the Koblenz office and the BDI up until 1959, when the former furnished the BDI committee with an order specifying correct liaison procedures, which the BDI welcomed as corresponding "fairly closely" with its point of view.[46]

On the *Land* level, the BDI regional offices and associations—such as textile, leather, and wood-processing—interested in defense contracts also sought representation in *Land* Advisory Offices for Contracts, which were partially financed by industry. In two of the *Länder* the BDI regional offices put up 5 per cent of the budget—in consideration of which they received all the memoranda, "were able to prevent errors in the decisions," and gained access to important committees in the Ministry of Economics. On the other hand, the BDI's Bavarian regional office dropped its membership in the Advisory Office for Contracts, and reduced its contribution from 6,000 DM to 3,000 DM out of a total budget of 240,000 DM, in part because the firms' experience in the awarding of contracts was such that they no longer needed the services of the advisory office.[47]

On the whole the BDI has been dissatisfied with the tenuous bonds to the ministries; but its attempts to strengthen them have had only mixed results. It has urged the Ministry of Defense to set up advisory councils in which industry and the academic community would be represented by members chosen —significantly—not by the Ministry but by itself and the German Research Society. It has also urged the establishment of

[45] For details of the scandals, see pp. 225–226. *JB*, 1958–1959, p. 253.
[46] *Ibid.*
[47] HGF, memorandum to executive officers of regional offices concerning a meeting on Jan. 30, 1959 (dated Feb. 27, 1959).

commissions of experts to work closely with various divisions in the Ministry, suggesting that the subcommittees of the BDI's defense committee could easily be transformed into just such bodies. The Ministry eventually did name a scientific and technical advisory council with commissions of experts—but the BDI complained in 1959 that there was still no rapport with its own organs even though the Ministry commissions were known to be overworked.[48]

The BDI has also attempted to increase its influence at other points of access on the federal and supranational level, but again cannot claim any major victory. It has submitted a memorandum on defense problems to Adenauer as chairman of the cabinet-level Defense Council. It has urged the inclusion of industrial experts in the Council, as well as in the committees and subcommittees of NATO and West European Union (WEU), when difficult economic or technical problems are to be discussed. But the response of the government has not been positive, apparently because of a wish to forestall accusations that industry was in control of the defense effort. The BDI, choosing the next best course, then tried to cement the link between German industry and NATO. Berg and various top industrialists several times visited NATO headquarters for a close study of its operations and for briefings by its officials. The BDI was given an opportunity to be in close communication with—although not to be directly represented on—such NATO organs as its Defense Committee and its Military Agency for Standardization, as well as with the Standing Armaments Committee of WEU, and the FINABEL committees (representing France, Italy, the Netherlands, Germany, Belgium, and Luxemburg) on military requirements.[49] One interesting reason why the German Association of the Chemical Industry wanted a representative on the WEU Defense Control Office—which checks for violations of the order prohibiting the Federal Republic from

[48] *JB*, 1957–1958, pp. 169–170; 1958–1959, p. 254.
[49] *JB*, 1955–1956, p. 184; 1958–1959, p. 255.

producing atomic, biological, and chemical weapons—was to make sure that the secrets of its civilian production were safeguarded.[50] But its efforts to obtain a voice there were in vain.

The BDI emphasizes not only its exclusion from advisory councils of this kind, but also the disadvantages of the defense buildup from the industrial point of view. It cites such handicaps to the employer who switches entirely to defense production as the loss of a consumer market which he cannot easily recapture, the high risks and low profits, the dependence on continued defense orders, and the obligation to make technical changes imposed by stringent government specifications.[51] Since, however, most manufacturers have not switched their entire line to defense, but have been able to fulfill both military and nonmilitary requirements, the complaint is not altogether justified.

Despite certain restrictions and frustrations, the BDI can scarcely complain that industry has not benefited from rearmament. It also has more links to the Defense Ministry than it will generally acknowledge. Indeed, in a speech to the Bundestag the SPD deputy Helmut Schmidt asserted that parliament had greater difficulty in obtaining financial estimates from the Ministry than did the BDI. He reported that in 1957 the Minister of Defense had given the BDI a survey of long-range Bundeswehr requirements, and followed it up with a press release beginning, "As a result of an understanding with the BDI, the Ministry of Defense announces . . ." According to the minutes of the Bundestag, when Schmidt read this he was interrupted by laughter and cries of "Hear, hear" from SPD ranks, and the interjection of a deputy: "Mr. Chancellor, who determines the guiding principles?"[52] The Chancellor remained silent.

[50] Verband der Chemischen Industrie, *Bericht über die Tätigkeit im Jahre 1956*, p. 44.

[51] *JB*, 1960–1961, p. 151.

[52] Bundestag, 3rd el. pd., 24th session, April 23, 1958, p. 1300.

ECONOMIC POLICY: TRADE

In the realm of economic policy the BDI is especially concerned with trade, tariffs, and investments in developing countries. Its preoccupation with trade is to be expected, since in 1962 the Federal Republic was "one of the three most important trading nations of the world, behind the United States and perhaps about on a par with Great Britain," with imports amounting to 49.5 million DM, and exports to 51 million DM.[53] Its imports include many basic and raw materials (steel, chemicals, timber, coal, oil, and petroleum products) as well as agricultural products; its exports are investment goods (machinery, cars, metal and electrotechnical products), steel, and chemicals.[54] More than half of German's exports and imports are with the noncommunist countries of Europe; in 1961 the proportion of trade with communist countries was 4.3 per cent (see Table V).

TABLE V

GERMANY'S TRADE, 1957 AND 1961*

Percentage shares in the Federal Republic's over-all foreign trade
(exports plus imports)

AREA	1957	1961
Common Market (the "Six")	26.4	31.4
EFTA (the "Seven")	23.3	24.1
U.S. and Canada	13.7	11.5
Communist countries	3.5	4.3
All others	33.1	28.7
Total	100.0	100.0

* *The Bulletin,* March 13, 1962.

In terms of bilateral trade the United States is the most important supplier of the Federal Republic, while France is the most important customer.[55]

53 *The Bulletin,* March 13, 1962; March 19, 1963.

54 *Ibid.,* March 13, 1962.

55 In descending order of magnitude, as a supplier: United States, France, Netherlands, Italy, Belgium/Netherlands, Great Britain, Sweden, Switzer-

For the BDI the volume of trade and the tariff level are paramount concerns. After World War II, while the Allies controlled foreign trade, the manufacturers' hands were tied; but after the Federal Government took over and the restrictions had been lifted, bilateral and eventually multilateral agreements with many countries led to a great liberalization in trade.

At the time the BDI was founded, a foreign trade committee was already in existence, and the BDI quickly set up a department of foreign trade of its own to service it. The principal tasks of these organs is to influence agreements concluded with other countries, through participation in negotiations, and to bring the industrial point of view to the attention of high government officials and members of the trade delegations. Normally the BDI is asked to send one or more representatives to the government delegation conducting the actual negotiations with another country. The BDI and its associations welcome this consultative role, but have criticized such procedural aspects as the government's repeated failure to grant enough time for consultation with industry when an agreement is pending.[56]

To stimulate trade during the early years of the Federal Republic, the BDI asked repeatedly for a swift buildup of the German diplomatic and consular corps. It has maintained close contact with diplomatic missions abroad, briefing diplomats and heads of the economic sections about to leave for foreign assignments, and keeping in touch with the latter while they are abroad. It has also organized conferences with the heads of the economic sections of foreign embassies in Bonn, and has sent

---

land, Austria; as a customer: France, Netherlands, Switzerland, United States, Italy, Belgium/Luxemburg, Austria, Sweden, Great Britain. *Ibid.*, March 19, 1963.

[56] Verband der Chemischen Industrie, *Bericht über die Tätigkeit im Jahre 1951*, p. 16. A BDI memorandum on another procedural matter, the question of Turkish debts, contended that since the lower civil service could not be expected to go far in solving a financial problem, the BDI would seek to hold conferences with the state secretaries of several ministries. BDI department of foreign trade, memorandum dated Dec. 17, 1958.

goodwill missions to confer with government officials in under-developed countries.

So much for the techniques. When it comes to the problems encountered by the BDI, and its success in promoting trade in various parts of the world, its lack of concern with the ideological coloration of the trading state, as compared to the accumulation of profits, is of importance. When politics and economics clash, friction is bound to be the result. This has happened in the Middle East, for example. Since Germany has traditionally been a trading partner with the Arab countries, the BDI was critical of the German-Israel agreement on reparations concluded in 1951, and lost no time in registering a protest against the economic burden and the threatened boycott of German goods by Arab countries if the agreement were to come into force. In 1952 Berg suggested to Adenauer that a good will mission made up of government officials and industrialists be sent to the Arab countries. The government took up his suggestion, and early in 1953 an economic delegation set out for Cairo. In addition, the BDI set up a commission to consider future economic relations with the Arab countries that had "promising" markets, and to forge closer cultural ties—an aim that has since been realized.[57]

TRADE WITH THE COMMUNIST BLOC

The BDI has clashed with the government on the question of trade with communist countries, again because German political and economic policies have not always coincided. In part as a result of governmental actions, trade with East Germany has never amounted to more than 2 or 3 per cent of the Federal Republic's entire commercial exchange.[58] The BDI had a hand in compiling the list of goods that might be shipped to East

[57] BDI, memorandum on session of main committee, Dec. 11, 1952; *JB*, 1952–1953, p. 85; Deutsch and Edinger, *Germany Rejoins the Powers*, pp. 171–172.

[58] There has been a gradual rise in exports from 12.9 million DM in 1948, to 79.9 million DM in 1960. *Bulletin*, No. 65, April 4, 1962, p. 545.

Germany under the Berlin Agreement of September 1951, and in 1952 it set up a committee to deal with interzonal trade. The government has taken the initiative on the whole, and the industrialists—many of them reluctantly—have bowed to political expediency so far as trade is concerned. Ernst Lemmer, the former Minister for All-German Affairs, once warned a BDI conference that out of political considerations manufacturers ought to give careful consideration to the kind of trade agreements that were to be concluded with the Eastern Zone (and with the rest of the Soviet bloc). In spite of exhortations to limit commercial relations with the Eastern Zone, some illegal trade has taken place—and Berg has denounced the manufacturers who were violating the law.[59]

The extraordinary political repercussions of the 1962 Leipzig trade fair have already been noted.[60] Normally, over 1,500 West German firms, including such giants as Krupp, Klöckner, and Daimler-Benz, have been represented at Leipzig. After the erection of the Berlin wall the great majority of these firms acceded readily to the BDI's request not to show their wares at Leipzig, although between 130 and 150 manufacturers broke the boycott in 1962. Ironically, it is largely the very employers—many of them from the Ruhr and Rhine areas—who have been trading with the Eastern Zone who are also helping to shore up the economy of West Berlin.[61] More and more the BDI has tended to conclude that because of the political situation its contacts with the Eastern Zone must be restricted solely to economic matters.

This is even more true of West German relations with the rest of the communist bloc. Trade with these countries rose steadily but slowly during the 1950's. Imports into the Federal Republic amounted to 3.4 per cent of the total in 1950, and to

[59] *JB*, 1951–1952, p. 49; *Bericht der Industrie- und Handelskammer Frankfurt am Main 1959/1960*, p. 155.

[60] See Chapter IX.

[61] *Industriekurier*, Feb. 17, 1959; *New York Times*, Jan. 28, 1962, Section I, p. 6; *Bulletin*, No. 65, April 4, 1962, p. 544.

4.6 per cent in 1959 while exports rose from 4.1 to 4.5 per cent in the same period. The most important trading partner has been the Soviet Union, followed by communist China, Poland, Czechoslovakia, Hungary, Rumania, Bulgaria, and Albania.[62] The communist bloc has been primarily interested in importing West German industrial products in exchange for raw materials and foodstuffs. But compared with the 1920's and 1930's, when bulk orders for machine tools and other industrial products were pouring in (in 1936 they amounted to 16 per cent of all German exports), trade with the East has been appreciably reduced since World War II. This is due first of all to the Soviet take-over of East European countries, and secondly to the German government's reluctance to encourage trade with communist countries.

When that reluctance took the form of an embargo on strategic goods after the Korean War, many businessmen did not conceal their dismay and resentment. They refused to support an embargo unless the same prohibition and yardsticks were applied to Western countries, and Germany was not put at a disadvantage in her traditional trade with the East. They backed efforts to increase trade in nonstrategic materials by liberalizing the provisions of the embargo, as well as by more aggressive promotion.[63] Even while orders from Western countries poured into the headquarters of West German firms, the latter continued to voice their concern over becoming dependent on trade with the West, arguing that Germany's leading economic position might be endangered in the future, and that it would then be necessary to compete with British and other Western firms in Eastern markets.

Yet the BDI warned these firms not to overestimate the possibilities of increasing trade with the East, and urged them to relinquish their nostalgia for old times. One expert estimated

[62] In monetary terms these import percentages represented the equivalent of 383,654,000 DM in 1950, and of 1,645,044,000 DM in 1959. Exports in 1950 amounted to 344,067,000 DM, and in 1959 to 1,860,846,000. *Bulletin*, No. 27, Feb. 8, 1961, p. 244.

[63] *JB*, 1951–1952, p. 46; Almond, *The Politics of German Business*, p. 90.

that perhaps 10 per cent of all industrialists still had these fond recollections.[64] Regardless of subjective feelings or politics, an important segment of industrialists was willing to sell to any and all customers. Alfried Krupp, for instance, said after a tour abroad that "his firm was interested in trade with the East bloc countries, and there was no reason why West Germany could not trade with them if other Western states could."[65]

In a sense this was also the BDI's position. While rejecting the conservative view that any trade with communists was a shoring up of their system, it asked for a realistic acknowledgment of the difficulties of expanding commercial relations with communist countries under state planning. Otto Wolff von Amerongen, head of the BDI committee on the East, warned that the possibilities were clearly limited by the fact that the Eastern bloc so strongly emphasized bilateral agreements, and that it wanted to export precisely those goods—such as coal and oil—that the Federal Republic could not use. He added that structural changes had led to increased industrialization in the Soviet Union and to a lesser dependence on imports of machinery and other finished goods, and that autarchical trends were strong in the Eastern bloc. But he nevertheless looked upon East-West trade as "a kind of testing ground for the entire relationship between East and West. Perhaps the *first* signs of a certain understanding will be visible in the trade sector between West and East, if the East bloc considers it as opportune."[66] (Italics in original.)

For political reasons, however, the West German government

[64] Interview with a BDI official concerned with East-West trade. He asserted that it was most difficult for the BDI to convince these men that they were living in the past. See also Almond, *The Politics of German Business*, pp. 91–95; Otto Wolff von Amerongen, "Ost-West-Handel im Schatten der Politik," *Offene Welt*, No. 65, March 1960, p. 58.

[65] M. S. Handler, "Adenauer's Germany: Nation in Transition," *New York Times Magazine*, June 10, 1956, p. 63. See also Muhlen, *The Incredible Krupps*; Wolfgang F. Stolper, *Germany between East and West* (Washington, 1960), pp. 64–65.

[66] "Ost-West Handel im Schatten der Politik," p. 61.

was reluctant to encourage extensive trade with the Eastern bloc, since that trade would run counter to its anti-Soviet policy, and would bring opprobrium from Western powers and from certain segments of the CDU that were sensitive to any new Russo-German alliance. Former Foreign Minister von Brentano said to the Bundestag in one debate on the East-West trade, "We are not of the opinion that we must conduct a political policy for the sake of business." The government feared that in any period of crisis Eastern markets would be closed, since the Soviet Union used trade for political purposes. "These markets," von Brentano went on, "are political markets. The relations in the final instance are political. How we shape our relations is a political and not an economic question." He urged representatives of business, with whose quests for increased commercial links he expressed sympathy, to remember that good balance sheets resulted from successful political policies. "There was a time in which the German economy had excellent balances, and the German people had to bear the consequences."[67]

Toward this official brief for the primacy of politics over economics the BDI had to be at least mildly critical, since so many of the major firms were trading with the East. It averred that if political ties were always given priority, economic ties would suffer. It acknowledged the leadership of the government, but asserted that business must be free to decide when to begin trading with the East on a purely economic basis.[68] One key association asked whether trade policies must be conducted more and more on the basis of political considerations, which all too often meant ignoring the legitimate wishes of business.[69]

The government must have chided business for making such public statements, for Berg was soon reaffirming his support for German foreign policy, averring that German industry acknowl-

[67] Bundestag, 2nd el. pd., 177th session, Dec. 6, 1956, pp. 9818, 9823.
[68] *Präsidialsitzung*, Sept. 3, 1954; *JB*, 1951–1952, p. 8; 1955–1956, p. 109.
[69] Verband der Chemischen Industrie, *Wirtschaftspolitik im Chemiebereich 1958*, p. 9.

edged the primacy of politics, and rejecting the thesis that foreign policy ought to be determined only by economic interests. On the other hand, von Amerongen again insisted that there was no primacy of politics over the economy, or vice versa, because foreign policy and foreign trade were so closely interwoven.[70]

The formation of the BDI's committee on the East *(Ostausschuss)* in October 1952 was an expression of the interdependence. In the absence of diplomatic channels of communication with communist bloc countries, the German government urged the BDI to fill the vacuum by setting up a committee to explore the possibilities of trade with the East. Despite its entirely private status, the government's blessing gave it a semiofficial aura and a good deal of prestige. Before 1955 the committee's numerous regional and functional subdivisions had the task of negotiation and of concluding trade agreements with Eastern bloc governments with the participation of the Ministry of Economics.[71] The committee's power can be gauged by the fact that a close friend of Erhard is its chairman; that unlike other BDI committees it consists of industrialists and important bankers; and that its executive committee includes directors of many of the largest firms, especially those located in the Rhine-Ruhr complex.

The committee claims the initiative in promoting trade with the East, and thereby in bringing about certain major adjustments in trade relations. However, it has also encountered some difficulties. In the spring of 1954 a delegation of German industrialists planned to visit Moscow and negotiate a trade treaty under the sponsorship of the committee; but just then Pfleiderer (FDP), in a speech to the Bundestag, assailed Adenauer's foreign policy and urged a more flexible policy vis-à-vis Moscow. One repercussion was Adenauer's request that the delegation cancel

[70] von Amerongen, "Aussenwirtschaft und Aussenpolitik," *Politisches Seminar,* 1958, p. 129.

[71] Almond, *The Politics of German Business,* p. 90.

its projected visit. It complied, and at a meeting of the BDI presidential board, the members expressed understanding of Adenauer's position, although they criticized the way in which he had made the request public. To the press, the BDI announced that the projected trip was to have had no connection with politics.[72]

A year later, German government officials journeyed to Moscow for talks on political and commercial issues, including a diplomatic exchange, the repatriation of prisoners of war, and an official trade agreement. No industrialist was on the delegation, and the BDI only reluctantly conceded the propriety of having foreign economic policies discussed by diplomats. Berg implicitly criticized the government in a statement that it would be dangerous to tie economic questions to political ones. Although the conference led to the establishment of diplomatic relations and the repatriation of prisoners of war, on the question of trade it was inconclusive. The final communique envisaged more talks by both sides.[73]

These were held in 1957 and 1958, when a government delegation spent eight months in Moscow working out trade and other agreements. This time representatives of the BDI's committee on the East participated. To negotiate the exchange of certain products, two groups of officials from major firms also went to the Soviet Union in the summer of 1958. The first group included Beitz of Krupp; in the second group were officers of Mannesmann, DEMAG, Thyssen, and Phoenix-Rheinrohr. Both groups drew criticism from the government, again because of timing; one group had the misfortune to arrive in Moscow as communist demonstrations were being staged in front of the German embassy. Adenauer promptly declared that he "hoped and wished the visitors would return." The delegations were recalcitrant, and had no intention of returning; but finally,

[72] *Präsidialsitzung*, Aug. 13, 1954; *Die Welt*, June 24, 1954.
[73] *Die Zeit*, Sept. 15, 1955; *Die Welt*, Sept. 13, 1955; *Der Spiegel*, XII, No. 27 (July 2, 1958), 17.

as a compromise, they returned home earlier than they had planned, and the Chancellor denied having given them any orders.[74]

These incidents illustrate Adenauer's sensitivity on foreign policy issues where the communist bloc is involved. He expected industry's undivided and loyal support for a Soviet-German policy which did not give sole priority to trade, and disagreed with the view of some industrialists who contended that increased trade would enhance the position of Bonn. Although on the one hand he refused to establish diplomatic relations with communist countries other than the Soviet Union because they recognized the Eastern Zone, on the other hand he did assent to the negotiations of trade agreements with bloc countries so long as those agreements did not involve diplomatic recognition. The Chancellor could not very well prohibit all trade with the East, since to do so would have led to a sharp break with an important element of industry; and he must have recognized that the committee offered certain advantages—for example, in serving as a West German counterpart of the trade monopolies through which the communist nations carry on commerce. It also functions as an advisory unit to German industries interested in trade with the East, and as an escort for foreign delegations on visits to German fairs and industrial plants. In return, the committee is invited to visit plants in the communist countries.[75]

Domestic pressures on Adenauer to reconsider his inflexible stand against diplomatic recognition of East European states mounted during the 1950's. Finally, late in 1960, Adenauer attempted to improve relations with Poland by sending Beitz, quite unofficially, to take soundings, not on a resumption of diplomatic relations but on increased trade relations, which might in turn become the basis for closer political ties.[76] Al-

[74] Hartmann, *Authority and Organization in German Management*, p. 249; *Der Spiegel*, XII, No. 29 (July 2, 1958), 17.

[75] *JB*, 1957–1958, p. 114.

[76] *New York Times*, Dec. 6, 1960, Jan. 24, 1961.

though there have been precedents, it remains somewhat un-orthodox for a government to send a representative of heavy industry to a parley with leaders of another government on matters not confined to economics. At any rate, the talks paid off. In 1963 a three-year trade agreement was finally concluded, which also provided for the establishment of a West German trade mission in Warsaw (Poland already had one in Bonn). Similar missions have been or will be established in several other East European countries.

In the meantime, at the end of 1961, the Soviets made direct overtures for a closer tie with the Federal Republic by tenta-tively proposing to open their huge markets to German indus-try. Their appeal was directed to a group of industrialists and to the FDP, both of whom are interested in a more flexible policy vis-à-vis the Soviet Union. They had in mind direct con-ferences with West German officials, but owing to the Berlin crisis and to the postwar tie with the West the reaction was negative.[77] The DI's response was to publish in its weekly maga-zine an article entitled "Siren Call from the East." The Soviet appeal was rejected because of its apparent design to split the West, especially in its efforts at economic unification, and be-cause of its attempt to shore up the faltering economies of sev-eral bloc countries. To the latter the East-West trade is more important than it is to those in the West, since most of the East European countries claim to send as much as 25 per cent of their exports to noncommunist countries. The DI added, how-ever, that if German firms were interested in boosting their exports to the East, they should be free to do so.[78]

A new crisis involving trade and political policy toward the Soviet Union erupted in 1962–1963. An initiative by the United States led to the decision at a NATO Council meeting on November 21, 1962, to place an embargo on the shipment of steel pipe to the Soviet Union. The German government com-

[77] *Ibid.*, Jan. 8 and 26, 1962.
[78] *UB*, No. 3, Jan. 18, 1962.

plied in an executive order dated December 14, with the warning that the order would be subject to revocation if the Bundestag should act on it adversely within three months. Three important Ruhr steel companies put heavy pressure on the deputies to reverse the order, since they had contracted in October to supply the Russians with 163,000 tons of pipe in the course of the coming year. They found a sympathetic hearing among some members of the SPD and FDP, who took up their cause in a parliamentary debate on the final day of the three-month deadline. The CDU, abandoned by its governing ally the FDP, and thereby deprived of a parliamentary majority, had to resort to a walkout in order to forestall legislative defeat.[79] The walkout left the Bundestag a few votes short of a quorum, and thus the embargo remained in effect by default. This incident is remarkable for the failure of the CDU to come to the support of industry when the latter was in conflict with the government's emphasis on loyalty to the NATO alliance. The walkout was distasteful to the CDU deputies with industrial ties, who consented to it only out of party loyalty. Equally remarkable were the positions of the FDP, which chose to court a breakdown of the governing coalition rather than lose industrial support, and of the SPD, which in seeking to discredit the government allied itself with big business.

Despite this political debacle, Khrushchev suggested to Beitz, the "roving ambassador," who in May 1963 was on a pilgrimage to Moscow, the possibility of West Germany's renewing and expanding her three-year trade agreement with the Soviet Union. Upon receiving Khrushchev's proposal, the Bonn government invited industrial leaders to air their reactions and recommendations at a conference. Steel leaders, still angry over the government embargo, asked the government to cooperate with industry and to guarantee an exchange of trade within the existing contracts. If West German industry became known as

---

[79] Bundestag, 4th el. pd., 68th session, March 18, 1963, pp. 3062 ff; *New York Times*, March 19, 1963.

an unreliable partner that failed to fulfill its contracts because of political expediency, they declared, trade was bound to suffer. They urged an expansion of trade with the East, and pressure on the Common Market authorities to permit West Germany to conclude an agreement that would not expire until the end of 1966. (The EEC Treaty stipulates that after January 1, 1966, the Common Market as a whole is to negotiate all trade agreements with countries outside the EEC.)[80] However, the government was also worried about the far from enthusiastic response of the Common Market partners, which were competing with East European countries for trade with West Germany, and which would suffer from an expansion of Soviet–West German trade. The Erhard government thus faced a challenge as it renewed negotiations on possible trade with the Soviets.

Trade with communist China has been as vital for German industry as that with the Soviet bloc. The BDI has been critical of the German government's support of the Western embargo on shipments to China, which it calls too inclusive. In 1956 an FDP speaker in the Bundestag decried the negative attitude of the government and asked it at least to set up a permanent trade mission with consular rights. Von Brentano retorted that years earlier the government had given the green light to the committee on the East to discuss trade questions, and even to conclude a general agreement with the Chinese trade agency if it so desired. The committee on the East, von Brentano averred, did not need the approval of the government to promote commerce with any country; only the conclusion of official trade treaties fell outside the jurisdiction of the committee.[81]

Von Brentano's remarks encouraged the committee to establish closer commercial links with the Chinese, although negotiations on increased trade had, in fact, been going on for a number of years. In 1957, after only three weeks of negotiations, an accord was reached with the China Committee for the Pro-

80 *Ibid.*, May 31, 1963; June 9, 1963.
81 Bundestag, 2nd el. pd., 177th session, Dec. 6, 1956, pp. 9811–9832.

motion of International Trade. The head of the committee on the East declared on a note of pride that this was the first semi-official contact with a country which had been Germany's best trading partner in the Orient before the war. If closer political relations eventually resulted, he wrote, then credit would be due to the committee as the "spearhead patrol for German foreign policy."[82] Although trade with China has been maintained on a rather limited scale the accord was not renewed in 1958, apparently because of internal economic difficulties.

However, as a result of the Sino-Soviet dispute, which led to reduced Soviet economic commitments in China, the Chinese in 1963 made overtures to Western countries, firms, and industrial associations, including the BDI committee on the East, for an increase in trade. In 1964 the German government responded positively, but had to move cautiously owing to the opposition of the United States to any economic strengthening of the Chinese regime. Unhappy about Erhard's failure to stand up to the United States, leading German industrialists wanted a comprehensive trade agreement or an exchange of permanent trade missions with the Chinese; but the Erhard government was ready to conclude only a limited goods agreement. An exchange of delegations—German industrialists in Peking and a Chinese purchasing mission in Bonn—was expected to lay the groundwork for the agreement. The German government's interest in increased trade had political overtones, inasmuch as China indicated a willingness to sign a Berlin clause which would signify her recognition of Bonn's right to represent the economic interests of West Berlin abroad. Such an action already undertaken by several East European countries would further weaken the contention of the Soviet Union and the Eastern Zone that Berlin is a third German state.[83]

[82] von Amerongen, "Aussenwirtschaft und Aussenpolitik," *Politisches Seminar*, 1958, p. 139; see also *JB*, 1957–1958, p. 114.

[83] *New York Times*, July 22, 1964.

TRADE WITH THE WEST

Trade with Western countries has not led to the complex political problems encountered by the BDI in its efforts to promote trade with the East. Joint commissions have frequently been established to foster bilateral commerce between Germany and her trading partners. One of these was Spain. Here the joint commission's German members included a representative of the BDI's department of foreign trade, the Spanish desk chief of the Ministry of Economics, the chief of the economic section of the German embassy to Spain, and several business and banking executives. The commission regarded its task as an advisory one to the governments and business communities of both countries. Among the problems discussed were ways in which the Spanish government could reduce its restrictions on foreign investment, boost imports, and advertise its famous sherry in Germany.[84]

Multilateral integration in the fields of trade and tariff has meant a host of new economic (and even political) problems, and has led to further BDI activities in the international sphere. As soon as a new public regional organization is created, private associations cluster around it *en masse*.

The first effort at integration was marked by the signing in April 1951 of the six-power European Coal and Steel Community (the Schuman Plan). German industry was split in its attitude toward this establishment. Suzanne Keller, in her study of German elites, arrived at the figures on support and opposition that are shown in Table VI. The not inconsiderable opposition among big and small business, and the greater support among middle-sized businesses, are of especial interest. Some of these figures obviously reflect a stereotyped response to supranational institutions in general, side by side with a thoughtful concern over the advantages and disadvantages to be expected under the ECSC.

[84] "Bericht über die Tagung des Arbeitsausschusses der Ständigen Kommission für die deutsch-spanische Wirtschaftliche Zusammenarbeit am 6.–8. Oktober 1958 in Madrid" (multigraphed).

TABLE VI

GERMAN ELITE OPINION AND THE ECSC*

OPINION	ALL ELITES	BIG BUSINESS	MEDIUM BUSINESS	SMALL BUSINESS
In favor	70	68	73	57
In opposition	19	24	19	25
No opinion	11	8	8	18
Total	100	100	100	100

* Source: "Attitudes toward European Integration of the German Elite," MIT Center of International Studies (Oct. 1957, multigraphed), pp. 2, 26.

Most industrialists supported the ECSC, but for a variety of reasons. Most of them tended automatically to back Adenauer's foreign policy, and to welcome Franco-German cooperation. Some hoped that Allied restrictions on cartels and concentrations would be abolished, while others hoped that there would be more free competition and fewer government controls. Among those directly affected, the steel-finishing industries hoped that steel would become cheaper and more easily available.[85]

A minority of industrialists, among them some tycoons from heavy industry whose interests were also directly affected, opposed ECSC. Steel manufacturers feared the competition of French and Belgian mills, especially in view of domestic wage and price pressures, and also the "creeping central planning of a bureaucratic agency" in which they might not be adequately represented, and which could be expected to set prices and impose restrictions. Coal producers feared for the survival of marginal pits. Both groups of producers opposed the clause in the ECSC treaty calling for the breakup of Ruhr concerns into smaller enterprises. They would have preferred to negotiate

[85] Almond, *The Politics of German Business*, p. 157; "German Views on the Schuman Plan," *The World Today* (London), VII, No. 7 (July 1951), 292–298; Ernst B. Haas, *The Uniting of Europe* (Stanford, 1958), pp. 162–176.

the treaty themselves, perhaps in the form of cartel arrangements, but could not publicly say so. Although they welcomed the tie to Western Europe, and likewise the investment funds they would receive from the High Authority, they—and the BDI concurred—did not want ECSC to serve as a model for further moves toward European integration. Instead, they called for unrestricted freedom of trade and convertibility of currencies.[86]

It is significant that the French industrial associations had similar doubts about ECSC, and opposed its ratification. They feared the consequences of an anticartel policy, the rise of a dynamic Germany, and the organization's implicit planning.[87] But despite some objections, under the leadership of France the six governments energetically pushed for ratification. Berg, at the BDI's 1951 assembly, coming out in support of the ECSC as a first step toward European integration, told the employers that their objections must be laid aside and that the Schuman Plan must be given a chance to work. Adenauer thanked industry for its support, and urged the employers to publicize the plan fully among the German people.[88]

Once ECSC had been launched, the criticism within the German business community died down somewhat, but not entirely. In September 1952 Berg asserted in a speech at Berlin that no decisions by ECSC officials should be reached on a national or party basis, and that Germany must have full and equal representation in its executive. Since France and Italy had received two of the top posts, Germany, he said, should receive the third one, in addition to that of president of the Common Assembly. Since the establishment of ECSC, German industry has in fact had no reason to complain, but has been well represented in its

[86] *Ibid.*; "Friends among the Germans," *The Economist*, June 12, 1954, p. 873; Ernst Hafer, "Kanzler und Wirtschaft," *Volkswirt*, June 29, 1951.

[87] Ehrmann, "French Trade Associations and the Ratification of the Schuman Plan," *World Politics*, VI, No. 4 (July 1954), 453–481; Ehrmann, *Organized Business in France*, pp. 407 ff.

[88] Hafer, "Kanzler und Wirtschaft," *Volkswirt*, June 29, 1951.

various organs. Etzel and Hellwig successively have held one of the German seats in the High Authority, and in the Consultative Committee such members as Berg and Burckhardt represented the interests of German industry.[89] The BDI and other industrial associations nevertheless have warned that the extraordinary powers of the High Authority pose the danger of a centralized European planning; they have demanded that industries not be limited in their right to make free decisions, and continued to oppose an extension of the Schuman Plan to other industries.[90]

As a matter of fact, the only other such plan to be set up has been the European Atomic Energy Community. Again concerned about the trend toward central planning, the BDI formed its own working group on atomic energy in the hope of limiting the power of EURATOM. But its attempt to prevent EURATOM authorities from obtaining a monopoly on the right to purchase atomic materials was not a success.[91]

The BDI hailed the establishment in January 1958 of the European Economic Community (Common Market), which it saw as encompassing the entire economic sector and thus implying a repudiation of limited economic unions. The BDI also expected EEC to eliminate any residual postwar discrimination

[89] Berg speech in *VR*, No. 38, Sept. 22, 1952. The German government also established an advisory council during the founding of the ECSC. The BDI was represented by Berg, Menne, and Lange, *Fünf Jahre BDI*, p. 178. However, according to Haas, Berg's anti-ECSC stand was resented by steel industrialists, who even considered withdrawing their association from the BDI. While the industrialists were mildly opposed to some ECSC policies, they felt that Berg was too critical, as evidenced by his resignation from the Consultative Committee. *The Uniting of Europe*, p. 173, note 21.

[90] *Fünf Jahre BDI*, pp. 178–179; BDI committee on international relations, session of April 21, 1955. The SPD asserted that if Berg then feared such planning, he had after all been warned earlier by the SPD, which had opposed the ECSC, that Jean Monnet, the guiding spirit of ECSC, intended such a course. *Neuer Vorwärts*, May 21, 1954. This criticism is irrelevant since Berg himself had voiced the same warning at an early stage.

[91] Verband der Chemischen Industrie, *Bericht über die Tätigkeit im Jahre 1956*, p. 22.

against Germany, to put her on an equal footing with other European powers, and to provide German industry with the ability to compete on favorable terms with other European industries in the fields of taxation, cartels, and transport.[92]

The BDI also wanted a voice in the drafting of the EEC treaty, recalling the mistakes in the ECSC treaty that might have been avoided—or so it reasoned—if business had been consulted more extensively in the preparatory stage. Hence the presidential board in January 1956 set up an *ad hoc* presidential commission to which it appointed leading BDI officers.[93] Its task was to establish contact with members of the German government delegation sympathetic to the BDI's objectives, and to work out proposals to be offered at the preparatory conferences. The BDI found these conferences unsatisfactory, complaining that it had not been consulted or been given sufficient data on the progress of negotiations.[94] Hence in talks with government officials the BDI insisted that industry could not take a definite position or make constructive proposals until it knew the details of the treaty. One member of the executive board asserted that approval of the treaty did not imply the agreement of industry with all sections, and another member urged continued efforts to influence the framing of several sections.[95] This was possible because a few government officials did listen to the BDI representatives, especially in matters concerned with foreign trade, and did accept some of their objections. But these officials obviously wanted to minimize interference by private associations if for no other reason than to speed the enactment of the treaty. Berg continued to criticize this exclusiveness, and was reported

[92] *JB*, 1955–1956, p. 25.

[93] Members were Berg (chairman), Kost (mining), Menne (atomic questions), Eckhardt (industry-agriculture), Boden (foreign trade), Riffel (cartels), Friedrich, and Schroeder. *Präsidialsitzung*, Feb. 7, 1956. See also *JB*, 1955–1956, p. 25.

[94] *Ibid.; JB*, 1956–1957, p. 34.

[95] Beutler report made on Feb. 8, 1957, to the executive board of the BDI's foreign trade committee. See its memorandum, Feb. 26, 1957.

to have protested personally to Adenauer that industrial associations in other EEC countries were being consulted more frequently than the BDI had been in Germany.[96]

The EEC Treaty was signed at Rome in March 1957 and went into effect in January 1958. During the early months of the fledgling organization, Berg expressed displeasure that industry again was not being consulted sufficiently. One complaint concerned the hiring of staff members. The BDI and DIHT urged that these be civil servants with experience in industry, citing the familiar argument that such persons would be better qualified than those who had merely administrative experience.[97] But the latter were hired, primarily in order to assure independence from pressure groups but also because not enough qualified personnel from industry were available to staff the headquarters at Brussels.

If the composition of the civil service was unsatisfactory, the BDI at least hoped for better representation at higher policy-making and advisory levels. It accordingly welcomed the appointment of a German official, Walter Hallstein, as president of the policymaking Commission of the EEC.[98] On the Economic and Social Committee, an advisory body to the Commission, it suggested that of the twenty-four seats allotted to Germany the employers' and the workers' representatives each be given twelve, and prepared a list containing the names of four men from the BDI, two from the DIHT, and one each from the other business associations. But the government decided to allot the

[96] Report by one informant. The BDI also complained to State Secretary Müller-Armack (Ministry of Economics) of the authorities' failure to consult it on the cartel provisions contained in the treaty. Memorandum of the BDI department on competition, Jan. 17, 1957. BDI associations also urged the EEC to issue regulations only after the business world was heard.

[97] DIHT, *Wirtschaft aufgerufen zur Bewährung, Tätigkeitsbericht für 1958/59*, p. 43.

[98] For example, on his plan to reduce the EEC timetable for lowering tariffs from 15 to 12 years. The BDI feared damage to German exports, and a reduced chance for a *rapprochement* between EEC and EFTA. *JB*, 1959–1960, pp. 29–30.

twenty-four seats on a tripartite basis to business, the trade unions, and the professions; and although the BDI then expected to receive five out of the eight business seats, in the end only three of these fell to industry. Of the latter, two went to BDI candidates (Wolfgang Pohle, then of Mannesmann, and Ernst Falkenheim of Shell) and the third to one from the BDA (Hans-Constantine Paulssen).[99] Of course, the BDI has maintained a close liaison with its representatives whom it keeps supplied with statistics and other data from its member associations. The Economic and Social Committee appears to have met with the general approval of the BDI, which has made no public criticism. Hallstein's statement that the EEC Commission and Council were ready to discuss their own plans with business and to listen to its wishes, has eased the initial tension on both sides.[100]

But there is still tension at times—as when the BDI complained of receiving an official draft of a Commission proposal (on the legal right of incorporation of business firms in the EEC countries) at so late a stage that no reply could be given before the proposal was submitted to the Economic and Social Committee. Pointing out that the Commission had had two years to prepare the proposal, the BDI demanded more consideration in the future.[101]

Attempts by industry to influence economic policy are made not only through the Committee, but also directly through its offices at Brussels. The amount of lobbying there is still not as extensive as in national capitals of the individual EEC countries, but will undoubtedly increase. One EEC staff member

[99] Interview with a BDI official. For list of members of the Committee, see *Taschenbuch für den Gemeinsamen Markt, EWG, Euratom, Montan-Union, 1959/60* (Frankfurt/M., n.d.). See also Gerda Zellentin, *Der Wirtschafts- und Sozialausschuss der EWG und EURATOM: Interessenräpresentation auf übernationaler Ebene* (Leiden, 1962).

[100] Hallstein, remarks made on Oct. 24, 1958, in a talk, "Der Gemeinsame Markt," to the Association of the Chemical Industry, published by the Association in a pamphlet (Frankfurt/M., 1958), p. 9.

[101] *JB*, 1959–1960, p. 77.

told this author that the cooperation between industry, the trade unions, and the staff had been good and that he met representatives of industry on an average of twice a day—although some other civil servants were more reluctant to expose themselves to outside pressure.

The BDI is represented through one of its officials in the Union of Industries of the European Community (UNICE), made up of national employer associations in the six countries, which was formed at the same time as EEC. The purpose of UNICE is to harmonize the policies of the member associations, and to transmit their views to the Economic and Social Committee and to other organs of EEC. A committee of the permanent representatives in UNICE meets weekly to discuss problems under scrutiny by EEC. These problems may then be submitted for appropriate action either to the national associations or to specialized UNICE committees on taxes, cartels, industrial relations, transport, trade, small and medium-sized business, atomic energy, and so on.[102]

In addition, nearly fifty industrial associations, ranging from producers of electric appliances to producers of ceramic tile stoves, maintain liaison offices in Brussels. Twenty-two of these have formed supranational associations to represent their interests in Brussels, since the EEC Commission will deal with them only at that level. The association officials in Brussels engage in lobbying; supply members with services such as analyses of costs, markets, tariffs, and cartels; and maintain liaison with ECSC and EURATOM.

Evidences of Parkinson's Law are emerging as new associations form their own secretariats, which are kept busy writing reports and scheduling conferences and membership assemblies. It is significant that these new bureaucracies in Brussels parallel EEC in attempting to perform a coordinating role. It has taken the establishment of EEC to bring about a harmonization among supranational associations in which substantive decisions must

[102] *JB*, 1956–1957, p. 42; 1958–1959, pp. 61–63.

be unanimous. Cartel agreements excepted, this coordination did not exist before World War II.

Industrial associations have also discovered that direct representation in Brussels may not always be the most effective channel for their demands, and therefore frequently ask their constituent firms to exert pressure via their own governments, whose representatives on the EEC Commission are in the best position to act on their behalf.[103]

The establishment of the European Free Trade Association by the Outer Seven has led to a schism in European trade. The BDI has deplored the rivalry of the two competing blocs, the more since the "Federal Republic's trading relations with the EFTA are as close as those with the European Economic Community."[104] Much else of course was at stake since about 28 per cent of German exports were going to EFTA countries, and since German industry feared an eventual exclusion of its products. German automobile manufacturers, for example, would have to compete with their British rivals in Switzerland and Sweden, two of their best European markets, if trade discrimination were imposed; and Sweden and Switzerland happen to rank fourth and sixth respectively as consumers of German goods.[105]

To deal with problems arising from the new rivalry, the BDI has set up a commission for European integration, composed of leading personnel from the BDI and its associations. In an attempt to compose the differences between EEC and EFTA, and especially between rival industries, it has called on both blocs to negotiate an agreement that will at least provide for an in-

[103] For a BDI study about the effect of the EEC on each industry see Ernst Otto, *Die Deutsche Industrie im Gemeinsamen Markt* (Baden-Baden, 1957).

[104] Beutler, "Economic Union in Europe Essential for West," *The Financial Times*, March 28, 1960.

[105] *Ibid.*, May 19, 1959.

terim solution to trade questions through mutual consultations and reciprocal tariff action.[106]

When negotiations were initiated by Great Britain for membership in EEC, rifts developed in Germany between Adenauer —who prized a Franco–German alliance above all—and Erhard, who hoped for a swift amalgamation of EEC and EFTA. The BDI was caught in the rift, and could not readily extricate itself. Berg, while decrying the split in the West European trade complex, also reminded his audience that Franco–German ties must not be forgotten. Taking a neutral position, Beutler wrote, "We look upon the European Economic Community as the starting point or the nucleus of an even more extensive all-European integration, which ought if possible to embrace all the member countries of OEEC. It has been a matter of great regret for us in the Federal Republic that Britain did not decide in 1957 to establish this close economic community together with the Six."[107]

Several industrial associations, including the automobile and chemical manufacturers, stood squarely behind Erhard. Late in 1959 they discussed the best approach to the Chancellor on behalf of a union of EEC and EFTA. One association suggested that several industrial branches should make a joint presentation of their views directly to the Chancellor, bypassing the BDI, which was basically committed to the Adenauer policy.[108] In 1963 the Adenauer government did deplore the French veto of Britain's entry into EEC. The BDI sustained Adenauer and Erhard, and criticized the setback to further European economic

[106] Berg, "Zwischen den Extremen wählen," Europäische Integration, I, No. 1 (Oct. 1959), 22–24. To assuage any fears by United States industry of tough competition should EEC and EFTA join forces, and to prevent the United States from altering its trade policy, the BDI asked Berg to make a speaking tour of the country in order to be heard by its industrialists. Vorstandssitzung, Oct. 3, 1958.

[107] "Economic Union in Europe Essential for West," The Financial Times, March 28, 1960.

[108] Vorstandssitzung of a BDI association, Dec. 15, 1959.

unity caused by the position of France. But these isolated efforts by industry could not speed up the slow pace of diplomatic negotiations between the nations involved.

TARIFFS

From a survey of the BDI's activities and policies in the area of trade, we now turn to the related subject of tariff policy. No question is more open to the activity of pressure groups than this one, since in any country the manufacturers not directly concerned with competition from foreign producers are few indeed.

In Germany, especially before the founding of EEC, government and private interests were often at loggerheads on the tariff question. Protectionist elements, in a valiant struggle to keep tariffs high, have insisted that weaker industries must be helped. Their often exaggerated demands have frequently been made through the BDI, which then transmitted them to national and international authorities. The German executive branch was the primary target, since it had the initiative in introducing legislative and administrative changes.

The ministries most often approached were those of Economics and Finance, both of which have divisions dealing with tariff questions. Consultations were generally between their civil servants and BDI staff officials; occasionally, to ward off objections, the ministries would not listen to outsiders. The bitterness of the Association of the Chemical Industry was extreme in 1955, when secrecy enveloped the 48th Order dealing with the lowering of tariffs on some 250 products. "The exclusion of the branch divisions and interested business circles," the Association declared, "is without parallel in German economic history of the last eighty years."[109] When the contents of the order were finally known, the presidential board of the Association complained of their potential adverse effects on its industry to Erhard, who promised to re-examine the order; but by then

[109] *Bericht über die Tätigkeit im Jahre 1955*, p. 12.

the draft had already been turned over to the Bundesrat as an urgent matter, and it was quickly passed by both houses.[110]

If there had been no parallels in the previous eighty years, as the Association maintained, there were certainly a good many others during the 1950's. As a result, the BDI began to insist on being heard in the ministries before a tariff bill went to the legislature. A letter to Erhard in 1956 expressed concern over reports that the Ministry was preparing new reductions without first hearing representatives of the businesses to be affected, as it had already done on two previous occasions. It reminded Erhard, lest he should conveniently have forgotten, of his promise to give industry an opportunity to be heard in every case, and demanded to know whether he was planning to take more tariff actions.[111] This haphazard and obviously unsatisfactory method of consulting industry could only be remedied through institutional safeguards, on the pattern of the hearings of the United States Tariff Commission.

The BDI objected generally to any across-the-board tariff reduction on all goods. In 1956–1957 it was common knowledge that Erhard, disturbed over domestic economic developments, was planning to lower tariffs across-the-board by 30 per cent, and that exceptions would require the consent of the cabinet. In full alarm, the BDI and its member associations, and especially the larger concerns, trained their heaviest ammunition against the plan. One tactic was a visit by Berg to Adenauer and leading ministers, followed up by memoranda and letters. In one of these to Adenauer, dated May 18, 1957, Berg attempted to placate the government by promising that there would be no further price rises and no further economic boom. But while Berg urged the cabinet to take the BDI's arguments into consideration, the government was under pressure from OEEC to lower tariffs since Germany had built up a sizable foreign trade advantage, and still had substantial import restrictions. When

110 *Ibid.*
111 Department of foreign trade memorandum, Feb. 20, 1956.

its own plea lost out, the BDI's presidential board advised German industry to submit its proposals to the government but to avoid publicity, lest the OEEC should make further demands.[112]

In the meantime the long delay over tariff reduction led the opposition in the Bundestag to ask Erhard some embarrassing questions: What interests were preventing a lowering of tariffs? Could not the Minister expect to receive the support of the majority of the Bundestag, or was he afraid of a defection by the business world during an election year? Rather meekly Erhard answered that he had not obtained the backing of his own party on this or the cartel question—but failed to give a reason why. It may be speculated that Adenauer, rather than the CDU, was the one who had failed to provide the necessary support—the more plausibly since the CDU had gone on record in favor of lower tariffs—and that it had been the pressure exerted by Berg in an election year that had swayed the Chancellor.[113]

Eventually Erhard was able to convince Adenauer that the economic situation called for drastic action on tariffs even before the 1957 election. Once the decision had been made, executive and legislative approval for a 25 per cent tariff cut was swiftly obtained. Although the BDI had suffered a defeat, it could take some comfort from the change in the amount of the reduction from 30 to 25 per cent. But the presidential board was up in arms, since Erhard had allegedly promised that the question would be settled only after the election, and then only with the support of industry. It hoped that Adenauer would not sign the decree until a list of exceptions had been prepared, and it asked those industries hardest hit by the decree to lose no time in submitting their lists of proposed exceptions to the Ministry of Economics. Its official objection to the government's action was couched in somewhat different terms—namely that tariffs should not become the primary instrument for influencing the business cycle.[114]

[112] *Ibid.*, May 22 and July 8, 1957; *Präsidialsitzung*, July 12, 1957.

[113] Bundestag, 2nd el. pd., 211th session, May 23, 1957, pp. 12263–12264. See also *FAZ*, May 25, 1956.

[114] *Präsidialsitzung*, July 12, 1957; *JB*, 1957–1958, p. 106.

In 1958 the government planned to cut the tariff further. The culprit this time, from the BDI's point of view, was the Ministry of Finance, which was secretly working on the draft of the bill. The BDI complained in a bristling letter to Erhard—a copy of which was sent to the Minister of Finance—that again the government had failed to consult the industrial associations, and that the Ministry of Economics had not discussed the bases of the reform with the BDI. But the plea for an expansion of the exemption list, for a hearing with government officials, and for an opportunity for the BDI's member associations to examine the planned changes in the tariff regulations, were not granted at the time.[115]

Later that year, however, a representative of the Ministry of Economics assured BDI officials that drafts of tariff legislation would be sent to the associations; it asked that the drafts be kept confidential, since the EEC was also involved. In order to give the associations more time to study EEC proposals, the Ministry promised to transmit them in the original French version without waiting for the German translation.[116]

The divisions between protectionist and free trade elements in industry (the latter of which are supported by Erhard) are bound to continue, as is the BDI's opposition in general to a free trade policy. In 1959, in a speech to the DIHT, Erhard was critical of businessmen who raised the cry of protectionism at the least whisper of a lowered tariff. The "free economy," he insisted, was no mere slogan, but a thing to be taken seriously: "Where freedom reigns there can be no rigidity." [117]

While Erhard was denouncing certain businessmen, a group of industrialists met and called on the government to take a firm position at the Geneva tariff conference. No "one-sided"

[115] Department of foreign trade memorandum, May 27, 1958.

[116] *Ibid.*, Sept. 29, 1958; June 30, 1959. A representative of the Ministry of Finance also agreed to give more cooperation to the industrial association in working out a German position on EEC drafts concerning tariffs. *Ibid.*, Feb. 21, 1959.

[117] *New York Times*, April 11, 1959.

concessions were to be accorded other members of GATT (General Agreement on Tariffs and Trade); rather, protection must be raised against imports from low-cost Asian countries. Erhard retorted that German manufacturers must make adjustments to meet such competition, and suggested greater production, better products, and lower prices.[118]

The trade unions backed Erhard's fight for a more liberal trade policy, arguing that increased imports would provide more choices to consumers, and charging that certain business quarters were not prepared to agree to this for fear of what would happen to their profits at home, while they planned to exploit the export market.[119] The trade-union attitude may be explained by the fact that the workers were enjoying a period of full employment and did not have to worry about layoffs because of a decreased demand for domestic manufactured products.

AID TO DEVELOPING COUNTRIES

It is well known that the United States has been dissatisfied with the extent of German assistance to developing countries and has been urging the Federal Government to accelerate and expand its bilateral and multilateral programs. The German government's reply is that much already has been and more will be done, when budgetary limitations are less stringent. There is also another problem. More than half of German private investments in foreign countries between 1951 and 1961 went to industrially advanced countries, and less than half to developing countries[120] (see Table VII). Industry has justified this pattern of investment on the basis of its traditional ties with other in-

[118] *Ibid.* Although Erhard disagreed with business on some fundamental aspects of tariff policy, he did encourage the industrial associations to be in close touch with German delegations to GATT and OEEC conferences.

[119] *Labor Headline News*, No. 1861, Dec. 22, 1958; No. 1981, Oct. 3, 1960.

[120] Between 1950 and June 1962, aid and investment came to a total of 19.2 billion DM, of which 15.2 billion DM went for bilateral and 4 billion DM for multilateral aid (the latter primarily through the United Nations). Industry did not engage in aid of the latter sort. *The Bulletin*, Oct. 9, 1962.

TABLE VII

GERMAN PRIVATE INVESTMENTS IN FOREIGN COUNTRIES, 1951 TO JUNE 30, 1961*

AREA	MILLION DM	PERCENTAGE
Europe	1253	36.9
EEC	(484)	(14.4)
EFTA	(633)	(18.5)
other	(136)	(4.0)
Africa	198	5.8
Asia	125	3.7
America	1737	51.2
USA	(449)	(13.2)
Canada	(307)	(9.1)
Latin America	(981)	(28.9)
Australia	83	2.4
Total	3396	100.0

* Source: BDI, *Jahresbericht,* 1961–1962, p. 36.

dustrial countries, and their geographic proximity, low risks, and minimum threat of nationalization. The BDI has argued that if the government wanted industry to make private investments in developing countries more attractive it must liberalize its credit, tax, and depreciation allowances, and provide firm financial guarantees where there is a risk of nationalization. Disputing the government declaration of May 1961 that private initiative would be given every chance in developing nations, the BDI argued that unless there was a change in the government policy, private investment would not increase significantly.[121]

In order to arrive at a more amicable working relation with the government and to increase joint aid and investment projects, at the end of 1959 the BDI organized a working group on developing countries. The group made some recommendations for technical assistance programs, and met with other economic organizations in an effort to promote collaboration between

[121] *JB,* 1961–1962, pp. 35–37.

business and government. It urged that greater use be made in foreign programs of industrial firms with experience abroad, and warned that the government ought not to compete with business in certain kinds of foreign aid, or to engage in solely commercial transactions; indeed, the government was called on to help build up the basic economy of a nation, and to assist massive private projects which could not be set up except with state aid. It also asked the government to staff its embassies abroad—especially those in Latin America, where relations were primarily economic—with more economic experts. It was pointed out that in Rio de Janeiro one expert worked alone on economic problems for many months and that a similar situation prevailed in other countries.[122] Through all these recommendations by the BDI runs a fear of government interference and of possible losses to busines firms abroad, as well as a certain hesitancy about committing itself to an expansion of development aid. But in the years to come the BDI will undoubtedly have to step up its commitments. To meet one objection of industry, in 1964 a Development Assistance Tax Law went into effect that provides for major tax exemptions to companies investing capital in developing countries.[123]

CONCLUSION

The BDI has not been greatly concerned with the political or military aspects of West German foreign policy so long as its own interests were not directly affected. It has supported, at times perfunctorily and at times energetically, the broad objectives of the Chancellor's policy since they happen to coincide with its own. This is true in the matters of German reunification, West European political integration, ties to the United States, NATO and the German defense buildup, and political policy toward the communist bloc. But whenever one of these

[122] According to a BDI mission to Latin America, *JB*, 1959–1960, p. 35; *FAZ*, June 21, 1960.
[123] *The Bulletin*, July 7, 1964.

policies poses a threat to the fortunes of industry, the BDI will immediately attempt to exert its influence on public decisions. Of course, on questions of foreign and domestic policy, such as European economic cooperation, trade and tariffs, the BDI is so deeply involved that it must take a position on each government proposal, which it will seek to mold to its own satisfaction. That the BDI has not always been successful in this goal, the preceding pages have made abundantly clear.

PART FOUR: CONCLUSION

XIV

The Political Power of the

Federation of German Industry

"The modern state, no matter what its form, is essentially a capitalist machine, the state of the capitalists, the ideal personification of the total national capital."[1] So wrote Friedrich Engels in the nineteenth century. Today, a century later, Marxists and many neo-Marxists are still in accord with this thesis, although they obviously would not include those states having a communist or socialist economy. But they do see a close connection in any state between economic and political power. For example, the political theorist Franz L. Neumann denies the existence of a "pure" economic power and a "pure" political activity: "Economics is as much an instrument of politics as politics is a tool of economics." Therefore, "the translation of economic power into social power and thence into political power becomes the crucial concern of the political scientist."[2] For the Marxists, the

[1] *Socialism: Utopian and Scientific*, as quoted in Michael Curtis (ed.), *The Great Political Theories*, Vol. II (New York, 1961), 175.

[2] *The Democratic and the Authoritarian State* (Glencoe, Ill., 1957), p. 12. Similarly Karl Loewenstein maintains "No political issue can be divorced from its economic implications, and no economic problem can be solved without political means." *Political Power and the Governmental Process* (Chicago, 1957), p. 350.

inevitable consequence of this process is that capitalists become the dominant group in the industrial state. Even such a non-Marxist as President Franklin D. Roosevelt, a firm believer in the neo-capitalist system, worked to strengthen organized labor to prevent this kind of domination, and in accepting the nomination for a second term, sounded a "Marxist" warning against big business as an "economic tyranny," whose managers were "privileged princes of these new economic dynasties, thirsting for power, [reaching] out for control over government itself."[3] For the period since World War II, C. Wright Mills saw the ruling group as composed of three power elites: government, the military, and business.[4]

Disagreeing with the Marxist and neo-Marxist thesis, the proponents of pluralism argue that although it contains a large element of truth, especially in regard to the interrelation of economics and politics, its oversimplification tends toward "the fallacy of the single factor."[5] There are, the argument runs, other dominant groups vying for power in an industrial state whose demands cannot be ignored. Oliver Garceau asserts that field research has not produced much evidence to support the neo-Marxist hypothesis that "postulates peak associations of interests dominating consistently the whole polity through the pressure politics of an exploiting minority of organized business."[6] The German sociologist Ralf Dahrendorf questions the identification of the managers of industry with the senior elite in the executive division of a government. He admits the possibility of fraternal relations, but argues that they are separate blocs.[7]

[3] As cited by *Fortune*, Jan. 1962, pp. 59–60.

[4] *The Power Elite* (New York, 1956).

[5] Hans Morgenthau used this phrase in another context in *Politics Among Nations* (3rd ed., New York, 1961), p. 158.

[6] "Interest Group Theory in Political Research," *The Annals*, Vol. 319 (Sept. 1958), 108.

[7] Class and Class Conflict in Industrial Society, pp. 141–142. In a study of New Haven, Conn., Robert A. Dahl asserts, " . . . the Economic Notables,

How does this difference of opinion between the neo-Marxists and the pluralists relate to the politics of the BDI in the German setting? At the beginning of this study, the following questions were posed: Does industry in Germany exert enough leverage on the decision-makers to dominate its politics? Do the competing interest groups counterbalance each other sufficiently to reduce the power of German industry to a tolerable level? Do the activities of the BDI benefit or harm the democratic state? Answers to these questions may suggest which school of thought is correct, so far as the political power of the BDI in postwar Germany is concerned.

The neo-Marxist view, which is frequently voiced by non-Marxists, may be typified by the British journalist Terence Prittie, a veteran observer of German politics, who has warned as follows concerning the power of German industry:

I listened to Professor Erhard giving an exposition on the anticartel law in Essen to the Federation of German Industry. He adopted a pleading tone when asking its members to trust him. This was quite understandable. That assembly of sober gentlemen, mostly bull-necked and with comfortably filled waistcoats, represented the orderliness, inventiveness, and ruthless energy of the *real rulers of present-day Germany*. . . . Here then, is the most serious danger inherent in this powerful class of industrialists [the Ruhr barons]: it has still not fused with the rest of the community, and it retains the peculiar arrogance which springs from social isolation. As long as that remains so, the immense power of the Ruhr could be once again misapplied. And that power is greater than before, and is still concentrated in the hands of a very few.[8] (Italics supplied.)

Within Germany itself, the SPD, the DGB, and some independent commentators share these views. Heinrich Deist told

---

far from being a ruling group, are simply one of the many groups out of which individuals sporadically emerge to influence the policies and acts of city officials." *Who Governs? Democracy and Power in an American City* (New Haven, 1961), p. 72.

[8] *Germany Divided*, pp. 298, 301.

the SPD congress in 1962 that the government was letting a small upper class dominate the country and impose an unfair distribution of income. He said:

In the Federal Republic today small but powerful interest groups have an influence on parliament and the government generally that would be unthinkable in any other modern democratic country. . . . The conservative, economic, financial, and tax policies of the present Government, working in cooperation with big business, have succeeded in maintaining an unjust division of income, property, and power. . . . The whole leadership in the Federal Republic is recruited from a narrow upper layer. The son of the worker, the white collar employee, the tradesman, and the small business man scarcely has a chance to rise to the top of our society.[9]

Deist averred that this situation must be replaced by a "healthy democratic order." Other Social Democrats have contended that the BDI's call for employers to go into politics indicated a special bid to replace the power from which such weakened social forces as the aristocracy and the landed gentry had abdicated. They have decried the anti-trade-union attitude of the BDI and its financial support of conservative parties, which they see as facilitating its accretion of power in the state.[10]

DGB spokesmen likewise argue that the BDI has a "tremendous" power in the Federal Republic, and that although occasionally it suffers defeats, or makes minor concessions, these are offset by a string of successes in economic, tax, and financial matters. They point out that its strength in the CDU is considerable as compared to the labor wing, so that even in social insurance and property affairs industry has scored a number of victories. They see the BDI managers as coupling pressure on the legislature and the executive with socioeconomic power; and

[9] *New York Times*, July 14, 1962.
[10] *Vorwärts* (n.d.), cited by *UB*, No. 41, Oct. 15, 1959. See also *Vorwärts*, Aug. 9, 1961.

since this political influence is not exposed to public scrutiny, they view it as a threat to democracy.[11]

While the FDP was in opposition it viewed the might of the BDI with some misgivings, warning of the "restorative forces" within a conservative coalition—made up of Adenauer's circle and the top officers of the BDI—and of the advantage they took of a weakened opposition: "They occupied the key positions in the state machinery and ensured for themselves control over the organs influencing public opinion."[12]

Kurt Pritzkoleit, a prolific writer on the economic aspects of postwar Germany whose political sympathies obviously lie with the SPD, has addressed himself repeatedly to the question, To whom does Germany belong? (One of his books has this title.) His answer is that it belongs to the big corporations, headed by wealthy families and a small number of *nouveaux riches*, and to the business associations, whose power has been permitted to increase by the failure of political forces to understand the process of economic growth. He argues that only an alert public and a responsible government can stem the tide of economic concentration and power.[13]

The response of the BDI to the charge that it dominates both the economic and political life of postwar Germany is to plead not guilty. In a speech to the 1958 BDI Assembly, Berg declared:

The BDI cannot and will not interfere with the right of political decision-making. That is, in our democratic order, a matter of the representative elected by the people. Under no circumstances can that right be undermined. The Federation regards as its first task the elucidation and balance of the numerous opinions within indus-

[11] Statements by DGB leaders, personal interviews. Cf. Otto Stammer, "Die politische Verantwortung von Unternehmern und Gewerkschaften," *Frankfurter Hefte*, VIII, No. 11 (Nov. 1953), pp. 850–851.

[12] *Das freie Wort*, April 4, 1958.

[13] *Wem gehört Deutschland*, pp. 675–676. His other books—emotionally charged but a mine of information—include *Bosse, Banken, Börsen* (München, 1954); *Das kommandierte Wunder* (München, 1959); *Männer, Mächte, Monopole* (München, 1956); *Die Neuen Herren* (München, 1955).

try. Thereby it makes the task easier for the state to ascertain the views of the various groups in the preparation of public decisions. Furthermore, the Federation views as one of its tasks the placing of expert advice at the disposal of the organs which must make political decisions. Thus it is perfectly clear that an expert can only be one whose views lean toward the general welfare.[14]

Berg went on to say that the BDI considered it a duty to set forth the views of industry on important economic problems. He consequently objected to the labeling of the BDI as a pressure group, since it had the same right as any other free association to voice its views.

In a similar vein, other top officers of the BDI have written that parliament, government, administration, and parties were dependent on business for advice because of the increasing number and complexity of economic problems. Such advice based on practical experience could then be incorporated into laws for the common good and would preclude mistakes and ill-considered legislation.[15] O. A. Friedrich has asserted that associations should not be feared as rivals to the state, since they were rivals of one another, and since the parties were strong enough to resist any undue pressure on their part. There was much more danger, he said, in that the associations would be dragged into the maelstrom of party politics or silenced as in the time of the Nazis. Accordingly they should be nurtured as a creative democratic force, with views worthy of serious consideration by political authorities.[16]

In public utterances the BDI tends to minimize its influence, and to picture itself merely as an organization devoted to the common good, while assailing the trade unions for the same actions of which it is accused by them. The BDI then asserts that in their wage and hour demands the unions fail to take

[14] *UB*, No. 21, May 22, 1958.

[15] Cf. Neumann, "Die Wirtschaftspolitik geht jeden an," *UB*, No. 36, Sept. 10, 1959.

[16] *Das Leitbild*, p. 36; *Gehen wir aufeinander zu*, pp. 50, 53.

into account the perspective of the general welfare, but show responsibility only toward their own members; that they prefer to work toward their partisan goals by fighting for political power and economic codetermination, instead of seeking an amicable understanding with management.[17]

The BDI's officers repeatedly deny the accusation that it has the country in the palm of its hand, insisting that its opponents exaggerate its effectiveness. Admitting that it is blessed with funds for propaganda, it argues that the parties—and notably the CDU in recent years—are more concerned with obtaining the electoral support of the masses of voters, to whom a legislative program, especially in matters of social and industrial relations, must be drafted to appeal especially. They argue that if the importance of the business community in rebuilding the postwar economy, in meeting the demands of consumers for goods and services, in raising the standard of living of the population under a free enterprise system, and in ameliorating social tensions, were fully taken into account, the BDI would have much more political influence than it now does.[18]

As reasons for what the BDI's officers see as its lack of political influence, it is argued, first, that there is no uniformity in that influence; on some legislative proposals it may be successful, but not on others. Second, its political thrust is weakened by internal conflicts: there are too many feuds between basic and consumer goods industries, between big and small firms, and between export-oriented and domestic-market–oriented industries; also, there are occasional feuds between industry and other sectors of business. Thus, the busines community will show strength in areas of consensus—such as Western unity and social legislation—but be weak in areas of discord, such as tariff, transport, and tax questions. A third reason is that the deputies sympathetic to industry are in a small minority, primarily because few employers are really interested in a political career,

[17] *UB*, No. 41, Oct. 15, 1959.
[18] *Ibid.; JB*, 1958–1959, p. 47.

and must contend with a powerful and cohesive agricultural bloc, a small business bloc, and the alliance of the SPD with the left wing of the CDU. Thus they tend to play what is primarily an advisory role. And on the executive level the BDI does not succeed in halting legislation detrimental to its interests.[19]

Not that the BDI considers itself ineffectual; far from it. The managing director of the DI, Dr. Ludwig Losacker, in a speech he made before assuming his present post, in fact admitted that the power of associations is such that they can influence the market and put the nonorganized into a helpless position. Then, speaking by implication of their political power, he urged associations to operate not anonymously but openly, so that the public would have more confidence in them.[20] A BDI department head told this author that he considered the BDI and the bankers the two most powerful groups because of their top-level connections with Adenauer. (It is worth noting that after the death of Pferdmenges in 1962 the banker Hermann J. Abs became the latter's trusted adviser.) Another senior official in the BDI asserted that in general its goals have been met, with only minor defeats. He described the chief task of the BDI to be not getting good bills passed but preventing bad ones from going through. Thus on many occasions the government, as a result of pressure from other organizations, may take an initiative that places the BDI on the defensive. If the BDI should find itself confronted by a government with an SPD majority, this would be even more true.

Between the officers of the SPD and DGB, backed by those writers who accuse the BDI of dominating the German political arena, and the officers of the BDI, backed by other writers who see it as merely one of several important associations legitimately presenting its views to public officials, there is obviously a wide gulf. Who is right? An answer may possibly be provided by a

[19] Personal interviews.
[20] Speech titled "Anonymität und Verantwortung," given at Bielefeld, Oct. 16, 1959 (typescript).

more general study of the Federation: its membership, financial strength, internal cohesion, ideological unity, leadership, public relations, party and government connections—and by a comparison of the BDI with competing associations.[21]

In membership the BDI cannot match the mass organizations such as the trade unions. However, the tens of thousands of employers who are members, at least indirectly, have social status in their own communities, and an influence greater than their numbers would indicate. Their financial strength is considerable, and is most telling in the financing of parties and of electoral campaigns. Although their internal cohesion is less than the leadership would desire, neither does it amount to a state of anarchy. It is perfectly true that on some measures the leadership cannot achieve a compromise among the competing industries; but on broad issues of policy it can usually obtain a degree of accord—either because all industries would benefit or because of a common ideology, or because it is centralized enough to command agreement. Thanks to its prestige, the leadership may marshal the support of other business associations if a particular show of strength vis-à-vis Bonn is necessary. To marshal such outside support the BDI has been increasingly active in its public relations campaigns. The promotion of the free enterprise system and of its own stand on public issues has been facilitated by a not unfriendly mass communications industry and has had a degree of favorable popular response.

The primary task of the BDI is to seek access to the political decision-makers wherever they may be found. With CDU and FDP leaders, BDI officials have maintained a close liaison in order to help mold the government's economic program. In this effort they have been successful, especially in regard to the CDU, although there have been numerous strains and stresses. In exchange for financial support and for supplying experts, the BDI

[21] Truman, *The Governmental Process*, pp. 506–507; Arnold Gehlen, "Industrielle Gesellschaft und Staat," *Wort und Wahrheit*, XI, No. 9 (Sept. 1956), 666.

expects the parties to support the objectives of industry, to nominate candidates from the business community, and then to give them seats in parliamentary committees handling industrial legislation. Some of these deputies have done yeoman service for the BDI, and have represented its interests effectively not only in the committees but also on the floor of the Bundestag and in party caucuses. Their efforts have been sustained by lobbying activities on the part of the BDI, its member associations, and the giant corporations. Thus, so far as its relations with the parties and with the legislature are concerned, it would seem that the BDI can look with some satisfaction upon its record of achievements.

This is no less true of its relations with the executive. The contacts of the BDI with former Chancellor Adenauer and many other senior government authorities, and with high- and low-level civil servants, have been remarkably cordial. The BDI has found it fruitful to approach Adenauer whenever economic policy would have affected its interests adversely. In many cases, it has won. In some, when Minister Erhard had the upper hand, it has lost. What influence it may be able to exert on Erhard as Chancellor remains to be seen. At any rate, its approach to the executive suggests that the BDI acts less on the basis of general policy than pragmatically on specific issues.

Since the end of World War II the business community has so prospered as to constitute an economic miracle, partly thanks to legislative policies adopted to resuscitate German industry. In recent years the government has drawn in the reins to prevent the boom from ending in economic disaster, thereby earning the temporary opprobrium of many industrial magnates.

How much power, then, does the BDI actually have in the Federal Republic? If power could be measured quantitatively, a precise answer might be given. But the number of variables, pressures, and counterpressures make this impossible. For example, in the cartel dispute the BDI was in the forefront of the opposition. But other groups were equally opposed, and their

arguments may have been more convincing to certain civil servants or legislators than those offered by the BDI. Even those
policy-makers might be unable to say how they had arrived at
their decision. S. E. Finer rightly observes that "it is very hard
to find any scientific proof that a particular measure is *due* to
the particular pressure of a specific group. In general no such
causal relationship can be established." Nor can it be established
"how much of what the group wanted it actually got."[22] The
extensive access enjoyed by many groups thus does not necessarily mean significant influence.

It is nevertheless possible to make certain generalizations
based on empirical case studies. It may definitely be said that
the BDI exerts power at all levels of the decision-making process, from supranational organizations down to local governments. It has been most effective at the national level, where a
CDU-led government has held sway since 1949. The renaissance
of industrial might was not predictable when after World War
II the Allies attempted to slash the power of the industrialists.
But a number of fortuitous circumstances have given the BDI
a commanding position on the political horizon.[23] On the other
hand, it is doubtful whether the SPD and DGB, or the writers
Pritzkoleit and Prittie, are correct in their sweeping assertions
that BDI officials are the "real rulers of present-day Germany."

Ample evidence has been set forth in this study that the BDI

[22] Ehrmann (ed.), *Interest Groups on Four Continents*, p. 295. Italics in
original. See also Dahl, "Business and Politics: A Critical Appraisal of
Political Science," *American Political Science Review*, LIII, No. 1 (March
1959), 18.

[23] Some of these views are reinforced by other observers of the German
scene. Deutsch and Edinger speak of the "very considerable influence [of
business] within the inner councils of the Adenauer government." *Germany
Rejoins the Powers*, p. 99. Hartmann asserts that "under the persistent
pounding of the 'elite' ideologists and with the recognition from other
social groups, many *Unternehmer* (employers) have agreed on staking out
claims well beyond their quarters proper. As this self-assuredness develops,
so do more appeals to fill the supposed vacuum of leadership in German
society." *Authority and Organization in German Management*, pp. 247–248.

must operate within certain prescribed limits. For in Germany as elsewhere, there are countervailing powers in a pluralistic industrial order. A multiple elite governs the nation. Within the CDU a number of groups vie for top stakes and a share of the nation's wealth, and no single one of them can claim a monopoly of power or wealth. Party chieftains must balance conflicting demands, and must work out compromises and concessions in order to keep business, labor, agriculture, and other forces well enough satisfied to stay within the party.

Perhaps the most important countervailing power is the executive branch itself. As Dahrendorf observes, "Managerial or capitalist elites may be extremely powerful groups in society, they may even exert partial control over governments and parliaments," but the governmental elite is the authority in the state.[24] Chancellor Adenauer, addressing the tenth annual assembly of the BDI in 1959, said that the BDI in the past decade had always been a "true helper" in the heavy work of reconstruction, but that never had he had the feeling that the state was therefore dominated by it or by any other interest group.[25] This is the kind of statement that a chancellor obviously must make; but it is substantially correct despite his various flirtations with the BDI. From now on, with other chancellors at the helm, the countervailing power of the executive may become even more effective, and the BDI may find less sympathy for its demands. Certainly if the SPD should eventually form a government—as it has in many *Länder*—this would be so.

Another important countervailing power against the BDI is that of organized labor, which in recent years has had some impact on economic policy. Not to be forgotten are such other interests as agriculture, the opposition parties, and the organs of mass communication. When they speak up, the government must lend an ear.[26]

[24] *Class and Class Conflict in Industrial Society*, p. 302.
[25] *Die Welt*, Oct. 21, 1959.
[26] See Hartmann, "Cohesion and Commitment in Employers' Organiza-

In their conflicting assessments of the BDI both schools of thought have been persuasive to a degree. This observer, however, must finally opt for the pluralistic view. Granted that the BDI is a powerful and prestige-laden association with many victories on its record, and granted that it operates in a political climate favorable to its interests, nevertheless it is not the only group of which this is true, but one that faces rivals with an equal appetite for power.[27]

Another generalization to be made is that the BDI is a very typical interest group as compared with those in the United States and elsewhere. The BDI uses the same language as the others ("We are working for the common good"), has similar aims, and employs the same techniques. It seeks to apply pressure where the focal decisions are made, just as interest groups do in other countries. However, the center of the decision-making process in Germany is not the same as in other political systems. In the United States, and in France before the Fifth Republic, access to the individual representatives in the legislature is or was sought; where there is a more disciplined and centralized party system, as in West Germany and Great Britain, the main targets are executive and key parliamentary leaders.

This study has focused on the BDI as one interest group in the Federal Republic. As studies are made of other interest

tions," *World Politics*, XI, No. 3 (April 1959), 475; Josua Werner, *Die Wirtschaftsverbände in der Marktwirtschaft* (Zürich, 1957) and *Die Verbände in Wirtschaft und Politik* (Zürich, 1959). Werner deals with Switzerland, but it has strong parallels with Germany.

[27] S. E. Finer comes to the same conclusion about the British counterpart of the BDI: "The notion of the FBI (Federation of British Industries) as the *éminence grise* of British politics must be adandoned. . . . Even with a Conservative Government in power the FBI is but one voice—albeit a very powerful one—among many, and today one of the other voices, however vicarious, is that of the trade unions." "The Federation of British Industries," pp. 79, 82. Paradoxically, Finer asserts that the FBI had more success under Labor than under the Conservatives because it could score successes on details rather than on principles. For a general description of British interest groups see also his *Anonymous Empire* (London, 1958).

groups in West Germany and elsewhere, it will be illuminating to search for parallels and differences among them; to anatomize the internal dynamics hidden behind their organizational fa- çade; to note their styles of operation, and their main targets. It will be more difficult—as this study illustrates—to assess their relative or absolute power and effectiveness in their political setting. To attempt an index of power among interest groups in any one country is likely to be either frustrating or mislead- ing, if not both.

No less difficult would be a study of group influence in the decision-making process. As has been noted in this study, it is easy enough to count the number of groups interested in a specific decision, but not the degree of their influence. Harry Eckstein's observation in his analysis of a British interest group, that many decisions are made independent of group pressures,[28] holds for West Germany as well.

From their academic perspective, political scientists have scrutinized another set of questions, which are particularly ap- plicable to the Federal Republic: Is the interplay of interest groups injurious or beneficial in a democratic state? Is there a danger that they may dominate it? And if they should be too powerful, how can their power be curbed? These questions are especially pertinent in a country without the democratic heri- tage of the English-speaking nations. Among German academi- cians, and other interested citizenry, there is still no consensus. As with attitudes toward the BDI itself, once again there are two major and conflicting views on the power of associations in Germany.

One view, held by a heterogeneous group of scholars, politi- cians, journalists, and civic leaders, is critical of the power of the interests. It argues that to maintain a flourishing democracy there must be a strong state, which can resist the encroachments of interest groups, correct inequities, prevent unfair activities, and protect the freedom of minorities and of the unorganized

[28] *Pressure Group Politics: The Case of the British Medical Association.*

individual. It must be strong enough to counter any interest group, any "hidden government" that may seek to dominate national politics if the time should ever come when the balance of associations breaks down. The concern of those holding this view is that the state should never become a football to be tossed about by interest groups.[29]

Implicit in these arguments, at least to some extent, is a faith —dangerous in Germany—in the possibility of an all-powerful state elevated above the hurly-burly of interest group activities. "In Germany the myth of a superhuman state facing the individual is not yet dead. Such a conception of the state leaves little room for the activity of interest groups," one observer writes.[30] The strong criticism of interest groups from this point of view is comparable to that heard in France, where certain observers are likewise skeptical, and where interest groups are held responsible for many crises in the parliamentary system. A number of Swiss authors, on the other hand, are less critical of the situation in their own country, where they see limits to the influence of associations. The least critical of all are Anglo-Saxon authors, for whom democracy is ingrained and who are acquainted, especially in the United States, with an effective system of checks and balances.[31]

In Germany a second view, reflecting the American pluralistic doctrine, is less critical of interest groups in a democratic state. Its proponents argue that, in a pluralistic system, associations do not constitute a danger to the parliamentary regime so long as

[29] Thus Werner Weber, J. H. Kaiser, and Helmut Coing argue in Beutler, Stein, Wagner (eds.), *Der Staat und die Verbände.*

[30] Hirsch-Weber in *Interest Groups on Four Continents,* ed. Ehrmann, p. 273.

[31] On France see the writings of, *inter alia,* Bernard E. Brown, Ehrmann, George E. Lavau, Meynaud; on Switzerland, those of E. Geyer, Erich Gruner, Hans Huber, Emil Küng, and Josua Werner; on Great Britain and the United States see (to cite but a few) Samuel Beer, Harry Eckstein, S. E. Finer, J. D. Stewart, and David Truman. This theme is elaborated by E. Tuchtfeldt, "Wirkungen der Verbände auf die wirtschafts-politische Willensbildung," 1960 (multigraphed), pp. 12–13.

a majority decision of the parties or the parliament is able to translate individual and group interests into a "general political will." The fewer the parties, according to this point of view, the more they can serve to aggregate the interests.[32] A legal scholar representing this school of thought disputes the assignment of collective guilt to all pressure groups for doctrinaire reasons: If they are really as dangerous as their critics say, he asks, why not disband them? In answer to his own question he asserts that groups foster interest in legislative affairs by giving their members the confidence that they can shape legislation—even though they can actually do so only to a limited extent.[33]

Proponents of this second point of view, however, have also not failed to criticize interest groups. They distinguish between those that publicize what are entirely legitimate political objectives, and can thus be controlled as well as criticized; and those that hide their influence—especially when it consists of financial contributions—and that manipulate the political leadership. They warn against the excessive power of some associations (the BDI, the DGB, and the agricultural bloc are often cited); against accords reached by business and labor at the expense of consumers and the public; against big associations that swallow up smaller ones; and against associations that seek to undermine and control the parties, which are dependent on them for specialists and for funds. Finally, they warn against having a parliament that no longer functions in the classical sense, but merely as the center of clashes between groups.[34]

[32] See, *e.g.*, Georg Strickrodt, "Gruppeninteressen und Staatsgewalt," *Neue Politische Literatur*, II, No. 5 (May 1957), 319–341; Scheuner in Beutler, Stein, Wagner (eds.), *Der Staat und die Verbände*, pp. 10–18.

[33] Herbert Krüger, "Die Stellung der Interessenverbände in der Verfassungswirklichkeit," *Neue Juristische Wochenschrift*, IX. No. 34 (Aug. 24, 1956), 1217–1221.

[34] See the discussion by Eschenburg, Otto Stolz, *et al.* in Beutler, Stein, Wagner (eds.), *Der Staat und die Verbände*; and the discussion at the 11th sociological convention, Weinheim, 1952, in "Der Staat der Gegenwart."

Despite the dangers expressed in these warnings, most German observers holding the second point of view no longer deny the right of interest groups to engage in political activity. Discussion in recent years has been primarily of the kind of limitations to be put upon group activities in a country where democracy is still a tender growth that needs careful nurture.

To the question of the kinds of limitations and controls to be imposed, and of the behavior required of interest groups in order to foster democracy and yet fulfill their goals, many thoughtful answers have been given. One of these is that in their internal organization, the groups must allow a maximum of democracy: members must be given complete freedom to express themselves, and groups must not seek a monopoly on decisions in their own particular sphere. In the relation of interest groups with political parties, the main problem is to forestall undue pressure. There must be a working relationship that will prove satisfactory to both in the nomination of candidates, in access to parliamentary factions, and in the use of experts in the legislature. It is especially important to ensure the prestige of the parties and their ability to function as a cohesive force in politics. To achieve this goal, it is suggested that a law be enacted to regulate the inner organization of the parties, and to make them less dependent on financial "angels" from the interest groups.

In relation to the legislature, it is argued, groups should be heard in advance of parliamentary debates, possibly through a system of public hearings, possibly through a national economic council with an advisory function. Through some such outlet, their pressure on parliament might be reduced to some degree.

In relation to the executive, it is urged that the anonymity of pressure groups be done away with, perhaps through lobbying regulations. Groups must expect the ministries to remain neutral and to promote national rather than special interests. The views of groups might be legitimately expressed by means of independent advisory councils to the ministries, in which all interests would receive equitable representation.[35]

But many of these prescriptions will never be palatable until a new spirit of democracy pervades the interest groups and the country as a whole. The German political scientist Wolfgang Hirsch-Weber points to the essence of the problem: "In the last resort, democracy requires that there be democrats. It should be clear that the governmental process in its present form is doomed if the strongest interest groups are not aware of a minimum of civic responsibilities."[36] Can the leaders and members of the BDI and other interest groups rise to the task of fostering a greater measure of democracy both internally and externally? The assignment is both challenging and imperative.

[35] Ludwig Bergsträsser in *ibid.*, p. 217; Stammer, "Interessenverbände und Parteien," *Kölner Zeitschrift für Soziologie und Sozialpsychologie*, IX, No. 4 (1957), 587–605; German Federal Republic, *Rechtliche Ordnung des Parteiwesens*; Hirsch-Weber in *Interest Groups on Four Continents*, ed. Ehrmann, p. 104.

[36] *Ibid.*, p. 105. Cf. Almond, who argues that "German business still lacks a tradition of democratic conviction and of civic responsibility." *The Politics of German Business*, p. iii.

APPENDIXES

BIBLIOGRAPHY

INDEX

APPENDIX A

List of BDI

Member Associations*

A. *Mining*
Mining Association
Petroleum Extraction Association

B. *Basic and Production Goods*
Stone and Gravel Association
Iron and Steel Association
Association of Steel Works and Rolling Mills
Association of Nonferrous Metals
Association of the Foundry Industry
Mineral Oil Association
Association of the Chemical Industry
League of German Sawmill Associations
Bureau of the Cellulose and Paper Industry
Association of the German Rubber Industry

C. *Investment Goods*
Steel and Iron Construction Association
Association of German Machine Construction
Automobile Industry Association
Association of German Shipyards

* Classification according to Statistisches Bundesamt, *Statistisches Jahr-buch für die Bundesrepublik Deutschland 1962*, pp. 160–161. List from BDI *Organisationsplan 1962*, p. 6. Some of the translations are free rather than literal.

Central Association of the Electrotechnical Industry
Association of the Precision Tool and Optical Industry
Steel Fabrication Association
Association of Iron-, Tin-, and Metal-Finishing Industries
Association of the Bicycle and Motorcycle Industry
Federation of the German Air and Space Industry

D. *Consumer Goods*
Association of the Ceramics Industry
Federation of the Glass Industry
Association of the German Wood and Related Products Industries
Industry Group Association
Association of Paper and Allied Products Industries
League of Graphic Associations of Germany
Association of the Synthetic Fabrics Industry
Association of the German Leather Industry
Association of the Leather Goods and Suitcase Industry
Association of the German Shoe Industry
Federation of the Clothing Industry
Association of the German Textile Industry

E. *Food and Related Products*
Federation of the German Food Processing Industry
Association of the Sugar Industry
German Brewers League
Association of the Cigarette Industry

F. *Construction*
Association of the German Construction Industry

APPENDIX B

List of BDI Presidential Board Members, 1962*

(and their industry affiliation)

President
Fritz Berg, owner, Firma Wilhelm Berg (metal finishing)

Vice Presidents
Dr. Otto A. Friedrich, chairman of board, Phoenix Gummiwerke (rubber)
Dr. W. Alexander Menne, board member, Farbwerke Hoechst (chemicals)
Carl Neumann, partner, P. C. Neumann (textiles)
Prof. Rolf Rodenstock, owner, Firma Optische Werke G. Rodenstock (optics)
Dr. Hans-Günther Sohl, chairman of board, August-Thyssen-Hütte (steel)

Members
Dr. Hanns Bauer, board member, Firma Glashütte Heilbronn (glass)
Dr. Curt Becker, partner, Firma Herrenkleiderfabrik C. A. Becker (clothing)
Dr. Edmund A. Bieneck, chairman of board, Didier-Werke (stone)
Erwin Bockelmann, chairman of board, BP Benzin–u. Petroleum (gasoline)

* BDI, Organisationsplan 1962, pp. 87–88.

Dr. Wilhelm Borner, board member, Schering (chemicals)

Dr. Helmuth Burckhardt, chairman of board, Eschweiler Bergwerks-verein (mining)

Dr. Richard Freudenberg, partner, Firma C. Freudenberg (leather)

Albert Honsberg, partner, Firma Gebrüder Honsberg (machinery, iron and tin finishing)

August Klönne, partner, Firma A. Klönne (steel & iron construction)

Dr. Wilhelm Koch, chairman of board, Vereinigten Deutschen Metallwerke (nonferrous metal)

Dr. Heinrich Nicolaus, manager, Firma Papierfabrik Günzach (paper)

Prof. Heinrich Nordhoff, chairman of board, Volkswagenwerk (automobile)

Dr. Karl Pfeiffer, board member, J. Berger Tiefbau (construction)

Dr. Hermann Reusch, chairman of board, Gutehoffnungshütte Sterkrade (steel)

Dr. Peter v. Siemens, board member, Siemens-Schuckertwerke (electrical machinery)

Bernhard Weiss, manager, Siemag-Siegener Maschinenbau (machine construction)

Alexander Wiedenhoff, board member, Rheinischen Stahlwerke (steel)

Dr. Oskar Wortmann, manager and partner, Firma G. Plange, Weizenmühle (food processing)

Executive Member

Dr. Wilhelm Beutler, BDI (Gustav Stein since 1963)

APPENDIX C

List of Bundestag Deputies from the Business Community, 1961*

(with occupation and committee assignment)

Name	Occupation	Committee
CDU/CSU		
Artzinger, Dr. Helmut	Personnel chief	Finance
Balke, Prof. Siegfried	Chemist; association executive	
Bieringer, Dr. Adolf	Factory owner	Petitions, Interior
Birrenbach, Dr. Kurt	Director	Foreign Affairs
Blumenfeld, Erik	Merchant	Foreign Affairs
Brand, Peter-Wilhelm	Merchant	Economic Affairs (DC)†, Foreign Trade
Burgbacher, Dr. Fritz	Professor	Atomic Energy, Public Property

* List of deputies and their occupations from DI, *Fraktion der CDU/ CSU (and FDP) im IV. Deutschen Bundestag* (mimeographed, with names of deputies allied with business underlined); committee assignments from *Amtliches Handbuch des Deutschen Bundestages, 4. Wahlperiode*, Part I, pp. 207–236. Omitted from list are bankers, artisans, and others associated with business but not underlined by the DI.

† DC = Deputy chairman of committee.

Name	Occupation	Committee
Burgemeister, Alfred	Merchant	Small Business
Delden, Rembert van	Factory manager	Foreign Trade
Deringer, Arvid	Lawyer	
Dichgans, Dr. Hans	Manager	
Diebäcker, Hermann	Association executive	Foreign Trade, Labor
Dollinger, Dr. Werner	Merchant	Finance
Dresbach, Dr. August	Former association manager	Finance
Elbrächter, Dr. Alexander	Chemist	Economic Affairs, Public Property
Finckh, Hermann	Factory manager	Foreign Trade, Development Aid
Fritz, Dr. Gerhard	Manager	Development Aid (DC)
Gassmann, Walter	Director	Social Affairs
Huthmacher, Eugen	*Land* Minister of Economics	Economic Affairs
Leonhard, Gottfried	Factory owner	Economic Affairs
Löhr, Dr. Walter	Manager	Foreign Trade
Mengelkamp, Theodor	Assistant manager	Budget
Missbach, Artur	Business adviser	Petitions, Housing
Nieberg, Wilhelm	Merchant	Interior
Philipp, Dr. Gerhard	Lawyer	Economic Affairs
Ruf, Thomas	Economist	Social Affairs
Schlick, Josef	Merchant	Finance
Schmücker, Kurt	Printing press owner	Economic Affairs
Sinn, Dr. Edmund	Merchant	Transport, Development Aid
Stein, Gustav	Lawyer	Economic Affairs
Steinmetz, Dr. Willy	Factory owner	Foreign Trade
Toussaint, Dr. Hans	Merchant	Finance
Verhoeven, Arnold	Assistant manager	Petitions, Cultural Affairs, Local Affairs, Debts

Name	Occupation	Committee
FDP		
Aschoff, Dr. Albrecht	Lawyer	
Atzenroth, Dr. Karl	Factory owner	Economic Affairs
Burckardt, Richard	Employer	Small Business
Dahlgrün, Dr. Rolf	Legal expert	Economic Affairs (C)‡
Funcke, Lieselotte	Assistant manager	Finance
Hoven, Dr. Viktor	Manager	Labor
Imle, Dr. Wolfgang	Association executive	Finance
Keller, Ernst	Employer	Foreign Trade (C), Public Property
Kohut, Dr. Oswald	Factory owner	All-German Affairs
Mälzig, Dr. Konrad	Factory owner, former minister	Housing, Public Property, Expellees
Margulies, Robert	Merchant	Foreign Trade, Development Aid (C)
Menne, Dr. Alexander	Board member	Economic Affairs
Rademacher, Willy	Moving line owner	Transport
Ramms, Egon	Shipping firm owner	Transport
Scheel, Walter	Employer	
Starke, Dr. Heinz	Association executive	

‡ C = Chairman of committee.

Bibliography

A majority of the BDI protocols, circulars, regional office and membership association publications, articles in newspapers, and DI publications cited are not listed here, but will be found in the notes.

NEWSPAPERS AND PERIODICALS

Der Arbeitgeber. Duesseldorf: Organ of the BDA. Fortnightly.

Die Aussprache. Bonn: Organ of the AsU. Monthly.

Deutsche Zeitung und Wirtschaftszeitung (since 1959: *Deutsche Zeitung mit Wirtschaftszeitung*). Cologne. Daily.

The Financial Times. London. Daily.

Frankfurter Allgemeine Zeitung. Frankfort. Daily.

Frankfurter Rundschau. Frankfort. Daily.

Das freie Wort. Bonn: Organ of the FDP. Weekly.

Handelsblatt. Duesseldorf. Daily.

Industriekurier. Duesseldorf. Four times weekly.

Junge Wirtschaft. Bonn: Organ of the Junge Unternehmer, an AsU branch. Monthly.

Material zum Zeitgeschehen. Cologne: Published by the DI. Irregular.

Mitteilungen des Bundesverbandes der Deutschen Industrie. Cologne: Published by the BDI. Monthly.

New York Times.

News from Germany. Published by the SPD. Monthly.
Schelldienst des Deutschen Industrieinstituts. Cologne. Twice weekly.
Der Spiegel. Hamburg. Weekly.
Stuttgarter Zeitung. Stuttgart. Daily.
Süddeutsche Zeitung. Munich. Daily.
Unternehmerbrief des Deutschen Industrieinstituts. Cologne. Weekly.
Der Volkswirt: Wirtschafts- und Finanz-Zeitung. Frankfort. Weekly.
Vortragsreihe des Deutschen Industrieinstituts. Cologne. Weekly.
Vorwärts (1948–1955: *Neuer Vorwärts*). Hannover–Bonn: Organ of the SPD. Weekly.
Die Welt. Hamburg. Daily.
Welt der Arbeit. Cologne: Organ of the DGB. Weekly.

BOOKS AND ARTICLES

Almond, Gabriel A. *The Politics of German Business.* Santa Monica, Cal., RAND Research Memorandum RM-1506-RC, 20 June 1955. Reprinted in condensed form in H. Speier and W. P. Davison, eds., *West German Leadership and Foreign Policy* (Evanston, Ill., 1957), pp. 195–241.

Altmann, Rüdiger. "Zur Rechtsstellung der öffentlichen Verbände," *Zeitschrift für Politik,* II (new series), No. 3 (1955), 211–227.

Amerongen, Otto Wolff von. "Ost-West-Handel im Schatten der Politik," *Offene Welt,* No. 65, March 1960.

———. "Aussenwirtschaft und Aussenpolitik," *Politisches Seminar,* 1958.

Apelt, Kurt. *Die Wirtschaftlichen Interessenvertretungen in Deutschland* (Leipzig, 1925).

Bardey, Ernst. *Unternehmer-Organisationen-: Wofür sind sie da?* (Stuttgart, 1959).

Beer, Samuel H. "Group Representation in Britain and the United States," *The Annals,* vol. 319 (Sept. 1958).

Bentley, Arthur. *The Process of Government* (Bloomington, Ind., 1949).

Berg, Fritz. "Zwischen den Extremen wählen," *Europäische Integration,* I. No. 1 (Oct. 1959), 22–24.

"Berg, der Interessen-Bündler," *Der Spiegel*, XIV, No. 45 (Nov. 2, 1960).

Bergsträsser, Ludwig. "Der Entwurf des Parteiengesetzes," *Politische Studien*, X, Heft 113 (Sept. 1959), 596–605.

Berle, Adolf A. and Means, Gardiner C. *The Modern Corporation and Private Property* (New York, 1932).

Bethusy-Huc, Viola Gräfin von. *Demokratie und Interessenpolitik* (Wiesbaden, 1962).

———. "Die Soziologische Struktur Deutscher Parlamente." Unpublished Ph.D. dissertation, University of Bonn, 1958.

Beutler, Wilhelm; Stein, Gustav; and Wagner, Hellmuth (eds.). *Der Staat und die Verbände* (Heidelberg, 1957).

Bowen, Ralph H. *German Theories of the Corporative State* (New York, 1947).

Bracher, Karl D. *Die Auflösung der Weimarer Republik* (Stuttgart, 1957).

———; Sauer, Wolfgang; and Schulz, Gerhard. *Die Nationalsozialistische Machtergreifung* (Köln and Opladen, 1960).

Brady, Robert A. *Business as a System of Power* (New York, 1943).

———. "Manufacturing Spitzenverbände," *Political Science Quarterly*, LVI, No. 2 (June 1941), 199–225.

Braunthal, Gerard. "Federalism in Germany: The Broadcasting Controversy," *The Journal of Politics*, XXIV, No. 3 (Aug. 1962), 545–561.

———. "The Free Democratic Party in West German Politics," *The Western Political Quarterly*, XIII, No. 2 (June 1960), 332–348.

Breitling, Rupert. "Das Geld in der Deutschen Parteipolitik," *Politische Vierteljahresschrift*, II, No. 4 (Dec. 1961), 348–363.

———. *Die Verbände in der Bundesrepublik* (Meisenheim, 1955).

Brettner, Hans. *Die Organisationen der industriellen Interessen in Deutschland* (Berlin, 1924).

Bueck, H. A. *Der Centralverband Deutscher Industrieller, 1876–1901* (3 v., Berlin, 1902, 1905).

Bundesverband der Deutschen Industrie. Hauptgeschäftsführung (cited as HGF). Protocols of presidential board sessions (*Präsidialsitzung*) and executive board sessions (*Vorstandssitzung*), 1950–1960.

———. *Jahresbericht des BDI* (Köln, 1951–1964).

———. *Kundgebung und Mitgliederversammlung des BDI* (Köln, 1951–1957).

———. *Organisationsplan* (Köln, 1950–1962).

Bundesvereinigung der Deutschen Arbeitgeberverbände. *Jahresbericht* (Köln, annual).

Bunn, Ronald F. "The Federation of German Employers' Associations: A Political Interest Group," *The Western Political Quarterly*, XIII, No. 3 (Sept. 1960), 652–669.

———. "The Ideology of the Federation of German Employers' Associations," *The American Journal of Economics and Sociology*, XVIII, No. 4 (July 1959), 369–379.

Burck, Gilbert. "The German Business Mind," *Fortune*, IL (May 1954).

Burneleit, Heinz. *Feindschaft oder Vertrauen zwischen Staat und Wirtschaft?* (Frankfurt/M., 1961).

Christlich Demokratische Union Deutschlands. *Bundesparteitag* (Hamburg, 1956, 1958, 1960).

———. *Düsseldorfer Leitsätze über Wirtschaftspolitik, Landwirtschaftspolitik, Sozialpolitik, Wohnungsbau*. Sonderdruck des Deutschland-Union-Dienstes, July 15, 1949.

Cleveland, Alfred S. "NAM: Spokesman for Industry?", *Harvard Business Review*, XXVI, No. 3 (May 1948), 353–371.

Cole, Taylor, "Functional Representation in the German Federal Republic," *The Midwest Journal of Political Science*, II, No. 3 (Aug. 1958), 256–277.

Committee on Comparative Politics, Social Science Research Council. *A Comparative Study of Interest Groups and the Political Process*, ed. by G. A. Almond. Report on the Planning Session held at the Center for Advanced Study in the Behavioral Sciences (Mimeographed; Stanford, April 5–10, 1957). Reprinted in condensed form in the *American Political Science Review*, LII, No. 1 (March 1958), 270–282.

Dahl, Robert A. "Business and Politics: A Critical Appraisal of Political Science," *American Political Science Review*, LIII, No. 1 (March 1959), 1–34.

Dahrendorf, Ralf. *Class and Class Conflict in Industrial Society*

(Stanford, 1959). Translation of *Soziale Klassen und Klassenkonflikt in der industriellen Gesellschaft* (Stuttgart, 1957).

Davison, W. Phillips. "The Mass Media in West German Political Life," *West German Leadership and Foreign Policy*, ed. by H. Speier and W. P. Davison (Evanston, Ill., 1957).

Dechamps, Bruno. *Macht und Arbeit der Ausschüsse: Der Wandel der Parlamentarischen Willensbildung* (Meisenheim, 1954).

Deutsch, Karl W. and Edinger, Lewis J. *Germany Rejoins the Powers* (Stanford, 1959).

Deutscher Industrie- und Handelstag. *Wirtschaft aufgerufen zur Bewährung: Tätigkeitsbericht für des Geschäftsjahr 1958/59* (Berlin, n.d. [1959]).

Deutsches Industrieinstitut. *Der deutsche Wirtschaftsfilm in Zahlen* (Multigraphed, n.p., 1959).

———. *Die deutschen Illustrierten.* Strukturbericht No. 7 (March 1958).

———. *Die deutschen Tageszeitungen.* Strukturbericht No. 8 (Aug. 1958).

———. *Films of German Industry* (Köln, 1959).

———. *Publications of the German Industrial Institute* (Mimeographed; n.p., n.d.).

———. "Der 17. September 1961 unter der Lupe," *Material zum Zeitgeschehen*, No. 10, Oct. 26, 1961.

———. "Die soziologische Struktur der deutschen Landtage," *Material zum Zeitgeschehen*, No. 7, July 3, 1962.

———. *Veröffentlichungen des DI 1951–1961* (Köln, 1961).

———. *Wirtschafts- und Sozialprobleme in der öffentlichen Meinung* (Hectographed; n.p., 1958).

DIVO. *Basic Orientation and Political Thinking of West German Youth and their Leaders* (Hectographed; n.p., 1956).

Dübber, Ulrich. "Aufgaben und Grenzen eines Parteiengesetzes," *Die Neue Gesellschaft*, V, No. 2 (March–April 1958), 118–126.

———. *Parteifinanzierung in Deutschland* (Köln, 1962).

Eckstein, Harry. *Pressure Group Politics: The Case of the British Medical Association* (Stanford, 1960).

Ehrmann, Henry W. "French Trade Associations and the Ratification of the Schuman Plan," *World Politics*, VI, No. 4 (July 1954), 453–481.

——. "Les groupes d'intérêt et la bureaucratie dans les démocraties occidentale," *Revue Française de Science Politique*, XI, No. 3 (Sept. 1961), 541–568.

——. *Organized Business in France* (Princeton, 1957).

——. "Pressure Groups in France," *The Annals*, Vol. 319 (Sept. 1958), 141–148.

—— (ed.). *Interest Groups on Four Continents* (Pittsburgh, 1958).

Eisermann, Gottfried. "Parteien und Verbände im neuen Bundestag," *Gewerkschaftliche Monatshefte*, IV, No. 12 (Dec. 1953), 750–755.

Erdmann, E. G., Jr., "Organization and Work of Employers' Associations in the Federal Republic of Germany," *International Labour Review*, LXXVIII, No. 6 (Dec. 1958), 533–551.

Erhard, Ludwig. *Prosperity through Competition* (New York, 1958).

Eschenburg, Theodor. *Aemterpatronage* (Stuttgart, 1961).

——. "Aemterpatronage im Parteienstaat," *Politische Studien*, V, No. 61 (May 1955), 23–27.

——. *Der Beamte in Partei und Parlament* (Frankfurt/M., 1952).

——. "Das Geld der Parteien," *Der Monat*, XII, No. 140 (May 1960), 31–37.

——. *Herrschaft der Verbände* (Stuttgart, 1955).

——. "Kritische Betrachtungen eines Zeitungslesers," *Der Journalist*. Supplement, May 1960.

——. *Probleme der modernen Parteifinanzierung* (Tübingen, 1961).

——. *Der Sold des Politikers* (Stuttgart, 1959).

Eyck, Erich. *Geschichte der Weimarer Republik*, Vol. II (Erlenbach, 1956).

Facius, Friedrich. *Wirtschaft und Staat: Die Entwicklung der Staatlichen Wirtschaftsverwaltung in Deutschland vom 17. Jahrhundert bis 1945.* No. 6, Schriften des Bundesarchivs (Boppard am Rhein, 1959).

Fack, Fritz-Ullrich. "Die deutschen Stahlkartelle in der Weltwirtschaftskrise." Unpublished Ph.D. dissertation, Free University, Berlin, 1957.

Die Finanzierung des Wahlkampfes 1957. Published by the SPD (Hannover, n.d. [1957]).

Finer, Herman. *Representative Government and a Parliament of Industry: A Study of the German Federal Economic Council* (London, 1923).

Finer, S. E. *Anonymous Empire* (London, 1958).

———. "The Federation of British Industries," *Political Studies*, IV, No. 1 (Feb. 1956), 61–84.

Fischer, Wolfram. "Das Verhältnis von Staat und Wirtschaft in Deutschland am Beginn der Industrialisierung," *Kyklos*, XIV, Fasc. 3 (1961), 337–363.

Flechtheim, Ossip K. *Die Deutschen Parteien seit 1945: Quellen und Auszüge* (Berlin, 1957).

———. "Gewerkschaften und Parteifinanzierung," *Gewerkschaftliche Monatshefte*, X (Oct. 1959), 583–586.

———. "Politische Entwicklung und Finanzierung der CDU," *Die Neue Gesellschaft*, V, No. 3 (May–June 1958), 182–189.

Friedmann, Werner. *Presse und öffentliche Meinung.* Heft 10, Schriftenreihe der Hochschule für Politische Wissenschaften (München, 1957).

Friedmann, W. (ed.). *Anti-Trust Laws, A Comparative Symposium.* University of Toronto Faculty of Law Symposium, Vol. III (1956), 191–229.

Friedrich, Carl J. *Constitutional Government and Democracy* (Boston, 1950).

———. "The Political Thought of Neo-Liberalism," *The American Political Science Review*, XLIX, No. 2 (June 1955), 509–525.

Friedrich, Otto A. *Gehen wir aufeinander zu* (München, 1958).

———. *Das Leitbild des Unternehmers wandelt sich* (Stuttgart–Degerloch, 1959).

Fünf Jahre BDI. Published by the BDI (Bergisch Gladbach, 1954).

Gable, R. W. "N.A.M.: Influential Lobby or Kiss of Death?", *Journal of Politics*, XV (May 1953), 254–273.

Garceau, Oliver. "Interest Group Theory in Political Research," *The Annals of the American Academy of Political and Social Science*, Vol. 319 (Sept. 1958), 104–112.

Gehlen, Arnold. "Industrielle Gesellschaft und Staat," *Wort und Wahrheit*, XI, No. 9 (Sept. 1956), 665–674.

German Federal Republic. *Die Bundesrepublik.* Sammelband 1960/61 (Köln, n.d. [c. 1961]).

———. Deutscher Bundestag. *Amtliches Handbuch des Deutschen Bundestages. 4. Wahlperiode* (Darmstadt, n.d. [c. 1962]).

———. Deutscher Bundestag. *Verhandlungen des Deutschen Bundestages. Stenographische Berichte.* All election periods.

———. Deutscher Bundestag. *Verhandlungen des Deutschen Bundestages. 2. Wahlperiode 1953, Register 2. Teil, Sprachregister. Stenographische Berichte der 1.–227. Sitzung.*

———. Presse- und Informationsamt. *Bulletin* (German ed.); *The Bulletin* (English ed.).

———. Presse- und Informationsamt. *Facts about Germany* (3rd ed.; Wiesbaden, 1960).

———. *Rechtliche Ordnung des Parteiwesens: Bericht der vom Bundesminister des Innern eingesetzten Parteienrechtskommission* (Frankfurt/M., 1958).

———. Statistisches Bundesamt. *Statistisches Jahrbuch für die Bundesrepublik Deutschland 1962* (Stuttgart, 1962).

"German Views on the Schuman Plan," *The World Today* (London), VII, No. 7 (July 1951), 292–298.

Grosser, Alfred. *Die Bonner Demokratie* (Düsseldorf, 1960).

Die Gründung des Ausschusses für Wirtschaftsfragen der industriellen Verbände. BDI Drucksache Nr. 2 (Bergisch Gladbach. 1949).

Grundmann, Werner. "Die Finanzierung der politischen Parteien," *Zeitschrift für die gesamte Staatswissenschaft*, Vol. 115, No. 1 (1959), 113–130.

Haas, Ernst B. *The Uniting of Europe* (Stanford, 1958).

Hallgarten, George. *Hitler, Reichswehr und Industrie* (Frankfurt, 1955).

Hamburger, Ludwig. *How Nazi Germany Has Controlled Business* (Washington, 1943).

Hamerow, Theodore S. *Restoration Revolution Reaction: Economics and Politics in Germany 1815–1871* (Princeton, 1958).

Hartmann, Heinz. *Authority and Organization in German Management* (Princeton, 1959).

———. "Cohesion and Commitment in Employers' Organizations," *World Politics*, XI, No. 3 (April 1959), 475–490.

Hauenstein, Fritz. "Die Gründerzeit der Wirtschaftsverbände," ORDO, IX (1957), 43–64.

Heck, Bruno. "Unabhängigkeit im Rundfunk," *Die politische Meinung*, IV, Heft 35 (April 1959), 47–58.

Heidenheimer, Arnold J. *Adenauer and the CDU* (The Hague, 1960).

———. "Campaign Finance Outside the United States." (Mimeographed; n.p., 1962).

———. "German Party Finance: The CDU," *The American Political Science Review*, LI, No. 2 (June 1957), 369–385.

———. *The Governments of Germany* (New York, 1961).

———. "Schattierungen im Röntgenbild der Christlichen Demokraten," *Die Neue Gesellschaft*, V, No. 3 (May–June 1958), 172–181.

Heinrichsbauer, August. *Schwerindustrie und Politik* (Essen, 1948).

Hennis, Wilhelm. "Verfassungsordnung und Verbandseinfluss," *Politische Vierteljahresschrift*, II, No. 1 (March 1961), 23–35.

Herrmann, Walther. "Industrielle Organisationen," *Handwörterbuch der Sozialwissenschaften*, ed. by Erwin von Beckerath *et al.*, Vol. V (Stuttgart, 1956), 268–272.

Herz, John H. "The Government of Germany," *Major Foreign Powers*, ed. by Gwendolen M. Carter and J. H. Herz (4th ed.; New York, 1962).

———. "Political Views of the West German Civil Service," *West German Leadership and Foreign Policy*, ed. by H. Speier and W. P. Davison (Evanston, Ill., 1957), pp. 96–135.

Heydte, F. A. Freiherr von der and Sacherl, Karl. *Soziologie der deutschen Parteien* (München, 1955).

Hielscher, Erwin. "Die Finanzierung der politischen Parteien," *Politische Studien*, V, No. 64 (Aug. 1955), 6–19.

High Commissioner for Germany, U.S. (HICOG). Reactions Analysis Staff. Office of Public Affairs. *Trend in German Opinions on Socialization of Industry*. Report No. 27, Series No. 2. July 27, 1950.

Hirche, Kurt. "Gewerkschafter im Bundestag," *Gewerkschaftliche Monatshefte*, VIII, No. 12 (Dec. 1957), 705–710.

———. "Gewerkschafter im Bundestag," *Gewerkschaftliche Monatshefte*, XII, No. 11 (Nov. 1961), 641–651.

Hirsch-Weber, Wolfgang. *Gewerkschaften in der Politik* (Köln und Opladen, 1959).

———. "Some Remarks on Interest Groups in the German Federal Republic," *Interest Groups on Four Continents*, ed. by H. W. Ehrmann (Pittsburgh, 1958), pp. 96–116.

—— and Schütz, Klaus. *Wähler und Gewählte: Eine Untersuchung der Bundestagswahlen 1953* (Berlin, 1957).

Jahn, Hans Edgar. *Gesellschaft und Demokratie in der Zeitwende* (Köln, 1955).

Kaiser, Joseph H. *Die Repräsentation organisierter Interessen* (Berlin, 1956).

Kaufmann, Karlheinz; Kohl, Helmut; and Molt, Peter. *Kandidaturen zum Bundestag: Die Auswahl der Bundestags-Kandidaten 1957 in zwei Bundesländern* (Köln, 1961).

Keller, Suzanne. "Attitudes of the French, German, and British Business Elite." Unpublished study, MIT, Cambridge, Mass., May 1958.

———. "Attitudes Toward European Integration of the German Elite." Unpublished study, MIT, Cambridge, Mass., Oct. 1957.

Key, V. O., Jr. *Politics, Parties, and Pressure Groups* (New York, 1946).

Kirchheimer, Otto. "The Composition of the German Bundestag," *Western Political Quarterly*, III, No. 4 (Dec. 1950), 590–601.

———. "West German Trade-Unions: Their Domestic and Foreign Policies," *West German Leadership and Foreign Policy*, ed. by H. Speier and W. P. Davison (Evanston, Ill., 1957), pp. 136–194.

Kitzinger, Uwe. *German Electoral Politics: A Study of the 1957 Campaign* (Oxford, 1960).

Krengel, Rolf. *Der Politische Standort des Deutschen Unternehmers*. No. 6, Schriftenreihe der Pressestelle Hessischer Kammern and Verbände (Frankfurt, n.d.).

Krüger, Herbert. "Die Stellung der Interessenverbände in der Verfassungswirklichkeit," *Neue Juristische Wochenschrift*, IX, No. 34 (Aug. 24, 1956), 1217–1221.

Lechner, Hans, and Hülshoff, Klaus. *Parlament und Regierung* (2nd ed.; München and Berlin, 1958).

Leitende Männer der Wirtschaft: Ein wirtschaftliches "Who is Who?" *1955.* Published by Spezial-Archiv der Deutschen Wirtschaft (Darmstadt, 1955).

Lewinsohn, Richard (Morus). *Das Geld in der Politik* (Berlin, 1930).

Liesebach, Ingolf, *Der Wandel der Politischen Führungsschicht der Deutschen Industrie von 1918 bis 1945* (Hannover, 1957).

Lipset, Seymour M. *Political Man: The Social Bases of Politics* (Garden City, N. Y., 1960).

Lochner, Louis P. *Tycoons and Tyrants: German Industry from Hitler to Adenauer* (Chicago, 1954).

Loewenstein, Karl. *Political Power and the Governmental Process* (Chicago, 1957).

Mayntz, Renate. *Parteigruppen in der Gross-Stadt: Untersuchungen in einem Berliner Kreisverband der CDU* (Köln, 1957).

Merkle, Hans L. "Der Unternehmer und die gegenwärtige Politik," *Politisches Seminar,* May 1960.

Meynaud, Jean. *Les groupes de pression en France* (Paris, 1958).

Millinger, Ludwig. *Wirtschaft und Funk.* No. 16, Schriftenreihe der Pressestelle Hessischer Kammern und Verbände (Frankfurt, 1957).

Mills, C. Wright. *The Power Elite* (New York, 1956).

Mommsen, Wilhelm. *Deutsche Parteiprogramme der Gegenwart* (2nd ed.; München, 1954).

Münster, Hans. *Die Presse in Deutschland.* Vol. I, *Die Moderne Presse* (Bad Kreuznach, 1955).

Muhlen, Norbert. *The Incredible Krupps* (New York, 1959).

Nettl, John P. "Economic Checks on German Unity," *Foreign Affairs,* XXX, No. 4 (July 1952), 554–563.

Neumann, Franz L. *Behemoth: The Structure and Practice of National Socialism* (New York, 1942).

———. *The Democratic and the Authoritarian State* (Glencoe, Ill., 1957).

Neumann, Sigmund. "Germany: Changing Patterns and Lasting Problems," *Modern Political Parties,* ed. by S. Neumann (Chicago, 1956).

Neunreither, Karlheinz. *Der Bundesrat zwischen Politik und Verwaltung* (Heidelberg, 1959).

Nipperdey, Thomas. "Interessenverbände und Parteien in Deutschland vor dem Ersten Weltkrieg," *Politische Vierteljahresschrift,* II, No. 3 (Sept. 1961), 262–280.

Office of Military Government, U.S. (OMGUS), Berlin. "German Opinions on Socialization of Industry," *ICD Opinion Survey.* Report No. 90, Jan. 23, 1948.

Otto, Ernst. *Die Deutsche Industrie im Gemeinsamen Markt* (Baden-Baden, 1957).

Parteien in der Bundesrepublik: Studien zur Entwicklung der deutschen Parteien bis zur Bundestagswahl 1953 (Stuttgart, 1955).

Paulini, G. *Wirtschafts-Behörden und -Organisationen* (Essen, 1956).

Piettre, André. *L'économie allemande contemporaine, 1945–1952* (Paris, 1952).

Der Politische Standort des Deutschen Unternehmers. No. 6, Schriftenreihe der Pressestelle Hessischer Kammern und Verbände (Frankfurt, n.d.).

Politisches Jahrbuch der CDU/CSU. 1st year, 1950; 3rd year, 1957 (Frankfurt, Recklinghausen, n.d.).

Politisches Seminar der Staatsbürgerlichen Vereinigung 1954 e.V. Sessions 1–9, 1958–1961 (Bergisch-Gladbach, n.d.).

Pollock, James K. *Money and Politics Abroad* (New York, 1932).

Potthoff, Erich. *Der Kampf um die Montan-Mitbestimmung* (Köln, 1957).

Preradovich, Nikolaus v. "Die politischen und gesellschaftlichen Führungsstrukturen in Deutschland seit den 18. Jahrhundert," *Politisches Seminar,* Nov. 1960.

Prittie, Terence. *Germany Divided: The Legacy of the Nazi Era* (Boston, 1960).

Pritzkoleit, Kurt. *Bosse, Banken, Börsen* (München, 1954).

———. *Das kommandierte Wunder* (München, 1959).

———. *Männer, Mächte, Monopole* (München, 1956).

———. *Die Neuen Herren: Die Mächtigen in Staat und Wirtschaft* (München, 1955).

———. *Wem gehört Deutschland* (München, 1957).

Reichsverband der Deutschen Industrie. *Mitglieder-Versammlung des RDI am 3. und 4. Sept. 1926 in Dresden.* Heft 32 (Berlin, n.d.).

———. *Organisatorischer Aufbau des RDI* (Berlin, 1929).

Remmling, Günter W. "Die Interessenverbände in der Westlichen Welt," *Zeitschrift für Politik*, IV (new series), No. 2 (1957), 169–186.

Roesch, Hans-Eberhard, "Die öffentliche Rechenschaftspflicht der politischen Parteien über die Herkunft ihrer Mittel," *Deutsches Verwaltungsblatt*, Sept. 1, 1958, pp. 597–602.

Sänger, Fritz. *Handbuch des deutschen Bundestages* (Stuttgart, 1954 [etc.]).

Schäfer, Dieter. "Die Tür weit offen halten-Die Wirtschaft in Rundfunk und Fernsehen," *Junge Wirtschaft*, VI, No. 6 (June 1958), 248–252.

Schardt, Alois. *Wohin Steuert die CDU?* (Osnabrück, 1961).

Scheuner, Ulrich. *Die staatliche Intervention im Bereich der Wirtschaft, Rechtsformen und Rechtsschutz.* Heft 11, Veröffentlichungen der Vereinigung der Deutschen Staatsrechtslehrer (Berlin, 1954), pp. 1–66.

Schriftgiesser, Karl. *The Lobbyists* (Boston, 1951).

Schröder, Dieter. "Wer bezahlt den Wahlkampf?" *Kölner Stadt-Anzeiger*, June 16–23, 1961 (also in *Süddeutsche Zeitung*, June 15–22, 1961).

Schulz, Gerhard. "Die CDU-Merkmale Ihres Aufbaues," *Parteien in der Bundesrepublik: Studien zur Entwicklung der deutschen Parteien bis zur Bundestagwahl 1953* (Stuttgart, 1955).

———. "Die Organisationsstruktur der CDU," *Zeitschrift für Politik*, III, No. 2 (Oct. 1956), 147–165.

———. "Über Entstehung und Formen von Interessengruppen in Deutschland seit Beginn der Industrialisierung," *Politische Vierteljahresschrift*, II, No. 2 (July 1961), 124–154.

Schwartz, Ivo E. "Antitrust Legislation and Policy in Germany—A Comparative Study," *University of Pennsylvania Law Review*, 105, No. 5 (March 1957), 617–690.

Schweitzer, Arthur. *Big Business in the Third Reich* (Bloomington, 1964).

Shirer, William. *The Rise and Fall of the Third Reich* (New York, 1960).

Shuchman, Abraham. *Codetermination: Labor's Middle Way in Germany* (Washington, 1957).

"Spannungsfeld Wirtschaft und Oeffentlichkeit," *Volkswirt.* Supplement, n.d.

Speier, Hans and Davison, W. Phillips (eds.). *West German Leadership and Foreign Policy* (Evanston, Ill., 1957).

Spiro, Herbert J. *The Politics of German Codetermination* (Cambridge, Mass., 1958).

"Der Staat der Gegenwart und die wirtschaftlichen und aussenwirtschaftlichen Interessentengruppen," *Kölner Zeitschrift für Soziologie*, V, Nos. 2/3 (1952/53), 204–229.

Staatsbürgerliche Vereinigung, *Wirtschaft und Kommunalpolitik* (Bergisch Gladbach [c. 1962]).

Stammer, Otto. "Interessenverbände und Parteien," *Kölner Zeitschrift für Soziologie und Sozialpsychologie*, IX, No. 4 (1957), 587–605.

———. "Die politische Verantwortung von Unternehmern und Gewerkschaften," *Frankfurter Hefte*, VIII, No. 11 (Nov. 1953), 844–854.

Stein, Gustav (ed.). *Unternehmer in der Politik* (Düsseldorf, 1954).

Stolper, Gustav. *German Economy 1870–1940* (New York, 1940).

———. *German Realities* (New York, 1948).

Stolper, Wolfgang. *Germany between East and West.* (Washington, 1960).

Strickrodt, Georg. "Gruppeninteressen und Staatsgewalt," *Neue Politische Literatur*, II, No. 5 (May 1957), 319–341.

Structure and Functions of the Top-Level Organisations of Industry and Trade in the Federal Republic of Germany. Published by the DI (Köln, n.d.).

Sweezy, Maxine Y. *The Structure of the Nazi Economy* (Cambridge, Mass., 1941).

Taschenbuch für den Gemeinsamen Markt, EWG, Euratom, Montan-Union, 1959/60 (Frankfurt/M., n.d.).

Thyssen, Fritz. *I Paid Hitler* (London, 1941).

Trials of War Criminals before the Nuernberg Military Tribunals. Vols. VI-IX (Washington, 1952).

Triesch, Günter. "Die Finanzierung der SPD: Die "Beitragspartei" —eine Propagandaschöpfung," *Die Politische Meinung*, Heft 28 (Sept. 1958), pp. 36–51.

———. *Die Macht der Funktionäre* (Düsseldorf, 1956).

Trossman, Hans. *Der zweite Deutsche Bundestag* (Bonn, 1954).

Truman, David B. *The Governmental Process* (New York, 1960).

Tschierschky, S. *Die Organisation der industriellen Interessen in Deutschland* (Göttingen, 1905).

Tuchtfeldt, Egon. "Wirkungen der Verbände auf die wirtschafts-politische Willensbildung," Diskussionsentwurf für die Tagung des Wirtschafts-politischen Ausschusses der Gesellschaft für Wirtschaft und Sozialwissenschaften in Würzburg am 29. und 30. April 1960 (Multigraphed).

Umfragen 1957: Ereignisse und Probleme des Jahres im Urteil der Bevölkerung. Published by DIVO-Institut (Frankfurt/M., 1958).

Umfragen: Ereignisse und Probleme der Zeit im Urteil der Bevölkerung, II. Published by DIVO-Institut (Frankfurt/M., 1959).

United States Government. President's Commission on Campaign Costs. *Financing Presidential Campaigns* (Washington, 1962).

"Unofficial Government: Pressure Groups and Lobbies," *The Annals of the American Academy of Political and Social Science*, Vol. 319 (Sept. 1958).

Unternehmermillionen kaufen politische Macht! Published by the SPD (Bonn, n.d.).

Varain, Heinz Josef. "Das Geld der Parteien," *Geschichte in Wissenschaft und Unterricht*, No. 8/1961.

———. "Kandidaten und Abgeordnete in Schleswig-Holstein, 1947–1958," *Politische Vierteljahresschrift*, II, No. 4 (1961), 363–411.

Die Waage: Ein Bericht über die Tätigkeit in den Jahren 1952–1957. Published by the Gemeinschaft zur Förderung des Sozialen Ausgleichs, e.V. (n.p., n.d.).

Wahrhaftig, Samuel L. "The Development of German Foreign Policy Institutions," *West German Leadership and Foreign Policy*, ed. by H. Speier and W. P. Davison (Evanston, Ill., 1957).

Wallich, Henry C. *Mainsprings of the German Revival* (New Haven, 1955).

Weber, Helmut. "Der moderne Staat und die Interessengruppen." Unpublished Ph.D. dissertation, Marburg University, 1954.

Weber, Max. *Wirtschaft und Gesellschaft*, Vol. I (4th ed., Tübingen, 1956).

Weber, Werner. *Staats- und Selbstverwaltung in der Gegenwart.* Göttinger Rechtswissenschaftliche Studien. No. 9 (Göttingen, 1953).

Der Weg zum industriellen Spitzenverband. Published by the BDI (Darmstadt, 1956).

Welter, Erich. *Der Weg der Deutschen Industrie* (Frankfurt/M., 1943).

Werner, Josua. *Die Verbände in Wirtschaft und Politik* (Zürich, 1959).

———. *Die Wirtschaftsverbände in der Marktwirtschaft* (Zürich, 1957).

Der Westdeutsche Markt in Zahlen. Published by DIVO-Institut (Frankfurt/M., 1958).

Wieck, Hans-Georg. *Christliche und Freie Demokraten in Hessen, Rheinland-Pfalz, Baden und Württemberg 1945/46* (Düsseldorf, 1958).

———. *Die Entstehung der CDU und die Wiedergründung des Zentrums im Jahre 1945* (Düsseldorf, 1953).

Wildenmann, Rudolf. *Partei und Fraktion* (Meisenheim am Glan, 1954).

Wilson, H. H. *Pressure Group: The Campaign for Commercial Television in England* (New Brunswick, N.J., 1961).

Winschuh, Josef. *Gerüstete Wirtschaft* (Berlin, 1939).

———. *Das neue Unternehmerbild; Grundzüge einer Unternehmerpolitik* (Baden-Baden, 1954).

World Political Science Congress. *Report on Proceedings, Meetings on Research in Party and Campaign Finance.* (Mimeographed; Paris, Sept. 27–29, 1961).

Wössner, Jacobus. *Die Ordnungspolitische Bedeutung des Verbandswesens* (Tübingen, 1961).

Zellentin, Gerda. *Der Wirtschafts- und Sozialausschuss der EWG und Euratom: Interessenrepräsentation auf übernationaler Ebene* (Leiden, 1962).

Zimdahl, Hans-Heinrich. *Wirtschaftssysteme und Parteiprogramme der wichtigsten Parteien der Bundesrepublik* (Frankfurt, 1955).

Index

Abs, Hermann J., 194, 290, 344

Adenauer, Konrad, Chancellor, viii, 17, 84, 104, 130, 151, 190, 209–211, 284–285, 346; and Berg, 193–203; and candidate nominations, 143; and CDU/CSU, 96, 98–100; economic policies, 201, 243, 245, 249, 252–254, 273–274, 276–278; and Erhard, 193–201; and FDP, 108; fiscal policies, 259, 260, 263, 265; foreign policies, 287–289, 295, 297, 301, 312, 318, 326; and interest groups, 201–202; on party financing, 112–114, 118, 127–130; and presidency, 196–197; social policies, 201; on tariffs, 328–329; on trade, 305, 310–311

Agriculture, in politics, 6–8, 141, 169–171, 207, 352

Agriculture, Ministry of, 169

Ahlen program, 96–97, 271

Allgemeine Elektrizitätsgesellschaft (AEG), 35

All-German Bloc of Expellees (GB/BHE), 107, 117–120, 122, 132, 245

Allied Powers, 23–25, 224, 236–237, 251–252, 274; see also France, Great Britain, Soviet Union, U.S.

Almond, Gabriel, 285, 293

American Federation of Labor–Congress of Industrial Organizations (AFL-CIO), 148–149, 284

Amerongen, Otto Wolff von, 308, 310

Arab countries, 305

Arbeitsgemeinschaft selbständiger Unternehmer (AsU); see Association of Independent Entrepreneurs

Arbeitskreise, 167–169

Aschoff, Albrecht, 156, 170

Association of German Machine Construction (VDMA), 32–33, 170

Association of Independent Entrepreneurs (AsU), 30–31, 94, 242, 244, 250, 264

Association of the Chemical Industry, 105, 162, 216–217, 254, 260, 301, 326–328

Association of the German Leather Industry, 268

Association of the German Textile Industry, 60

Association of the Iron and Steel Industry, 197, 251

Atlantic Bridge, 289

Atlantic community, 289–291

Atlantic congress, 289

Atomic armament, 294; see also Defense policy

Atzenroth, Karl, 166n

Aumer, Hermann, 179

Automobile industry, 226–227, 280–281, 325

Automobile Industry Association, 42, 208, 221n, 326